DUTY, HONOR OR COUNTRY
GENERAL GEORGE WEEDON AND THE AMERICAN REVOLUTION

MEMOIRS OF THE
AMERICAN PHILOSOPHICAL SOCIETY
Held at Philadelphia
For Promoting Useful Knowledge
Volume 133

DUTY, HONOR OR COUNTRY

GENERAL GEORGE WEEDON AND THE AMERICAN REVOLUTION

Harry M. Ward

Professor of History, University of Richmond

THE AMERICAN PHILOSOPHICAL SOCIETY

Independence Square ● Philadelphia

1979

Library of Congress Catalog Card Number 78-73168
International Standard Book Number 0-87169-133-7
US ISSN 0065-9746

CONTENTS

Illustrations

Maps

PREFACE

In many ways George Weedon is representative of the military leaders of the American Revolution. Weedon received his military baptism in the French and Indian War; he was middle-aged when the Revolutionary War began. While most of Washington's generals in civilian life were businessmen or gentlemen farmers, Weedon was both. Like Israel Putnam, he came to his patriotism by way of his tavern-keeping before the war. Weedon acquired professionalism and competence from long and hard experience in the field, and he had a down-to-earth quality with which his troops identified.

Beyond his importance as a military leader in two wars is the fact that George Weedon was one of four Virginians (including Gates, Muhlenberg, and Scott) who held the rank of general early in the war and served to the end. Mercer was killed at Princeton; Andrew Lewis resigned at the beginning of the war; Charles Lee and Adam Stephen left in disgrace; Woodford died in captivity. Weedon, at the start of the Revolutionary War, was a regimental commander in the Virginia force that repelled Governor Dunmore's little army from Virginia. As a brigade commander in the Continental Army, he had important responsibilities in the northern battles and campaigns. Later when in command of Virginia militia, he affected, as much as any single person, the course of the British invasion of Virginia before Yorktown. During the siege of Yorktown, he led the Virginia militia at Gloucester, helping to checkmate Tarleton's force and to prevent Cornwallis's escape across the York. His career measures the quality of the military leadership in Virginia and in the Continental Army.

Of significance also is Weedon's keen observation of all aspects of military life, operations, and support. His running commentary, as seen in his letters, is one of the most perceptive of Revolutionary War times. His sense of humor—albeit often risque—is unsurpassed by any that is found in the writings of his contemporaries in the war. Weedon wrote among the most detailed descriptions of battles of the

vii

Revolution. He was a frequent correspondent with Virginia authorities, members of Congress, and various military officers. Weedon's relationship with Nathanael Greene reveals the human qualities of the two men. General Weedon's views on the war suggest reasons why there was so little support for it after 1778, especially in Virginia, and why the war dragged on so long. Weedon's biography also affords a picture of life not only as it was in the army, but also in Virginia among the aristocracy, the merchants, and the people at large.

Unfortunately much of Weedon's private correspondence is missing, or at least has not surfaced. No letter to his wife is extant. If only there were a few letters to Kitty Weedon—as there were to Lucy Knox from bulky Henry Knox, whom Weedon resembled in many respects—there could be a fuller portrait. Nevertheless, the known letters and papers of Weedon form one of the most valuable sources for the study of the American Revolution; for unlike Washington, who did not open himself up personally in his correspondence, Weedon was always candid and blunt. Although in quantity the Weedon manuscripts fall short of the voluminous papers of Washington, Greene, and Knox, they are next in importance—along with the papers of Steuben, Gates, and perhaps others—as a source on the Revolutionary War.

A biography of George Weedon poses the problem of the obligations of the professional soldier. Loyalty itself was compounded: first to "country" (Virginia), then to the cause of independence, and last to the emerging nationalistic idea of "country." There was also the duty of a soldier. Underneath it all was honor: integrity of character and service. Could the claims of duty, honor, and country conflict? Reared in the code of a gentleman, George Weedon considered personal honor in the strictest sense and held that his was irreproachable in any way. In the service of the public honor was nonetheless inviolable in the character of a gentleman, whose motives were unquestionable. In the public arena honor was involved in a kind of contract, as it was in private life. When the public violated that contract, as Weedon would consider it had, he had to face the dilemma that confronted many officers in Washington's army, whether there was a degree of transgression on honor that weighed against obligations of duty and patriotism.

My interest in General Weedon arose when preparing a history of Richmond, Virginia, during the Revolution. Everywhere Weedon's name appeared. Other investigation of military aspects of the Revolution sharpened my curiosity as it became evident that Weedon had a major role in the Revolution. Douglas Southall Freeman's own fascination with Weedon in his biography of Washington provided a stimulant. Correspondence and conversation with Professor Richard B. Morris of Columbia University, who had interest in Weedon from his own work, gave me early encouragement.

I would particularly like to thank George H. S. King of Fredericksburg for his contribution to this study. Mr. King is a descendant of a cousin of George Weedon and is an authority on the old families of Fredericksburg and the Northern Neck. His article on George Weedon in the *William and Mary Quarterly* (1940) served as a starting point. Mr. King contributed several documents that would not otherwise have been located and provided typewritten material relating to George Weedon and the Sentry Box that proved invaluable. Charles G. McDaniel, also a relative of the general, who is now the owner and occupant of the magnificently restored Sentry Box, has been a gracious host, explaining various Weedon memorabilia. John Weedon, of Vienna, Virginia, and Hugh Mercer of Savannah, Georgia, were helpful. Ralph Happel of Fredericksburg and formerly of the National Historical Parks Commission, John D. Hutchinson, curator of the James Monroe Museum, and Edward H. Cann, Grand Master of the Fredericksburg Masonic Lodge No. 4 provided important service. Two natives of Fredericksburg, now in Richmond, were valuable resource persons: Professor Welford D. Taylor of the University of Richmond and Michael Sanchez-Savaadra, curator of the Valentine Museum.

Professor Hiley H. Ward of Temple University, my journalist twin-brother, while in Minnesota tracked down the Allyn K. Ford collection to the Minnesota Historical Society. It turned out that the Society was preparing a microfilm publication of this multifarious collection. Sue E. Holbert, assistant curator of manuscripts at the Society, arranged for the author to obtain a copy of the microfilm many months before it was released to the public. Appreciation is also expressed to Alan F. Perry, archivist for the Center for the Documentary Study of the American Revolution at the National Archives; Murphy DeWitt Smith, associate librarian of the American Philosophical Society; Dr. Lance J. Bauer, librarian, Brown University Library, and Stuart C. Sherman, librarian of the John Hay Library of the same institution; Bruce Henry of the Huntington Library; Harry D. Mackey of Camden, New

Jersey; and Arlene Kleeby Shy, assistant curator of manuscripts at the William L. Clements Library. I am also indebted to other institutions for their expert staff assistance: New-York Historical Society; New York Public Library; Pierpont Morgan Library; Historical Society of Pennsylvania; Duke University Library; Massachusetts Historical Society; Harvard University Library; Chicago Historical Society; Alderman Library of the University of Virginia; the Library of Congress Manuscripts Division; and Mills College Library, Oakland, California.

I would like to acknowledge the fine services rendered at the Virginia State Library, where most of the work on this biography was accomplished, citing specifically Milton R. Russell, head reference librarian, Mrs. Ethel M. Slonaker, in charge of interlibrary loans, and Dr. John W. Dudley, Conly Edwards, John Salmon, and Dennis Hallerman of the archives division. At the Virginia Historical Society, William M. E. Rachal, Howson W. Cole, Waverly K. Winfree, and Virginius C. Hall gave invaluable assistance.

A critical reading of the manuscript by Professor Georgia B. Christopher of the University of Richmond led to its improvement. Professor Don Higginbotham of the University of North Carolina and Dr. Lynn L. Sims, executive director of the Richmond Independence Bicentennial Commission, read the manuscript in its entirety and contributed significantly to clarification of a number of points relating to military affairs. For the writing of this biography, the University of Richmond granted the author a summer fellowship and a sabbatical, and the Virginia Society of the Cincinnati, of which George Weedon was founder and president, generously provided financial aid.

ABBREVIATIONS IN NOTES

AKF	Allyn K. Ford Collection, Minnesota Historical Society
APS	American Philosophical Society
CL	William L. Clements Library, University of Michigan
FCCM	Fredericksburg Common Council Minutes
FLB	Fredericksburg Lodge Book
HCOB	Fredericksburg City Hustings Court Order Book
HL	Henry E. Huntington Library
HSP	Historical Society of Pennsylvania
LC	Library of Congress
NA	National Archives
NYHS	New-York Historical Society
NYPL	New York City Public Library
UVL	University of Virginia Library
VHS	Virginia Historical Society
VSL	Virginia State Library
WC, APS	Weedon Correspondence, American Philosophical Society
WL, BUL	Weedon Letters, Brown University Library
WML	College of William and Mary Library
WPC, CHS	Weedon-Page Correspondence, Chicago Historical Society

I. THE YOUNG SOLDIER

LIKE MANY young planters of Virginia at the start of the French and Indian War, George Weedon was thrilled at the prospect of going off to war. Not yet twenty-one years old, he could scarcely foresee that entering military service to fight on Virginia's frontiers would be an induction into a fraternity that would provide the leadership in a war for American Independence.

George Weedon had spent all of his young life in Westmoreland and Stafford counties in Virginia's Northern Neck between the Potomac and Rappahannock Rivers. George Weedon's great-great grandfather of the same name had arrived as an indentured servant in 1650, but soon was free and in possession of a farm in Westmoreland County at the mouth of Rozier's Creek on the Potomac. Over the years lands were sold and bought and divided among heirs. George Weedon's grandfather, Jordan, died as a young man in 1716, and his father, George, died at age twenty-four. George Weedon's mother, Sarah Gray Weedon, was the daughter of a neighboring planter, Nathaniel Gray.

George Weedon was born a few months after his father's death (late 1734).[1] George Gray was made the guardian of his nephew. Sometime before 1743 George Weedon's mother married William Strother. In 1747, a "Division and allomt. of the Estate of George (Weedon, Sr.) Dec'd" was returned to court. The entailed estate of George Sr., 326 acres, was left "unsettled" by the court, and presumably there was no contest to George Weedon's inheriting it. Weedon's step-father, William Strother, was ordered to keep his step-son "on the profitts" of the Weedon estate until he came of age and to give him three years of schooling.[2]

---

[1] 24 June, 1735, Westmoreland County Records and Inventories (1723-1746): pp. 154-155, VSL.; 26 November, 1731, Westmoreland County Orders (1731-1737): p. 150 and 24 June, 1735, p. 173, VSL.; 23 March, 1734, Westmoreland Deeds and Wills (1723-1738): p. 253, VSL.; Crozier, 1962: p. 40.

[2] 25 February, 1746/7, Westmoreland County Records and Inventories (1746-1752): p. 46, VSL.

During his early youth, Weedon lived with his widowed mother either on the family plantation, just south of Rozier Creek at its head, or across the creek on the Nathaniel Gray plantation. While his mother was married to William Strother, Weedon probably lived with her on the Strother estate. Yet Nathaniel Gray's will of 1743 mentions that Sarah Strother "shall be no ways disturbed nor Molested of or from that place where she now dwells during her natural life," implying that mother and son were living on the Nathaniel Gray estate at that time. The relationship between Weedon's step-father and Nathaniel Gray was close, and Gray made his "loving Friend" his sole executor.[3] Strother died in February, 1750, and later Weedon would acquire some of Strother's land on the bank opposite his own on Rozier's Creek,[4] forming part of what would later be declared as a 535-acre estate.

In growing up in upper Washington Parish in Westmoreland County, George Weedon, therefore, probably at various times lived on the Weedon, Gray, and Strother estates. He had the company of three step- or half-sisters—Sarah, Margaret, and Patty[5]—and half-brothers, James and William Strother. Weedon had an attachment to William Strother (eldest son of William Sr.), as he left him lands in his will. William married Winifred Baker and died in King George County in 1797 very poor. James Strother later became a carpenter and house joiner in Frederick County and died about 1773; he may have been the same James Strother killed by the Indians in Kentucky in that year.[6]

The area of the Northern Neck where George Weedon lived as a boy by the 1730's had taken on some of the rudiments of civilization. A second growth of timber now had replaced many of the thick forests. The Indians, who had been decimated by disease and war, had disappeared beyond the Blue Ridge Mountains.[7] Tobacco was the main livelihood,

---

[3] 6 March, 1743, Westmoreland County Deeds and Wills (1738-1744): pp. 303-304, VSL; Fothergill, 1925: p. 114.

[4] 29 August, 1749, 7 February, 1749-50, 28 August, 1750, and 12 September, 1750, Westmoreland County Deeds and Wills (1747-1753): pp. 192-194 and 235-236, VSL; 25 February, 1746/7, Westmoreland County Order Book (1743-1747): p. 204 and 28 August, 1750, (1750-1752): p. 5, VSL; 28 August, 1750, Westmoreland County Records and Inventories (1746-1752): p. 134, VSL; Nicklin, 1930: p. 43.

[5] Power of attorney to George Gray, 8 June, 1756, Stafford County Deed Book, Liber P (1755-176-): p. 105, VSL.

[6] For references to William and James Strother, see 1768-1773, William Allason Papers, Ledger Books G and H, *passim*, VSL.

[7] Hatch, 1966: p. 1687; Haynie, 1959: p. 133.

and wasted fields dotted the landscape. Hogheads of tobacco, rolled from the countryside or carried down the streams, could be seen glutting the wharfs of thriving river ports.

Yet the life of the people of the Northern Neck in the early eighteenth century was simple. Most were small planters, hardly more than yeoman farmers, living on estates of several hundred acres[8] squeezed in and around the plantations of the great river barons. There were few conveniences. Much toil went into the raising of tobacco and subsistence crops. The plantation produced its own food and manufactured the various necessities, including clothes. Wheat had to be beaten out with sticks or trodden out by oxen. It is true that the small planter had several servants or slaves, but he was usually his own overseer and manager. Sons of the plantation owners had to learn the skill of keeping accounts. A favorite pastime for a stocky, rough-hewn lad like George Weedon was hunting for wild game that was still abundant.

Young George Weedon spent convivial Sundays, mingling with neighbors after service, at Round Hill Church, where infrequently Augustine Washington and his sons also attended. George Weedon was probably baptized by the Rev. Roderick McCulloch, rector of Washington Parish from 1731 to 1744, who is said to have christened George Washington at Wakefield.[9]

As with other sons of the minor gentry, George Weedon had little opportunity for a formal education. His family was not wealthy enough to send him to England. Nor did he aspire to a career in law or the church that would have sent him in pursuit of an education outside of Virginia or at the fledging College of William and Mary. George Weedon undoubtedly had at least three years of schooling as provided by the court decision after his mother's marriage to William Strother. He may have been tutored by the Reverend McCulloch, and he may also have attended the little school established in Westmoreland County by McCulloch's successor, the

---

[8] Brown, 1965: p. 51.

[9] Round Hill Church was built in the 1720's. A new church (at Pope's Creek) near the Washington estate was not erected until 1744, and whenever Augustine and his son George attended church, while living at Wakefield, it must have been at Round Hill Church, ten miles away (Davison, 1963: pp. 1196-1199; "Reverend McCulloch," 1929: p. 346). By mid-century there were three churches in Westmoreland County: Round Hill, Pope's Creek, and Leeds (Meade, 1857: p. 162).

Reverend Archibald Campbell, who came to Virginia from Scotland in 1741.[10]

Weedon received training in mathematics and may have learned the one hundred ten *Rules of Civility and Decent Behavior in Company*. An abridgment of this work, which was first compiled in sixteenth-century France, was a staple in the education of young gentlemen in the Northern Neck.

George Weedon had a natural ability for the turn of a phrase and descriptive narration. Yet Weedon's spelling indicates that much of his education was acquired by oral communication—for example, he spelled words as they sounded in colloquial usage ("ware" for "were," "clair" for "clear," etc.).

From the early 1750's to about 1763, George Weedon may have stayed frequently with George Gray, his uncle, on the plantation known as Pine Hill in Stafford County. In Stafford County Court in 1756, as he prepared to return to military duty on the frontier, Weedon gave George Gray a power of attorney for all his affairs, and

> in Case of mortality it is then my desire that the Negro wench and Children I now own is to be left as follows. The wench to my Mother The Negro Girl late to my Sister Margaret Strother The Negro boy Bob to my Sister Patty Strother and the Land in the Forrest to be sold and after all my Creditors satisfied the remainder of what it fetches to Mother & the Land on the River to my Mother to dispose of to whom she thinks best after her death.[11]

From his uncle's plantation, George Weedon could partake of the life in the cultural and trade center of Fredericksburg and broaden his connections with the merchants of the town and the gentry in Stafford and Spotsylvania Counties along the Rappahannock.

At the beginning of the French and Indian War, George Weedon had slight interest in being a gentleman farmer or in setting up some business of his own. His thoughts were on serving in the impending war. In early 1755, Virginia volunteers were hastened off to the frontier.[12] Although

---

[10] Meade, 1857: p. 159; Johnson, 1929: pp. 114-115; Haynie, 1959: p. 154.

[11] 8 June, 1756, Stafford County Deed Book, Liber P (1755-1756-): p. 105.

[12] Dinwiddie to Captains Mercer, Waggoner, and Stewart, 15 January, 1755, Brock, 1883: 1: p. 452; John St. Clair to General Braddock, 9 February, 1755, Pargellis, **1936**: pp. 61 and 64.

anxious to join this army, Weedon, true to the character of a
Virginia gentleman, awaited a commission.

By June, 1755, five hundred Virginians, mainly rangers
from the western counties, were stationed at Wills Creek on
the upper Potomac, and of these, three hundred would join
the Braddock expedition.[13]

Braddock's inglorious defeat only further excited fears of
Virginians, as their frontiers lay exposed. "Flying Parties of
French and their Indians," reported Governor Dinwiddie,
were "robbing and murdering many of our Inhabitants."[14]
Refugees swarmed into the interior from the back settlements
on the upper Potomac. Virginians now had a war of invasion,
and would not rest until the barbarous foreign and heathen
enemy would be driven back to the north side of the Ohio
River. "On to Fort Duquesne" was a rallying cry; the chief
objective would be to capture that fort at the gateway to the
Ohio Valley. The chance for military distinction enthralled
the younger sons of the gentry as it had not done since the
filibustering zeal for the ill-fated Cartagena expedition of
1740.

After the Braddock debacle, the Virginia Assembly
appropriated £20,000 for frontier defense and provided for
keeping 1,200 men in the field, including three companies of
rangers and a garrison of fifty at Fort Cumberland. Thus
about 1,000 men had to be recruited by volunteers or draft.
Meanwhile military stores and £10,000, furnished by the
crown, had arrived. In August, Washington was appointed
commander in chief of the enlarged Virginia Regiment. The
troops, for the purpose of defense only, were to serve until
spring, and could not be marched out of the colony.
Recruitment proceeded slowly, and it was soon apparent that
only half of the quota could be raised.[15] Anyone that could
raise and pay and equip (until reimbursed) a band of recruits
was virtually assured an officer's commission. It was by this
means that George Weedon, who would later demonstrate his
talents at recruitment during the Revolution, received a

---

[13] Washington to Adam Stephen, 18 November, 1755, Adam Stephen Papers, LC; A
Return of the Virginia, Mary-land & North Carolina Troops, Encamp'd at Wills
Creek, 8 June, 1755, Pargellis, 1936: pp. 88-89.

[14] Dinwiddie to Governor Shirley, 12 November, 1755, Brock, 1885: 2: p. 263.

[15] Dinwiddie to the Lords of Trade, 15 November, 1755; Dinwiddie to the Earl of
Granville, 15 November, 1755; and Dinwiddie to Sir Thomas Robinson, 24
December, 1755, ibid.: pp. 270, 275, and 307 resp.; Freeman, 1949-: 2: p. 111; Koontz,
1925: p. 58.

commission as an ensign. Weedon recruited twelve men whom he delivered to Washington at Williamsburg.[16]

Every officer of the Virginia Regiment was to provide for himself "a Suit of Regimentals of good blue Cloath; the Coat to be faced and cuffed with Scarlet, and trimmed with Silver: A Scarlet waistcoat, with Silver Lace; blue Breeches, and a Silver-laced Hat, if to be had, for Camp or Garrison Duty." In addition, each officer had to have "a common Soldiers Dress, for Detachments, and Duty in the Woods."[17]

In rank and seniority (commission dáted September 14, 1755), Weedon was last on a list of forty-six officers of the Regiment (including last of sixteen ensigns).[18] But, with the usual expected turnover among the officers, a young officer who persevered could anticipate a rapid advance. Young Weedon returned to Fredericksburg and waited anxiously to join his brother officers, many of whom he knew and liked from Stafford, Spotsylvania, and Caroline Counties, including new friends, Captain Charles Lewis of Caroline County, brother of Fielding Lewis of Fredericksburg, and Ensign William Daingerfield, Jr. of "Coventry" in Spotsylvania County.

Weedon was ordered to return his recruits to Fredericksburg and place them under the command of Major Andrew Lewis.[19] Colonel Washington meanwhile went to Fort Cumberland on Wills Creek to inspect the garrison and the two hundred men—Virginia and Maryland survivors of Braddock's campaign who had not deserted. On his return, Washington stopped at Fredericksburg a few days to coordinate plans for marching the new troops to Winchester and Fort Cumberland.[20] On October 8 he ordered Lewis to take all recruits then collecting at Fredericksburg under Captains Charles Lewis and Henry Woodward, Lieutenants John Edward Lomax and Peter Steenbergen, and Ensigns Edward Hubbard and George Weedon, to march to Winchester, "using the utmost Dispatch in your March." Captain Robert Spotswood was left in Fredericksburg to receive any further recruits.[21]

---

[16] 2 September, 1755, Washington Papers, Ser. 4. Reel 29, LC.

[17] Orders, 17 September, 1755, Fitzpatrick, 1931-: 1: p. 175.

[18] 26 May, 1757 (refers to August-September, 1755), Hamilton, 1898-: 1: pp. 144-145; "Journal of Lewis," 1892: pp. 211-214.

[19] Washington to Captain Robert Spotswood, 6 September, 1755, Hamilton, 1898-: 1: pp. 171 and 171n. (same orders to Weedon).

[20] Freeman, 1949-: 2: pp. 117-118.

Weedon and his recruits were among a band of eighty men that Major Lewis led out of Fredericksburg on October 10. One hundred sixty-seven miles away was Fort Cumberland, the most advanced English garrison on the frontier (now Cumberland, Maryland).[22] The men got so drunk on the first day's march that orders were given to make camp after covering only seven miles. The next day they fared better—eighteen miles. In the evening there was a hearty meal of a roasted bullock that had been picked up from the countryside and "plenty of bread;" afterwards, commented Charles Lewis, "we had a good entertainment, a merry landlady and daughter." Averaging better than twenty miles a day the next three days, Major Andrew Lewis's detachment arrived sober but fatigued at Winchester, where Washington greeted them.[23] At Winchester Weedon received pay (to October 1) for the ten recruits that had accompanied him (one sergeant and nine men). Several desertions had taken place on the march and presumably two deserters were Weedon's men. Weedon was now given charge of eighteen men.[24]

Major Lewis led the new troops out of Winchester on October 20, and after marching thirteen miles, camp was made on the "top of a mountain." After a fifteen-mile march on the twenty-second, they were joined by Washington and Captain George Mercer. The ragtag band ploughed through a driving rain and snow. Everywhere there were deserted houses and evidences of Indian depredations—especially gruesome was the body of a man killed by the Indians half out of his grave and gnawed by wolves. At last, cold and hungry, they arrived at Fort Cumberland at nightfall of October 25.[25] The next day Washington's orders mentioned that "The Recruits that came up under the command of Major Lewis, are to be commanded by Capts Henry Woodward and Charles or Joshua Lewis; Lts [Peter] Steenbergen and [John] Campbell and Ensigns [Edward] Hubbard and Weedon."[26]

---

[21] Washington to Major Andrew Lewis, 8 October, 1755, Fitzpatrick, 1931-: 1: p. 190.

[22] Ambler, 1936: p. 93. Ft. Cumberland was built in October, 1754 by Governor Sharpe of Maryland and named for the duke of Cumberland, victor at Culloden.

[23] "Journal of Lewis," 1892: pp. 205-207.

[24] Account of Cash expended for the Expedition at Winchester . . . and receipt from Weedon, 16 October, 1755 and Receipt, 20 October, 1755, Washington Papers, Ser. 4, Reel 29, LC.

[25] "Journal of Lewis," 1892: pp. 207-209.

[26] Orders, 26 October, 1755, Fitzpatrick, 1931-: 1: p. 223.

Perched on a hill at Wills Creek on the north side of the upper Potomac in Maryland, Fort Cumberland was a desolate place. One hundred feet square, its defenses boasted only eleven four-pounders. Washington immediately got into his famous feud with the commander of the Maryland troops at the fort, Captain John Dagworthy, who refused to recognize anyone other than himself as supreme commander. Washington left October 27 to take up this matter and the regulation of the Virginia troops with Governor Dinwiddie and the Assembly. With Washington gone, the acting Virginia commander, Adam Stephen, also could not get along with the intractable Maryland commander. Dagworthy, who held a royal commission, directed that none of Stephen's men could leave the fort without permission,[27] an order which, needless to say, Stephen ignored.

Another hundred Virginia troops, with five officers, arrived on November 13, bringing the Virginia Regiment to about five hundred troops. Scouting parties were frequently dispatched, and came back with reports of finding burned and scalped bodies of men, women, and children—grim reminders of an invisible presence of "our very cautious enemy." There were also details sent out to hunt and to gather corn and other food from the farms.[28] Weedon undoubtedly participated in several of these excursions, a responsibility usually assigned to a subaltern. He may also have logged some time at several nearby forts garrisoned by twenty to thirty soldiers of the Virginia Regiment.[29]

By mid-December it was evident that most of the Indians, as was their custom, had abandoned the warpath for the winter, and so the Virginia soldiers could enjoy a little relaxation. On Christmas eve, Colonel Stephen had the twenty-four officers, including Weedon, to his quarters for dinner, followed by "drinking loyal healths and dancing 'till 11 o'clock." On Christmas Day, the officers again dined with Colonel Stephen. After dinner they spent the evening until midnight in drinking, singing, enacting "part of a Play," and dancing.[30]

---

[27] Freeman, 1949-: 2: pp. 134-135, 138-139, and 145.

[28] "Journal of Lewis," 1892: pp. 210-214.

[29] *Ibid.*, p. 211; Koontz, 1925: pp. 111-112. Nicholas's Fort was five miles from Fort Cumberland; Cocke's Fort and Fort Ashby, south of Fort Cumberland on Patterson's Creek, were nine and twenty-five miles distant from Fort Cumberland, respectively.

[30] "Journal of Lewis," 1892: pp. 215-216; Adam Stephen to Washington, 26 December, 1755, Hamilton, 1898-: 1: p. 162.

Washington visited Winchester in early January, 1756, and arranged the Virginia Regiment into sixteen companies. Ensign Weedon now served under Captain Thomas Cocke and Lieutenant William Stark in the fifth company.[31] Washington soon returned to Alexandria, and in February would make a long trek to Boston in order to convince General William Shirley, commander of His Majesty's forces in America, to decide in his favor in his rivalry with Captain Dagworthy for command at Fort Cumberland. In mid-January Colonel Stephen sent Ensign Weedon, along with seven other officers home on recruiting assignment.[32] Weedon was absent from service in the field until June.

George Weedon had now cut his teeth on military service. Except for the long marches, of which Weedon would often complain during the Revolution, he enjoyed the out-of-doors life and the camaraderie of fellow officers. Without knowing it, he was becoming addicted to military life.

While Weedon was in Fredericksburg recruiting, the Indians in spring, 1756, swept with fury through the western counties of Virginia and threatened to pass through the Blue Ridge Mountains. Numerous skirmishes were fought with the Indians, and in April John Fenton Mercer and sixteen men were killed and scalped by the Indians while on a scouting mission. Militia from the western counties rallied, but came and went, and in May Washington had only 331 effectives. The legislature authorized the building of a chain of forts in March, and throughout 1756 construction was underway that would afford a one-hundred-mile defense perimeter on the eastern slope of the Allegheny Mountains. Main emphasis was placed on the construction of Fort Loudoun, at Winchester, east of the chain of forts, which would now become the command post rather than Fort Cumberland.[33] Weedon, returning to the Regiment in June, probably had alternate duties during the summer and fall at Fort Cumberland and Fort Loudoun, where he could assist in the fort's construction. On July 12, 1756, Ensign Weedon was assigned to the seventh company, serving with Captain Thomas Cocke and Lieutenant Mordicai Buckner.[34] News came in August that England and France were at war, and a grand parade was held

[31] Orders, 9 January, 1756, Fitzpatrick, 1931-: 1: pp. 272-275.
[32] Stephen to Washington, 18 January, 1756, Hamilton, 1898-: 1: p. 169.
[33] Freeman, 1949-: 2: pp. 180-181, 193ff and *passim*.
[34] Orders, 12 July, 1756, Hamilton, 1898-: 1: p. 298.

at Fort Loudoun, whereupon the Declaration of War was read, followed by drinking of toasts and the firing of artillery and musketry.[35]

With new Indian raids on the frontier in September, 1756, many Virginians felt that the Virginia Regiment was not doing its job. A venomous series of letters appeared in the *Virginia Gazette*, under the pseudonym of "Virginia Centinel" impugning the character of the Virginia officers. Number X accused them of being "drunken debauchees." On October 7, the officers of the Virginia Regiment addressed a letter to Colonel Stephen, charging Governor Dinwiddie with complicity in the publication of "Centinel X," and stated that they would no longer serve as officers after November 20, "unless we have public satisfaction as the injury received." Washington, arriving to view the work at Fort Loudoun, met with the officers and convinced them he needed more time to investigate and put the case before the Virginia Assembly. The officers agreed to a deferment in a letter to Washington of November 12, signed by thirty-four officers, including Weedon, but they were adamant that they must be vindicated in the public's eye: "Nothing less will be sufficient than the Thanks of the Assembly in the Publick prints for what We have already done & are still willing to do." Washington was advised to "answer ev'ry Article" and to make the case that the "Centinel" or his informers were "malicious, wilfull and . . . cowardly Lyars." The officers, as "Men of Spirit," would "not bear patiently any Thing unbecoming the Character of Gentlemen."[36]

Dinwiddie and the Assembly avoided the issue, and "Centinel X" faded into the background. During the winter it appears that Weedon took a leave of absence.[37]

In May, 1757, because of the colony's financial difficulties and the insufficient number of recruits, Governor Dinwiddie ordered a rearrangement of the Virginia Regiment and a reduction of officers. There were to be ten companies of one hundred men each, and the officer complement was to be seven captains, twenty lieutenants, and ten ensigns.

---

[35] Ambler, 1936: p. 113.

[36] Officers of the Virginia Regiment to Washington, 12 November, 1756 Hamilton, 1898-: 1: pp. 382-385; Freeman, 1949-: 2: pp. 221-223.

[37] Koontz, 1925: p. 116. Weedon was not present at a council of war on 30 October, 1756 at Fort Loudoun, which Adam Stephen and fifteen officers attended.

Dinwiddie, however, always allowed Washington flexibility, and Washington settled on twelve companies. In the new arrangement of June, 1757, Weedon was promoted to lieutenant—one of twenty-four. He received his commission on July 26, 1757.[38]

In June Governor Dinwiddie ordered out one-third of the militia from six counties to be sent to Fort Loudoun. They were to be collected at Winchester and Fredericksburg. Eight or ten of Washington's subalterns were to go to the places of rendezvous to receive the militia draftees.[39] It is probable that Weedon was assigned to this duty at Fredericksburg. By July, 114 of the four hundred men that had been collected at Winchester and Fredericksburg had deserted.[40]

On July 29, Lieutenant Weedon, "commanding the company, lately Captn. Cocke's, now joined to Captn. [Joshua] Lewis's," received orders from Washington to march the company from Fort Loudoun to Conococheague Creek, which empties into the Potomac about thirty miles to the north. The Conococheague Valley, running into the lower part of Pennsylvania, had been the scene of massacres by the Indians the year before.[41] Weedon remained on active duty—presumably being sent on similar scouting missions—until October 26, 1757, when he went home again on recruiting assignment.[42]

Meanwhile the British ministry prompted the colonies to raise troops for an all-out offensive. High on the agenda was a campaign against Fort Duquesne. The Virginia Assembly responded under a new governor, Francis Fauquier, and voted to continue Washington's regiment and to raise a second regiment to be commanded by William Byrd. Each regiment

---

[38] Instructions to Washington, 16 May, 1757, Brock, 1885: 2: pp. 622-623; Washington to Dinwiddie, 12 June, 1757, Fitzpatrick, 1931-: 2: p. 56; Hamilton, 1898-: 5: p. 163n.

[39] Dinwiddie to Washington, 20 June, 1757, Brock, 1885: 2: pp. 643-644.

[40] Freeman, 1949-: 2: p. 359.

[41] Washington to Captain Thomas Waggoner, Fort Loudoun, 29 July, 1757, Fitzpatrick, 1931-: 2: pp. 106-107; Sipe, 1927: pp. 291-292.

[42] A Return for the month of November, 1757 of the Virginia Regiment, Fort Loudoun, 1 December, 1757, Washington Papers, Ser. 4, Reel 31, LC; Returns . . . Company commanded by . . . Lewis for September, October, and November and Absent Officers Monthly Return, First Virginia Regiment, for October, November, and December (1757), Virginia Militia Records, 1754-1758, VSL.

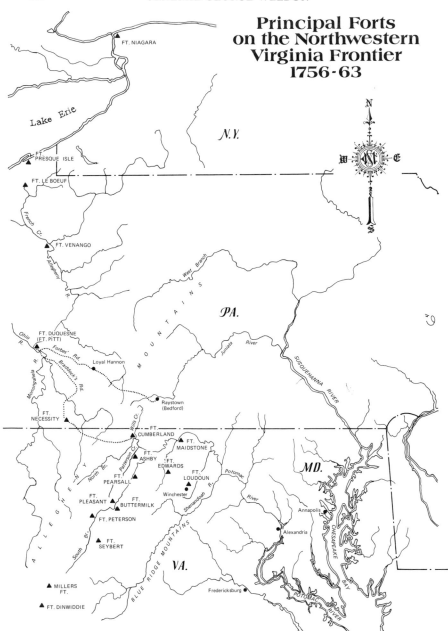

Principal Forts
on the Northwestern
Virginia Frontier
1756-63

Map 1.   Principal Forts on the Northwestern Virginia Frontier, 1756-1763.
Drawing by Paul Nickerson, Richmond City Planning Commission.

was to consist of one thousand troops, and Washington was to deploy eight hundred men for the expedition.[43]

By April, 1758, Lieutenant Weedon was back on active duty at Patterson's Fort, a small stockade on the South Branch of the Potomac. On April 9 he headed a scouting party and tracked what were thought to be Indians until dark. Next day Captain John Baker dispatched Ensign Coleby Chew to continue in pursuit of the Indians. Chew followed their tracks "from pretty near the place where Lt. Weedon left them last night." Coming across two of their prey, Chew's party fired on them, killing both, only to find out that the two dead savages were really soldiers disguised as Indians, who had been on a scouting mission themselves.[44]

In June Washington gathered his troops at Winchester. Of these, five companies and artificers left for Fort Cumberland on June 24, 1758. As Byrd's Second Virginia Regiment was still being organized—and never would be up to full strength—it came up several weeks later.[45] Andrew Lewis took two hundred Virginians to Raystown (present day Bedford, Pennsylvania), thirty miles northeast of Fort Cumberland, where they were to be used to begin cutting a new road to Fort Duquesne. By July 12, 535 Virginians, six companies, were at Raystown under the command of Adam Stephen.[46] Weedon was probably still on special garrison duty and therefore did not accompany the troops to Raystown at this time. By September most of the men of both Virginia regiments—a total of 1,484—were in the expeditionary force commanded by General John Forbes as it edged westward, cutting a road as it went through the mountains.

Either Weedon was present in the Forbes expedition or remained on garrison duty at Fort Cumberland, Fort Loudoun, or one of the lesser forts. In any event he was with the First Virginia Regiment immediately before and after the

[43] General Forbes to General Abercromby, 22 April, 1758 and Forbes to Pitt, 19 May, 1758, James, 1938: pp. 68-69 and 91 resp.

[44] Captain John Baker to Washington, 10 April, 1758, Hamilton, 1898-: 2: p. 276.

[45] Colonel Henry Bouquet Memorandum, 12 June, 1758, Stevens et al., 1940: Series #21643: p. 92.

[46] A Return of the Six Companies of the First Virginia Regiment Encamped at Rays Town, inclosed in a letter of Adam Stephen to Washington, 13 July, 1758, Washington Papers, Ser. 4, Reel 31, LC; Freeman, 1949-: 2, p. 316; Morgan, 1973: pp. 37-38.

Forbes expedition.[47] Muster lists do not indicate the names of officers below company commanders, unless a notation regarding special duty is written in. None of the muster lists for the Forbes campaign have Weedon's name, or, for that matter, the names of most of the other subalterns.

If Weedon did join the Virginians with Forbes, he may have taken part in the unfortunate defeat of a detachment under the British regular, Major James Grant, on September 14. At that time, 805 men, including 168 of the First Virginia Regiment under Major Lewis, were sent ahead of Forbes's army to reconnoiter and check any scouting parties. They were ambushed only a few hundred yards from Fort Duquesne. The casualties were high: 270 killed and forty-two wounded, including six officers and sixty-two men of the Virginia troops killed; Grant and Lewis were captured.[48] If Weedon was with the Virginia troops in Pennsylvania, he may also have been among the five hundred Virginians led by Washington in a skirmish with the French and Indians near Fort Ligonier.[49]

Forbes's combined army of Royal Americans, Highlanders, and provincials from Virginia, Maryland, North Carolina, and Pennsylvania entered the abandoned and destroyed Fort Duquesne on November 25, 1758. Already orders from the governor of Virginia had arrived, directing the Virginia troops to return to the colony. Enlistments in the Second Regiment expired on December 1. Most Virginia troops, however, did not reach Fort Loudoun until mid-December. A detachment was kept on at Fort Duquesne, now renamed Fort Pitt.[50].

The objective of the Virginia participation in the war had been achieved with the taking of Fort Duquesne. Only several hundred troops were needed to serve at frontier posts, and most of the officers would retire or go home on extended leave.

---

[47] Weedon received £9 4s. 7d. in pay and was one of the fifteen officers on a pay voucher, 15 June, 1758, at Fort Loudoun (Washington Papers, Ser. 4, Reel 31, LC).

[48] Expedition against Fort Duquesne, n. d. (14 September, 1758) and Forbes to Pitt, 20 October, 1758, James, 1938: pp. 237-240; Colonel Mercer to Colonel Bouquet, 10 and 14 September, 1758, Stevens et al., 1940: Series #21643: pp. 164 and 168 resp.; Alberts, 1965: p. 210; Freeman, 1949-: 2: pp. 342-346.

[49] Freeman, 1949-: 2: pp. 357-358; Sipe, 1927: pp. 399-400.

[50] Captain James Craik to Washington, 20 December, 1758 and Robert Stewart to Washington, 29 December, 1758, Washington Papers, Ser. 4., Reel 32, LC. The time of service for the First Virginia Regiment was extended to May, 1759. Forbes left 200 Virginians at Fort Pitt.

Washington's announcement that he would leave the army evoked a response, on December 31, 1758, of twenty-seven officers at Fort Loudoun, with Weedon's name heading the list, expressing their regret over Washington's intention.[51] Washington resigned his commission on January 16, 1759, and was succeeded by Colonel Byrd.

George Weedon found the routine of garrison duty dull and the wilderness isolation unnerving. Undoubtedly, like most of the officers, he spent much of his time in 1759 at home. By February, 1759, Virginia troops at Fort Pitt and other frontier posts consisted of only a remnant of the First Regiment and four companies of rangers. Possibly Weedon stayed on the frontier long enough to accompany Colonel Adam Stephen and three hundred Virginia troops from Winchester to the supply depot at Fort Bedford in May, 1759. Stephen's force soon dwindled, but in June they acted as an escort for a supply train along Forbes's Road to Fort Pitt.[52]

Events on the Pennsylvania frontier in 1759 offered assurance to Virginians that the war was nearing an end. The Indians had given up their siege of Forbes's Road, and the several Indian conferences, which involved Weedon's future brother-in-law, Hugh Mercer, as commandant at Fort Pitt, seemed to indicate that a pacification of the Ohio Indians was well under way.[53] There was good news that Sir William Johnson had taken Fort Niagara on July 25, 1759, and subsequently, that the French had abandoned in ruins the three forts in Pennsylvania that formed a link between Fort Pitt and Fort Niagara—Venango, Le Boeuf, and Presque Isle. Briefly in autumn, 1759, Indian hostility flared up in the west and the south. The Virginia legislature voted to raise 1,500 men until December 1. Hostilities subsided, and in December the Assembly allowed all Virginia troops to disband except for 150 troops for the frontier garrisons.[54]

The conquest of Quebec and other victories in the north left the French with only a tenuous hold in the west. Montreal and Detroit would be the next British objectives. There was a substantial French force at Detroit and the western Indians,

[51] The Humble Address of the Officers of the Virginia Regiment to Washington, 31 December, 1758, Fitzpatrick, 1931-: 3: pp. 143-146.

[52] Wainwright, 1959: pp. 160 and 163; Baker-Crothers, 1928: pp. 145-147.

[53] E.g., Stevens et al., 1943: Series 21655: pp. 27ff.; Darlington, 1920: p. 99.

[54] Baker-Crokers, 1928: pp. 145-147.

disorganized and always unpredictable, were still a threat. For frontier security and as bases of operations, the French forts should be rebuilt and maintained by British arms. This task fell to Brigadier General Robert Monckton, who now commanded the Southern military department. Monckton arrived at Fort Pitt on June 29 and immediately ordered Colonel Henry Bouquet to march 400 Royal Americans and 100 Virginia troops from Fort Pitt to Presque Isle, 105 miles away. The Royal Americans would relieve British troops at Niagara, and the Virginia soldiers would work on rebuilding Fort Presque Isle. Hugh Mercer would follow with a detachment of Pennsylvanians to aid the Virginians and to work at the other forts.[55]

Lieutenant Weedon joined the Virginia troops at Fort Pitt in early summer, 1760. Two of his good friends were with him, William Daingerfield and Captain John McNeill of Augusta County. McNeill would later will his sword to Weedon.[56] At Fort Pitt Weedon first became acquainted with his future brother-in-law, Hugh Mercer. Weedon was in Bouquet's detachment which set out July 7. Guided by George Croghan and his Indian scouts, who were probably drunk as usual, the troops lost valuable time in taking a wrong trail. The summer's heat was intense as the soldiers filed northward along a barely discernible path. The pack horses almost died and the sweat and the puss from their sore backs damaged the provisions. Yet the relief party made steady progress and reached Presque Isle, on Lake Erie, in ten days.[57]

As soon as the detachment arrived at Presque Isle, Bouquet sent Weedon and six of his men to Fort Niagara to get pilots for boats and whatever provisions could be spared. It was a hazardous trip, braving choppy waves and summer storms, on small boats around the shore of the lake to the opposite side and then following the Niagara River to its mouth on the south side of Lake Ontario, where the old stone fortress was located. The Royal Americans were also sent out at the same time for duty at Fort Niagara. Weedon found the fort teeming with English traders waiting for permission to move

---

[55] Mercer to Monckton, 19 July, 1760, *Aspinwall Papers*, 1871: p. 276; Wainwright, 1959: p. 171.

[56] Kegley, 1938: p. 312.

[57] Bouquet to Monckton, 18 July, 1760, *Aspinwall Papers*, 1871: p. 274; Quattrocchi, 1962: pp. 199-201; Wainwright, 1959: pp. 171-172.

westward. Having accomplished his assignment by July 29, Weedon returned to Presque Isle, arriving August 4, followed by thirty Royal Americans with three *bateaus* carrying twenty barrels of pork and some tools.[58]

Work proceeded slowly in building the fort at Presque Isle. Colonel Bouquet reported on September 2 that it had rained for twenty-four days, and "we have raised only the first story of the Blockhouse."[59] Hostile Indians were again in the vicinity, and a Virginia escort party for a pack train was ambushed by a small band of French and Indians about two miles from the camp. Another party of soldiers on the other side of the fort was also fired upon. Bouquet, however, refused to send a force out, "the Woods being so full of Branches and fallen Trees as to be nearly impracticable, and much better known to the Enemies than to us."[60]

By the end of September the blockhouse at Presque Isle was almost completed. The Pennsylvanians had finished a smaller one at Fort Le Boeuf, and some of the Virginia troops had also erected a fort at Venango.[61]

Frontier duty in building a fort out in nowhere was not the kind of excitement that George Weedon liked. There was no action, and no glory. He wondered why he had stuck it out so long in the service when so many other officers had retired, but being an officer meant more to Weedon than to others of more prominent families. It was a mark of distinction and a badge of a gentleman. He would keep his strong sense of duty, at least as long as he was needed, and he would hold on to his commission. Yet he was getting homesick for his friends and society in Virginia, and reflected on how good it would be to return to civilization. Like all good soldiers, however, Weedon kept his sense of humor. He found time to pen a long letter to Charles Lewis that is remarkable not only for describing life at a frontier post but for its odd humor and revelations on Weedon's colorful personality.

---

[58] Bouquet to Monckton, 19 July and 6 August, 1760, *Aspinwall Papers*, 1871: pp. 275 and 294; Major William Walters to Bouquet, 29 July, 1760, Stevens *et al.*, 1941: Series 21645: p. 129; Cuneo, 1959: pp. 131-132.

[59] Bouquet to Major Gates, 28 September, 1760, *Aspinwall Papers*, 1871: p. 311.

[60] Bouquet to Monckton, 3 September, 1760, *ibid.*: pp. 312-313.

[61] Wainwright, 1959: p. 172.

Prisque Isle on Lake Erie Sept. 20th, 1760
My Dear Charles

Your agreeable favour of the 26 July I have this moment Rec'd, and hope I need not be at much pains to Convince you that I shall let no opportunity slip my Earnest Endeavours to keep in the graces of so worthy a Correspondence. I see how the land lyes and if I dont weather the point D—n my Eyes, silence you for long letters mr. Fatty, have at ye. I tell you as an Indian told me, that my name is Tom Hickman and Value no man, and to show you I dont, I snatch at this opportunity that offers within 2 hours after the Receipt of yours, tho' was you to know my Situation, ye fat sides of yours would work like a pair of Bellows. I am at this time Commander in Chief of a Bullock Guard kept on an Island 6 miles long and about 4 miles broad, and Expect (from Indian Intelligence) to be attackd within 3 hours, but as the information comes from that fraternity my hand don't shake so much as it would from any one Else. My Only Enemy, as yet has been the Musketoes, which have Surrounded me, flankt me, attack'd me in Front & Rear, but by the help of a little Smoke I as yet Keep my Ground. My table is made of the Smoothest kind of polish'd Burch barke. My Ink is Gun Powder mash'd and mixt with Lake Erie Water Double distill'd through the Devils Crooked A--. My pen is made of the Quill of Lake Ontario Flocking fowl and all these Difficultyes do I Surmount to Write to my much esteem'd friend C. L. but am Sorry I cant Gratify his Expectations, for I am Sure you Expect a D--nd deel of News. You know if I had any I should not be Backward, and when you consider the place I am in you'll not be Surprised at my Silence on that head. You might depend that I would send you a Catfish was I at P. Burgh or any thing Else that that place could afford. I was only there Eight days before I marcht with Capt. McNeill, Daingerfield, Lawson and 100 R. F. of the Virgns. to take Post here where we have Remained Ever since. We have been pretty much Troubled with Scalping Partyes from Detroyat (but Virginians never give way you know). Capt McNeill was the Other day Attackd by a Party of french and Indians within two miles of the Camp. They Killd one and took two prisoners of his advance Guard before he Could get up, but as he fired on them with his Party, they Immediately ran of; you see they have not forgot their old methods at F. Cumberland, when we ware their in 56 upon Salt Chunk &c.

I am sorry that Larkin dont Visit you oftener but I can tell you his Reason, he wants to make people believe he's Damnably Interested in the Service, but dont give him too much Encouragement or then he will Eat & Drink you out of house and home, for he is very fickld, and far from being Bashfull. I wish you was with us their would be no Occation for you to be as Spry as Jack Asby, for we go all by Water here, unless Its some few Carrying places which are Quite Levell, so if you ware with us, you would not be Obliged Perhaps to have a Litter on acct. of your Toes. I thank my god I have at last got to be a grate man, that is I have got to be Comodore of the Red Flagg on Lake Erie, by going to Niagara Sience I have been here. The Particulars of my Voyage I keep till I see you. On my Passage Collected a good many Curious stones which I'll send you by the first Opportunity.

I am Glad to hear of the Augmentation of Fredcricksbg, but believe if it augments in Buildings it Diminishes in Inhabitants for have not heard a Sylable from any of them these three months. Scott I can Acct. for, but none of the rest. Do let me know whats become of them in your next. Pray where is that damn fellow Yates gone to. I am afraid miss Catty Reynolds has Piss'd in his Eyes. Wel he was good worthy lad as Ever I had the pleasure of Cultivating an Acquaintance with, & one that mist no Oppertunity to let his friends hear from him. Oh woman, Woman, Curst Confounded Woman, to Deprive me of my Constant Correspondant C. Y. [Charles Yates] by the evacuation of Urine, and as for Scott you'll find him at Mrs. Thornton's spring a playing Jackstones, at any hour of the Night. Do my dear Charles, have his Body Decently Buried, and pay him all the honours of a True Backanalian, His Body lyes in a small ditch abt. 20 yards from the spring.

I observe as how, you are Ever Striking me in the teeth with mrs. Champ, Miss Thornton as was. I'll tell you what it is Charles. I dont want to Batter Vauxhall abt. your Ears, on Acct. of mrs. Lewis. Therefore would have you mention her to me no more, for if you do may depend I will Raze the Walls of Vauxhall Levell with the Ground. I have already brought two 24 lbs. to bare on you and an 18 Inch Mortar is Ready for to salute you with a shell, if you persist in your Insults.

No doubt but you have heard of Montgomery's leaving Carolina, & believe you are as able to judge the Ill Consequences as I can tell you, we have had no News from Colo. Byrd sience he left us. Everything wares the face of Expedition in this Quarter, but we have had so much to do that I believe Detroyat will not be ours this Campaign.

General Amherst has marcht for Montreal Some time with an Army of 15000 men and well Supply'd with all kind of Stores. I expect to have a deel of News for you in my next, till which time

> I am Dear Charles
> Your Ever Obt. & Hble Servt.
> Geo. Weedon
> C. R. F. on L. E.

N. B. pray my kind Complyts. to Mrs. Lewis & Oblg GW[62]

It was not that George Weedon was especially vulgar, but he did like to add relish to descriptions, and his being in the army so long had not led to refinement. Frustrated without other creative outlets, Weedon let himself go in his letter writing, often achieving an impressionistic quality and leaving his readers a bit baffled. Weedon's letter to Charles Lewis points to Weedon's need for close friendships and his going to lengths to poke fun at his friends. He missed his old friends and the pleasures of sharing with them table and bottle.

Weedon and the Virginia troops at Fort Presque Isle were sent to Fort Pitt on October 1, 1760. He stayed on duty there until the end of November, when he returned to Virginia with some 300 Virginia troops on the Pennsylvania frontier ordered back because of the Cherokee War.[63] Weedon could hardly know where his military career would take him in the future, but he must have left the western Indian frontier with a sigh of relief. Three years later, the Indians of Pontiac's Rebellion would destroy the "French" forts, butchering many of the defenders, and even roasting alive a young lieutenant over a slow fire for several nights.[64]

Weedon seems not to have served in the Virginia expedition against the Cherokee Indians in 1761, even though his Virginia Regiment, under Adam Stephen, was ordered to join other Virginia troops for this purpose in April, 1761. Weedon apparently took leave, and would probably have joined the expedition if peace were not in the making in late 1761.[65]

Stephen's regiment was disbanded on March 1, 1762, and Weedon at that time received £91 5s. in pay.[66] He and other officers were also to receive a full year's pay, voted by the Assembly in January, 1762, "over and above what shall be due them till disbanding said Regiment."[67]

---

[62] Weedon to Charles Lewis, 20 September, 1760, Lewis Family Papers, University of Virginia.

[63] Bouquet to Monckton, 1 October, 1760 and 29 November, 1760, *Aspinwall Papers*, 1871: pp. 332 and 353 resp.

[64] O'Meara, 1965: pp. 226-227.

[65] Fauquier to William Byrd, 25 April, 1761, Draper Collection, Virginia Papers (microfilm zz, vol. 4), VSL; Morton, 1960: **2**: p. 735; Corkran, 1962: pp. 263-266.

[66] An Account of Cash paid Officers of the Virginia Regiment ... disbanded 1 March, 1762, "Journal of Lewis," 1892: p. 217.

[67] Hamilton, 1898-: **3**: pp. 231-232n.

But disbandment was for a brief duration. On March 29, 1762, Governor Fauquier received a copy of the declaration of war against Spain, and the following day he asked the assembly to create a new regiment and to provide additional troops for a British expedition being formed in the South under Amherst.[68]

On the reconstituting of Stephen's regiment, George Weedon was awarded a promotion to Captain Lieutenant[69]— well deserved because of his persistence in staying in the service at isolated garrisons. It does not appear, however, that he saw any further active service during the war.

When the preliminary articles of the Treaty of Paris became known in December (formally signed on February 10, 1763), the Virginia Regiment was finally disbanded.[70] At that time, Weedon let it be known he was willing to send "a Servant or an Express" to General Amherst to apply to being taken into the pay of the crown.[71] Whether Weedon, other than to seek a pay readjustment, seriously considered entering into the regular British service is not determined. But the long stints of army life made him think of himself as a professional military man.

Among the reasons for disbanding the Virginia Regiment were that Parliament put a clamp on Virginia's issuance of paper money and that, with the war being over, the partial funding by Great Britain of colonial war expenses had ceased. When Pontiac's Rebellion proved threatening to the colony later in 1763, the Virginia government simply called out militia from the frontier counties.

For Weedon's service in the French and Indian War he was eventually awarded bounty lands. As a Captain Lieutenant he was entitled to 3,000 acres, according to provisions of the Proclamation of 1763. This the Virginia government made good, after Independence in 1780, by issuing him six warrants for 500 acres of land each.[72]

[68] Morton, 1960: 2: pp. 735-736; Koontz, 1925: p. 95; Peckham, 1964: pp. 203-204.

[69] Francis Fauquier . . . to George Weedon, 22 May, 1762, printed in Greene, Katherine G., 1926: p. 343.

[70] 4 and 7 December, 1762, Hillman, 1966: 6: p. 242.

[71] Captain Robert Stewart to Washington, 15 November, 1762, Hamilton, 1898-: 3: pp. 240-241.

[72] At a Court held in Spotsylvania County, 17 February, 1780, certificates #676-681, French and Indian War Bounty Warrants and Land Bounty Certificates, VSL. Weedon was not entitled to any of the 200,000 acres set aside "on the Great

At long last a civilian, Weedon could enjoy uninter-
ruptedly the easygoing bachelor life, renewing old friendships
and making new acquaintances of the gentry and merchants
in and around Fredericksburg. No longer would his
romancing be suspended by having to return to some lonely
outpost. Always somewhat a ladies' man, he had a whole field
to play among the young—and not so young—belles of the
vicinity. He struck quite a figure in wearing the latest fashions
of knee breeches, silk stockings, and white gloves.

The town of Fredericksburg, with a population of 3,000 in
1765 and ranking next only to Norfolk and Williamsburg as a
commercial center, had "all the trade of the Back settlements
who send Down here great quantitys of Butter, Chees, flax,
hemp, flower, and some tobacco which they rol Down many
miles."[73] A number of mines were located nearby. The town
could boast a brewery among its small industries. Fairs, horse
races, theatrical productions, and tavern conviviality
enlivened the social scene. Gregarious and even a hail-fellow-
well-met sort, George Weedon would be very happy to live in
this budding metropolis.

A year or so after he left active military service, Weedon
came to the realization as he neared his thirtieth birthday, that
it was time to seek a wife. In early 1764 (or possibly late 1763)
he married Catharine Gordon, daughter of John and Margaret
(Tennent) Gordon of Fredericksburg. Catharine's parents had
married in 1739,[74] and she was six or seven years younger than
George. John Gordon, who had kept a tavern in Fredericksburg for twenty years, died in 1750. He left his wife several
lots, with a tavern-house and other buildings, in Fredericksburg, which were to be sold when the two daughters,
Catharine and Isabella, reached twenty-one years of age or
married, the proceeds then to be divided among his wife and
children.[75] Mrs. Gordon had been keeping the tavern, known

Kanhaway" reserved for "the first adventurers," who served before the battle of Great
Meadows in 1754. (See *Virginia Gazette* [Rind], 22 March, 1770). The Proclamation of
1763 is printed in Hening, 1820-1823: 7: pp. 663-669.

[73] "Journal of a French Traveller, 1765," 1921: p. 747.

[74] Crozier, 1905: 1, pts 1-2: p. 85. An entry for 21 February, 1731 mentions "John
Gordon of Fredericksburg, ordinary keeper." (p. 122.)

[75] —February, 1649-1650, will dated 13 December, 1749, "exhibited" 6 February,
1749-1750, appraisal 6 March, 1749-1750, Spotsylania County Will Book B (1749-
1759): pp. 26-28, VSL.

as Mrs. Gordon's Tavern, on the property since her husband's death.[76]

After their marriage, George and Catharine settled at the Gordon property in Fredericksburg, and George Weedon took over the management of the tavern. Weedon was already popular about town and was named Captain of the Spotsylvania militia in March, 1764.[77] Now he had a place that would be a center of attraction to his friends and offer hospitality to the socially prominent of Virginia who might be passing by. Aspiring to social distinction, Weedon would have to discard some of his army brusqueness and polish up the social graces. Now, too, he was a businessman.

---

[76] E.g., 6 June, 1759 and 6 March, 1769, William Allason Papers, VSL.

[77] Crozier, 1905: p. 519.

II. TAVERN AND TRACK

For more than a decade before the Revolution, George Weedon plunged into a whirl of business and social activity. His tavern gained renown throughout Virginia. The wealthy elite, from George Washington to the governor himself, stopped at the tavern, famous for its food and drink specialties and entertainment. Weedon was a major supplier of meat in the Fredericksburg area. He had to keep tabs on his plantation on the Potomac and, at the end of the period, to administer the estate of his uncle, George Gray. He was recognized as a leading sportsman-promoter in the colony. As expected of a prominent citizen, he participated in the affairs of the church and the Masonic Lodge.

The Weedons lived in the tavern still owned by Catharine's mother, Margaret Gordon. The sale of the Gordon property that was to take place upon the marriages of the two daughters, according to John Gordon's will, did not occur until ten years after the daughters married. In 1774 Weedon bought the tavern property from Mrs. Gordon, with Catharine's interest being considered, for £371 10s. 4d.[1] Presumably he also had to make a settlement with Hugh Mercer for the share in the property of his wife, Isabella. The tavern property covered a half block—lots 25 and 26—on the corner of Caroline Street on the west, William Street on the south, and Sophia on the east.[2]

Weedon's tavern property had two dwelling houses, one facing Caroline Street and the other, connected to the first, on the east side. The first house probably had one story originally, with a second added during the period April–August, 1774, when Weedon had extensive brick and shingle work done and when he had a stairs built in the kitchen.[3] Specific description of the property is found in the records of the

---

[1] Ledger Book #2, VSL.

[2] At the present site of the Woolworth store, and, earlier in the twentieth century, the site of the Wakefield Apartments and Simpson's garage. A fire in 1807 destroyed the tavern property and other buildings in the vicinity.

[3] Ledger Book #1, WML and #2, VSL.

Mutual Assurance Company in 1796.[4] Presumably at that time the structures were essentially the same as in 1774, for it does not appear that Weedon did any more work on the property after he rented it in 1776. By 1796, however, there is no indication of a stable, which Weedon had when he operated the tavern. The first dwelling house facing Caroline Street, was 46½ feet long and thirty feet wide, built of brick and covered with wood; the second house, one story high—forty-four feet long and twenty-five feet wide, built of wood and covered with wood. A small wooden shed was added to the first house on the north side at some time. Weedon's billiard room was located in the adjoining second house.

There is no way of determining how many rooms there were in the two buildings, but it is assumed the rooms were small and at least consisted of a dining room, a sitting room, a room used as a post office, several bedrooms (one used by the Weedons), and the billiard (and game) room. It would seem that the tavern could accommodate a few lodgers at a time, and these were more often than not servants of wealthy visitors who stayed with friends elsewhere. Weedon's tavern, in addition to a stable and stable yard, had a smokehouse (salthouse), a small slaughterhouse, a well with pump, and perhaps other small outbuildings.[5] "Iron work" was done on the stable in 1774.[6]

From 1772 to 1776 Weedon rented a house to Tulley Whitehurst, which may have been part of the tavern property, but most likely was elsewhere. In 1764 Weedon and Hugh Mercer, as partners, purchased lot 203 from Roger Dixon and his wife Lucy and at the same time drew "as prizes in Dixon's Lottery" lots 240 and 250[7] (later the location of the Sentry Box) on lower Caroline Street.

Weedon had an overseer, Price Thomas (hired at £35 a year and one-tenth of the wheat crop), to run his plantation on the Potomac, which he now called Crab Cove plantation and which had a tobacco house. Nine Negroes were maintained on the plantation, and occasionally several slaves were hired from George and Nathaniel Gray, Jr. The plantation was diversified. Cattle, swine, and sheep were raised, which

---

[4] Declarations, 1 April, 1797, Mutual Assurance Co., 3, #6, VSL.

[5] Indenture George Weedon and William Smith, 17 February, 1776, Fredericksburg District Court Papers (xerox), supplied by G. H. S. King.

[6] Ledger Book #2, VSL.

[7] Crozier, 1905: p. 238; Weedon's Will, 25 and 26 November, 1793, Fredericksburg Hustings Court Will Book A (1782-1817).

provided meat "for my Own use in Fredericksburg" and also for Weedon's meat business. At Crab Cove, corn, wheat, and tobacco were grown. In Weedon's ledger books there are also accounts listed with "Fishingshore," which for want of identification may be assumed as part of the Crab Cove plantation or Weedon's or someone else's fishing interests in the vicinity. In 1773 Weedon bought for £270 one hundred thirty-five acres of land, "call'd Washington's tract," from Nathaniel Gray, Jr. At that time Francis Gray was living on this land.

With the death of his uncle, George Gray, in 1773, Weedon became administrator of the estate, which included two plantations: Pine Hill in Stafford County, where Weedon may have spent his teen-age years with his mother, and an estate in Culpeper County (leased from James Duncanson). His responsibilities as administrator of George Gray's estate included various business transactions, smallpox inoculation, hiring tutors for the orphans, tobacco inspection, and obtaining "sundries." Weedon even billed the estate in 1775: "To your part punch to treat the Officers."[8]

Besides the partnership in the three lots in Fredericksburg, Weedon was involved in another transaction with Mercer when he sold Mercer his rights (French and Indian War bounty claims) to 3,000 acres in Fincastle County (Kentucky), seventeen miles above the Falls of the Ohio (near Louisville). As mentioned before, the claims to these lands would not be confirmed until 1780, after Mercer's death. Mercer probably arranged to pay Weedon what George Washington was offering veterans to buy their claims, i.e., £5-7 per one thousand acres.[9] In all, Mercer had claims to over 11,000 acres along the Ohio River from purchases from Weedon and James Duncanson and his own claims for lands under the Proclamation of 1763. He still retained 900 acres in Pennsylvania. Mercer had three full lots in Fredericksburg (numbers 50, 63, and 123), five half acres, at least two houses, and a stable on his hillside half acreage. In 1774 he purchased George Washington's Ferry Farm (about 600 acres), on the north side of the Rappahannock River overlooking both Falmouth and, across the river, Fredericksburg.[10]

---

[8] Ledger Book #2, VSL; *Virginia Gazette* (Purdie and Dixon), 24 March, 1774.

[9] Freeman, 1949-: **3**: pp. 246-247.

[10] Hugh Mercer's Will, 20 March, 1776, probated 20 March, 1777, photograph, VHS

In 1772, Hugh Mercer formed a partnership with Dr. John Julian "in the Practice of Physick and Surgery."[11] Their shop was next door to "Mrs. Julian's Tavern," which was located several blocks away from the present building styled in the Fredericksburg tour as "Hugh Mercer's Apothecary Shop." Mercer never owned this property on the corner of Caroline and Amelia, but he was to own the property directly opposite it. He could, however, have leased what is the current "Apothecary Shop." It is also possible he used one of his houses on the three lots, on Amelia crossed by Princess Anne and Charles Streets, as the apothecary shop.[12]

George Weedon and Hugh Mercer became fast friends. Hugh married Isabella Gordon about the same time that George married her sister, Catharine—before April 10, 1764.[13] Two of the Mercer children (fourth and fifth) were named after George Weedon: George Weedon Mercer and Hugh Tennent Weedon Mercer (the other children were Ann Gordon, John, and William). Hugh Mercer had come to Fredericksburg shortly after his discharge on January 15, 1761, from the Pennsylvania regiment. As noted before, he had met Weedon at Fort Pitt and Fort Presque Isle. A refugee from Scotland, having served as a surgeon in the abortive uprising of Bonnie Prince Charlie in 1745–1746, Mercer had first settled in the Conococheague Valley in Pennsylvania. Since he had fought for the English in America, he now felt it was safe to practice his professon in a more settled area. He admired Washington and this was probably a factor in his decision to move to Fredericksburg.[14]

(from Spotsylvania County Will Book E [1772-1798]: p. 169); Embrey's Index . . . Deeds, Wills . . . (1782-90), Grantee, H-Z; Freeman, 1949-: pp. 346-347; Hugh Mercer to Washington, 21 March and 6 April, 1774 and Washington to Mercer, 28 March and 11 April, 1774, Washington Papers, Ser. 4, Reel 33 and Ser. 5, Reel 115, resp. LC. The price was £2000, Virginia currency, to be paid in five annual installments.

[11] *Virginia Gazette* (Purdie and Dixon), 9 July, 1772; advertisement, 1 July, 1772.

[12] For the particulars on the history of the ownership of Hugh Mercer's "Apothecary Shop" in Fredericksburg and evidence that this shop never belonged to Mercer, see John T. Goolrick, "Letter to the Editor," *The Free Lance Star* (Fredericksburg), 9 April, 1936. Useful in locating property in Fredericksburg is a map, "Plan of Fredericksburg, Virginia," 1890, VSL. It includes lot numbers.

[13] Crozier, 1905: p. 310.

[14] See Waterman, 1941. Though well written, this biography has much that is fiction; e.g., a lengthy meeting between Hugh Mercer and John Gordon in 1764 when supposedly Mercer was introduced to Weedon. Gordon had actually died fourteen years before.

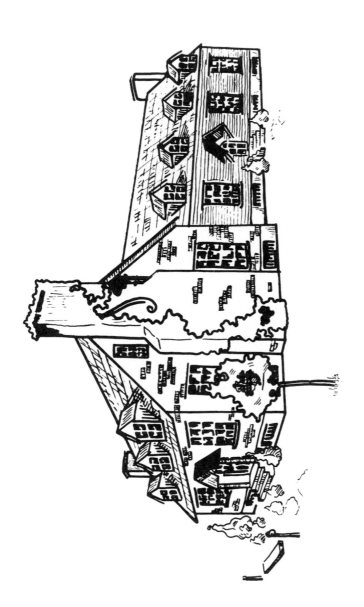

Fig. 1. Old Stage Office or Weeden's Tavern. A sketch by B. N. Goodman. From G. H. S. King. 1940. "General George Weedon." *William and Mary Quarterly*, ser. 2, 20: p. 242. With permission of Virginia State Library.

As a side occupation to his tavern-keeping, George Weedon in the late 1760's went into the business of selling meat. Demand increased, and Weedon formed a partnership in Fredericksburg with Charles Washington, brother of George Washington. The success of the enterprise may be measured by the fact that for 1772–1773 there were ninety-nine customers on account. A pasture was rented from Francis Thornton that served as a stockyard. On one day alone thirty-three head of cattle were purchased from Messrs. Davidson and Frazer for £100. Slaughtering was done by contract with "Charles the Butcher." Meat, off the hoof, was also brought in from the Crab Cove plantation. For a while there was a third partner, James Ward. After 1773, when it seems that the partnership was dissolved, Weedon continued supplying meat on his own, but on a more moderate basis. Beef, lamb, and mutton were usually sold by the quarter. A quarter of lamb remained at a constant price of £2 6s. The price of beef depended upon the grade and cut. A hind quarter of beef varied from as low as 12s. 11d. to £1 8s. 3½d. A side of lamb usually brought 5s. A barrel of pickled beef sold for £4 4s. Messrs. Weedon and Washington dealt exclusively with beef and lamb (and mutton), although rarely they supplied "some bacon." Among the customers were James Madison, William Woodford, and William Paul (brother of John Paul Jones).[15] One of the best customers was Fielding Lewis, who purchased meat to feed the ever flowing stream of guests at his house in Fredericksburg and also to stock his vessels in the Rappahannock.[16]

As tavern-keeper, George Weedon bought large quantities of rum, wine (chiefly Madeira), arrack, and "strong beer," which he used for the tavern or resold to friends. Rum was the most popular beverage in the colony, and was usually mixed into some sort of fruit punch. It is impressive how great a quantity of limes and lemons Weedon bought for his own use and for resale. "Six boxes of lemons" or a "barrel of limes" was not an unusual shipment received.

At the tavern, friends, neighbors, and an occasional lodger gathered around in the evening; and, relaxing in Weedon's black walnut chairs, they enjoyed warm conversation and beverages of their choice. Old comrades-in-arms frequently stopped by the tavern to reminisce on their adventures in the French and Indian War. Persons dropped by to see if they had

[15] Ledger Book #1, CWM.
[16] Duke, 1949: p. 77.

any mail in Weedon's post-office room, and probably often lingered to have a drink or chat with the proprietor or guests.[17] Occasionally in the evenings there was a puppet show or other special entertainment. Weedon was very proud of his billiard table, which may have been the only "public" table in Fredericksburg at the time. Some of the guests sat around and played cards or backgammon. Some came early for dinner and passed the evening at the tavern in the small talk or more aggressively playing and betting at the games. It can be imagined that some of the guests, typical of many wealthy Virginia gentlemen of the time, had been drinking all day since their first toddy or julip at breakfast and were so much in their cups by late evning that when the less inebriated were ready to depart sometime before midnight they had to be prodded out of their stupor. Most guests kept an expense account with the tavern, which was recorded as "Club in . . ."[18] Travelers and guests could expect a variety of food, drink, and services at Weedon's tavern, a sampling of which is given below from the one surviving tavern ledger book, chiefly for the period 1772–1775:

Dinner and Club	Club in Punch
Supper and Club	Club in Cards and Punch
Lodging	Turtle Dinner and Club
Stablage—Oats and Hay	Breakfast and Julip
Oats and Hay	Club at Puppet Show
Breakfast	Club in Beer
Breakfast and Bitters	Club in Punch and Billiards
Club in Bumbo	Club in Wine
Club in Arrack	Bumbo and Grog
Club in Arrack Punch	Club in Cards
Boys Dinner and Bumbo	Guinea Bowl of Arrack
Boys Dinner and Beer	Dinner and Bumbo
Boys Dinner and Lodging	Grog and Lodging
Club in a Meridian	Club in Cards and Bumbo
Turtle Dinner and Club	Dinner and Beer
Club Porter and Beer	Diet and Loding
Bottles Madeira	Club in Liquor
Bumbo at Backgammon	Bowl of Bumbo
Club in Cards and Punch	Bowl of Punch

---

[17] E.g., Washington picked up a letter "By exprs. at Weedon's" (for 1 s. 6 d.). Fitzpatrick, 1925: 2: p. 189, 18 March, 1775.

[18] For the best definition of "club" and a comment on Washington's spending an evening at the Weedon tavern on 8 March, 1769: "THE CLUB: It was a common practice among Virginia gentlemen of this time, when dining or supping at a tavern, to do so in groups either at a private table or, at a large tavern like Weedon's, in a

Many persons made it a habit to stop at the tavern. Old army veterans such as William Daingerfield, Jr., George Taylor, and John Lewis were regulars. John Lewis was the most persistent—averaging a "club" visit once a month. Other frequent patrons were Fielding Lewis, Mann Page, Sr., Mann Page, Jr., James Mercer, and Dr. Charles Mortimer. Less frequent, but regular, were visits by Joseph Jones (a burgess from King George County), Benjamin Grimes, Thomas Digges, James Duncanson, George Baylor, Henry Mitchell, William Woodford, and William Horner. Alexander Spotswood (grandson of Governor Spotswood) of Nottingham near New Post, four miles from Fredericksburg,[19] dropped in once in a while. Hugh Mercer, who drank either bumbo or beer, was a regular in taking a "Club," but probably came by frequently, not putting anything on account and probably sponging a few drinks on the house from his brother-in-law.

Notables from out of town stopped on the way to the fair or the various races in the Northern Neck. Some of these were Charles Carter, Ralph Wormeley, Thomas Ludwell Lee, John Jamison, and John Tayloe. John Earl of Dunmore, Governor of Virginia, stabled his horses at Weedon's on August 17, 1773, and again on a return trip, September 15–17, 1773, at which time he purchased twenty-nine gallons of rum from Weedon. Fielding Lewis, William Woodford, James Mercer, Joseph Jones, and William Fitzhugh were attracted by a good game of billiards or cards. Fitzhugh, whose estate of Chatham was across the Rappahannock from Fredericksburg, may have been the house "shark" at billiards, as he had his own table to practice on. Fielding Lewis seems to have been an inveterate backgammon player.

When George Washington infrequently came to Fredericksburg to visit his mother and the Lewises, he usually dined at the Lewises, "Spent the Evening at Weedon's," and then returned to the Lewises for lodging. He recorded four such occasions (in 1769, 1771, 1772, and 1774), not including other

private room. They would be served as a unit by the innkeeper and then would *club* for the cost of the food, drink, and room; that is, they would divide the total bill equally. On this evening GW (Washington) paid 2s. 6d. as his share of the club and lost 1s. 6d. at cards." (Jackson, 1976: 2: 133n.)

Besides several slaves, including Bob, Weedon had the assistance of a housekeeper (or cook), Mrs. Susannah Keyton, who is known to have worked for the Weedons from 1773 to 1776. Her yearly wages were £7 10s. and probably included board. Weedon also supplied red wine for use of the "Church Warden at Fredericksburg."

[19] Riley, 1963: p. 188n.

visits to Weedon's tavern of an official nature.[20] Washington probably had met with Weedon in Fredericksburg before his first recorded visit at the tavern in 1769, most likely at a dinner party at the Lewises or at the tavern. Some sort of continuing acquaintance is implied in a letter of Captain Robert Stewart (in Jamaica) to Washington, January 25, 1769: "I am truely glad that honest Weedon (for whom I have a great regard) is well and still maintains the same happy flow of Spirits and Joyous turn for which he was always remark'd."[21]

Weedon, accompanied by Charles Washington, visited Mount Vernon for the week of April 7–13, 1769. George Washington had other guests at the time: William McGachin, a "sea captain," and a Mr. Buchanan. Washington sat around with his guests for four days, and then went off fox-hunting for each of several days. When Weedon and Charles Washington went home on the 13th,[22] they must have begun to get the impression that they had overstayed their invitation. There is no indication that Weedon was ever again a guest of George Washington—though obviously Washington continued to have a high regard for Weedon.

George Weedon probably found a more intimate reception when visiting other patrons of his tavern, including Fielding Lewis[23] and the gentry along the Rappahannock—the Pages, Thorntons, Fitzhugh, Daingerfield, and others. In 1766, along with William Woodford and Larkin Chew, he was a godfather of William Daingerfield's daughter, Elizabeth.[24]

Public meetings were held at Weedon's tavern to discuss important issues of the day. Shortly after the passage of Patrick Henry's "Virginia Resolves" opposing the Stamp Act, during the Fredericksburg Fair in June, 1765, a group of leading citizens met at the tavern to weigh the implications of the "Resolves."[25] Although opinion was divided as to the extent resistance should take, there was a consensus that the duties violated the constitutional liberties of Virginians.

[20] 8 March, 1769, 24 October, 1771, 15 September, 1772, and 13 May, 1774, Fitzpatrick, 1925: 1: p. 315; 2: pp. 79 and 151, resp.

[21] Captain Robert Stewart to Washington, 25 January, 1769, Hamilton, 1898-: 3: p. p. 335.

[22] 7-13 April, 1769, Fitzpatrick, 1925: 1: p. 320.

[23] Duke, 1949: p. 54.

[24] Information from G. H. S. King, concerning the bible at Kenmore (Cambridge, 1763). Elizabeth Daingerfield was born 8 February, 1766; married Colonel Charles Magille, 21 April, 1789; died February 1791.

[25] Letter of James Mercer, 14 September, 1766, *Virginia Gazette* (Purdie and Dixon), 3 October, 1766.

Undoubtedly in 1768–1769 there was discussion in Weedon's tavern on the Townshend Duties and efforts to re-create an "association" for boycotting British goods.

On August 2, 1770, George Washington met with the veteran officers of the French and Indian War at Weedon's tavern. He dined at the tavern and stayed until sunset. The purpose of the gathering was to work out details for the precise acreage the officers were entitled to in their claims. The officers agreed to apportion among themselves the costs of surveys and other expenses. They appointed Washington to act as their agent and attorney to consult with the governor and council.[26] Again on November 23–24, 1772, Washington attended a meeting of the officers at Weedon's tavern dealing with the distribution of the bounty claims.[27] This collective bargaining had some success. In December, 1773, the governor and council agreed that the officers could relocate their grants "wherever they shall desire, so as not to interfere with Legal Surveys or actual Settlements," and every officer was "allowed a distinct Survey" for every thousand acres.[28]

Weedon's tavern also was used for other public functions, such as land auctions[29] and meetings of creditors to place demands against a person or estate.[30]

Nothing excited Weedon's interest more than horses. Whenever he and his guests settled down to dinner and an evening of drinking, talk always seemed to turn to horses and horse racing. Many of the patrons at Weedon's tavern were racehorse owners and breeders. Weedon himself was an excellent judge of horseflesh. He was a habitué of the race track in Fredericksburg, and was known to attend the track at Leedstown.[31]

Soon after he took over management of the tavern, George Weedon became a promoter of horseracing in Fredericksburg. He helped to introduce subscription racing. The *Virginia Gazette* ran advertisements in September, 1766, placed by

---

[26] 2 August, 1770, Fitzpatrick, 1925: 1: p. 391.

[27] 22-23 November, 1772, *ibid.*: 2: p. 87; Hillman, 1966: 6: p. 516, December, 1772.

[28] 15 December, 1773, Hillman, 1966: 6: p. 553.

[29] *Virginia Gazette* (Purdie and Dixon), 3 January, 1771; *Virginia Gazette* (Rind), 10 January, 1771.

[30] E.g., creditors against William Taliaferro of Orange County, original meeting for 20 January, 1770, but extended to 3 April, 1770 (*Virginia Gazette* [Rind], 14 December, 1769 and 26 February, 8 March, and 15 March, 1770); against estate of John Campbell of New Post, 15 March, 1773 (*ibid.*, 4, 11, and 25 February, 1773); *Virginia Gazette* (Purdie and Dixon), 26 August, 1773, advertisement 17 August, 1773.

[31] E.g., "cash paid at Leedstown" to Captain James Wignell, Ledger Book #2, VSL.

Weedon that at the Fredericksburg races on Thursday,
October 9, 1766, there would be a purse of £20 "ready money,
to be run for by any horse, mare, or gelding, not more than
quarter blooded, the best of three four mile heats" and on
Friday, October 10 there would be a purse of £10 for a race of
horses that did not have "any mixture of the English" breed in
the best of three two mile heats.

> The horses that are to start for either of the above purses are to
> be entered, shown, and measured, at Capt. *George Weedon's*
> on, the Monday preceding the races, paying for the first purse
> 20*s.* and for the second 10*s.* which entrance money is to be
> given to the second best horse, &c. running for each purse,
> acording to the rules of racing, to be adjudged by Gentlemen
> appointed by the subscribers, who are also to regulate every
> matter on the field, and determine any dispute that may arise.

No less than three horses had to enter and start the race.
George Weedon promised that there would be "sundry other
diversions" at the races. It was also announced that, "on the
first race day," there would be handed "about a subscription
for future races at *Fredericksburg,* on such terms as may be
most agreeable to the Gentlemen present, who are encouragers
of the turf."[32]

Weedon's efforts to put subscription racing on a permanent
basis succeeded, and in about a year the Fredericksburg Jockey
Club was formed. Weedon was elected secretary, and the
quarterly meetings of the FJC were held in his tavern.
Members of the FJC were admitted only by ballot. By 1774, the
FJC had forty-four members, which represented most of the
leading sportsmen of the area.[33] Among Weedon's duties as
secretary of the FJC was serving as treasurer, selling tickets,
and arranging for advertising. During the races he acted as
concessionaire, supplying punch and "sundrys" at the races.

The peak year for the FJC was 1774. Attendance at the races
had so increased that a stand was built on the race ground.
The finances of the FJC were on "so good a Footing that
Gentlemen who start their Horses . . . may depend on receivng
the full Value of the purse in ready Cash, as soon as the Race is
determined." At the April match race, Mann Page Jr.'s
Damon defeated Moore Fauntleroy's mare Miss Sprightly for
two hundred guineas; two weeks later at the second match

---

[32] *Virginia Gazette* (Purdie and Dixon), 12 and 26 September, 1766.
[33] *Ibid.,* 20 January, 7 and 14 April, and 21 July, 1774; Morton, 1960: p. 309.

race Maxmilian Robinson's Roundhead outdistanced Miss Sprightly for a purse of one hundred pistoles. On the second day of the fair, May 24, Fauntleroy's Miss Alsop beat William Fitzhugh's Kitty Fisher for £50, and the next day Alexander Spotswood won with Fearnought for the entrance money. Weedon was in charge of seeing to it that proper weights were carried by the horses according to their ages. As was the practice for many years, the horses had to be entered with Weedon on a date a few days before the races, with the proper certification.[34]

For the October races, Weedon set the deadline for subscription money at September 10, and pleaded that "those who have not Guineas will please send me other Money." The race for the Jockey Club Plate on Tuesday, October 4, was open to members only. The subscription purse of one hundred guineas went to William Fitzhugh for his Regulus in a two of three heats triumphed over Spotswood's Eclipse in a five horse field. Moore Fauntleroy's horse in this race threw his rider. Bets ran high, and Wormeley Carter lost £20. The Give and Take Purse of £50 was run the next day—John Tayloe's bay mare, Single Peeper, the winner. William Daingerfield's Ariel ran sixth out of the eight starters in the first hear. On Thursday, the Town Subscription Purse of £50, "free for any horses," was run for the best of three of four heats, four miles each; only one horse in the field finished the race with the winner, William Fitzhugh's Kitty Fisher. On Friday, the Jockey Club and Town Subscription race of £50, requiring an entrance fee of one guinea, was won by William Fitzhugh's gelding, Volunteer.[35]

The next year, 1775, the Revolutionary movement absorbed the attention of Virginians and contributed to a sense of austerity. Many FJC members were active participants in the patriot cause, serving in the Virginia conventions, the committees of safety, and as military officers. Measures were passed by the committees of safety to curtail frivolity, especially gambling. To hold the Fredericksburg races would be a risky business financially, and unpatriotic. The *Virginia Gazette* carried a notice on February 24, 1775 that George Weedon had called a meeting of the FJC for March 14, "at which time some matters of consequence will be left to their

---

[34] *Ibid.*, 17 February, 1774; Carson, 1965: p. 127.
[35] *Virginia Gazette* (Purdie and Dixon), 11 and 25 August, 1774; Riley, 1963: p. 189n.; Carson, 1965: pp. 128-129.

consideration."³⁶ Apparently a decision was made at the meeting to postpone the races indefinitely.

Fairs were held in Fredericksburg twice a year—since 1770 in May and September.³⁷ The Fredericksburg Fair, dating back to 1738, had become the leading attraction of its kind in Virginia. Visitors from out of town checked in at Weedon's tavern for refreshments, "sundrys," and even, if they ran out of money, for cash advances. Weedon's stable offered fodder and shoeing for the horses.³⁸

No particulars are known of Weedon's slaves at this time. His ledger books do not indicate that he did any trading in slaves, except for hire. An item in the *Virginia Gazette* in March, 1770, advertised for a runaway, "a tall slender Mulatto man named CHARLES EVANS," hired by Weedon in 1769 from William Watkins. Evans, "rather a brighter Mulatto than common," had on a red jacket when he ran away and was thoroughly "acquainted on James River."³⁹

George Weedon was as exasperated as other Fredericksburg residents with the prevalence of horse thievery. Two horses belonging to Alexander Donald were stolen out of Weedon's stableyard on Tuesday night, September 8, 1767. Weedon apparently had custodial care of some blooded horses that he kept in Fielding Lewis's pasture. William Woodford had "a dark bay horse," between six and seven years old and bred by Colonel Edward Carter of Albemarle County missing from Lewis's pasture and offered a 20s. reward in May, 1768, to anyone who would deliver the horse to himself or to "Capt. George Weedon in Fredericksburg."⁴⁰ Weedon advertised in the *Virginia Gazette* in January, 1771: "STRAYED or stolen . . . a bay mare about 13 hands high, with a roached mane and bob tail, her brand I have forgot, though believe it was WF. She trots and canters very well, and is about 9 years old. Whoever will bring her to me shall receive 15s. reward."⁴¹ Eight months later Weedon advertised again for a missing horse, "STRAYED, or STOLEN, from Captain George Weedon's Pasture," and he offered a reward.⁴²

³⁶ *Virginia Gazette* (Purdie and Dixon), 24 February, 1775.
³⁷ *Virginia Gazette* (Rind), 2 August, 1770.
³⁸ Riley, 1963: 179n.; Ledger Book #2, VSL.
³⁹ *Virginia Gazette* (Rind), 7 and 15 March, 1770.
⁴⁰ *Ibid.*, 12 May, 1768 and *Virginia Gazette* (Purdie and Dixon), 1 October, 1767.
⁴¹ *Virginia Gazette* (Rind), 31 January, 1771.
⁴² *Virginia Gazette* (Purdie and Dixon), 3 October, 1771.

Although the death penalty had long been on the books for horse stealing and even for being an accessory to the act,[43] it was difficult to trace a stolen horse taken out of the area where the crime was committed, and juries were reluctant to convict a person of a capital offense for horse stealing. Had the law been less severe and had the punishment fitted the crime, enforcement might have been more effective. George Weedon finally had to disclaim any responsibility for horses under his care that were stolen. In the *Virginia Gazette* in October, 1772, he served notice that

AS HORSE-STEALING is become so common, and the Difficulty of Conviction so great (as proved by a recent Instance) in Justice to myself, I am obliged to inform all Gentlemen who put up with me that I cannot be answerable for the forthcoming of Horses put into my Pasture or Stable hereafter, the Profits being very inadequate to the Risk.

In the Instance now alluded to, I was within five Minutes of being answerable for two Beasts worth a Hundred Pounds, and though my Stable and Yard are as well secured as possible, a Villain found Means to possess himself of two valuable Mares, the Property of Mr. *Henry* Whiting and Mr. John *Throckmorton* of *Gloucester*.

He was taken within fifteen Minutes after he had committed the Robbery, with the Creatures in his Possession; and yet he has escaped! It may be relied on that the best Care which human Prudence can suggest shall be taken, as formerly; but I will not be answerable for Robberies. GEORGE WEEDON[44]

In the same issue of the newspaper it was announced that

THE Gentlemen of this Place [Fredericksburg] and *Falmouth* have raised, by Subscription, the Sum of FIFTY POUNDS, which is deposited with Mr. *George Weedon*, as Reward for apprehending and bringing to Justice any Person or Persons who shall, after the Date hereof, steal any Horse, Mare, or Gelding, the Property of a Subscriber. Twenty five Pounds to be paid on the County Court's committing the Thief for farther Trial, and twenty five Pounds on Conviction at the General Court.

Keeping the horses of noted gentlemen as becoming a frustrating experience. George wondered if it was worthwhile.

---

[43] September Session, 1744, Hening, 1820-1823: **5**: pp. 247-249 and October Session, 1748, *ibid.*: **6**: p. 129.

[44] *Virginia Gazette* (Purdie and Dixon), 18 and 22 October, 1772.

George Weedon attended Saint George's Church and persuaded his brother-in-law, Hugh Mercer, to do the same, even though Mercer had been a staunch Presbyterian. As the only church in town, Saint George's was the center of religious life, and, to be a member of the established society, it was desirable to affiliate with the church. The extent of George Weedon's association with the church was simply in being a member; he did not become a church warden until 1789.[45] But he was always willing to lend a hand in any community activity of the church. In 1768 he was one of twelve persons serving as managers for a lottery to raise £50 to build a new church and to purchase an organ. Three thousand tickets (there would be 213 prizes and 2,787 blanks) were issued. First prize was £500; and two prizes for £250 each. The drawing was scheduled for December 28, but not enough tickets were sold, and it was postponed to June and then to October, 1769. It is doubtful if the lottery was ever held; there were no further notices on a drawing,[46] and a new church was not built.

As a prominent Fredericksburg citizen, Weedon joined Masonic Lodge Number Four, one of the three oldest in America (founded in 1752 and chartered in 1758 by the "Grand Lodge of Scotland"). The Lodge at the time met at the Market House on the corner of Caroline Street and Market Alley. Originally Weedon was a member of the Kilwinning Port Royal Cross Lodge in Caroline County (founded in 1755), even though he was never a resident of Caroline County.[47]

At the regular anniversary meeting in December, 1763, to commemorate "our Patron," Saint John the Divine, Weedon and Adam Hunter were listed as "visiting Brothers." At this meeting Weedon petitioned to become a member of the Fredericksburg Lodge, and, after a vote, he was "admitted as such by the unanimous Consent of the Lodge having agreed to the Laws of this Lodge & paid the Sum of one Pistole the usual Sum for such admission."[48] Weedon entered as a full member and therefore bypassed the initial stage of

---

[45] Quenzal, 1951: p. 16; Quinn, 1908: p. 203.

[46] *Virginia Gazette* (Rind), 14 July and 11 August, 1768; 20 April and 24 August, 1769.

[47] Campbell, 1954: pp. 468-469. The charter, due to an oversight, was not recorded until 1767. (5 January, 1767, FLB, VSL.)

[48] 26 December, 1763, FLB, VSL.

apprentice.[49] The next day he took part for the first time in the annual procession that led from the Market House a few hundred yards, past the gallows and pillory, to Saint George's Church, where a sermon was preached in the "forenoon."[50] Next year Weedon was elected a senior warden, an office he would hold intermittently many years; at other times Weedon served as junior warden. After 1770, no person could serve "successively" in an office more than one year.[51] George Washington, Fielding Lewis, William Woodford, and Charles Dick were among the members of the Fredericksburg Lodge.

On each Saint John's Day, after the Lodge heard the annual sermon, they went to Weedon's tavern to dine in the early afternoon. In the evening a ball was held in the Market House.[52]

The Lodge met monthly on the last Saturday until 1769 and thereafter the first Friday. Quarterly dues were applied towards "Liquors & all other necessarys."[53] Weedon seems to have procured the liquors and other items for the Lodge meetings, as he submitted large bills, usually £17 or £18, for reimbursement.[54] Weedon sold tickets to the annual ball and received a commission of 4s. on each ticket; starting in 1768 he was allowed "one Dollar" for each ticket sold.[55]

By 1774, the Weedons were tiring of being so much in the public's eye, with little privacy of their own. The hustle and bustle of Fredericksburg society and the responsibilities of running the tavern and the Jockey Club gave them pause to wonder if it was all worth the while. In the tavern business, the burdens of trying to please everyone and cater to different tastes and demands were at the least exhausting, and gratitude was as fleeting as many of the patrons. Competition had stiffened, with more than a dozen other taverns doing business in the Fredericksburg area.[56] As Weedon's ledger books

[49] E.g., Lewis Willis and Anthony Strother entered as apprentices, *ibid*, 25 December, 1756.

[50] 27 December, 1763, *ibid*.; Riley, 1963: p. 79, 27 December, 1774.

[51] 27 December, 1764, 19 December, 1770 and *passim*, FLB, VSL.

[52] "Dinner and Club" entries, Ledger Book #2: *passim*, VSL; 28 November, 1767, 3 December, 1768, and 25 November, 1769, FLB, VSL: Quinn, 1890: pp. 9-10. The first ball was held in 1757. Ledger Book #2 contains a number of entries for Masons' "Dinner and Club" at Weedon's tavern. In 1769 the Masons decided not to have a ball, and instead voted that they "shall sup" at Weedon's."

[53] 28 March and 17 April, 1767, FLB, VSL.

[54] Ledger Book #2: *passim*, VSL.

[55] 3 December, 1768, FLB, VSL. In March, 1768, the Lodge went in procession to Falmouth "and Constituted a Lodge there." (*Ibid.*, 30 March, 1768).

[56] Darter, 1957: p. 106.

indicate, money was scarce and some customers simply did not pay up, preferring to continue their accounts on credit. Weedon, going on forty years old, must have wished for a more free and easy existence. After all, he had enough assets to get by. He and Catharine were childless. They had no desire to travel. Weedon might give more attention to his slaughtering business and take a first hand interest in his Westmoreland plantation. Although trouble was stirring between the colonies and the mother country and a break was conceivable, little did Weedon realize that, past his prime, new adventure and military glory awaited him. Nor could he be aware that his new career would be, in a sense, a personal tragedy.

III. THE REVOLUTION COMES TO VIRGINIA

In the summer of 1774, the revolutionary movement came alive in Virginia. George Weedon relished excitement, and these were volatile times. Everywhere in America citizens were smarting under the late brash efforts of intimidation by Parliament. Spontaneously resistance developed, and event quickly followed event.

A new and younger leadership was vying for control of Virginia politics. If George Weedon was not in the forefront in the political leadership of the revolutionary movement in Virginia, his friends and acquaintances and the circle of Virginia veteran officers of the French and Indian War were. He was of the same generation. George Weedon had a great affection for Virginia, his country. Even in service in the backwoods of Pennsylvania he had known no other loyalty. The honor of Virginia—and George Weedon as well—was at stake. He would participate in the revolutionary movement both because this was what Virginians were doing and because by principle he had no other choice. To say that Weedon was simply a follower, however, does him an injustice. As his later correspondence reveals, his mind and being were committed to the revolutionary cause. But he was also aware that should war break out he might reap material benefit. There would be preferment in military service based on his past experience, and veterans of war could expect a bountiful reward in land or other compensation. Weedon was losing interest as a tavern manager and businessman. Military service would be a welcomed change and would give Weedon an opportunity to exert a leadership he could not or would not exert in political life.

Although shying from political ambition, Weedon, nonetheless, was very much in the fray. Local citizens found his tavern a lively place for news of revolutionary activity elsewhere and also a center for organizational discussions for resistance in the Fredericksburg area. J. F. D. Smyth, writing at a later time, recalled that during his tour of Virginia in 1774 he stayed "at an inn or public house kept by one Weedon, who is now a general officer in the American army, and was then

41

very active and zealous in blowing the flames of sedition."[1]

Weedon joined with other residents of Fredericksburg and Spotsylvania County on June 1 in voting to support the people of Massachusetts in their measures protesting the Coercive Acts and in forming a committee of correspondence.[2] Three weeks later the committee resolved that no obedience should be given to any act of Parliament that interfered with the internal affairs of Virginia, which "we will oppose . . . with our Lives and Fortunes." It was proposed that all trade with Great Britain should be severed until the obnoxious acts of Parliament should be repealed.[3]

Meanwhile resistance gained momentum. An extra-legal convention met at Williamsburg in August, 1774, and adopted non-importation. A Continental Congress convened in the fall and established an "Association" for coordinating local economic sanctions. The colonies and the localities were requested to set up committees for the enforcement of a total boycott: non-importation, non-exportation, and non-consumption.

On December 14 and 15 a gathering of freeholders of Spotsylvania County met in Fredericksburg and elected a committee of safety, consisting of twenty-seven persons. Although Weedon was not elected a member of the committee, he must have attended the general meeting, as a person's patriotism was measured according to whether or not he was present.[4] It was also voted at the meeting that merchants would be asked to subscribe to the association, that a warehouse be rented for the collection of grain to be sent to the relief of the people of Boston, and—what interested Weedon the most—that the county raise independent companies "of public spirited Gentlemen to be ready on all occasions to defend this Colony and to act in Conjunction" with similar forces of other counties "when it shall be judged most necessary." A committee (again Weedon was not a member) was appointed to draw up regulations for the independent companies, and a subscription was "set on foot" to purchase

---

[1] Smyth, 1784: **2**, p. 151.

[2] Quoted in Duke, 1949: p. 85; Benson, "Wealth and Power," 1970: pp. 80-81; "Fredericksburg in Revolutionary Days," 1919: pp. 76-77. The committee: Fielding Lewis, Charles Dick, Charles Mortimer, Charles Washington, William Woodford, James Duncanson, William Porter, George Thornton, and Charles Yates.

[3] *Virginia Gazette* (Purdie and Dixon), 7 July, 1774.

[4] The loyalty of persons not attending the general meetings at Falmouth, across from Fredericksburg, was suspected. E.g., see William Allason to Thomas B. Martin, 6 February, 1775, *Richmond College Historical Papers*, 1917: **2**, no. 1: p. 113.

gunpowder, lead, and flints.[5] The Spotsylvania Independent Company was immediately formed, and George Weedon served as captain under Colonels Hugh Mercer and Alexander Spotswood.

In late March, 1775, Weedon eagerly awaited news from the second Virginia Convention that met for a week in Richmond. From delegates who passed through Fredericksburg on their way home, Weedon learned of the heated debates at the convention, of Patrick Henry's fiery speech, and of the narrow decision to put the colony on a military footing. The convention had taken upon itself to re-instate the militia system, which had expired by law.

Over the weekend of April 22–23, alarming rumors drifted into Fredericksburg that on the previous Thursday night marines from Governor Dunmore's ship, anchored five miles below Williamsburg, had crept into the town and stolen the powder from the magazine. Monday morning, April 24, Weedon and other Fredericksburg citizens heard verification of the rumor. This was the day for a muster of the Spotsylvania Independent Company. When the question of what should be done was put to the troops, they unanimously voted against "submission to so arbitrary an Exertion of Government" and proposed that "a Number of public spirited Gentlemen should embrace this opportunity of shewing their Lead in the grand Cause" by marching on Williamsburg to secure the arms still in the Williamsburg magazine. A rendezvous of the Company as "light Horse" was set for Saturday morning. Letters were sent to the commanding officers of companies of "adjoining counties," asking that they send troops to Fredericksburg. George Washington and other interested persons were also informed of the decision. The letters bore the signatures of Hugh Mercer, Alexander Spotswood, George Weedon, and John Willis.[6]

For several days armed men from all walks of life, in hunting shirts and with tomahawks dangling from their belts,[7] straggled into Fredericksburg, which now began to resemble an armed camp. A letter arrived from Peyton Randolph, Speaker of the House of Burgesses, writing on

---

[5] 14-15 December, 1774, Spotsylvania County Committee Resolves, VSL.

[6] Hugh Mercer, Alexander Spotswood, George Weedon, John Willis to Captain William Grayson, 24 April, 1775 and The Independent Company to Washington, 26 April, 1775, Hamilton, 1898-: 5: pp. 162-163.

[7] Michael Wallace to Gustavus Brown Wallace (in Glasgow), 14 May, 1775, Wallace Papers, UVL.

behalf of the corporation of Williamsburg, stating that
Dunmore had agreed to return the powder, and hence there
was no need to march on the capital. Randolph also advised
waiting for further directions from the Continental Congress,
which was about to convene. On Friday news arrived of the
battle of Lexington and Concord.[8]

On Saturday, a council of war of 102 members was formed
in Fredericksburg. After deliberating for two days, the council
of war heeded Randolph's advice and decided against a march
on Williamsburg. But the troops were to keep themselves in
readiness to answer a summons to duty at a "minute's" notice.
A resolution of the council of war condemned the powder
seizure and extolled the patriot cause; yet it desired to avoid
"the horrors of a civil war." The resolution concluded by
proclaiming "GOD SAVE THE LIBERTIES OF AMERICA,"
instead of the usual phrase, "GOD SAVE THE KING." On
Monday, the military assemblage broke up, and the troops
went home. Letters were sent to halt other militia from the
neighboring counties who were on their way to Fredericksburg.[9]

Had Patrick Henry gone to Fredericksburg during the
crisis, the troops there might well have joined him and the
Hanover militia in their trek towards Williamsburg of May 2.
News of Henry's success in receiving a bill of payment for the
powder from the governor's representative, Carter Braxton,
served to quiet tempers, although the air was still charged
with Dunmore's threat to free and arm the slaves. George
Washington, as he prepared to leave for the Continental
Congress, approved of the caution of the Fredericksburg
military proceedings.[10] Several weeks later a letter from
Edmund Pendleton in Philadelphia addressed to "William
Woodford . . . To the Care of Capt. Weedon" indicated
Congress's approval of the caution of the Fredericksburg
military leaders, while also not censoring Henry's action,
because to do so would invite factionalism.[11] Meanwhile,
Weedon helped to lead the Spotsylvania Independent

---

[8] 28 April, 1775, Riley, 1963: p. 94; Duke, 1949: p. 92; Eckenrode, 1916: p. 50.

[9] Fredericksburg Committee, 29 April, 1775 and Alexander Spotswood to Col.
George Washing, 30 April, 1775, Force, 1837-: 4th Series: 2: pp. 443 and 447; Burk,
1816: 4: pp. 10-12.

[10] Washington to Captain Charles Lewis and Lieuts. [George] Gilmer and [John]
Marks . . . 3 May, 1775, "Papers . . . Gilmer, " 1887: 6: p. 81.

[11] Edmund Pendleton to William Woodford, 30 May, 1775, Burnett, 1921-1938: 1:
p. 102.

Company in its drills to be ready for any further emergency.[12]

Although events were tranquil in Virginia during most of the summer, Virginians were acutely aware that war was erupting. Lord Dunmore in June established headquarters at Gosport on the Elizabeth River near Norfolk. There he busied himself in trying to put together a military force out of a handful of sailors and marines, sixty men of the British Fourteenth Regiment, and assorted Scottish clerks and runaway slaves. Some plundering by British ships in August and the subsequent capture and burning on September 2 of a British warship grounded by a storm at Hampton marked the beginning of hostilities in Virginia. The patriot committees of counties around Norfolk proceeded to "blockade" the town.[13]

News arrived that Congress had taken charge of the war in the north, and Weedon took pride that his former regimental commander was now the commander in chief of the Continental Army. The brave defense at Charlestown Heights across from Boston on June 17 stirred the martial zeal among the men of the Virginia independent companies. The time was soon forthcoming when they, too, would also be in the thick of battle.

But first Virginia had to organize for war. Lord Dunmore's actions and the war in the north pulled the moderates over the fence to the side of revolution. The Virginia Convention reconvened in Richmond on July 17 and sat until August 26. Of the ordinances passed by the convention the one that interested George Weedon the most was that which created a regular military establishment that superseded the independent companies. Three regiments were voted. In the initial balloting for commander of the first regiment (and hence the commander in chief of the colony's force), Weedon's brother-in-law, Hugh Mercer, led by one vote, but lost in the run-off to Patrick Henry. Thomas Nelson was elected to the command of the second regiment. But Nelson declined, and the Convention then decided to form only the first and second regiments, with William Woodford being selected as commander of the second regiment. Besides raising a regular military force, the "July Convention" also voted appropriations to erect a manufactory of arms near Fredericksburg,

[12] Riley, 1963: p. 96.
[13] Eckenrode, 1916: pp. 58-60.

which in a few months was ready to make gun barrels, bayonets, ramrods, and other equipment.[14]

Although Weedon and his brother-in-law had not received commissions in the new military establishment, it was only a matter of time before they would. In anticipation of entering regular military service, George Weedon planned to lease his tavern. Looking about for prospects, he placed an advertisement in the *Virginia Gazette* in September, 1775:

> The subscriber intending to quit publick business after the first day of *January* next, would rent his house and lot in this town upon reasonable terms, which would suit any person inclinable to keep TAVERN, it being situated in the centre of the town, and has been long accustomed by the first gentlemen of this and the neighbouring colonies. It is large and commodious, there are all convenient outhouses, including a storehouse on the main street, an exceeding good garden, a well of fine water within a few steps of the door, a billiard table &c &c. Any person inclining to rent the same shall have . . . all the liquors on hand, consisting of best *Madeira* wine, old arrack, port wine, and spirits with any part of the household and kitchen furniture; they giving bond, with approved security, for payment of the same.
>
> All persons indebted to me are desired to settle their accounts, and give bonds for such as they cannot conveniently discharge; and those who have any demands against me will be pleased to make them known. George Weedon[15]

But there were no immediate takers, and Weedon had to bide his time and await the first reasonable offer.

The newly formed Virginia Committee of Safety took over the direction of the military force during the adjournment of the convention. In October the Committee ordered Woodford's Second Regiment and some of the Culpeper militia to the vicinity of Norfolk to keep a check on Dunmore. In November Dunmore moved his force, which included loyalists and Negroes (the total estimated as low as 150 and as high as 500), to Great Bridge on the South Branch of the Elizabeth River, twelve miles below Norfolk.[16] At nearby Kemp's Landing, on November 14, the British dispersed about 300 militia. Dunmore then set up an outpost at Great Bridge.

---

[14] *Proceedings* . . ., 1816: *passim*; Hening, 1820-1823: **9**: pp. 72 and 81-82; Sellers, "Virginia Continental Line," 1968: pp. 50 and 61-62; Meade, 1969: **2**: pp. 33-34; Duke, 1949: pp. 97-99.

[15] *Virginia Gazette* (Purdie), 15 February, 1775, advertisement 6 September, 1775.

[16] W. B. Wallace to Michael Wallace, 12 November, 1775, Wallace Papers, UVL.

Woodford's force moved up to Great Bridge and there, on December 9, the Virginia troops withstood an assault by Dunmore. Woodford reported to the Virginia Convention that "This was a second *Bunker Hill* affair, in miniature, with the difference that we kept our part and had only 1 man wounded in the hand." He put the enemy's casualties at over a hundred. Dunmore retreated to his fleet. A North Carolina force of 250 arrived a day after the battle, and several days later the American troops occupied Norfolk.[17]

When the Virginia Convention reconvened on December 1, it created nine regiments, and George Weedon could now expect to enter active duty in the Third Regiment, which would be formed from the Fredericksburg and Northern Neck area. The Congress, on December 28, asked for six Virginia regiments to be taken into the Continental service, and the Third Regiment was one of these.[18] George Weedon was among the candidates for a commission and who was recommended as one willing to serve and was "well thought of."[19]

On January 12, 1776, the Virginia Convention elected the field officers of the Third Regiment—Hugh Mercer, Colonel; George Weedon, Lieutenant Colonel; and Thomas Marshall, Major.[20] Congress took the Third Regiment into Continental service on February 13, and approved the selection of officers.[21] Weedon's commission of the same date, bearing the signature of John Hancock, indicated that the commission was "to continue in force until revoked by a future Congress."[22]

Weedon finally succeeded in finding someone to rent his tavern property. William Smith of Falmouth signed an indenture on February 17 with Weedon for a lease for the tavern lots, the tenement, the outbuildings, and "the use of a Billiard Table." Weedon, however, retained the use of the salthouse and slaughterhouse in the stableyard, which he

---

[17] William Woodford to the President of the Virginia Convention, 9 and 10 December, 1775 and Robert Howe to [the Virginia Convention?], 13 December, 1775, Anderson, 1915: 1: no. 1: pp. 115-116, 120-121, and 125, resp.; Eckenrode, 1916: pp. 64-68, 74-79, and 116.

[18] Flagg, 1912: p. 185; Burgess, 1927-1929: 3: p. 1240.

[19] Edmund Pendleton to William Woodford, 24 December, 1775, Mays, 1967: 1: p. 141.

[20] Virginia Convention, 12 January, 1776, Force, 1837-: 4th Series: 4: p. 120; *Virginia Gazette* (Purdie and Dixon), 12 January, 1776 and (Dixon and Hunter), 13 January, 1776.

[21] Ford, 1904-1937: 4: pp. 131-132.

[22] Weedon's Commission, Philadelphia, 13 February, 1776, AKF.

reserved the right to enclose. Smith could take possession April 20 on a three year lease: £100 "of lawful money of the said Colony of Virginia" for the first year; and for each of the next two years, £120. Smith had to keep in good repair all buildings, fences, and, of course, Weedon's prize possession, the billiard table.[23] Smith advertised in the *Virginia Gazette* that the tavern under his management would open April 22, 1776, and that he "has laid in a good stock of liquors." The advertisement also noted, "A good COOK WENCH wanted, on hire."[24] Smith would prove to be a durable tenant and would stay on many years after the expiration of the initial lease. Weedon was a regular patron at Smith's tavern whenever he was in town and used the opportunity to inspect how his tenant treated his property. Eventually Smith fell considerably behind in the rent and let the property run down, for which Weedon was compelled to take him to court. With the lease of the tavern property, the Weedon moved into a house rented from James Duncanson on the corner of Caroline and George Streets, a block away from the tavern.[25]

Dunmore's ships still hovered off Norfolk, and the burning of that city on January 1, 1776, further brought to Virginians the reality of war and hastened the independence movement in the colony. Williamsburg became the military headquarters of the Virginia forces. Hugh Mercer and other newly appointed officers were in the capital in January, and George Weedon may also have been there while seeking his commission. Definitely in March, Mercer and Weedon, with some troops collected for the Third Regiment, were in Williamsburg. On March 5 Mercer and Weedon took an oath to uphold the Articles of War and received their commissions. On March 11 Weedon was the "Field Officer of the Day."[26]

At Williamsburg, a major problem of Colonel Mercer and his officers was the backcountry rifle company of Captain

---

[23] Indenture of 17 February, 1776, Fredericksburg District Court Papers.

[24] *Virginia Gazette* (Purdie) 5 April, 1776.

[25] *Virginia Gazette* (Dixon and Nicolson), 14 June, 1780 carried an advertisement of Duncanson offering this property for sale: "the subscriber's valuable lots in Fredericksburg in the centre of the town on the main street where General Weedon at present resides. There are three different tenements on the lots [#21 and #22], which are occupied by as many families. With a yard and garden paled in, annexed to each, including a commodious store house, with five rooms, and a large ware house adjoining of 40 feet square . . . ." Duncanson, who had moved to Culpeper County, did not sell this property, and still had it at the time of his death in 1791.

[26] 11 March, 1776, "Orderly Book . . . Stubblefield," 1887: p. 148; Waterman, 1941: p. 102.

George Gibson. The surley riflemen, known as "Gibson's Lambs," considered themselves above drill and other discipline. As an old veteran of frontier warfare, Mercer knew how to handle the situation. One day he managed to line up the rifle company, and surrounded it with two other companies, muskets cocked. The "Gibson's Lambs" were then disarmed of their guns and knives, and two of the riflemen were put in irons; the rest of the company was confined to barracks. Weedon thus received a lesson from his Scottish brother-in-law on how to quell "Seditious and Mutinous Spirit." Having straightened out the "Lambs," Mercer later apologized to Captain Gibson for his high-handedness.[27]

On February 27, Congress established a southern military district, and two days later appointed Charles Lee to the command.[28] Before Lee arrived in Virginia, Mercer took the Third Regiment to Dumfries and then to Alexandria to collect arms and equipment and to provide defense of the Potomac River.[29] Lee assumed command of the Virginia forces in Williamsburg on March 29. He found among the remnant of the small army soldiers wandering in and out of the town without discipline. The most stern punishment that he could order was thirty-nine lashes. On April 2 Lee called all the "regular forces" from their stations to Williamsburg.[30]

The Third Regiment immediately departed for the capital, but heavy rains making "the Roads almost impassable" forced a stopover at Fredericksburg. There the Regiment stayed for about two weeks, drilling and parading in the Market House Square. On Sunday the troops had to attend "Divine service." George Weedon undoubtedly assisted on the parade field. He and other officers were virtually indistinguishable from the men since they were also required to wear hunting shirts when under arms.[31]

In ordering the Third Regiment to Williamsburg, General Lee planned to replace it in the Northern Neck with Colonel

---

[27] 11 and 17 March, 1776, "Orderly Book . . . Stubblefield," 1887: pp. 145n., 150, and 154.

[28] Alden, 1951: pp. 109-110.

[29] Hugh Mercer to Charles Lee, 1 April, 1776, *Lee Papers*, 1871: 1: p. 371.

[30] Hugh Mercer to Charles Lee, 10 April, 1776, *ibid.*: p. 406; 6 and 18 April, 1776, Diary of Dr. Robert Honeyman, LC; Bowman, 1943: p. 66.

[31] 3 and 11 April, 1776, Campbell, 1860: pp. 13 and 22; Orders, Third Virginia Regiment, 30 March (Alexandria) and 11 April (Fredericksburg), 1776, Bounty Warrants, Revolution, (Thornton Papers), VSL.

FIG. 2.   General Hugh Mercer. From: *Life of General Hugh Mercer* by John Goolrick. With permission of Virginia State Library.

Daingerfield's Seventh Regiment. Learning, however, that the Seventh was expected to march out of the colony for Continental duty, Lee countermanded his earlier order and directed the Third Regiment to return to Alexandria.[32] Mercer informed Lee that he would resume his "former station" at Alexandria, which was a place of "easy access of Ships of Force," considerable military stores, and "fitting out the principal Marine of Virginia."[33] Another reason for ordering the Third Regiment up the Potomac may have been the abortive anti-rent uprising in Loudoun County led by James Cleveland, a well-to-do-tenant. Prince William County militia had already been sent into Loudoun County, and it was perhaps considered necessary by the frightened local planters that an additional show of force be present to overawe the insurgents. On April 16, with Mercer staying behind at Fredericksburg or going on ahead, Weedon marched the five companies of the Third Regiment to Dumfries, about ten miles south of Alexandria. All soldiers of the regiment had been informed that no furloughs would be granted. The regimental company commanders were a spirited lot— Captains Philip R. F. Lee, William Washington, Gustavus Brown Wallace, Thomas Johnson, and John Thornton. Thornton acquired a dubious reputation for dragging an Episcopal minister out of the pulpit and kicking him for preaching submission to taxation and the king.[34] A young cadet in the regiment was James Monroe.

There were rumors that the Third Regiment would soon be ordered to the Carolinas. Before General Lee left for the south on May 13, leaving Andrew Lewis in command in Virginia, he dispatched the Eighth Regiment southward. Lee had concurred with the Virginia authorities that the Northern Neck defense should be left to the militia and two regular companies. Towards the end of May the Third Regiment was sent to Williamsburg to await further orders.[35] On May 14 the Virginia Convention in Williamsburg passed a resolution instructing its delegates to the Continental Congress to vote

[32] Charles Lee to Colonel Mercer, 10 April, 1776, *Lee Papers*, 1871: 1: p. 409.

[33] Colonel Mercer to Charles Lee, 14 April, 1776, *ibid.*, p. 419. On the anti-rent disorders, see Benson, 1970: pp. 343-348.

[34] 15 April, 1776, Orders (Fredericksburg) and note, Bounty Warrants, Revolution, (Thornton Papers), VSL.

[35] David Griffith to --, 19 April, 1776, Griffith Papers, VHS; Sellers, "Virginia Continental Line," 1968: pp. 125-126.

for independence. Weedon probably took part in the grand review of the troops and the ensuing festivities held at the capital two days later.[36]

Dunmore's fleet left Hampton Roads on June 1, and General Lewis, anticipating an attack on Hampton, sent most of the troops at Williamsburg down the James. But the only contact made by the Virginia force at Hampton with the enemy was to pick up the bloated pox-ridden corpses of fifteen to twenty Negroes that had been dumped overboard from Dunmore's ships. The British force anchored off Gwynn's Island in Chesapeake Bay at the Piankatank River just south of the mouth of the Rappahannock River. General Lewis then posted three companies of Colonel Daingerfield's regiment, which had not left for Continental service as planned, on both sides of the Piankatank River, to which he would later add more troops, including some of the Third Regiment. Mercer was sent to command this force.[37]

Congress, however, promoted Mercer to brigadier general on June 5, and Mercer returned to Williamsburg on the sixteenth,[38] leaving soon afterwards for New York City to assume command of the "Flying Camp"—militia of the middle colonies to be used for defense against British invasion. Weedon, by authority of General Lewis and the Virginia Convention, took over as acting commander of the Third Regiment on June 19. Marshall moved up to acting lieutenant colonel; and Philip R. F. Lee, the eldest captain, to acting major.[39] Promotion in the Continental Line had to be approved by Congress. Weedon, for the time being, stayed in Williamsburg. There were administrative responsibilities to which he had to attend. Several companies of the Third Regiment had yet to arrive from Alexandria, and "Necessarys and Arms" also had to be obtained. Weedon regularly served as officer of the day at Williamsburg.[40]

To be detained in Williamsburg, however, was not to Weedon's liking. He was eager for assignment in the field and

---

[36] Evans, 1975: pp. 57-58.

[37] Brig. Gen. Lewis to Charles Lee, 3 and 12 June, 1776, *Lee Papers*, 1872: 2: pp. 52-53 and 63, resp.; Campbell, 1860: p. 43 and *passim*; Sellers, "Virginia Continental Line," 1968: pp. 125-128; Rowland, 1892: 1: p. 232.

[38] David Griffith to Col. Leven Powell, 16 June, 1776, "Correspondence of Leven Powell," 1901: no. 1: p. 40.

[39] 19 June, 1776, Campbell, 1860: p. 53; Boatner, 1966: pp. 371 and 701; Heitman, 1914: p. 389.

[40] David Griffith to Hannah Griffith, 2 July, 1776, Griffith Papers, VHS; 21 and 24 June, 1776, Campbell, 1860: pp. 54-55.

to see some action. Perhaps there might be another fight with Dunmore's little army. But Dunmore could scarcely afford a direct engagement with his ill-trained and diseased force of what now numbered no more than 400 troops. Weedon wanted duty with Washington's army, which was then awaiting Howe's expected return to the mainland from Nova Scotia.

Yet from all appearances, Dunmore's motley band intended to remain on Gwynn's Island. They were building fortifications, barracks, ovens, and windmills on the island, which was about five miles in length and inhabited by only a dozen or so poor families. Numerous British small craft anchored at the island; and a sloop, a schooner, and a pilot boat were placed between the island and the mainland as a guard against an American attack. By the end of June, four Virginia regiments were stationed on shore opposite the island. Although two eighteen-pound and four nine-pound cannon had been brought up, there was need for boats and more men if an American attack was to be launched against Dunmore's new stronghold. General Lewis had held back some troops at Hampton, York, Jamestown, Burwell's Ferry, and Williamsburg in case of the remote possibility that Clinton and Cornwallis might invade Virginia on a rebound from their siege of Charleston. There was some action, however, as British landing parties from tenders sent up the Nantichoke and Wicomico Rivers plundered some of the plantations and took Negroes, in spite of stiff resistance from local militia.[41]

On the morning of July 8, General Lewis set out from Williamsburg for the American encampment opposite Gwynn's Island to take personal command of the American operations. George Weedon, Mordecai Buckner, William Christian, and Adam Stephen—all regimental commanders—accompanied General Lewis. Arriving at camp at 7 p.m., the officers immediately sat down to plan a bombardment for the next morning which was to be followed by a landing on the island if boats were available. At 8 a.m. of July 9, the anniversary of Braddock's defeat, General Lewis gave orders to fire on the enemy fleet and camp. He himself put the first match to one of the eighteen pounders. The shot miraculously hit the *Dunmore* as its broadside lay exposed to the American battery. The Earl caught a splinter in his leg. At the next blast

---

[41] Sellers, "Virginia Continental Line," 1968: pp. 129-130; Caley, "Dunmore," 1939: pp. 811-852.

a boatswain on the stern was killed and several gunners were wounded. The firing ceased at 9 a.m., but was resumed on both sides at noon. After withstanding the bombardment for another two hours, the *Dunmore* slipped around the island. The only American fatality was Captain Dohickey Arundel, who was killed by the bursting of his homemade mortar.[42]

Towards evening ten companies from the First and Fourth Regiments arrived. Eventually thirty canoes were rounded up from nearby creeks. Early on the tenth a detachment of Virginia troops crossed over to Gwynn's Island in these boats, at a time when Dunmore's force was embarking from the opposite side of the island. The Americans discovered many dead or dying Negroes abandoned by Dunmore. A child was found "sucking at the breast of its dead mother."[43]

The day after the "battle" of Gwynn's Island, Dunmore's ships steered up the Bay into the Potomac, stopping on the north side of St. George Island. Several Virginia companies were sent up the Potomac to assist in the defense of the Maryland shores.[44]

George Weedon remained at the American camp "near Gwynn's Island" for several days; then he returned with General Lewis to headquarters at the "Spring Field" camp near Williamsburg. One of the disciplinary problems was "Gaming to excess," and Weedon and other officers were instructed to conduct an investigation and to put "a total stop" to gambling. The field officers on July 18 met with General Lewis to report on their regiments and to discuss plans for the future. On July 25 the Declaration of Independence was proclaimed in Williamsburg and presumably read to the troops at the same time.[45]

A fourteen-year-old servant boy named Tom, who served as a barber to Weedon's and Woodford's regiments, ran away. Weedon advertised his description, noting that he still had four years to serve and that he absconded with a case of razors. Weedon posted a three-dollar reward for Tom's capture.[46]

---

[42] David Griffith to Col. Leven Powell, 8 July, 1776, "Correspondence of Leven Powell," 1901: no. 1: p. 42; John Page to Charles Lee, 12 July, 1776 and Col. Adam Stephen to Charles Lee, 13 July, 1776, *Lee Papers*, 1872: 2: pp. 131-137; *Virginia Gazette* (Purdie), 12 July, 1776; *Virginia Gazette* (Dixon and Hunter), 20 July, 1776.

[43] *Virginia Gazette* (Dixon and Hunter), 20 July, 1776.

[44] Diary of Honeyman, p. 53, LC; Sellers, "Virginia Continental Line," 1968; pp. 132-133.

[45] 17 and 19 July, 1776, Campbell, 1860: pp. xi, 52, and 63.

[46] *Virginia Gazette* (Purdie), 26 July, 1776.

George Weedon got an assignment which was reminiscent of the uneventful kind that he had put up with so long during the French and Indian War. At the end of July he and the Third Regiment were ordered up the Potomac to keep an eye on Dunmore's force. On August 4, Weedon made camp at Yeocomico Church in Westmoreland County. The extreme heat, "Dirty roads, cursed Ferrys, D--n Musketers, and one plague or other has almost cracked my Brain," he wrote to James Hunter, Jr. in Fredericksburg. At this "out of the way place" there was

> nothing but racoon Oyshters, Crabs fattened on dead Negroes, and Lathefryed Beef can be had; for want of a Bird spit have never tryed a dish of rost Musketers, otherwise they are full large. Our business here was to Counteract Dunmore in his Motions. He lay Aposite us, near the mouth of St. Mary's on the Maryland side, however he continued there but a short time after our ariveing and Forming a disposition. He last Friday took his departure with 55 sail only, where for God only knows . . . . He has fill'd all the Wells with Desected Negroes, Leggs, Arms, heads, hands etc, etc, may be fished up . . . . I am just setting off for Maryland, and shall return again tonight. The cost is now clair, and all the Entrenching Tools laid aside, and last night moved my Camp from the Arse of the world, to this place, where we have a free Air, hog Belly's, and Empty Caggs, however the Church, will I am in hopes make up for all . . . .[47]

After sailing out of the Potomac, Dunmore's ships anchored briefly at Lynnhaven Bay near the mouth of the James River. Because of the lack of manpower, with the smallpox having taken a large toll, a dozen of the British vessels were burned. On August 7, the British fleet left the Virginia shores; half of the ships headed towards New York and the other half southward.[48] Virginians rejoiced that they had at last compelled Dunmore's force to leave the colony.

Weedon and his troops returned to Williamsburg during the second week in August. Colonel Weedon received authorization from the Virginia Council to apply for arms at the gun factory in Fredericksburg on condition he deliver up inoperable arms, which were to be used by the "Marine Companies in York and James River" after they were

---

[47] Weedon to James Hunter, Jr., 4 August, 1776, typescript from manuscript in Mills College Library, Oakland, California.

[48] David Griffith to Leven Powell, 5 August, 1776, Griffith Papers, VHS; Caley, "Dunmore," 1939: pp. 864-871.

repaired.[49] Before old arms could be exchanged for new ones, the First and Third Regiments were ordered to join Washington's army at Long Island. On Tuesday, August 13, 1776, the same day that Congress elected Weedon a colonel in the Continental establishment, Weedon and the Third Regiment began their trek northward.[50] Probably he had a chance for a short visit with Catharine at Fredericksburg and maybe obtained some new arms at that time.

Jefferson, in Philadelphia, sent Weedon's and Marshall's commissions to John Page, since he heard that the Third Regiment was "on the hither." Avidly he wrote, "would to god they were in N.Y."[51]

---

[49] August, 1776, Journal of the Council, McIlwaine, 1926-1929: 1: p. 30.

[50] David Griffith to Leven Powell, 5 August, 1776, Griffith Papers, VHS; John Hancock to Gen. Andrew Lewis, 22 August, 1776, PCC, NA; 13 and 16 August, 1776, Force, 1837-: 5th Series: 1: pp. 973 and 1606; Tyler, 1931: p. 2.

[51] Jefferson to John Page, 20 August, 1776, Boyd, 1950-: 1: p. 500.

IV. RETREATING CONTINENTALS

George Weedon was well aware that the battle for New York was imminent. The British army was in full force on Staten Island, where they had been for over two months. Washington had drawn his army to Manhattan and Long Island and would challenge an invasion. Weedon at the time had no reason to question Washington's plan for strategically defending such an important place like New York City, but he knew that more at stake than the control of the populous trading port and the Hudson was the success and failure of the American cause. A victory might deter further British attempts to conquer the rebellious colonies. Defeat would bring despair and even possibly capitulation. The Virginia regiments were sorely needed for the defense of New York.

The sooner Weedon and his regiment got to New York the better, and then it might be too late. Weedon led his troops hurriedly over back roads. He planned to take his regiment through York, Philadelphia, Mercer's Flying Camp in New Jersey, and on to Long Island. When Congress heard of the route of the Third Regiment, President Hancock wrote Weedon on August 28 to change his course at York and to follow a direct route to New Jersey because smallpox had broken out in Philadelphia. This letter was followed by another two days later—after Congress had learned of the Battle of Long Island—ordering Weedon to march straight to Manhattan.[1]

Weedon found his brother-in-law in New Jersey, but departed immediately for New York, carrying a dispatch from Mercer to Washington. Weedon went ahead of his regiment and arrived at Washington's headquarters on Manhattan Island on September 11, the same day that Captain Daniel Morgan's rifle company debarked in New York, having been

---

[1] 28 August, 1776 and President of Congress to (Weedon), 30 August, 1776, Burnett, 1921-1938: **2**: pp. 62-64.; *cf.* 28 August, 1776, Letter Books and Transcript Journals, PCC, NA; Sellers, "Virginia Continental Line," 1968: pp. 152-153. Congress on 4 September voted one month's pay and supplies for Weedon's regiment. (Transcript Journals, PCC, NA.)

paroled from imprisonment in Quebec. Two days later the Third Regiment came up "in good spirits,"[2] but upon taking muster, Colonel Weedon found that of the 603 men of his regiment only 408 were fit for duty.[3]

Weedon's Virginians were disappointed to find Washington's army "in great disorder." Captain Gustavus B. Wallace of Weedon's regiment observed that Washington had only fifteen hundred troops instead of ten thousand, as he had heard.[4] Actually Washington could count on 16,124 effectives out of a paper army of nearly 28,000.[5] Wallace probably took into account only the troops in the vicinity of Harlem Heights above the city, where the Third Regiment was stationed. Greene's and Putnam's divisions were in lower Manhattan and Heath's troops were strung along the Harlem River from Harlem to King's Bridge. Washington and his councils of war of September 12 and 14 had decided to evacuate lower Manhattan but had delayed, awaiting word from Congress.[6]

During the night of September 13, Howe landed troops at an island in the East River. Weedon's regiment was among the American force marched and countermarched from 3–7 a.m. along the eastern banks of Harlem Heights, in case Howe should move up the East River and into the Harlem River and attempt a landing. In early evening, September 14, six enemy ships were spotted moving in the East River; and again it was anticipated that Howe intended to land in upper Manhattan north of Harlem, in an effort to cut off that part of Washington's army below. Again Weedon's troops were out on patrol that night.[7]

Early on Sunday morning the fifteenth, under cover of five

---

[2] Washington to Brig. Gen. Mercer, 11 September, 1776, Fitzpatrick, 1931-: **6**: p. 43; Sellers, "Virginia Continental Line," 1938: p. 153.

[3] Ninety-four sick; 8 on furlough; 15 confined; 17 "On command;" 5 artificers; 56 absent sick. (Return of Col. George Weedon's Regiment, 13 September, 1776, Revolutionary War Rolls, 246, Reel 97, NA.) William McWilliams was adjutant. In William Washington's company of the Third Regiment: Lt. Col. Thomas Marshall and his son, Lt. John Marshall; also Lt. James Monroe. Irishman William Croghan, nephew of the famous George Croghan, was assigned at this time to Weedon's Third Regiment. (English, 1896: **2**: p. 1003).

[4] Gustavus B. Wallace to Michael Wallace, 15 September, 1776, Wallace papers, UVL.

[5] Ward, 1952: **1**: pp. 240 and 247.

[6] At a Council of War, 12 September, 1776, Washington Papers, Ser. 4, Reel 38, LC: Gustavus B. Wallace to Michael Wallace, 15 September, 1776, UVL; Freeman, 1949-: **4**: pp. 188-189.

[7] Sellers, "Virginia Continental Line," 1968: p. 155.

frigates, the British army debarked at Kip's Bay (at present 34th Street). Howe, contrary to the persistent advice of General Henry Clinton, had decided to push the Americans out of New York City instead of cutting them off in the rear— undoubtedly one of the British commander's greatest blunders. Northern troops who were to oppose the British landing fled without firing a shot. Washington rushed down from Harlem Heights to the scene of the action. Although Weedon and the Third Regiment remained on Harlem Heights, Weedon has given a rare portrait, gleaned from soldiers after the retreat, of Washington as he tried to stay the flight from the British advanced units. The retreat became a rout in spite of the efforts of Washington, "his Aide de Camps, & other Genl. Officers." The troops

> ware not to be raly'd till they had got some miles. The General was so exhausted that he struck Several Officers in their flight, three times dashed his hatt on the Ground, and at last exclaimed 'Good God have I got such Troops as Those.' It was with difficulty his friends could get him to quit the field, so great was his emotions . . . .[8]

Howe did not press his advantage, and, at least, the fleeing Americans made it safely to Harlem Heights.

At dusk the British line extended from Kip's Bay to Bloomingdale (94th Street), where Clinton took a position on King's Bridge Road (at 5th Avenue). Israel Putnam's New Englanders and William Smallwood's Maryland troops checked this British right flank on King's Bridge Road. The main American lines stretched across the Harlem Heights plateau (three lines crisscrossing about four miles from near present 130th Street to about 170th Street), with the rocky cliffs of the Hudson and Harlem Rivers on each side. A short distance to the south an advanced guard was placed at Point of Rocks, which fronted a plain known as the Hollow Way that reached southward to Vandewater's Heights (now Morningside Heights). Throughout the night the British heavily bombarded American emplacements on the East River.[9]

Washington rose early on September 16 and sent a party of rangers under Colonel Thomas Knowlton of Connecticut to

---

[8] Weedon to John Page, 20 September, 1776, WPC, CHS.

[9] Gustavus B. Wallace to Michael Wallace, 16 September, 1776, Wallace Papers, UVL; George Clinton's Report, 18 September, 1776, Hastings and Holden, 1899-1914: 1: p. 352.

reconnoiter the British advance position, which had moved up to the Hollow Way. About noon, Knowlton's men, pushing through the thick forest of the Hollow Way, were fired upon by "red coats." Washington heard the firing and rode down to the front line at Point of Rocks. As he pondered a decision, he heard the echoing taunt of a British bugler sounding a call of fox hunters, signifying the killing of the fox and the end of the hunt. It did not take long for Washington to make up his mind to engage more troops in the skirmish. A detachment of Rhode Islanders were sent to aid Knowlton in an assault from the front, and Major Andrew Leitch and three rifle companies of Weedon's Third Regiment were sent along the flank to get at the enemy's rear. Weedon himself with the remainder of the Third Regiment was ordered to defend a pass in the valley "that divides those heights [Morningside Heights] from N. York and the Country below." Knowlton was to withhold fire until Leitch's Virginians had reached the rear of the enemy advanced party. But both Leitch and Knowlton attacked too soon. The Americans, from the front and the flank, pressed the attack, and drove the enemy from the Hollow Way and up a hill into a buckwheat field (116th Street on Morningside Heights). The enemy detachment was forced to retreat another quarter mile, when a large British reinforcement was spotted coming to their aid. Thereupon Washington ordered back the American force. During the two to three hours fighting, Weedon with his Third Regiment and some Maryland, Connecticut, and Massachusetts troops were in the thick of the fray. Weedon, it seems, took post with other officers (including Generals Greene, Putnam, and George Clinton) in a cordon-like formation in order to urge the men forward and to prevent skulkers from escaping the flight.[10]

George Weedon had a narrow escape. A "spent ball" struck the guard of his sword, knocking away part of the hilt. Fortunately he had only a bruised thigh. Estimate of casualties varied. The British admitted to nine killed, 130 wounded. One report put the American losses at forty wounded, "a few" killed. The Third Regiment had four killed (two sergeants and two privates), an ensign wounded, and

---

[10] Tench Tilghman to James Tilghman, 19 September, 1776, *Memoir*, 1876: pp. 138-139; *Virginia Gazette* (Dixon and Hunter), 4 October, 1776; Washington to the President of Congress, 18 September, 1776, Fitzpatrick, 1931-: **6**: pp. 67-68; Smith, 1881: pp. 94-95; Johnston, 1878: pp. 251-252; Tyler, 1931: p. 3; Freeman, 1949-: **4**: pp. 198-200; Ward, 1952: **1**: pp. 248-252. The three rifle companies of the Third Regiment were commanded by John Thornton, Charles West, and John Ashby.

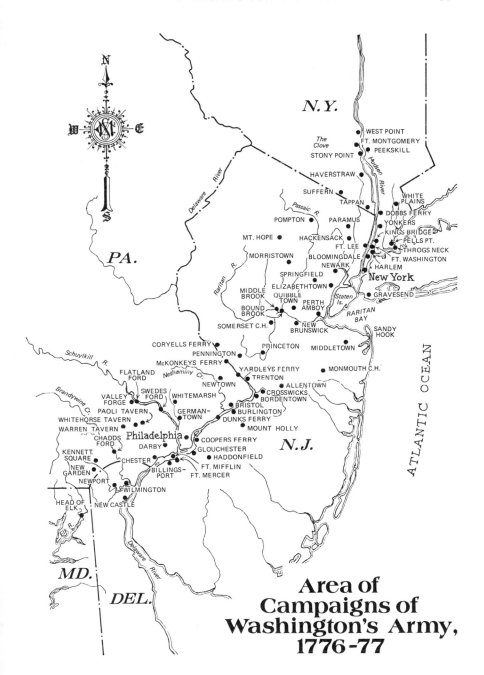

Map 2.   Area of Campaigns of Washington's Army, 1776-1777. Drawing by
Paul Nickerson, Richmond City Planning Commission.

twelve privates wounded or missing. As Weedon wrote after the battle, "upon the whole" the enemy "got Cursedly thrashed." The saddest loss for the Americans were the deaths of Knowlton and Leitch. Leitch received two balls through his belly and one through his hip, and would linger on for several weeks.[11]

On the evening of the battle, after reestablishing lines on Harlem Heights, Washington ordered Weedon's and several other regiments "to retire to their quarters and refresh themselves; but to hold themselves in readiness to turn out at a moment's warning."[12] The next day, in the general orders, the commander in chief "most heartily" thanked the troops that had been commanded by Major Leitch "and the others who so resolutely supported them. The Behaviour of Yesterday was such a Contrast, to that of some Troops the day before, as must shew what may be done, where Officers and Soldiers will exert themselves . . . ."[13] Although not specifically mentioned in the general orders, Weedon and other officers of the Third Regiment could take pride in Washington's praise.

For the next week Weedon kept a working party under Lieutenant Colonel Thomas Marshall busy putting up breastworks on the eastern edge of the plateau at Morris Heights overlooking the Harlem River.[14] Meanwhile the two armies, separated by the Hollow Way and only two miles apart, maintained an uneasy watch on each other. Weedon wrote on September 20: "We are now very near Neighbours, and view each other every hour of the day." Although he expected a general action at any time, Weedon felt relieved "since we have got Elbow room." He would have preferred for the American lines to be three miles further up Manhattan, "as it's not our business to run any risque of being Surrounded." He thought that the "Navigable Rivers & Creeks" and the narrowness of the island gave the enemy an advantage. The soldiers of the Third Regiment were

[11] Weedon to Page, 20 September, 1776, WPC, CHS; *Virginia Gazette* (Purdie), 4 October, 1776; Trumbull, 1899: p. 196; Lydenberg, 1930: p. 99.

[12] Orderly Book, 21 August-4 October, 1776, 16 September, 1776, #853, Reel 2, NA; General Orders, 16 September, 1776, Fitzpatrick, 1931-: **6**: pp. 56-57; Gen. George Clinton to N. Y. Convention, 18 September, 1776 and William Ellery to Gov. Cooke of R. I., 11 October, 1776, in Stevens, 1880: pp. 370 and 372.

[13] General Orders, 17 September, 1776, Fitzpatrick, 1931-: **6**: pp. 64-65.

[14] General Orders, 30 September, 1776, *ibid.*, p. 134; Orderly Book, 21 August-4 October, 1776, 20 and 30 September, 1776, #853, Reel 2, NA; Sellers, "Virginia Continental Line," 1968: p. 163.

exhausted, "being kept in Constant alarm, besides the Necessary Guards, picketts, fatigue parties, &c all upon the Back of a very long March."[15] Indeed the fatigue of the troops was evident in the muster of the next day. Of a total of 602, only 383 were present and fit for duty (147 sick, 53 absent, 17 on command).[16] They had spent a sleepless night gazing into the southern horizon brightened by the conflagration that swept a large part of New York City.[17]

As it became apparent that the enemy was not planning a direct attack, the troops were able to relax a bit. Cartridge paper that Weedon had ordered from Virginia arrived.[18] On the twenty-sixth Washington ordered Weedon's regiment, until brigaded, to join General Thomas Mifflin's brigade on the left flank at the Point of Rocks and the Hollow Way.[19] For several days Weedon served as president of a general court martial.[20]

Weedon learned of Major Leitch's death on the morning of October 2. Leitch, after the Battle of Harlem Heights, had been sent by Weedon to a house at Hackensack Bridge, nine miles away. Everyone had thought that Leitch would recover, as his intestines had been uninjured by his three wounds. But lockjaw set in, and he "laboured" only four days afterwards, wrote Weedon's chaplain, David Griffith, whose duty it was to inform Leitch's widow. "America has lost as Brave & prudent Officer as ever Defended her Rights," said George Weedon, and Leitch's courage would be an example "to all Military Characters who step forth in her cause. We paid him our last Tribute of respect on the 4th Inst. by Intairing him with all the Honours of war."[21]

Four weeks on Harlem Heights seemed like an eternity. With the army stationary, lack of discipline and demoralization were blatantly evident. The close fraternization of officers

---

[15] Weedon to Page, 20 September, 1776, WPC, CHS.

[16] General Return of the Army at King's Bridge and its Dependencies, 21 September, 1776, Force, 1837-: 5th Series: 2: pp. 451-452.

[17] See Lydenberg, 1930: p. 99, 21 September, 1776.

[18] William Hartshorne to James Hunter, 17 September, 1776 and Andrew Lewis to James Hunter, 27 September, 1776, James Hunter Papers, UVL.

[19] General Orders, 26 September, 1776, Fitzpatrick, 1931-: 6: p. 120.

[20] General Orders, 28 and 29 September, 1776, ibid., pp. 125 and 131, resp.; 28 September, 1776, Orderly Book, 21 August-4 October, 1776, #853, Reel 2, NA.

[21] David Griffith to Richard Henderson, 3 October, 1776, Griffith papers, VHS; Weedon to John Page, 10 October, 1776, WPC, CHS; Extract of a letter, 17 September, 1776, in Virginia Gazette (Dixon and Hunter), 11 October, 1776.

and men had to be overcome. There was talk among the Virginia officers of resigning. Captain Wallace of Weedon's regiment complained that the encampment was "the most disagreeable place I ever saw—there is nothing to eat but Beef & Beef." The scant supply of bacon was too salty.[22]

Being acutely aware of the deficiency in the Virginia regiments of men present and capable of active duty, Weedon asked Washington for permission to recruit from the Flying Camp, which, with the invasion of New York, had joined Washington's army. Weedon informed the commander in chief that some Maryland troops from the Flying Camp, the enlistments of whom were to expire at the end of October, wanted to join the Third Regiment. Washington refused Weedon's request, principally because to enlist troops in regiments from states other than their own would create a "hardship" on states attempting to complete their levies. But Washington was willing to defer to any advice on the subject from Congress.[23] On October 14, the Third Regiment had only 371 fit for duty out of a full complement of 601.[24] From October 4 to 14, Weedon again headed a general court martial.[25]

Weedon, nevertheless, considered the American lines on Harlem Heights "very Formidable and I think sufficient to defend against twice our Number." But he soon changed his opinion. In the evening of October 12, Howe took his main army up the East River to Throg's Neck, where the East River enters Long Island Sound. It appeared that the British would extend a line in Washington's rear to the Hudson and thereby cut off the American army. The British vanguard at Throg's Neck was checked by a deadly fire from Pennsylvania riflemen, later reinforced by Connecticut and New York troops. Howe reembarked his army on October 18 and sailed three miles eastward to Pell's Point, which afforded a less marshy landing place. A small Massachusetts brigade disputed the British landing, and thereby gave Washington

---

[22] Gustavus B. Wallace to Michael Wallace, 28 September, 1776, Wallace Papers, UVL.

[23] Washington to President of Congress, 2 October, 1776, Force, 1837-: 5th Series: **2**: pp. 841-842; Sellers, "Virginia Continental Line," 1968: pp. 163-165.

[24] Weedon's Return of the Virginia Brigade-Third Regiment, Service Records (Weedon), NA.

[25] General Court Martial Proceedings, Heights of Haerlem, 10 October, 1776, Washington Papers, Ser. 4, Reel 38, LC; General Orders, 4, 7, 10, and 14 October, 1776, Fitzpatrick, 1931-: **6**: pp. 157, 178, 192, and 207, resp.

valuable time. Washington meanwhile had decided to escape the British flanking movement and to seek more favorable ground at White Plains, thirteen miles away.[26]

During the last days on Harlem Heights, Washington had been busy reorganizing his army. At first it was intended that Weedon and the Virginia troops would be attached to General Putnam's command. As Washington prepared to march his army northward, the Virginia regiments, on October 17, instead were ordered to join Lord Stirling's brigade and to go on ahead. Stirling had ten days before been exchanged for Governor Browne of New Providence and had arrived at Washington's headquarters on the ninth. Stirling's brigade set out on the eighteenth, marching along the western side of the Bronx River. The main army followed more slowly, making a series of entrenched camps from Fordham Heights to White Plains. Twenty-eight hundred American troops were left in what would now be enemy territory at Fort Washington on the upper tip of Manhattan overlooking the Hudson.[27] Most of the American army arrived at White Plains by October 22, and Washington opened headquarters there on the twenty-third. Weedon pointed out "we . . . have now got so situated that they must come to our own Ground to do anything Decisive."[28]

Howe made his headquarters at New Rochelle, directly up the coast from Pell's Point. Weedon noted that "his right extends towards Rye, the left to East Chester and Frogs Point, with a large Fleet before them." Howe "advanced four or five miles towards us, Fortifying as he came," and "we are now but four miles asunder, and Skirmaging every day, in all of which we have had the advantage." One of the skirmishes involved a detachment of Weedon's men, although he himself remained at White Plains. On the night of October 22, 150 troops from the First and Third Virginia Regiments joined with Delaware Continentals in attacking a camp of five hundred Tory Rangers, five miles southeast of White Plains. The sortie was successful: a dozen or so rangers were killed, thirty-six that

[26] Weedon to Page, 26 October, 1776, WPC, CHS; Trumbell, 1899: p. 200; Ward, 1922: 1: pp. 255-256.

[27] Weedon to Page, 10 and 26 October, 1776, WPC, CHS; Trumbell, 1899: p. 199; General Orders, 17 October, 1776, Fitzpatrick, 1931-: 6: p. 216; Sellers, "Virginia Continental Line," 1968: pp. 165-166; Dawson, 1886: pp. 234 and 238; Ward, 1952: 1: p. 256.

[28] Quoted in Freeman, 1949-: 4: p. 226n.; Weedon to Page, 26 October, 1776, WPC, CHS.

were caught sleeping were captured, and the Americans returned with the enemy's colors and much needed muskets and blankets. Weedon boasted that none of the Virginians were killed; but there were three Americans killed and about twelve wounded overall. Major Robert Rogers and his Tory Rangers, Weedon pointed out, "has never since dared to Venture from the main body."[29]

In further reporting for the benefit of the folks back home in a letter of October 26 to John Page, Weedon commented on skirmishing of other units of the army with Hessian troops.

> We have got into the way of Catching the Hessian Gentry of late. General Mercer got 12 of them with Eight Regulars not long since from staten Island, since which another party he sent over, brought of[f] seven and Kill'd several. General Lee had a little bout with them last Tuesday Evening. He Buried ten, and took three prisoners. One of our light Horse Brought in one of their Grandiers [Grenadiers] last night, with the most infernal pair of Whiskers I ever beheld. The last Division of these people arrived at N. York last Sunday, and ware Immediately sent up to the Army on the sound. Those that Lee took, & Kill'd, ware part of the last Division. They have all been made to believe no Quarter would be given them by the Americans, and had laid their Accts with the rope, as soon as they fell into our hands. They say they have been brought here against their inclination, being told by their prince they ware only to Garrison the King of Englands Towns while he sent his people over to scourge the Rebbles.

As the two large armies faced each other, Weedon despaired of leading his bedraggled soldiers—exhausted, poorly supplied, and soaked to their bones from nearly a week of heavy rains—into what seemed to be an impending major battle.

> Something of Consequence must take place in a day or two. I wish it was over, for the Sufferings of my poor men makes me feel exceedingly. For these five Weeks we have been under Arms every morning before day, exclusive of the other necessary duties of the Army, which has been uncommonly harde. They have been Oblige to engage it, entirely Naked, some without shoes or stockings, Several without Blankets and almost all without Shirts. If I live to write you again, expect to give you News of the Utmost importance . . . .[30]

---

[29] Weedon to Page, 26 October, 1776, WPC, CHS; Tyler, 1931: p. 4.

[30] Weedon to Page, 26 October, 1776, WPC, CHS.

But a brisk dawn and clear skies on October 28 roused the spirits of Weedon and his men, and they were in the mood for a good fight.

The American lines extended three miles over a series of hills above the "plains," with the swollen Bronx River on the right and a swamp on the left where Stirling's brigade, including Weedon's troops, were posted. Shortly after dawn, the British army marched directly towards Washington's force. A Hessian advance party passed the American right and crossed the river, where they met a sharp fire from Connecticut troops under Brigadier General Joseph Spencer. The American detachment was driven up Chatterton's Hill, a half mile west from Washington's lines. General Alexander McDougall brought reinforcements, and a siege of the hill continued for a while with heavy bombardment of the American position. Then 4,000 British and Hessian troops stormed the hill and were met by stubborn resistance. Casualties were high on both sides, and eventually the Americans had to withdraw from the hill. The clash, which lasted for most of the day, was witnessed by Weedon and his troops as distant spectators along with most of the American army. At dusk the British army checkmated Washington's army both from the front and at the American right from Chatterton's Hill.[31]

For several days the armies remained stationary. About the only excitement was the burning of the town of White Plains—attributed to either American pickets or British troops. The British planned to attack at dawn on the thirty-first, but were unable to because of rain. Washington used this opportunity to slip his army beyond the Croton River to an even stronger position at North Castle Heights, two miles north of White Plains. During this maneuvering, Stirling's brigade, including Weedon's Virginians, held the old lines in order to conduct a delaying action against an expected British attack.[32] As the American artillery commander, Henry Knox, summed it up, "the enemy are determined on something decisive & we are determin'd to risque a General Battle only on the most advantageous terms."[33] But Howe had second thoughts. On November 4–5, the enemy broke camp and

---

[31] 28-31 October, 1776, Lydenberg, 1930: pp. 105-106; Sellers, "Virginia Continental Line," 1968: p. 168; Tyler, 1931: p. 5; Scheer, 1962: pp. 54-55; Champagne, 1975: pp. 116-118.

[32] Scheer, 1962: pp. 54-55.

[33] Henry Knox to William Knox, 1 November, 1776, Knox Papers, MHS.

headed towards the southwest to the Hudson, stopping for
several days at Dobbs Ferry, and then back to Manhattan to lay
siege to Fort Washington.

Waiting to see what the intentions of the enemy were,
Washington kept his army intact at North Castle Heights for
several days. Weedon made his camp at John Fushee's and was
disconcerted that the Third Regiment still was well below
strength. Only 290 men of 603 rank and file were present and
fit for duty: four officers reported sick, one was recruiting in
Virginia, and two companies were without captains.[34]
Washington decided to divide his army. Lee was left at North
Castle, and Heath was sent to Peekskill to cover the
Highlands. With the remaining troops, Washington headed
for New Jersey. George Weedon's Virginians, still in Stirling's
brigade, went with Washington on November 8 to Peekskill
and the next morning embarked on boats and sailed down the
Hudson five miles, landing on the west bank. On the tenth
Weedon and his men, as part of Washington's force, marched
southward along the Hudson, on the sixteenth reaching
Woodbridge, across from Staten Island, where they heard the
cannonading of Fort Washington.[35]

The outcome of the British attack on Fort Washington—its
fall and surrender of 2,800 men—was something to which
Weedon could say "I told you so." Although Weedon felt the
war could only be won by marshalling the full strength of the
Americans against the British in major battles, he realized that
Washington's force at the time was inadequate for such a
confrontation. Nevertheless Washington should still
consolidate his forces and wait for the best opportunity. He
was critical of Washington's emphasis on tactical defense, of
establishing fortifications inviting British assault, and
especially of retaining Fort Washington behind British lines,
even though the fort was on the highest ground on Manhattan
Island and might thwart a flanking movement against
Washington should he move southward toward New York.
Weedon brought up the matter with his brigade commander,
Lord Stirling, and General Greene, on whose discretion
Washington had relied in making the decision to hold
Fort Washington. Weedon experienced a rebuff that he

[34] Return of the Third Virginia Regiment, 5 November, 1776, Force, 1837-: 5th
Series: 3; pp. 515-516.

[35] "Diary of James McMichael," 1892: pp. 138-139; Freeman, 1949: 4: pp. 241
and 256.

thought was uncalled for. But he did not protest further and harbored his complaint in his breast for many years until after Greene's death and long after the war when he wrote John Page about it:

Fort Washington never was tenable against so powerful an Army as Genl. Howe commanded, and in my conception of things no Act of providential Agency was ever more wonderfully conspicuous than in the circumstances which diverted our beloved General from personally defending the place. I shudder at the present moment when I think of it, and cant help mentioning to you a conversation between Lord Stirling & myself upon our Army Crossing North River after the Enemy begain their retrograde movement from White plains. His lordship came to me the morning after crossing and asked me to ride down to a place call'd English Neighbourhood nearly oposite to the Fort where Genl. Green held his Quarters & spend the day with him. I readily agreed to his proposal and instantly took horse. The road by its' bends, and turns frequently opened the North River to us and all the Country on the East side, and at intervals a full view of the British Colums moving down. At one of those places siting side by side on our Horses Chating on the events of the Campaign, I observed to his Lordship we had it now in our power to end it most gloriously on the part of America by evacuating Fort Washington before the enemy could sit down before it, and leave them an Empty shell that had answered every purpose as a place of diversion. My Old friend gave me a Stern look, and pushing up the cock of his hatt with his right hand said 'Colo. Weedon when I was a Field Officer I never took the liberty of adressing my Superiors, besides Sir do you know the Natural Strength and importance of that post.' I beg'd his Lordships pardon & observed we ware alone, that I did not mean it as a piece of advice, it was only my private Opinion, for reasons that ware Obvious to my mind. I thought it military policy to Enuncuate it. Which at Dinner Lord Stirling observed to Green with a laugh that "Weedon was for evacuating his Hobby horse," the Genl. asked me seriously my reasons. I observed to him that Gen. Howes Army was powerful, ware well provided with all kind of stores necessary for carrying on a siege, that his military fame would be blasted if he retreated into N. York & left that post in his rear, that the Fort was not tenable against regular approaches, it had not Casements to shelter the men off duty from the weather, and from the Enemies Shells, that there was no water in the Fort, but what was stored in hogsheads. That by cuting off our communication with North River the Garrison would be greatly distressed indeed, and further that I conceived it our policy to guard against every Circumstance that led to a Sacrifice of men & stores.

I was so laughed at for my Ideas, that towards the last I was a little miffed, Damned the place for a pudding bag, and remarked I was sorry I had given my opinion, but Subsequent events would prove who ware right. To be sure the Natural strength of the place is great, but for my own part I never considered it in a better light than field workes to answar certain purposes, and not as a place of defence against regular advances.[36]

Weedon was right. The commander in chief realized that "Bunker Hills" would not win the war. His troops, many of whom were young and inexperienced, could not be depended upon to be heroes in such encounters. For the time being Washington would have to avoid a head-on confrontation with the British army and keep his own army together as much as possible.

After the evacuation of Fort Lee (across the Hudson opposite Fort Washington) on November 18, the commander in chief took most of his troops to Newark, where he established temporary headquarters on the twenty-third. Stirling's brigade (five Virginia regiments and a Delaware regiment—1,200 men) and a Pennsylvania detachment were sent to Brunswick to guard against a possible British landing at Amboy or Brunswick further up the Raritan River. At Brunswick Weedon and his troops relaxed a bit. A lieutenant in the Pennsylvania detachment wrote: "Here our soldiers drank freely of spiritous liquors. They have chiefly got a disorder, which at camp is called the Barrel Fever, which differs in its effects from any other fever—its concomitants are black eyes and bloody noses." That same day Stirling's brigade, except for the riflemen, marched to Newark to join Washington's force.[37]

Howe split up his army. Clinton and 6,000 troops were sent to Newport, Rhode Island, and Cornwallis was dispatched to chase Washington in New Jersey. As Cornwallis approached Newark on the twenty-eighth, Washington retreated with his force, now numbering only about 3,400 effectives. Weedon's regiment brought up the rear as the American troops marched

---

[36] Weedon to John Page, 23 July, 1789, WPC, CHS. For evaluation of Washington's actions in the New York campaign, with emphasis on both his defensive strategy and defensive tactics, see Weigley, 1973: pp. 9-12.

[37] "Diary of James McMichael," 1892: p. 139; Freeman, 1949-: 4: pp. 261, 265, and 268.

FIG. 3. George Weedon, *ca*. 1776 reputedly by John Trumbull, location of picture not known. With permission of the Virginia State Library.

to Elizabethtown and then to Brunswick over "a deep Miry road and so many Men to tread it made it very disagreeable marching." Morale ran low among Weedon's men. Wrote Captain John Chilton of the Third Regiment to his brother: "You will wonder what is become of the great Army of Americans you have been told we had . . . . I really can't tell. They were in some degree imaginary." The time of service of militiamen, who enlisted for two to five months, was "mostly out" before the Battle of White Plains "and I suspect that the thinness of our troops was one reason why we were not allow'd to fight them that day. The same reason prevents us now . . . until we get them to a place advantageous to us."[38]

Cornwallis came in pursuit. While Washington's force retreated towards the Delaware River, Weedon and his men were posted with Stirling's brigade at Princeton to conduct a delaying action should Cornwallis continue to advance. But there was some respite as Cornwallis's troops, thoroughly drenched and exhausted from a twenty-mile march in the rain, paused at Brunswick, affording valuable time to Washington to ready his army for battle—if Lee's overdue division from New York should arrive. Washington, who reached Trenton on December 3, reconsidered his tactics and on the seventh marched his army towards Princeton, but on the way they were met by Stirling's brigade in rapid retreat. Howe had arrived at Brunswick with reinforcements and had sent Cornwallis forward with a substantial force. Washington and his army returned to Trenton, and at night, December 7, and early the next morning, the American force crossed the ferry into Pennsylvania. Washington had barely avoided a battle, as Cornwallis, who had been delayed repairing a bridge over Stony Creek, reached Trenton only moments after the last Americans had crossed the river.

Early on December 9 Washington stationed detachments of Stirling's brigade at different landing places should the British attempt a crossing. Eventually the American front spread twenty-five miles along the "nose" of the Delaware, from opposite Burlington to north of McKonkeys Ferry. The fox had eluded the hunter, and on December 14, Howe announced the end of the campaign until the winter was over. But the British were to occupy New Jersey with posts

---

[38] John Chilton to Charles Chilton, 30 November, 1776, Keith of Woodburne Papers, John Chilton Letters, VHS.

along an eighty-mile line from the Delaware to the Hudson— at Bordentown, Pennington, Trenton, and Brunswick.[39]

It was indeed a crisis that tried men's souls as Washington's army faced the bleak prospects during the first week n Pennsylvania. The river offered almost no barrier to the enemy. The morale of the soldiers was low. Blankets and tents were in short supply, and some of the men had neither.[40] The countryside threatened to be hostile as the Howe brothers issued a proclamation giving pardon and protection papers to all who would swear allegiance to Great Britain. Enlistments were soon to expire, and Washington lamented that by January 1 there would be no one to oppose the enemy "except the Virginia regiments" and the "shattered remains" of Smallwood's Maryland regiment.[41]

The situation brightened when, on December 20, General John Sullivan led into camp 2,000 troops, formerly commanded by Lee, now a British prisoner. Gates soon came in with 500, and Colonel John Cadwalader brought in about 1,000 Philadelphia Associators. Washington could now count on 6,000 effectives. If he were to do anything decisive, he would have to do it before January 1, when so many of his troops would go home.

Meanwhile the army was formed into three corps. Stirling's brigade—now consisting of only eighty-one officers and 592 men, including only 160 men (which by December 22 dwindled to 134) and twenty-one officers of the Third Virginia Regiment—was lumped with the troops of Mercer, Stephen, and Roche de Fermoy. This corps, 2,000 in all, was posted from Yardleys Ferry up to Coryells Ferry; General Ewing, with five hundred men, patroled the area from Yardleys Ferry down to the ferry to Bordentown; Cadwalader had 1,800 men spread from south of Bordentown to Dunks Ferry.[42] George Weedon, as his correspondence indicates, had duty at Washington's headquarters at Newtown.

George Weedon knew that Washington intended some counterstroke against the enemy, especially now that part of the British Army was fragmented in New Jersey. The arrival

[39] Ward, 1952: 1: pp. 283-284; Stryker, 1898: p. 27.

[40] "Diary of James McMichael," 1892: p. 139.

[41] Washington to Lund Washington, 10 December, 1776, Fitzpatrick, 1931-: 6: pp. 346-347.

[42] Return of the Forces . . ., 22 December, 1776, Force, 1837-: 5th Series: 3: pp. 1401-1422; Tyler, 1931: pp. 7-8; Ward, 1952: 1: pp. 285-286 and 289-290.

of reinforcements for Washington made this all the more a probability. Weedon, of course, did not as yet sit on the commander in chief's war councils, but few secrets could be kept from a field officer at Washington's headquarters.

So far George Weedon had seen long marches, dreary encampments, and action himself in only one battle that was more of a skirmish—that of Harlem Heights. The time had come for more aggressive tactics. Some blow must be struck to give credibility to the American Army.

V. AN ACTIVE DEFENSE

Howe's forward strategy in setting up posts in New Jersey for the winter invited an attack in detail. He was falling into the kind of errors that Washington had made during the New York campaign. Yet the British commander had good reason to be contemptuous of Washington for ever being the aggressor, and it did make sense to have garrisons in New Jersey as a show of British strength and to protect the loyalists of the area.

The idea of an attack on Trenton seemed definite a week before the decision was finally made on December 23. The plan called for a three-pronged operation on Christmas night. Cadwalader with 1,800 men would cross near Dover and attack Donop's Hessians at Mount Holly. Upstream, Ewing with 800 troops would cross at Trenton Ferry and hold the bridge on Assunpink Creek to prevent escape of the Hessians in Trenton. A force of 2,400 under Washington, including Stirling's brigade, would divide into two corps—under Greene and Sullivan—and would cross at McKonkeys Ferry above Trenton. George Weedon and his Virginians, still nominally in Stirling's brigade, formed the reserve in Greene's division.

When the embarkation began, the moon was full. A few hours later a blinding snowstorm set in. By 3 a.m., as Weedon noted, in spite of the density of ice cakes in the river, Greene's force completed its landing, nine miles above Trenton. "The Noble Example" set by Washington, Weedon observed, "made all other Difficulties & hardships Vannish." Following the Pennington Road which curved leftward, Greene's division, with Stephen's brigade leading the way, moved "in so private a manner that the Enemy never suspected our Approach." Between 7 and 8 a.m., according to Weedon, Greene's troops were halted within 500 yards of the British pickets, just outside of Trenton. The right wing arrived, and Washington took an observation post on a nearby hill.

The action started about 8 a.m., when an advanced party from the Virginia Fifth Regiment drove the Hessian pickets into Trenton. Artillery was brought up and pointed down the

75

two main streets, King and Queen. Weedon's Third Regiment now came up, and had the honor to be the first to charge down the two streets, followed by the rest of Stirling's brigade. In a bold dash, Captain William Washington and Lieutenant James Monroe of Weedon's regiment took possession of the two cannon on King Street, which several German soldiers had rolled out at the sound of the alarm. Captain Washington and Monroe were both wounded and carried from the field. The enemy made several unsuccessful attempts to form. "Our men entered the Town in a trot, & pursued so close that in less than an hour we made ourselves master of all their Field ps— (six in Number)." Sullivan's troops attacked from the southern end of the town, and other American units aided in blocking an escape. With the Hessians in confusion and entrapped, it was all over in about an hour from the time the first shots were fired. There were 919 prisoners taken, according to Weedon, thirty of whom were officers. "The whole loss on our side, I believe I sustained, which was not more than three privates kill'd & these two brave Officers wounded."

Colonel Weedon escaped injury, but when he returned to "our Old Quarters" at Newtown on the night after the battle he had caught the "flu" or worse, and on December 29 reported that "I am at present unfit for duty." Yet Weedon was exuberant over the astounding victory at Trenton and proud of his role and that of his men. It was the best Christmas, "with more real enjoyment," than any other he had spent. Weedon had praise for all the American troops in the battle, and he thought the victory might be a turning point.

> The behaviour of Our People in General, far exceeded any thing I ever saw. It's worth remarking, that not one Officer or privt was known that day to turn his back. Should our present Expedition prove Equally Successful, we shall have these Robbers that have so long lived upon the fat of the Jarsay Farms, once more over the Hudsons river.

Weedon himself "was honored with his Excellencies Orders to take charge of the prisoners with my Regt."[1]

Weedon's responsibility for the Hessian prisoners of war also meant conducting them to Philadelphia. He accompanied the German officers, who, after taking their parole in

---

[1] Weedon to Page, 29 December, 1776, WPC, CHS; Brown, 1959: pp. 25-26; Cresson, 1946: p. 29; Lancaster, 1955: p. 246; Ward, 1952: 1: pp. 294-298.

Fig. 4. The Capture of the Hessians at Trenton, Weedon at far right. Yale University Art Gallery.

Newtown on Tuesday morning, December 30, headed for Philadelphia in five canvas-covered wagons. The Hessian enlisted men also left Newtown at the same time as the officers and were marched under guard of Weedon's Third Regiment, assisted by a detachment of Pennsylvania riflemen. Virginians read of the occasion in the *Virginia Gazette* of January 24, which picked up a notice from Philadelphia, dated January 4: "Last Tuesday night Col. George Weedon, of Virginia, arrived in this city, with the Hessian officers taken at Trenton . . . . he this day delivered them to the Council of Safety, with six standards. They are allowed their parole of honour, and declare themselves perfectly satisfied with their fate. We hear the Colonel sets off again, in a day or two, for the continental army in Jersey."[2] Weedon probably joined the Hessian officers on the night of their arrival at the Indian Queen Inn, where a sumptuous dinner and wine and punch were provided for the captives at the expense of Congress.[3]

In Philadelphia, the enlisted men-prisoners were confined to the city barracks. At the time of the arrival of the captives or on January 4 when Weedon turned them over to the Pennsylvania government (the actual date is unclear), Weedon presumably led the parade of the Hessians through the streets of Philadelphia. A large crowd viewed the triumphal procession as it marched up Chestnut Street past the State House, where Congress had sat before fleeing to Baltimore. One spectator recalled: "They made a long line—all fine, hearty looking men and well clad, with large knapsacks, spatterdashes on legs, their looks were *satisfied*. On each side, in a single file, were their guards, mostly in light summer dress, and some without shoes, but stepping light and cheerful."[4] A Hessian corporal wrote in his diary:

> Big and little, old and young, stood there to see what sort of mortals we might be. When we came directly in front of them they looked sharply at us. The old women howled dreadfully, and wanted to throttle us all, because we had come to America to rob them of their freedom. Some others, in spite of all the scolding, brought brandy and bread, and wanted to give them to us, but the old women would not allow it, and still wished to strangle us. The American guard that had us in charge had

---

[2] *Virginia Gazette* (Dixon and Hunter), 24 January, 1777.

[3] Stryker, 1898: pp. 212-213.

[4] *Ibid.*, quote p. 213.

received orders from Washington to lead us all about the town,
so that everybody should see us; but the people crowded in on
us with great fury, and nearly overpowered the guard.

The prisoners were marched back to the barracks. Both the
Hessian officers and men were soon sent to the western
counties of Pennsylvania and then to Virginia. In December
the officers were brought to Fredericksburg, and while there
were given a surprise party by a group of socially prominent
ladies of the town[5]—an event which Catharine (Kitty) Weedon
must surely have attended.

Relieved of his duty as commander of the guard of the
prisoners, Weedon lingered on in Philadelphia to recuperate
and to enjoy the pleasures of table and hearth. A stay in
Philadelphia also afforded Weedon the opportunity to check
on the large number of his regiment allegedly in the
Philadelphia hospitals. Many men in his regiment, however,
had not availed themselves of Washington's promise of a
bounty and re-enlisted, and were on their way home.

Because of the Hessian guard duty, Weedon and the Third
Regiment missed the Battle of Princeton on January 3.
Nevertheless, Weedon followed Washington's maneuvering
closely and relayed the details to John Page. Cornwallis had
marched to Trenton on January 1 and had "found the Bird
had flown;" when he reached Princeton the battle was over,
and Washington had again withdrawn. Weedon expressed his
optimism: "we now have the Greatest hopes of Closing this
Campaign with the Total Destruction of Howes Army as they
are so Dispersed." He cited the heroism of the Virginia troops
at Trenton and elsewhere, who, though they "had suffered
much in men & officers thank God they behaved like men
fighting for their just rights and privileges." Weedon
entreated Page as a member of the Virginia Council to work
for greater support of the men in the field: "Numbers we do
not dread, support us, but, you have the Means in your hands
and let not slip the Golden Opportunity of establishing your
Independence, and bidding defiance to British Oppression."
At the conclusion of the letter, Weedon remarked, "it's added
that General Mercer is wounded, this I am afraid is true, as
evil tidings to me, has generally wanted no Confrontation."[6]

---

[5] Lowell, 1884: pp. 16 and 103-105; quote on pp. 104-105.
[6] Weedon to Page, 6 January, 1777, WPC, CHS.

The news of Mercer's fate was all too true. Weedon had not seen much of his brother-in-law, although the two must have met occasionally during several weeks before the Battle of Trenton. During the New York and New Jersey campaigns, both men were in separate parts of the army; and before Princeton Mercer had returned to command a newly constituted Flying Corps of mostly Maryland and Pennsylvania regiments. Mercer's troops had been placed in advance of the American Army. Pushing along Stony Brook through a wooded area he had come upon a Quaker meeting house at the end of a blind road. There he ran into Colonel Charles Mawhood's detachment of seventeenth and fifty-fifth Foot, and his horse was shot from under him. While Mercer was trying to rally his men, the enemy charged and Mercer was clubbed with a musket and bayoneted seven times. After Mawhood's troops retreated into Princeton, Mercer was found on the ground insensible from the cold and wounds. His aide, Major John Armstrong, carried him to Thomas Clark's house in the rear where two Quaker women nursed him. Briefly when the British marched by Mercer was made a prisoner, but since he was dying he was let alone. Washington sent his nephew and aide-de-camp, Colonel Charles Lewis, to attend the mortally wounded general. Mercer died January 12.[7] His body was brought to Philadelphia three days later, and next day a funeral procession left City Tavern for Christ Church Yard, where the fallen hero was buried "with all the honors of war."[8]

It is not known whether Weedon, who at the time of Mercer's death had gone to the army's headquarters at Morristown, attended Mercer's funeral or not. To Weedon, Mercer's death was a stunning personal loss, and his thoughts turned to his brother-in-law's widow and five children.

About January 9, Weedon was ordered to go to Virginia to recruit. When he visited Morristown, however, to check on his troops before returning home, he received a different assignment. Washington's General Orders of January 13, 1777 read: "Till an Adjutant General is appointed, the duty of that office will be discharged by Col Weedon, who is obliging

---

[7] Reed, 1847: 1: pp. 279-280 and 290; Keene, 1908: pp. 212-213; Carson, 1965: p. 92.

[8] 16 January, 1777, Duane, 1877: p. 112; Reed, 1847: 1: p. 291n.; Carson, 1965: p. 92n. On 26 November, 1840 Mercer's body was removed to Laurel Hill Cemetery. Col. James Innes was in Mercer's funeral procession (1777) and described it in a letter to Mrs. Gordon, mother-in-law of Mercer and Weedon.

enough to undertake it, Pro-Tempore. He is to be regarded and obeyed as such."[9] Undoubtedly a fringe benefit of Weedon's new post was better living quarters; for a field officer at Morristown was expected to live among his troops, who, according to Chilton, were "stationed on the side of a Mountain without Tents," with the "Ground covered with Snow." The Third Regiment moved to Hanover Township in February and stayed there until April.[10]

The office of adjutant general was a prestigious assignment and had been held by General Horatio Gates. Recently it had been brought down a notch or two, having been given to a promising officer of field rank. Weedon's predecessor, Colonel Joseph Reed, had resigned. Weedon himself did not take to the endless paper work and administrative details. He preferred command in the field. So Washington continued to search for a permanent adjutant general. Weedon served for only six weeks, to about February 28, a week after he was promoted brigadier general. Captain Isaac Budd Dunn and then Lieutenant Colonel Morgan Connor, both of the Pennsylvania line, were temporary successors, with Colonel Timothy Pickering assuming the post on a permanent basis in June.

As adjutant general, Weedon's duties consisted mainly of personnel record keeping, preparing and distributing orders, and to some extent facilitating administration among the departments. His tasks were largely perfunctory, but at times he could exercise his own discretion. He showed special interest in matters relating to the detention of British prisoners, issuance of proper passes, and disposition of militia in New Jersey for preventing supplies falling into the hands of the enemy.[11]

George Weedon was one of ten colonels elected brigadier general by Congress on February 21. The order of the election,

---

[9] General Orders, 13 January, 1777, Fitzpatrick, 1931-: 7: p. 5; Sellers, "Virginia Continental Line," 1968: pp. 216-217.

[10] John Chilton Diary, January-April, 1777, *passim*, VHS.

[11] Fascimile, 14 January, 1777, Charles McDaniel, Fredericksburg; Weedon to Capt. Eyre, 21 January, 1777, Gratz Collection, HSP; Weedon to the N. J. Council of Safety, 24 February, 1777, Misc. Collection, Revolution, LC; Weedon to Brig. Gen. Clinton, 28 February, 1777, Sparks MS, Weedon Letters, Harvard University Library. Greene wrote Weedon, asking who sent Col. Schuyler and his detachment to his post at Basking Ridge, and he also gave Weedon a report on troop maneuvering and skirmishes. Weedon had written earlier and this was probably the first in the long correspondence between the two. (See Greene to Weedon, 24 February, 1777, Weedon Letters, HL.)

though not rank, was as follows: Poor, Glover, Paterson, Wayne, Varnum, De Haas, Weedon, Muhlenberg, Cadwalader, and Woodford.[12] Next day Congress settled the respective rank of the new brigadier generals. Those in Continental service were to "take rank according to the dates of their commissions, and the rank they held in the army at the time of their promotion; and that such as do not hold continental commissions, stand after them in the order in which they are elected." Congress determined that Colonel William Woodford, who had resigned as colonel of the Second Virginia Regiment a month or so before, would not have rank according "to his former commission." Of the new brigadier generals, Woodford ranked last, after Muhlenberg, Weedon, and Cadwalader, in that order. Woodford would have to serve under Muhlenberg and Weedon, whom he had out-ranked as far back as the French and Indian War. Contentions over rank among the general officers would become increasingly acrimonious and would plague the command system throughout the war. This was the beginning of what would become the bitter Weedon–Woodford controversy. The promotions by Congress on February 19 (major generals) and 21 (brigadier generals) angered other officers as well. Brigadier General Andrew Lewis, feeling himself slighted by not being promoted to major general, resigned; and Benedict Arnold threatened to do so. Cadwalader flatly declined to serve. On April 1 Congress added three new brigadier generals: Hand, Scott, and Learned.[13]

The promotions of Muhlenberg, Weedon, and Woodford were announced in the Virginia newspapers at about the same time as it was reported that Colonel Mordecai Buckner of the Sixth Virginia Regiment was cashiered for cowardice.[14] The disillusionment over the Buckner affair was coupled with the irritation over the affront to Woodford, Virginia's first hero of the war. Edmund Pendleton, friend and neighbor of Woodford in Caroline County who, as head of the Virginia Convention and the Committee of Safety, had secured for Woodford command of the Virginia troops against Dunmore

---

[12] 21 February, 1777, Ford, 1904-1937: **7**: p. 141.

[13] 22 February, 1777, *ibid.*; Extracts of Minutes of Congress, Washington Papers, Series 4, Reel 40, LC; Washington to Brig. Gen. Andrew Lewis, 3 March, 1777, Fitzpatrick, 1931-: **7**: pp. 234-235; Freeman, 1949-: **4**: pp. 394-395.

[14] *Virginia Gazette* (Purdie), 7 March, 1777. For the Buckner affair, see Josiah Parker to Weedon, 24 January, 1777, WC, APS.

in the fall of 1775, commented: "it must hurt the delicacy of a good Officer to have a man under him to-day, command him tomorrow; But these Gentlemen, however worthy I think them, had no such claim and I am persuaded would have been happy in Ranking under him."[15]

Woodford, unlike Weedon later, was willing to put country above honor. He wrote a long letter to Weedon on March 17, responding to Weedon's letter of February 11, "in which you complain of my neglecting you." Woodford had no intention of forfeiting a friendship of twenty years.

> I have heard within these few Days of the late promotions. Let me, with much Sincerity, give you Joy, & assure you that I shall serve with pleasure under my old Friend. I am Sir determined to disappoint my Enemys in their Aim, & if they had appointed me a Corpl. I would have acted. I judged for myself before, but let the impartial & unprejudiced publick, who I have Faithfully served Judge for me in the present case. Because I have offended a particular party who have done me injustice, that shall no longer prevent me from rendering my best services to my Country.
>
> * * * * * * *
>
> N. B. advise me in your next, whether I shall bring some Brandy to camp.[16]

Perhaps it was Washington's prompting that led Woodford to accept his appointment:

> By some Resolves of Congress, just come to my hands, I find as I hoped and expected your name in the new appointment of Brigadiers, but perceived at the same time that you were named after *Muehlenberg* and *Weedon*; the reason assigned for this your having resigned your former rank in the service of the Continent.
>
> You may well recollect, my Dear Sir, that I strongly advised you against this resignation. I now as Strongly recommend your acceptance of the present appointment. You may feel somewhat hurt in having two Officers placed before you (though perhaps never to command you) who once were inferior, in point of rank, to you, but remember that this is a consequence of your own act, and consider what a Stake we are contending for. Trifling punctilios should have no influence

---

[15] Edmund Pendleton to Richard Henry Lee, 9 March, 1777, Mays, 1967: 1: p. 206.

[16] Woodford to Weedon, 17 March, 1777, AKF. The same letter, with slightly different wording is in Letters from General Officers, PCC, NA.

upon a man's conduct in such a cause, and at such a time as
this. If smaller matters do not yield to greater, If trifles, light as
Air in comparison of what we are contending for, can withdraw or withhold Gentlemn from Service, when our all is at
Stake and a single cast of the die may turn the tables, what are
we to expect! It is not a common contest we are engaged in,
every thing valuable to us depends upon the success of it, and
the success upon a Steady and Vigorous exertion. Consider
twice therefore, before you refuse.[17]

In view of Weedon being faced with a similar decision as
Woodford later when the situation was reversed, it would have
been good for him to have seen this letter of Washington's.

George Weedon heard from prominent Virginians on his
promotion. Mann Page, Jr. sent his congratulations.[18] So did
John Page, who used the opportunity to voice his "contempt
of American spirit" in the lack of support for the war and to
call for harsher penalties for deserters. He asked Weedon
humorously, "have you ever tried my spiked rollers? I think
Harlaem Heights must have been a fine place for them."[19]
Richard Parker of Westmoreland County, lieutenant colonel
in the Sixth Virginia Regiment, which would now be under
Weedon's brigade command, also offered his congratulations.
"It ever gives me pleasure to find merit rewarded," he said,
"and I have no doubt of your distinguishing yourself in the
post you now enjoy, as well as you have hitherto done in that
you formerly held."[20]

Weedon was sent to Philadelphia in early March to check
on invalid soldiers in the Pennsylvania hospitals. While in
Philadelphia he was also to contact all colonels there and
order them to march whatever men they had raised to
Morristown.[21] Weedon wrote Washington on March 10 that
he had sent recovered soldiers to Morristown, but Washington
on the twenty-seventh replied that none had arrived in camp.
The commander in chief also informed Weedon that he could
not promote Major John Thornton and Major William
Augustine Washington, whom Weedon had asked to be
named lieutenant colonels, because "(considering the
connexion between us)" it would "be looked upon as the
effect of partiality."

[17] Washington to Woodford, 3 March, 1777, Fitzpatrick, 1931-: 7: pp. 239-240.
[18] Hugh B. Grigsby Papers and Notes, Sec. 70, folder 1, VHS.
[19] John Page to Weedon, 21 March, 1777, Balch, 1857: pp. 87-88.
[20] Richard Parker to Weedon, 30 March, 1777, ibid., p. 89.
[21] Washington to Weedon, 8 March, 1777, Fitzpatrick, 1931-: 7: pp. 265-266.

In his letter of the tenth (which has been lost) Weedon told Washington that he was going to take an extended furlough and return home to Fredericksburg. Washington did not take kindly to Weedon's suggestion and he condemned the tendency of some officers to think that they could leave whenever and for as long as they pleased.

> You conclude your letter, my good Sir, with an assurance, that you shall see me early in the Summer; surely you meant this by way of Joke or trial only. Can you possibly conceive, that my consent would be obtained for such an absence as this? Could I stand justified, do you think, in the opinion of the public, to suffer the Officers of the States to be absent so long, at the most important and active part perhaps, of the Campaign? No Sir, it is neither to be done, nor expected; no man wishes more to gratify officers than I do, nor can any Man feel more for their private inconveniencies, because no Person suffers more by an absence from home than myself; but when I forego all the advantages of private Interest, and have more cause to regret my confinement and may suffer more by it, from a peculiarity of circumstances than any other man in the Service, from a sense of duty to the public, it cannot be presumed that, that sense which totally restrains my own wishes, can give unbounded indulgences to others. I must therefore inform you, that I cannot consent to your being longer from the Army than the 10th of May, that will allow you as many Months, as I should be sincerely thankful, for Weeks, to go home and return in.[22]

Weedon took Washington's enjoinder for a shortened furlough to mind.

For two months, George Weedon enjoyed some leisure among family and friends at Fredericksburg. Unlike some officers and men, he had not sent for his wife and had not seen Kitty since he had left for the northern campaigns. But the leave of absence from the army was not to be as "nonchalant," to borrow D. S. Freeman's description, as Weedon thought it would be. His personal obligations had enlarged; besides Kitty and her mother, there was now a responsibility towards Isabella Gordon Mercer, Hugh's widow, and her five children—William, John, Ann Gordon, George, and Hugh. The private burden would eventually rival his public sense of duty. The Mercer properties, including a plantation across the Rappahannock from Fredericksburg (purchased from George

---

[22] Washington to Weedon, 27 March, 1777, *ibid.*, pp. 322-323.

Washington), and Weedon's own Crab Cove plantation had to be managed. The schooling of the Mercer children and the sorting out of Hugh Mercer's financial affairs had to be attended to. Yet Weedon did not have the time on this furlough to do much about these matters. With the fresh epaulets of a general on his shoulders, military considerations were foremost on his mind, and he was eager to return to the army where he could display, so he thought, his immeasurable ability to command a large body of troops.

The folks back in Fredericksburg were eager for news of the army. Weedon kept in touch with congressman Mann Page, Jr. in Philadelphia for word on the overall military situation.[23] His friends wanted to hear the true story of the heroism of Virginians in the war to the north. Weedon visited, when he could, his former tavern, now known as "Smith's," which was as popular as when he was the proprietor. He recounted the exploits of the army and, not so much to the liking of his listeners, how inadequate had been the support of Virginians back home. Apparently Weedon corrected some impressions, but at times was thought to strain credibility. Wrote Landon Carter: "It seems the story about Genl. Mercers barbarous usage by the enimy after a Surrender is all contradicted by Genl. Weedon. But as the same Person contradicts What C. G. has told everybody else and from W. I. I begin to fancy he is mistaken."[24]

Weedon inspected James Hunter's manufactory of arms on the outskirts of Fredericksburg, and he assisted in forwarding what few recruits there were to the army.[25] Lieutenant Colonel James Innes of the Fifteenth Regiment visited Fredericksburg and wrote that "the positive Mandates of Genl. Weedon— hurry me to Camp."[26] Weedon applied to Governor Patrick Henry for arms to be sent from Williamsburg, but Henry said that he "must suspend the delivery" because he heard that ten thousand arms had arrived in Philadelphia.[27]

During spring, 1777, Washington required that all the soldiers be inoculated against the smallpox. Instructions went out to military and civil officers in five states, including

[23] Mann Page, Jr. to Weedon, 22 April, 1777, WC, APS.

[24] 17 April, 1777, Greene, 1965: 2: p. 1092.

[25] Granville Smith to William Grayson, 8 April, 1777 and Gen. Philip Schuyler to Washington, 16 April, 1777, Washington Papers, Series 4, Reel 41, LC; Mann Page, Jr. to Weedon, WC, APS.

[26] Innes to Tucker, 23 May, 1777, quoted in Carson, 1965: p. 93.

[27] Gov. Patrick Henry to Weedon, 5 April, 1777, Balch, 1857: p. 90.

Virginia, to assist in the project.[28] Weedon took it upon himself to order inoculation of recruits collecting at Dumfries for reasons that the disease might be contracted en route to Philadephia, that the treatment was cheaper in Virginia, and that there were already too many persons to inoculate at Baltimore, Wilmington, and Philadelphia. Most of the Virginia officers complied with Weedon's directive.[29]

Weedon had hoped to visit Williamsburg, but could not find the time. He wrote John Page his regrets for not doing so, and said he was sorry "for not trying the Rollers," which Page had recommended tongue-in-cheek in his letter to Weedon of March 21. "Harlem Heights was to rocky" for the roller skates, Weedon noted. For the benefit of the legislature, Weedon argued for greater attention to military affairs. "You have often heard me complain of the bad consequences that might attend Opperations supported by an Army on the establishment ours was last Campaign," he said.

Did I ever expect to see the American Cause depending on the Efforts of such another, Cantuck [Kentucky] should be my Asylum at once, and no other man but our present General, who is the Greatest that ever did or ever will adorn the Earth, could have supported himself under the many disappoint-ments and disgraces he was subjected to from this irregular System of Carrying on a war, against the most Formidable Enemy in the world. To have Laurels in reach, and not be able to pluck them must be Vexing to an exaulted mind. But I trust in God his troubles on this head is partly at an End. Desertions have been to frequent and to much Encouraged by the reception they meet with in this Country, an Object I think worthy the attention of the Legislative body. Shurely some Method might be fallen on to bring them foarth from their sulking holes. The backwardness of the recruiting Service is a little alarming . . . and its clair to me that nothing but a draft will effect the Quotas of the states.[30]

About a week after May 10, the date Washington told him to be back with the army, Weedon rode into camp at Morristown just in time, for Washington was readying the army for a new campaign. Had Weedon arrived a few days earlier, he would have assumed command temporarily of the American wing at

---

[28] Weig, 1950: p. 8.

[29] Mann Page, Jr. to Weedon, 22 April, 1777, WC, APS; William Grayson to Washington, 1 April, 1777 and Col. David Mason to Washington, 17 April, 1777, Washington Papers, Series 4, Reels 40 and 41, LC.

[30] Weedon to John Page, 15 April, 1777, WPC, CHS.

Princeton from Major General Israel Putnam, who was sent to command American troops in the Highlands along the Hudson River.[31]

On May 20 Washington arranged the army into five divisions. Adam Stephen and Nathanael Greene commanded divisions totaling 3,442, including 2,925 Virginia troops. Weedon's Second Brigade (2d, 6th, 10th, and 14th Regiments) and Muhlenberg's First Brigade (1st, 5th, 9th, 13th Regiments and Colonel Moses Hazen's regiment) were placed under Greene; Stephen's division included Woodford's Third Brigade (3d, 7th, 11th, and 15th Regiments) and Scott's Fourth Brigade (4th, 8th, and 12th Regiments and William Grayson's and John Patton's "Additional Regiments"). Both Scott and Woodford appear to have returned to Morristown only a short time before Weedon.[32] Muhlenberg, formerly a Lutheran pastor, had stayed in camp. All four Virginia brigade commanders had colorful personalities. Woodford had the reputation of being a dandy, and dressed to the hilt. Scott, from Powhatan County, was a flamboyant orator and the most politically inclined. Muhlenberg, like Scott, had easy rapport with his troops, which made up for limited physical stamina. The new brigade commanders were soon making detailed reports and supervising personally the exercise and drill of their troops.[33]

For the new campaign Washington would avoid a pitched battle as much as possible, but he would seize any opportunity to attack the enemy in detail. Because he would be greatly outnumbered if the British came in force, it was essential that he maintain a strong defensive position. Expecting the British army would march on Philadelphia or into the eastern states, Washington moved the army in easy stages from May 25 to 31 twenty miles south to Middlebrook, in the Watchung Mountains and eight miles northwest of Brunswick, where Washington anticipated the British army would first head if they intended to attack Philadelphia.[34]

---

[31] Washington to Maj. Gen. Putnam, 12 May, 1777, Fitzpatrick, 1931-: 8: pp. 50-51.

[32] Washington to Capt. Gibbs, 3 May, 1777 and Washington to Brig. Gen. Woodford, 10 May, 1777, ibid., pp. 11 and 40; General Orders, 22 May, 1777, ibid., pp. 99-100; Greene, 1871: 1: p. 380; Stewart, 1973: 2: p. 764.

[33] Washington to Brig. Gen. William Maxwell (Circular), 20 May, 1777 and Washington to Brig. Gen. William Smallwood (Circular), 26 May, 1777, Fitzpatrick, 1931-: 8: pp. 97 and 127-129, resp.; Washington to Weedon (Circular), 26 May, 1777, WC, APS.

[34] Freeman, 1949-: 4: p. 425; Ward, 1952: 1: p. 325.

On the twenty-sixth an enemy advance party of 700 men was discovered near the village of Bound Brook, two miles east of Middlebrook. Weedon's brigade "moved along the mountains" to the left in order to cover Anthony Wayne's brigade, which was sent out to attack the British detachment. Wayne encountered the British troops, and after several rounds of fire, with fixed bayonets, his force pursued the British detachment for three miles "into their redoubts." As one soldier declared, had the British detachment stayed to fight Wayne, Weedon's party would have cut off their retreat."[35]

Back at camp, George Weedon found time to give an optimistic report to John Page.

> The Army is now drawn together at this place [Middlebrook], at least that part of it, which have been Cantoned all Winter in this state. The whole of them [are] now Encamped in Comfortable Tents on a Valley covered in front and rear by ridges which affords us security. His excellency our good Old General, has also spread his Tent, and lives amongst us. Every Department of the Army is properly Arranged, and strictly Attended to—so different in our situation in every respect, to what it was last Campaign, that a friendly heart can not help being highly elated on reflection. Our men all happily over the small pox, and remarkable healthy, well Armed, well Cloathed, and from our Commander in Chief down, to the private Centinal, in the highest Spirits. Was our Difficiencies but completed and sent on, we would hang heavy on Sir Williams hands go where he would.

Weedon did not believe the enemy would attack from Canada, a view which, of course, would soon be disproved by Burgoyne's invasion. But as for Washington and Howe, "preparations are making on boath sides for a Vigorous Campaign, let which will open it, it will be Active."[36]

By June 13 Howe had assembled an army of 18,000 at Brunswick. To determine what action the American Army should take, Washington held a council of war on June 12, attended by the four commanders of divisions attached to the main army (Greene, Stirling, Stephen, and Lincoln) and nine brigadier generals, including Weedon. It was Weedon's first council of war. Washington pointed out that it was "beyond

---

[35] Extract of a letter from Middle Brook Camp, dated 26 May, 1777, *Virginia Gazette* (Purdie), 13 June, 1777.

[36] Weedon to John Page, 31 May, 1777, WPC, CHS.

doubt" that Howe had one of two objectives—either defeat the American Army or take Philadelphia. The council voted to call back all but one thousand Continentals from Peekskill, near the Highlands, to reinforce the army and to maintain a post at Morristown.[37]

In a letter of June 13 Weedon again described the improved capacity of the American army and considered it ready for battle.

> The enemy have assembled all their troops at Brunswick, and a formidable appearance they make. New York, Long Island, Staten Island, Amboy, and the communication from thence to Brunswick, are drained in a great measure of troops. Howe has come over himself, and seems determined to put his much talked of plan in execution. However, if we can but give him a rap over his fingers, the campaign will be pretty well settled; and I have great hopes this may be done, as our army are in the highest spirits, and well found with every necessary implement for the purpose. It is now as well arranged as any army in the universe, and it is a pleasure and honour to belong to it. Every thing goes on with the greatest regularity: The troops are well clothed, well armed, and there is the greatest abundance of good provisions; the hospitals are furnished with every accomodation necessary for the sick (of which, thank God, we have but few), the ablest surgeons on the continent employed to attend them, and, in short, so differently circumstanced from what we have been accustomed to, that the continental army is visited and admired by thousands from all parts of the world. Business in the fighting way accumulated; the drum sounds to arms.[38]

From June 13 to 20 General Howe conducted three maneuvers in an effort to draw out Washington from his strong position. Washington put his army on the alert for marching orders, with General Weedon's brigade to be in the advance.[39]

For the first maneuver, Cornwallis was sent to Somerset and Von Heister to Middlebush to entice Washington to battle on the plains and to cut off General John Sullivan, who was still on outpost duty, at Princeton. The enemy then established a nine-mile front from Somerset to Brunswick. Washington ordered Sullivan to Rocky Hill and then to Flemington to

---

[37] At a Council of General Officers . . . Middlebrook, 12 June, 1777, Ford, 1894: pp. 2-3; also Washington Papers, Series 4, Reel 42, LC.

[38] Extract of a letter from General WEEDON, dated camp at Middle Brook, 13 June, 1777, *Virginia Gazette* (Purdie) 27 June, 1777.

[39] General Orders for Marching the Grand Army, 14 June, 1777, AKF.

attack the British right flank. American troops were also placed on the other side of the Delaware. Washington refused to be drawn down from Middlebrook, and Howe found himself checked frontally at the Delaware, in the rear by Washington, and on the flank by Sullivan.

Next, Howe retreated through Brunswick to Amboy, hoping that Washington would follow. Washington sent Greene's division, including Weedon's brigade, Wayne's brigade, and Morgan's riflemen to attack the rear of the enemy. Sullivan's division was to take a flank position between Brunswick and Amboy. Greene, Wayne, and Morgan pursued the rear guard of the enemy through Brunswick, into their redoubts across the Raritan River, and as far as Piscataway. But because of a mix-up in orders, Sullivan and Maxwell did not come up, and the American force led by Greene had to abandon the pursuit. The British now took up a strong position at Amboy. During the enemy's retreat to Amboy, Colonel Lewis Willis, under orders from General Weedon, took a small horse patrol to scout the route of the retreat.[40]

With Howe's force concentrated at Amboy, Washington, on June 24, was lured from the hills to Quibble Town (now New Market), about eight miles northwest from Amboy. He sent Stirling's division to Short Hills (Metuchen), three miles from the enemy. On the twenty-sixth Howe suddenly began his third maneuver by marching his army in two columns towards Woodbridge and Bohampton, intending to defeat Stirling and then seize the passes leading to Middlebrook; with this accomplished he would force Washington into battle on British terms. After some fighting with the British vanguard under Cornwallis, Stirling escaped, and Washington's army headed back to the hills of Middlebrook. Howe now decided to abandon the New Jersey invasion, and on June 30 he collected his whole army on Staten Island, whence he could launch an invasion by sea.[41]

Not knowing what would be the destination of Howe's army, Washington marched and countermarched his army in

---

[40] Col. Lewis Willis to Charles Yates, 10 July, 1777, "Letters of Lewis Willis," 1894: pp. 429-430; Ward, 1952: 1: pp. 326-327; Boatner, 1966: pp. 857-858; Scheer and Rankin, 1957: p. 259. On 22 June Col. Spotswood's regiment, in Weedon's brigade, was ordered to take post in Gen. Wayne's encampment "and mount a Subaltern guard at the gap near the encampment." (General Orders, 22 June, 1777, Fitzpatrick, 1931-: 8: p. 285.)

[41] Scheer and Rankin, 1957: pp. 259-260.

New Jersey for nearly a month—time that he might have better used remaining in one position in order to drill the troops and to make preparations. From July 3 to 12 the army was back at Morristown. There Weedon took his turn as brigadier general-officer-of-the-day and sat on a board of officers to determine rank of officers in the Virginia regiments.[42] The commander in chief noticed the long hair of the men in Weedon's brigade, and asked that they have their hair cut short and bobbed so that they would look more "soldier like," have cooler heads, and put up with less nuisance in rainy weather.[43]

Since it was very possible that Howe would move up the Hudson to join Burgoyne's army as it advanced southward from Fort Ticonderoga, the American army proceeded northward towards the Hudson. At "Clove Camp" (at a pass in the Pallisades in lower New York) Weedon wrote (presumably to Richard Henry Lee at the Congress) on July 18 that the army was "elated" upon hearing of the "Glorious enterprize" of Major William Barton, who with forty-five men captured the whole British garrison at Newport, Rhode Island and its general, Richard Prescott.[44] The next several days the army moved up to near West Point.

There was still no news on what General Howe intended. But it was evident that if he planned to form a junction with Burgoyne he should have been in the Hudson by now. Washington, therefore, felt that Howe's destination must be either New England or Philadelphia, with the latter being the stronger possibility. Without delay, the American Army rapidly headed southward. Although it was reported that some British ships were thirty miles from the mouth of the Delaware on the twenty-sixth, Washington, fearing that Howe might still double back northward, held his army on the Jersey side of the Delaware River. Greene's division, including Weedon's brigade, made encampment at Coryells Ferry on the twenty-eighth; Stephen's and Lincoln's divisions

[42] Orderly Book, 11 June, 1777-25 April, 1777, General Order, 5 July, 1777, #853, Reel 3, NA; At a Board of General Officers at Headquarters, Morristown, 9 July, 1777, Memorials Addressed to Congress, PCC, NA.

[43] Stewart, 1973: 2: p. 783.

[44] Weedon to [Richard Henry Lee?], 18 July, 1777, "Clove Camp in New Jersey," Sparks MS, Harvard University Library.

settled in at Howells Ferry; and Sullivan's division took position near Morristown.[45]

Three days later, upon receiving confirmation that the British fleet was sighted off the Delaware Capes, Washington took the army across the Delaware River. But news on August 1 that the British had left Delaware Bay and were along the Jersey coast only added to the confusion. To await further word, Washington rested his army five miles above Philadelphia, while he went to Philadelphia to discern the views of Congress. At the Germantown encampment, the general officers were asked for advice on the fortifications of Philadelphia. Several of the generals replied in lengthy papers; Weedon, it seems, did not prepare a written response. Overall, the generals felt, as did Greene, that "security of the country must depend upon our superiority in the field." Some posts along the river should be improved, but care should be taken to avoid committing too many troops to garrisons.[46] It seems that Greene now was in agreement with Weedon.

Suspecting again that the British destination was the Hudson River, Washington started the army on a march to Coryells Ferry on August 7. But three days later it was learned that the British fleet was off the Maryland coast, south of the Capes of Delaware. Washington was even more perplexed. He could hardly believe Howe was heading for the Carolina coast during the hot summer, when disease threatened. It made a lot more sense that the British general would turn about and make for the Hudson and form a junction with Burgoyne. All Washington could do for the present was to wait, and, therefore, he decided to hold his army at the crossroads on the Old York Road, along Neshaminy Creek twenty miles north of Philadelphia.[47]

At this "camp at the Crossroads" on the twelfth, George Weedon became more acquainted with General Greene, as he attended meetings with Greene at the division headquarters.[48] Weedon did not know why, but there was

---

[45] John Chilton Diary, April-July 1777, VHS; General Orders, 24 and 25 July, 1777 and Washington to the President of Congress, 27 July, 1777, Fitzpatrick, 1931-: 8: pp. 464-465 and 486-487, resp.; Freeman, 1949-: 4: pp. 446-447.

[46] Board of General Officers [including Weedon], 7 August, 1777, Washington Papers, Series 4, Reel 43, LC; Ford, 1894: pp. 5-19, 163-175, and *passim*; Friend and Gaines, 1931: p. 315; Freeman, 1949-: 4: pp. 448-449.

[47] Freeman, 1949-: 4: pp. 450-451.

[48] E.g., in determining the location of the division armory. 17 August, 1777, "Orderly Book of Muhlenberg," 1910: p. 357.

something about the asthmatic Rhode Islander that attracted him—an attraction that would be acknowledged by Greene and permitted to ripen into friendship. But there was little time for camaraderie at the Neshaminy camp as there were too many details that needed attention. Weedon fretted over the absenteeism of a number of officers in his brigade, and sent an order to Williamsburg, Virginia to be published in the newspapers, declaring that the officers return to their respective regiments immediately: ". . . Particular attention must be paid to this order, as a different conduct cannot be justified in the active part of a campaign."[49] From August 14 to 19 Weedon served on a board of general officers concerning the settlement of rank of Pennsylvania field officers.[50]

Weedon did manage to catch up on some of his correspondence. He advised his friend, John Thornton of Fall Hill, who, as a Lieutenant Colonel in Colonel Charles Mynn Thurston's Continental Regiment, was recruiting in Fredericksburg, that he should stick with his assignment no matter how "disagreeable" the "Service." He assured Thornton, "Nothing would afford me more pleasure than having you with me, the expense would be nothing, for as long as I have a Biscuit, half should be at your Service with a very sincear welcome." Weedon said that John's brother, George, had just arrived in camp, "as fat as a porpoise. He dines with me to day. I wish you were with us, to test the old Copper bowl, which is to be fill'd."[51]

To John Page Weedon wrote of the present stalemate of affairs and of the possibility that a British raiding party might set ashore in Virginia. The enemy's destination

> remains a perfect Mistory to us, and various are the Conjectures respecting them. In this situation it is natural for every one to be concerned for their own State tho I cant say I ever much expected their making an Object of Virginia further than sending in a marauding party for fresh provisions &c, &c, which might have distressed individuals and laid wast part of

---

[49] *Virginia Gazette* (Purdie), 12 September, 1777, advertisement, Camp, Cross Roads, 20 August, 1777.

[50] 19 August, 1777, Washington Papers, Series 4, Reel 43, LC. Edmund Pendleton in a letter to Gen. Woodford asked: "How breathes Weedon this Hot Weather . . . ." (Mays, 1967: 1: p. 219.)

[51] Weedon to Lt. Col. John Thornton, 12 August, 1777, "Revolutionary Letters," 1928: pp. 246-247.

our Country. This supposition held good no further than supposing them to operate to the Southward, however we are still in the dark with reguard to their designs, and every Oppinion about them is no more than Mear Speculation.

Weedon noted that the enemy had been six weeks at sea and nearly eight weeks had passed since the first troops and horses had boarded their ships. His vulgar sense of humor again surfaced: "If the weather has been as hot at sea, as we have had it on shore, I think they will come from between Dicks with pritty fair skins."

The Neshaminy camp, Weedon explained, was located "in a plentiful Country which furnish Our Troops with Sundry little Necessaries from which they reap great Advantages. Our Hospitals decrease every day, and in a General way the Army may be said to be very healthy, and higher Spirits never prevailed Among any set of men." There should be a battle soon: "We have lay here inactive these ten days on Mr. Howes Account but as he will have nothing to say to us, I am in hopes this Army will speak with some of his Troops before long." Weedon also gave Page various intelligence on the northern theater of the war. "Burgoyne's *Dance*," he said, "is nearly Over." He mentioned General Nicholas Herkimer's battle in New York and that the enemy had lost "Several of their chief men"—including "two Natural Sons of the late Sir William Johnstons," William and Peter Johnson. Weedon expected that the arrival of Gates, Lincoln, and Arnold to the northern army "will change the face of affairs very shortly." Colonel Daniel Morgan, "with his Core of Morganites (between 5 & 6 hundred) are gone to show them a little Allegany play . . . and am not without hopes of Seeing Mr. Burgoyne Dance yet."[52]

On August 22, Washington gave orders to prepare to march the next day towards the Hudson in order to join the northern army against Burgoyne. The council of war, which included Weedon, the day before had made this recommendation even though it was then thought that Howe's destination was Charleston. Reluctant to assume full responsibility himself, Washington sent Alexander Hamilton to Philadelphia to secure the approval of Congress, but while Hamilton was calling upon Congress, news came in that the British fleet was sighted in upper Chesapeake Bay. Now there was no doubt that Howe would attack Philadelphia from the south. Word

---

[52] Weedon to John Page, 22 August, 1777, WPC, CHS.

of the American victory over a British detachment at Bennington that arrived the same day buoyed American spirits and lessened any urgency that the main army march northward. Weedon had to give up plans of meeting with other general officers to regulate the price of liquors supplied the army. Washington's whole force was to be moved as quickly as possible to the heights around Newport and Wilmington, Delaware in order to oppose Howe's expected advance on Philadelphia. On August 23 the American Army covered sixteen miles and encamped at Germantown.[53]

The commander in chief thought it would be good for the morale of the army and the local citizenry to march through Philadelphia. Precautions were tight: any soldier leaving the ranks during the parade was to receive thirty-nine lashes "at the first halting place afterwards" and "not a Woman belonging to the Army is to be seen with the troops on their march through the City."[54]

Early Sunday, August 24, the army started out in one column for Philadelphia. At 7 a.m. the Continentals, with sprigs of green leaves in their hats, filed down Front Street and then up Chestnut Street to the Common, to the sounds of drums and fifes accentuating the shuffle of boots upon the cobblestone streets. Washington, Knox, Lafayette, in their fine blue and buff uniforms, and their aides rode at the head of the procession. The Virginia brigades of Muhlenberg, Weedon, Scott, and Woodford (in that order), at one hundred yard intervals, marched near the front of the parade. From the Common, the army turned southward and crossed the Schuylkill at Middle Ferry to the heights of Darby, where they encamped.[55] For two hours the citizens of Philadelphia had a glimpse of the patriot soldiers, and everyone seemed impressed by the seriousness of the marching men. Even John Adams, after viewing the parade, wrote Abigail that "we have an army well appointed between us and Mr. Howe . . . so that I feel as secure here as if I was at Braintree." But Adams, true to his critical nature, pointed out that "our soldiers have not yet quite the air of soldiers. They don't step exactly in time.

---

[53] At a Council of General Officers . . ., 21 August, 1777, Ford, 1894: p. 329; 22 August, 1777, *Valley Forge Orderly Book*, 1902: p. 12; Ward, 1952: 1: pp. 330-331 and 334.

[54] 23 August, 1777, *Valley Forge Orderly Book*, 1902: p. 19.

[55] General Orders, 23 August, 1777, Fitzpatrick, 1931-: 9: pp. 124-125; Sellers, "Virginia Continental Line," 1968: pp. 246-247; Gottschalk, 1937: p. 40.

They don't hold up their heads quite erect, nor turn out their toes so exactly as they ought. They don't all of them cock their hats; and such as do, don't all wear them the same way."[56]

Even as Howe was debarking his troops at the Head of Elk the American Army took position at Red Clay Creek near Newport on the main road to Philadelphia. As the Virginia Line marched through Newport, Captain John Chilton, who would be killed at the Battle of Brandywine, observed "here we saw some fine Girls not much unlike our first Virga. Nymphs." On the twenty-ninth Greene's division took post on the outskirts of the Red Clay Creek camp at White Clay Creek, although division headquarters was at the main encampment at Red Clay Creek.[57] General Weedon kept busy in sending out fatigue parties.[58]

It was the end of a frustrating summer. At first the two armies had played a cat and mouse game, with neither side falling into the mousetrap of the other. Then the British Army had disappeared, and the American Army had crossed up and down New Jersey vainly trying to outguess the British plans. Now the enemy had landed and their objective was clear. The American Army, in the best condition that it had ever been, could fight a defensive action from a position of its own choosing. Both armies were in full force, and there would be a pitched battle. It was evident to George Weedon and about everyone else that a decisive victory for the American Army would likely bring about the end of the war.

---

[56] Quoted in Lancaster, 1955: p. 293.

[57] Diary of John Chilton, 25-28 August, 1777, VHS.

[58] 30 August— 5 September, 1777, *Valley Forge Orderly Book*, 1902: pp. 27-34.

VI. NEAR GLORY

Tension filled the air as the two armies lay within ten miles apart. Skirmishing between scouting parties occurred, and on September 3 the American troops took their "alarm posts" for several hours until a rumored enemy advance proved false. Washington announced that the enemy had "advanc'd some little way into the Country." Should they press on towards Philadelphia "their all is at stake—they will put the Contest on the event of a single battle—If they are overthrown, they are utterly undone—The War is at an end—Now then is the time for our most Strenuous endeavours."[1]

Washington learned on the seventh that the British had divested themselves of all excess baggage, tents, and clothing; and so he ordered the same for his troops. All the men were to keep only what they had on, a blanket, a shirt, and a "great" coat if they were fortunate enough to have one.[2] At the camp near Newport, Washington approved a court martial acquittal of Lieutenant Henry Whiting of the Eleventh Virginia Regiment and Ensign Robert Jouett of the Seventh; they had been charged with "pillaging an orchard near General Weedon's quarters and with abusing the guard Genl. Weedon had set to protect it."[3]

The enemy made a feint as if to attack on the eighth, but Washington suspected Howe's real intention was to conduct a flank movement and get between his army and Philadelphia. On the advice of his council of war, Washington, before dawn on the ninth, moved his army nine miles northward along the Brandywine Creek and took a position on high ground around Chadds Ford, where the shallow water afforded the best crossing for the British Army. The commander in chief established his headquarters at Birmingham Meeting House, three and a half miles to the rear. He made sure that every soldier had a gill of rum—a sure indication that battle was expected. Weedon's and Muhlenberg's brigades, in Greene's

---

[1] 5 September, 1777, *Valley Forge Orderly Book*, 1902: p. 34; Diary of John Chilton, 3-6 September, 1777, VHS.

[2] General Orders, 7 September, 1777, Brown, 1910: p. 165.

[3] General Orders, 7 September, 1777, Fitzpatrick, 1931-: **9**: p. 191.

Map 3. "Plan of the Battle of Brandywine" (Weedon's map). With permission of the Chicago Historical Society.

division, were posted on the east side of the Brandywine, straddling Chadds Ford, with Wayne's and Armstrong's brigades close on each side. Maxwell's 800 light infantry were put on the enemy's side of the ford. Guarding other fords further upstream to the American right were Stirling's, Stephen's, and Sullivan's divisions and Hazen's regiment. On the tenth the enemy appeared in full at Kennett Square, about six miles west of Chadds Ford.[4] Should Howe's army cross at Chadds Ford, it would have to contend with Weedon's Virginians.

Boxed in by steep banks and hills, fog hugged closely to Brandywine Creek during the morning of September 11. General Weedon and his Virginians awaited anxiously for any sound or sight of the enemy. Maxwell's light infantry on the other side of the Brandywine set out on a probing mission about nine o'clock. They soon came across a vanguard of Major Patrick Ferguson's riflemen and the Queen's Rangers. After exchanging fire, Maxwell's force retreated slowly until it reached Chadds Ford. Close behind the British advance party marched General Knyphausen with 5,000 seasoned British, Scottish, Hessian, and Tory soldiers. Forming a line on the hills overlooking the Brandywine, Knyphausen's troops opened up an artillery duel with the Americans on the other side of the creek.

Weedon and his men were eager for a fight. Charles Moile Talbot of the Sixth Virginia Regiment said that he "never saw men with Higher Spirits when the firing began on the outguard. Our troops fairly Liped for Joy."[5] Robert Hanson Harrison, Washington's secretary, visited Weedon's and Muhlenberg's troops and commented that if the British should cross the ford, "I trust they will meet with a suitable reception and such as will establish our Liberties."[6]

When Knyphausen made no attempt to cross at Chadds Ford and the rest of the British Army did not come up, Washington suspected the main British force would attempt a turning movement by crossing upstream on the American flank. Indeed, about 11 a.m. Washington learned that

[4] John McKinly to Caesar Rodney, 9 September, 1777, Ryden, 1933: p. 224; letter of Greene, 10 September, 1777, quoted in Greene, 1871: 1: p. 446; 9 September, 1777, *Valley Forge Orderly Book*, 1902: p. 42; Freeman, 1949-: 4: pp. 471-472; Ward, 1952: 1: pp. 341-342.

[5] Charles Moile Talbot to Charles Talbot, 11 September, 1777, Friend and Gaines, 1931: p. 318.

[6] Robert H. Harrison to Washington, 11 September, 1777, Washington Papers, Series 4, Reel 44, LC.

Cornwallis had led a British column of 6,000 troops upstream past the American right. Once again, as in the Battle of Long Island, Washington had committed a fatal error in not protecting an open flank.

Washington ordered Stirling's and Stephen's divisions to Birmingham Meeting House on the road where the British could be expected to advance after crossing the Brandywine. Washington prepared orders to send Greene's, Wayne's, and Sullivan's divisions across the creek at Chadds Ford to attack Knyphausen's force. But he received conflicting intelligence, and withdrew this order. Then suddenly news came that Cornwallis with the main British force had crossed and were advancing on Washington's rear. Sullivan was sent out to meet Cornwallis's force. Washington went to Greene's position at Chadds Ford, and ordered Greene's division to join Sullivan—Washington himself riding on ahead of Greene's two brigades. Sullivan was on the left of the enemy, and Stirling's and Stephen's divisions, down from the Meeting House Hill, were barely holding at the right. Sullivan took battlefield command of all three divisions. The scene of the battle was less than a mile from the Birmingham Meeting House. Weedon's and Muhlenberg's brigades "went on in a Trott to gain the Meeting House Hills." Although running along the east side of Limekiln Road, over many thickets and fences, Weedon's men covered four miles in forty minutes.

While Weedon and his men were on their way to the scene of action, his former Third Regiment (in Woodford's brigade in Stephen's division) was mistaken for the enemy during the confusion and fired upon by other American troops; many of his former comrades, with whom he had served from the long trek from Virginia through to the Battle of Trenton, fell at the hand of friend as well as foe. Commenting afterwards, Weedon said that Colonel Marshall of the Third Regiment, under "orders to hold the Wood as long as it was tenable, & then retreat to the right ... received the Enemy with a Firmness which will do Honour to him & his little corps, as long as the 11th of September is remembered." One hill had exchanged hands eleven times within an hour, and Woodford himself was wounded in the hand.

As Weedon came upon the field of battle about five in the afternoon, he was met by Colonel Charles Cotesworth Pinckney, who bore a request from Sullivan that Weedon and his men halt on a ploughed field to the right to contend with the enemy's outermost flanking movement. Weedon's brigade defended this position, fronting a pass through the forested hills. Weedon, in the thick of the fighting himself, had to make quick decisions. As Sullivan's troops and the Virginia units earlier on the scene of action fell back, Weedon opened his ranks to let them pass through, and then tightly closed them once more. For twenty minutes, Weedon and his men held off the enemy by hand to hand bayonet combat. Sullivan said afterwards that for this brief but crucial period only Weedon's brigade engaged the enemy, in which they "did themselves Honor." Faced with this stubborn resistance and with twilight setting in, Cornwallis decided to call off his troops and make encampment.

Back at Chadds Ford, Wayne's and Maxwell's troops had "gallantly repulsed" several "violent Attacks" from Knyphausen's force, but were compelled to retreat. All of Washington's force was collected together and made a "general retreat" to Chester, twelve miles east of Chadds Ford, and the next day the army moved northward, crossing the Schuylkill and encamping at the Falls and at Germantown. In a narrative of the Battle of Brandywine, which he composed a few days later and sent to John Page, Weedon stated that the American loss was no more than 600 killed and missing, while that of the enemy was "Enormose!" Another such battle, he wrote, "would establish the rights of America & I wish them the Honor of the Field again tomorrow on the same Terms."[7] As was his custom, Weedon avoided mentioning his own role. Of course it would have been preposterous to have conjured up any similarity to the heroic deed of the Spartan Leonidas— even if Weedon had this knowledge of classical antiquity. Literally he had "held the enemy at the pass," allowing the rest of the army to re-form for an orderly retreat.

Washington's general orders immediately after the battle omitted praise of the Virginia brigades. Weedon, according to one traditional story, complained to Greene, who took up the matter with Washington. The commander in chief supposedly told Greene: "You, sir, are considered my favorite officer. Weedon's brigade like myself, are Virginians; should I

[7] [Weedon's narrative of the Battle of Brandywine], 11 September, 1777 [written about 14 September], sent to John Page, WPC, CHS; Col. Pinkney's Statement, 24 September, 1777 and Candidus [Gen. John Sullivan] to Messrs. Powars & Willis [Sept., 1777] in Hammond, 1930-1939: 1: pp. 473-474 and 557; Lt. Col. Alexander Hamilton & John Laurens to Maj. Gen. Sullivan, 21 September, 1777, Syrett, 1961-: 1: p. 329; Whittemore, 1961: pp. 60-62; Wildes, 1941: pp. 119-123; Herndon, 1969: p. 316; Thane, 1972: p. 110; Freeman, 1949-: 4: pp. 473-488; Ward, 1952: 1: pp. 344-354.

applaud for their achievement under your command, I shall
be charged with partiality; jealousy will be excited, and the
service injured." Another version has it that Greene refused to
carry Weedon's complaint to Washington.[8] But Greene made
a point of praising Weedon and his brigade in his divisional
orders issued at camp at Germantown on the thirteenth.[9]
There was some public recognition; even a Boston newspaper
noted that "in the infantry the brigades which composed
Greene's and Wain's Divisions particularly Weedon's and
Woodford's [actually in Stephen's division] behaved
admirably. They sustained a close and heavy fire from the
enemy for a long time without starting an inch."[10]
  Rumors back in Virginia had it that Weedon was killed at
the Battle of Brandywine. Landon Carter jotted down in his
diary, September 30:

> Colston it seems on Saturday the 27 heard at a race from Billy
> Pearson a noted tory in the days of the Ballentines, the
> Hamiltons, and the Blanes, that Howe had beaten G[eorge]
> W[ashington] killed Genl. Weedon and may others and had
> got to the lower ferry within 4 miles of Philadelphia. He had
> heard it from an honest man Just from Fredericksburg, but
> new not any Particulars. I was nobly abused because I would
> not believe anything of the Matter and egregiously so when
> Stoughton, my flax dresser, the day before heard a man the day
> before crossing the Piscataway say the same thing as from
> Fredericksburg.

But Carter confirmed his suspicion when "a young man"
visiting the plantation said that "Not at all" was there
anything to the rumor of Weedon's death. Others whom
Carter talked to said the rumor was disproved by a letter of
Washington to Colonel Edmund Pendleton and that the story
had been concocted by Tories.[11]
  For two days after the Battle of Brandywine, Weedon and
other brigade commanders sent out parties to look for
stragglers. Some of Weedon's officers were directed to go into
Philadelphia to see whom they could find.[12] On the fifteenth
the army recrossed the Schuylkill and marched five miles
towards the enemy, making camp between Warren and White

---

[8] Greene, 1871: 1: p. 457.

[9] 13 September, 1777, *Valley Forge Orderly Book*, 1902: pp. 45-46.

[10] Quoted from *Almond's Remembrancer*, in Stewart, 1973: 2: p. 810.

[11] 30 September, 1777, Greene, 1965: 2: pp. 1131-1132.

[12] 12-13 September, 1777, Brown, 1910: pp. 168 and 170.

Horse Taverns. Two regiments of Weedon's brigade formed the rear guard.[13]

On the eighteenth the army encamped in two lines at Swede's Ford on the Schuylkill. Howe's army had taken position at South Valley Hill. Washington dispatched Wayne's infantry division to harass the enemy's rear in the woods; two days later Howe surprised Wayne at Paoli, twelve miles west of Philadelphia, and the fierce hand to hand encounter resulted in one of the worst American disasters of the war.[14] From September 20 to 23 the American Army maneuvered, finally taking a position up the Schuylkill to within four miles of Pottsgrove (later Pottstown). George Weedon was one of fourteen general officers attending Washington's council of war on the twenty-third. The commander in chief called the meeting to determine whether any action should be taken since the British were now moving towards Philadelphia. It was the unanimous decision of the council to await the arrival of McDougall's force from Peekskill, a thousand New Jersey militia under General Dickinson, and Wayne's and Smallwood's troops before moving against the enemy.[15]

At the same time that Cornwallis took possession of Philadelphia on the twenty-sixth, Washington brought his army to Pennypackers Mill (later Schwenkville).[16] The commander in chief announced to a council of war that the American force now consisted of 11,000 (3,000 being militia) which could be pitted againt Howe's army of eight thousand. A detachment from McDougall's command and Wayne's troops were at the "Trap" on Reading Road, and 2,000 Virginia militiamen were soon expected in camp. Ten members of the council of war voted for an attack whenever the additional troops should arrive; five favored no delay. Weedon and Maxwell were not recorded as voting. Weedon was brigadier-general-officer-of-the-day, and probably did not devote full time to the meeting. Certainly he favored an attack, and the sooner the better.[17]

---

[13] General Orders, 14 September, 1777, Fitzpatrick, 1931-: **9**: pp. 225-226.

[14] 18 September, 1777, Lydenberg, 1930: p. 148; Washington to the President of Congress, 16 and 17 September, 1777 and Washington to Gen. Anthony Wayne, 18 September, 1777, Fitzpatrick, 1931-: **9**: pp. 230-231 and 235.

[15] Council of War . . . near Potts Grove, 23 September, 1777, *ibid.*, pp. 261-263.

[16] 26 September, 1777, Lydenberg, 1930: p. 150.

[17] 23 September, 1777, *Valley Forge Orderly Book*, 1902: p. 150; Council of War, 28 September, 1777, Ford, 1894: pp. 340-342.

Since the council of war was unanimous for an attack at some time, Washington prepared for an offensive. This would be the first time during the war that Washington would march against a whole British army. On October 1 it was learned that Howe's army had encamped in battle order at Germantown. Weedon said that the enemy "got wind of our intentions." From September 29 to October 2, the American Army took post at the crossing at Skippack Creek, and then it went down Skippack Road to Metuchen Hill, twenty miles above Philadelphia.[18] Here Weedon's brigade major, Valentine Peers, for the second time, was hailed before a court martial, accused of "repeated neglect of duty" for not "bringing his men into parades." Peers was convicted and sentenced to receive a severe reprimand from General Greene in the presence of the officers of the division.[19]

Weedon was again brigadier-general-officer-of-the-day on the third as the army made its final preparations to do battle with the British at Germantown. In his general orders, Washington, more emotional than usual on the eve of battle, revealed a sensitivity of rivalry with General Gates and the Northern Army: "This army, the main American Army, will certainly not suffer itself to be out done by their northern Brethren; they will never endure such disgrace . . . . Covet! a share of the glory due to heroic deeds."[20]

At nightfall, Weedon's brigade in Greene's division along with the rest of the army, leaving packs behind, began the fourteen-mile march to Germantown. For the order of battle, with the army advancing in four columns, Greene's and Stephen's divisions formed the left wing; Sullivan's and Wayne's the right; Conway's brigade marched in front of the right wing and were to file as if to attack the enemy's left flank; McDougall's troops similarly proceeded in front of the left wing and were to lead the attack on the enemy's right flank; Stirling's division of Nash's and Maxwell's brigades were to be held in reserve; Maryland and New Jersey militia were to attack the enemy's right flank and rear; Armstrong's Pennsylvania militia were to attack on the enemy's left flank and rear.[21]

---

[18] Fitzpatrick, 1931-: **9**: *passim; Valley Forge Orderly Book*, 1902: *passim;* Freeman, 1949-: 4: pp. 500-501.

[19] General Orders, 3 October, 1777, Fitzpatrick, 1931-: **9**: p. 304.

[20] *Ibid.*, p. 305; Brown, 1910: pp. 188-189.

[21] Weedon to Page, 4 October, 1777, WPC, CHS; Fragment of Diary of William Knox, September-October, 1777 Knox Papers, Mass. Hist. Soc.

At daybreak, amidst an intense fog, the American army reached Chestnut Hill on the outskirts of Germantown. Sullivan made contact with the enemy pickets, and Conway halted his flank movement. The enemy advanced, but the Americans held. No sound came from Greene's advance or from Armstrong's Pennsylvania militia. Sullivan sent Wayne to the left where Greene should have been. The British light infantry was beaten off, and the Americans advanced through the buckwheat fields and over the high fences which slowed them down. Eventually there came a retort of small arms from Greene's troops. During the last part of the march his division had taken a circuitous route, and hence had arrived late. Now with the full American force in the battle, according to Weedon, the enemy was pushed back two miles. It was still dark because of the fog. "Indeed the misfortunes of that day," said Weedon

> was owing to the most horrid Fogg I ever saw. That with the Smoak together rendered it impossible to Distinguish our men from the Enemy at a greater Distance than Sixty yards, and many favourable Advantages ware lost, from not being certain who ware friends & who Foes and from the Different Divisions and Brigades not being Able by that means, to Co-operate with each other. Our men behaved with the Greatest intrepidity for three hours, Driving them from their Camps, Field pieces, Stone Walls, Houses &c. Trofies lay at our feet, but so Certain ware we of makeing a General defeat of it, that we pass them by in the pursuit, and by that means lost the Chief part of them again, for when the unlucky Idea struck our men to fall back, the utmost exertions to rally them again was in vain. And a few Minutes evinced the Absolute Necessity of drawing them off in the best manner we could . . . ."

At one time Wayne's and Stephen's men mistook each other for the enemy. Maxwell halted at the Chew house, where a British regiment fired from walls so thick that even Henry Knox's artillery did not have any effect. This afforded a costly delay in getting reinforcements to the front lines. Confusion became rife. Troops retreated, and soon there was panic. The battle was over by 10 a.m.

Greene came under criticism for arriving too late during the battle, but Washington did not blame him. That American troops were worn out from the long night march before going into battle was undoubtedly a major reason for the failure at

Germantown. Some officers, utterly exhausted, were found asleep in buildings along the retreat. General Stephen was stretched out beside a fence drunk.[22] Stephen supposedly gave the order to retreat prematurely, which may have contributed to the panic of the American troops. Charles Moile Talbot, a sergeant in the Sixth Regiment of Weedon's brigade said, "but by bad Conduct on the Left wing of our Lines the Enemy Retook the Ground."[23] This reference seems to have been to Stephen's troops. George Weedon, however, thought the retreat was precipitated at another quarter of the American lines.

> When I thought Victory was Declaring in our favor, by some means or other the Right wing gave way, which encouraged the Enemy to Rally and press forwards. The left shortly after was also Broke, and a General repulse took place instead of a Victory the most important (had we obtained it) that ever America experienced.

Yet Weedon felt that "Tho' we got disappointed . . . the day was well sold." Although "the enterprize miscarried" it was "well worth the undertaking" because the British light infantry "(the flower of the Army) was cut to pieces." Weedon estimated the British casualties at 750 to 1,200 [24]

From the fourth of October to the eighth, Washington's army made camp once again at Pennypackers Mill. The commander in chief complained that for the thirteen brigades there were only six brigadier generals, including Weedon, present, and of the six General Francis Nash was dying of wounds.[25] Weedon's brigade was positioned at Pawlin's (Paul's) Mills. On October 8 he penned a long description of the Battle of Germantown, which he thought the Americans could have easily won:

> The Grand cause was in my opinion in one Quarter of an hour of being finally settled that day, to the eternal honor of America. They confess themselves had we Continued the Attack fifteen minutes longer, a general retreat over the Schuylkill would have taken place, to Chester on Delaware

[22] Weedon to Page, 4 October, 1777, WPC, CHS; Thayer, 1960: p. 204; Freeman, 1949-: 4: pp. 506-513.

[23] Charles Moile Talbot to Charles Talbot, 4 October, 1777, Friend and Gaines, 1931: p. 318.

[24] Weedon to Page, 4 October, 1777, WPC, CHS.

[25] Washington to the President of Congress, 7 October, 1777, Fitzpatrick, 1931-: 9: pp. 321-322.

where their Shipping lay. It was ordered by General Howe just as we gave way. But so sportive is fortune, and the Chances of war so uncertain, that when Victory was in our hands, we had not Grace to keep it.

In this letter to John Page, Weedon reflected on the condition of the army, and again he rued the missed opportunity at Brandywine:

Such disappointments as these tryes the Philosophy of a man and happy is he who is so much a pridestinarian as to suppose all is for the best. I confess this has tryed my principals that way, and It's with Difficulty I can bring myself to think with Mr. Pope tho' a strong Advocate for him heretofore. Barran Hills for our Camps, & Low Dutch Cottages for our Quarters, has been our fair since, while the Tyrants of the land, are in the most Ellagant Buildings even down to a lance Corporal, but Patience is a jewel and sooner or later Sir William [Howe] must march of, and make room for honest men, as he possessed them by the Craft & Subtalty of Quakerism, no ways inferiour to that of the Devil, tho' not with impunity, as from exact returns which have fallen into our hands since the Battle of the Brandywine his loss on that day in Kill'd and wounded amounts to 1,973. We have other Coroborating Accounts which Confirm the same. False intelligence saved his Bacon that day, or in all probability America would have had just cause to adore the Name of Brandywine to the latest posterity. While the British Army is by these Engagements diminishing fast, Ours are reinforcing, And by Saturday Night we shall be stronger than the first day we opened the Campaign. Strange infatuation to persist in Subduing a people whose resources are Constantly at hand, and inexhaustable.

Weedon also gave Page a full report of news from the northern theater of the war and of a planned expedition under General Spencer against the British in Rhode Island. The excuse Weedon made for finding the time to write such a long letter was that "a fever & Cold" rendered him "unfit for other duty." In conclusion Weedon reminded Page that Virginia should not ignore military defenses.

Do not relax because the Seat of war is a little removed from you. It may be your time Next. Lay up good Magazines . . . Arms, Ammunition, Provisions &c. Fortifye the mouth of your rivers. Encourage Military Art, and spair not cost or pains to make yourselves a warlike Nation. Your Enemies in that case will Dread you.[26]

---

[26] Weedon to Page, 8 October, 1777, WPC, CHS. Weedon also wrote Page a long letter on 15 October, giving a detailed report of the northern theater of the war—at Saratoga and the lower Hudson River forts.

To George Weedon, twice within a month defeats had been
snatched from victory. Brandywine could have been won with
better intelligence. Germantown could have been a victory
with a little more persistence. Of course Weedon had the
advantage of hindsight as did everyone else. At no time did he
raise his voice against the majority of the general officers in
the strategic planning. At the time of battle Washington had
to make numerous tactical decisions, and one small human
error could cost the battle. Weedon did not impugn
Washington's judgment; he only regretted that by slight
circumstance the American Army would have been victorious.
Weedon knew, too, that Washington—and the army as a
whole—was inexperienced in bringing the enemy to pitched
battle. From the lessons of Brandywine and Germantown
there would be more caution—and a lengthening of the war.

Tents were struck on the eighth, and the army marched
eight miles eastward and took post near Kulpsville. Two days
later Weedon again wrote Page, and about the only news that
he had was of the Northern Army. Benedict Arnold had been
wounded in the leg—"a compound fracture which will
endanger the Limb." General Lincoln had also received a leg
wound. "Two brave & Active Officers, whose services in the
pursuit, is now lost to us."[27]

The army shifted a few miles along Skippack Road to the
southeast on the sixteenth. Weedon led four to five hundred of
his troops to probe the enemy's outer pickets, and at 4 p.m. on
the seventeenth stopped at Whitemarsh. According to the
young British officer John André, Weedon "made large fires
along a considerable extent of ground" and then withdrew at
10 p.m. "He termed this a manoeuvre."[28] Of Weedon's tactical
mission, Colonel Martin Pickett simply recorded that "one of
our brigades" marched to the "Enemies Lines to endeavour to
draw them out or feel their probe a little."[29]

Back at camp on the eighteenth, General Weedon noticed a
little levity. Captain Peter Priest of Benjamin Harrison's
Virginia volunteers suffered a painful embarrassment, which
caused amusement among the Virginia troops. According to
Martin Pickett, it seemed that Priest "got slightly wounded by
accident from one of our own Guns which went of struck the

---

[27] Weedon to Page, 10 October, 1777, WPC, CHS; Brown, 1910: p. 195.

[28] Lodge, 1903: 1: p. 110; Muhlenberg, Orderly Book, HSP.

[29] Martin Pickett to William Edmonds, 18 October, 1777, Martin Pickett Letters,
VIIS.

lower part of his testikles I think but skin deep & went through one side of his Peanus which I hope he will soon get well of without any damage to his reputation."[30] In the evening there was a *feu de joie* celebrating the capitulation of Burgoyne's army.[31]

With news that the British Army had crossed the Schuylkill River, the American Army, "to be at his heels,"[32] marched several miles southeastward, again along Skippack Road, and settled in at Whitpain township, fifteen miles from Philadelphia. Here the army was to remain until November 9. Weedon's brigade—and Greene's division as a whole—was kept in readiness to march at an instant's notice.[33]

After a delay of several days, the court martial of Brigadier General Anthony Wayne, called at his own request, began on October 25. George Weedon and three other brigadier generals (Muhlenberg, Conway, and Huntington), three colonels, and two lieutenant colonels formed the tribunal. Wayne was accused of failing to "annoy" the enemy and of not taking adequate measures for covering his retreat at the time of the Paoli affair. A week later the court found Wayne not guilty.[34]

On October 26 Weedon received a letter from Washington, asking his "sentiments" on a series of questions: chiefly whether an attempt should be made to "dislodge" the enemy; if the British stayed in Philadelphia, should the Continental army keep to the field; what measures were needed to "cover the country" and what actions should be taken regarding promotions, apprehending deserters, and regulations concerning rations, liquor, and prices?[35] A council of war met three days later to consider these questions. The important recommendations made by the fourteen general officers, including Weedon, were that instead of attacking the enemy the army should shift "a little to our left" and that the decision whether or not to canton the army be deferred.[36]

The army moved down Skippack Road a mile to Whitemarsh on November 2. Here Washington could keep a

---

[30] *Ibid.*

[31] Lodge, 1903: 1: p. 110.

[32] Martin Pickett to William Edmonds, 18 October, 1777, Martin Pickett Letters, VHS.

[33] *Valley Forge Orderly Book*, 1902: pp. 99-100.

[34] 24 October, 1777, *ibid.*, pp. 101-102; Brown, 1910: pp. 213-214; General and After Orders, 24 October and 1 November, 1777, Fitzpatrick, 1931-: **9**: pp. 421-422 and 491.

[35] Washington to Weedon, 26 October, 1777, WC, APS.

[36] Council of War, 29 October, 1777, Fitzpatrick, 1931-: **9**: pp. 442n. and 461-464.

better eye on the main roads to Philadelphia. The major event at Whitemarsh was the court martial and cashiering of Weedon's former commander during the French and Indian War, Major General Adam Stephen, for being drunk at the battles of Brandywine and Germantown. At a council of war on November 8, with Weedon attending, it was decided unanimously not to attack Philadelphia even if the enemy moved against the Delaware forts.[37] By mid-November new militia in large numbers were coming into camp, and some of Gates's troops from the north also arrived. An overly optimistic estimate put Washington's total strength at Whitemarsh and vicinity at 15,000 Continentals and eight to nine thousand militia and the enemy's numbers at nine to ten thousand.[38] Were this to be so, Washington might find it worthwhile to provoke another general engagement despite the winter weather.

Belatedly General Greene convinced Washington that Fort Mifflin on Mud Island, five miles from Philadelphia, and Fort Mercer at Red Bank on the New Jersey side, were essential to control of the Delaware River. The British attacked both forts, and Fort Mifflin fell on November 16. The siege of Fort Mercer was more stubborn, and Washington decided to relieve the siege by sending Greene's enlarged division (including 800 militia) to reinforce the fort. Aiding Greene were Morgan's riflemen and Huntington's, Varnum's, and Glover's brigades—a total force of 5,300. Meanwhile Cornwallis crossed the river at Chester with about 3,000 troops for the purpose of storming Fort Mercer. Greene reached Fort Mercer just before Cornwallis, and, upon conferring with the commander of the post, he ordered an evacuation. Greene retreated, but he planned to fight Cornwallis in south New Jersey. On the twenty-second Greene's force, including Weedon's brigade, camped at Mount Holly, ten miles east of Philadelphia.[39]

Three days later, Weedon, who with his brigade was now apparently detached ahead of the rest of Greene's division, dashed off a letter to Washington from Haddonfield "a few minutes" after his arrival. He informed Washington of a brief skirmish with the enemy the night before and of the British

[37] Council of War, 8 November, 1777, *ibid.*, **10**: pp. 23-24.

[38] David Griffith to Hannah Griffith, 13 November, 1777, Griffith Papers, VHS. Richard Claiborne was appointed Brigade Major to Weedon's brigade.

[39] Greene to Washington, 2 November, 1777, Washington Papers, Series 4, Reel 45, LC; Thompson, 1974: p. 38; Thayer, 1960: p. 205.

advance along Great Timber Creek. From a few prisoners, Weedon learned that there were no British troops left at Red Bank and only a small British detachment at Billingsport. "The prisoners say they intend Crossing the Delaware at Coopers Ferry. We shall look about us in the Morning and shall communicate any thing of Importance."[40] Washington also heard from other sources that Cornwallis was heading back to Philadelphia, which news, he wrote Greene, "corresponds with the information sent you by Genl. Weedon." Therefore, he ordered Greene's "whole force" to rejoin the main army as soon as possible. Greene was a little miffed in not bringing Cornwallis to battle: "We have a fine body of troops & in fine spirits & every one appears to wish to come to action."[41]

Weedon arrived back at Whitemarsh just in time for a council of war. Washington asked whether an attack should be made on Philadelphia. Eleven officers, including Weedon, were opposed; five—Scott, Woodford, Stirling, Wayne, and DeKalb—in favor. Scott argued that an advance party of Weedon's and Muhlenberg's Virginians—Greene's division— should be sent against Philadelphia: "those men with him [Greene] are the Flower of the army" and "it will require the best men we can pick to effect the landing if opposed."[42] Deferring to the majority of the council, Washington held the army at the strong defensive position at Whitemarsh, and awaited the next move from the British.

Still, some consideration had to be given to a winter cantonment. On November 30, the commander in chief proposed three sites to his generals: on a line from the Schuylkill River to Bethlehem; on a line from Reading to Lancaster; or on the Wilmington Road. Six generals favored the first alternative; nine, including Weedon, the second; four had different ideas, of whom only Pulaski advocated for a campaign.[43] The possibility of attacking Philadelphia lingered in Washington's mind. Could not this be done with the aid of a sizable number of militia? He thus solicited further comments from the generals. Washington notified

---

[40] Weedon to Washington, 24 November, 1777, Gratz Collection, HSP.

[41] Washington to Greene, 25 November, 1777, Fitzpatrick, 1931-: **10**: p. 104; Thayer, 1960: p. 210.

[42] Charles Scott to Washington, 25 November, 1777, Washington Papers, Series 4, Reel 45, LC.

[43] Washington to Joseph Reed, 2 December, 1777, Fitzpatrick, 1931-: **10**: p. 133.

General Weedon on December 3 that he wanted his "sentiments" by the next morning.[44] Weedon complied with a lengthy argument for avoiding too much reliance on militia. "Reasons Sufficiently cogent, must diminish your force every day you keep the field at this season of the year," Weedon pointed out. "Your principle dependence must then be on the Militia, to carry this important matter into execution. Glory and our Countries good is no doubt what every upright Soldier would wish to obtain, but we may be too keen in pursuit of it, and like the Dog in the fable, Suffer the Substance to escape while we Grasp at the Shadow." Weedon called attention to the difficulties in attempting to bring in a large force of militia and to provide for them during the winter. He also revealed a contempt for the use of militia with the Continental army.

> Everyone that reflects on human nature and considers mankind at large must know how reluctively [sic] they relinguish the ease and more calmer pleasures of domestick & social life to share the hardships and Fatigue of a Camp, even in more plesent weather than what winter generally affords us. Men that are not taught and compell'd to obey, will never render Service. And Obedience and perserverance is not to be expected from a permiscuous body of men drawn together from all Quarters of the Globe, were they to assemble. But you would find one half would desert on their way to Camp. Others probably might arrive a day or two before their time of service expired. No object on earth would keep them afterwards nor could any influence them after their time was out. What would follow must be distressing to an exaulted mind. You would find your regular Troops by this time diminished.

After further discourse Weedon concluded:

> The Eyes of the Continant are turned towards you. Much Spiculation on the practicability of the expedition terminating with success, which you at last find yourself, Oblige [you] to relinguish [it], leaving the unthinking world (who want nothing more to blast reputation than a miscarriage, without enquiring into its causes) at liberty to Sensure boath you & [the] Army. Your Excellency is perfectly acquainted with my Sentiments respecting this Army. It is Sir the Business of America and should be nursed and Cherished as the salvation of her Liberties. The Troops that compose it are not more than mortal and cannot work miracles. The bravest spirits may be

---

[44] Washington to Weedon, 3 December, 1777, WC, APS.

exausted by uncommon, and constant fatigue. And Sir, there is not in my opinion an Object of the Continent that justifies Subjecting them, at this particular time, to a winters Campaign, unless there was a . . . certainty of obtaining that Object, and with it a permanent and honorable end to any further Hostilities. I give it therefore as my Opinion, that keeping this Army in the Field for the purpose of attacking Philadelphia, under the uncertainty of sufficient Aid and support of Militia, is by no means advisable.[45]

While Washington was pondering a decision, he learned on December 4 that the British planned to attack. Washington drew his army into a battle plan, with Weedon's brigade, in Greene's division, on the left.[46] The enemy, in full strength, marched for battle shortly before dawn of the 5th and halted at Chestnut Hill, three miles from the American camp on the hills at Whitemarsh. The next day the British drew closer to the American lines, and heavy skirmishing followed, principally involving Morgan's riflemen and Irvine's Pennsylvania militia. Then "the two Armies lay like Saul & the Philistines," said Weedon. Although Weedon's troops seem to have had no contact with the enemy, they were ready for battle. Weedon wrote Richard Henry Lee on the sixteenth an account of "our Operations as are worthy your Attention while I continue with the Army." Howe, Weedon said, "kept us in one continued alarm" from the fourth to the eighth of December. "As his design" on the fourth "was to attack us a general Action was every moment expected;" but "after reconnoitring our position" Howe changed his ground to our left the Next day, where our camp was more Accessible, but did not come on."[47] On the night of the eighth the British withdrew and returned to Philadelphia.

Since the enemy now gave positive evidence of retiring for the winter, Washington decided to do the same. Valley Forge was deemed as the best place for winter encampment for a number of reasons, not the least of which was the superiority of natural defenses. Although George Weedon preferred a winter encampment at a greater distance from the enemy, one advantage, he noted in his letter of the sixteenth to Richard

---

[45] Weedon to Washington, 4 December, 1777, Washington Papers, Series 4, Reel 46, LC.

[46] 3 December, 1777, *Valley Forge Orderly Book*, 1902: p. 147.

[47] Weedon to Richard Henry Lee, 16 December, 1777, Lee Family Papers, VSL; Lydenberg, 1930: pp. 159-161.

Henry Lee, was that the Valley Forge site could check enemy access to a "Country plentifully supply'd with provisions & forrage."[48] In any event, hutting the army for the winter, as Weedon explained to John Page, was a necessity.

> Disagreeable as this Measure is, we are Oblige to adopt it, in preference to Quarters in order to afford what Cover and protection we can to a plentiful but Distressed Country. The Devastation which Mark the rout of the British Army on all Occations, is shocking to behold, and am happy to see with what charefulness the Officers and Soldiers submit to this method of Cantonment in order to Check such ravagements. Debilitated as our Troops are from the exceeding hard Service during this whole Campaign, their Zeal for the Country dose not abate, and tho' they suffer greatly for want of Shoes and other Necessaries they seem determined to Surmount all Difficulties and turn hardships into Diversion.

Weedon hoped that rumors circulating in camp that the French had joined in the American cause were true. "Every Account seems to Confirm a french war, which god of his infinite Mercy grant may be true, that the Labouring Ore may be taken of our Sholders till we could be restored by repose to our former Health & Vigor."[49] Before the army left Whitemarsh, Weedon had many details to attend to, most important of which was to examine several brigade court martial sentences.[50]

On December 11, Washington's wearied troops marched down Skippack Road and turned southward. The next day they crossed at Swede's Ford to the south side of the Schuylkill and halted at a defile known as the Gulph. There they remained a week, braving the almost continual winter storms.

Drums sounded "Forward" at 4 p.m. on the nineteenth, and the army began the eight-mile trek over frozen roads to Valley Forge.

---

[48] Weedon to Richard Henry Lee, 16 December, 1777, Lee Family Papers, VSL.

[49] Weedon to Page, 17 December, 1777, WPC, CHS.

[50] *Valley Forge Orderly Book*, 1902: p. 153.

VII. "BANDED ABOUT LIKE A FOOT BALL"

As the soldiers plodded through the snow and ice at a mile an hour towards Valley Forge, billeting officers went on ahead to stake out houses for quarters of the general officers. During the morning of December 19, an officer chalked the name of George Weedon on the door of Abijah Stephens's stone house on Little Trout Run. Abijah and his wife, Priscilla, were informed that the general and his guard would be arriving later in the day.

The Stephenses were Quakers and more prosperous than most farmers of the area. They had put in a large supply of buckwheat meal, and a few days before had killed a fatted beef. As Henry Woodman was to relate many years later in a story handed down from his parents and grandparents, who were to farm in the area, the Stephenses were

> in some ways, prepared to receive them. They immediately prepared a large tub-full of buckwheat batter, and when sufficiently leavened, they commenced baking cakes, to be in readiness when the soldiers arrived, and at the same time, put all their iron pots, of all sorts and sizes into requisition to boil scraps, shins and other pieces of beef, to make a large quantity of soup or broth for them.

About the time that the cakes were baked and the soup was ready, "thickened with buck wheat cakes and vegetables," some common soldiers straggled up to the house. "Almost famished with hunger, they soon began like ravenous animals to devour the food provided for them." As soon as they started, however, General Weedon "and suite" arrived, and Weedon's

> first introduction was a haughty display of his imperious temper, in driving the poor, fatigued, and famished men out of the house, striking some of them with his sword, using the most blasphemous language, calling them impious names for entering the house, and daring to eat before his arrival, and uttering oaths not to be repeated; and such was their terror and

fear of him, that they fled from his presence as from a dangerous pestilence, or the fury of a lion.

This "cruel treatment" was more than Mrs. Stephens could take. She had the soldiers carry buckwheat cakes and a large iron pot and several smaller ones, filled with soup, out of doors. The food was quickly devoured. Woodman also says that the Stephens family threw food out of the house to soldiers walking guard duty outside the house. Thus George Weedon's sojourn at Valley Forge began irritably. He did as probably any general officer would have done in insisting upon military protocol. But it was his misfortune that his momentary brashness towards his soldiers would affect his reputation, at least locally.

Another charge by Woodman is that Weedon had his slaves come up from Virginia with wagon loads of supplies, which he sold to the army at exorbitant prices. This allegation is not substantiated, although it is possible that Weedon might have had his slaves bring up the surplus of his crops from the Crab Cove plantation. Selling supplies by soldiers to the army, although requiring permission, was not an unusual practice. But it is unlikely that Weedon did so, given the distance and that he had all but given up any mercantile pursuits.

One other libel against Weedon by Woodman was that the general had fences taken up for firewood and for building huts and that he stripped the land of the timber and all the hay, grain, straw fodder, and vegetables. He supposedly left the grindstone alone in order for his men to grind knives and other utensils taken from the household. Again this is fact taken out of context, and, as will be shown, Weedon did what he could to stem the excesses of his men.

It is interesting that Woodman thought Weedon's first name was Joseph and that he came from Nansemond County, Virginia. Woodman insists that Weedon was nicknamed "Joe Gourd," because he had used "drinking utensils" made of gourds[1] at his former tavern. There is no other evidence that Weedon had acquired this nickname, although in a pension claim long after the war, a Virginia veteran referred to General

---

[1] Woodman, 1922: pp. 49-52 and 66-67. Henry Woodman (1795-1879) heard the story from his parents, and they in turn from their parents. Woodman's grandfather was a soldier in the North Carolina Line at Valley Forge, and his grandmother was a local farm girl. The grandparents settled on a farm at Valley Forge where Henry Woodman grew up. Woodman became a school teacher and a Quaker preacher. Pinkowski, 1953, pp. 36-37, accepts the story uncritically, as do other works. Douglas S. Freeman accepts the "Joe Gourd" designation unconditionally.

"Joe Weedon." Many of Washington's officers had nick-
names, so, as for Weedon, this was a probability.

Woodman's story of Weedon, undoubtedly embellished
from the telling of several generations, must have had some
foundation in fact—if for no other reason than that Weedon
was remembered, but it does an injustice to Weedon. The
condition of the men startled the residents of the countryside,
and the more substantial means of the officers must have been
a striking contrast. Weedon's vulgarity and insistence on
earthly comforts certainly antagonized the Quaker family.
And he was not in the best mood. The prospects of another
dreary winter cantonment had not raised his spirits. As a hero
of Brandywine, he may have had a rather inflated view of
himself, which may also explain his adamance in the
controversy over rank soon to erupt. In any case, Weedon, who
had no liking for Quakers because of their pacifism and
habits, must have rubbed the gentle farm folk the wrong way.

Weedon's quarters, on Little Trout Run, was a half mile
beyond the outer entrenchments on the south side of Valley
Forge. All the major generals, seven brigadier generals, and
Colonel Morgan took quarters outside the campground.
Weedon's and Muhlenberg's brigades were on the east side of
the front line. In all, eight brigades formed this line. Two
other sides of the triangle, the Schuylkill River to the north
and Valley Creek to the west, offered ample protection.[2]
Weedon's brigade totaled 1,219: Second Regiment (Febiger),
364; Sixth (Gibson), 209; Tenth (Stevens), 401; and Fourteenth (Lewis), 245. On paper, Washington at Valley Forge
in December had a force of 19,900.[3]

For several weeks the soldiers were busy constructing log
huts which housed twelve men each. To get water Weedon's
men had to walk a mile to the creek. For days at a time the
men subsisted on frozen potatoes and flourbread, a kind of
hardtack, and, as one surgeon at Valley Forge said of himself,
the cold and smoke made eyes protrude "from their Orbits like
a Rabbit's."[4]

With the troops demoralized and lacking in food and
clothing, it is small wonder that George Weedon had almost

[2] Wildes, 1938: pp. 151-157.

[3] Febiger Orderly Book, 1778, 1 January, 1778, Harvard University Library; 'Order
of Battle at Valley Forge, 26 November, 1777, "Virginia Troops," 1932: pp. 138-139.

[4] "Valley Forge . . . Waldo," 1897: pp. 309, 312, and 314; Lydenberg, 1930: p. 162;
Military Journal of Ewing, 1928: p. 25; Lancaster, 1955: p. 330.

insurmountable problems in exacting discipline from his brigade. On the matter of the fence rails, Weedon at first tried to cajole and then had to take stern measures. Part of the problem was that most wood was wet from rain and snow, and fence rails burned easier. Several times Weedon issued orders against stealing the rails. With pressure from Washington, he finally ordered ten lashes for each offender. No fences were "to be burned on any pretext whatever. . . if unfavorable necessity compels us to do it, license must first be obtained from the Commander-in-Chief."[5]

Temptation to desert increased with the inactivity of the army and its suffering. Yet examples had to be made of offenders. John Reily (Reely) of the Virginia Second Regiment in Weedon's brigade was sentenced to death by a brigade court martial for deserting the guard and taking two prisoners in irons with him. His hanging on January 10 was attended by detachments of forty men from each brigade.[6] Among other desertion cases there was one involving a wide conspiracy. A division court-martial sat on January 20 "for the Tryal of those prisoners Confined by Brigadier Weedon on Suspicion of Mutiny and Desertion." From this case five men of the Second Regiment and one of the Tenth were sentenced to one hundred lashes; a soldier of the Second was to be reprimanded at a division parade; and Mary Johnson, "charged with laying a plot to Desert to the Enemy," was sentenced to one hundred lashes and to be drummed out of the army.[7]

Among Weedon's men there were problems of intoxication, gambling, and assault. One troublesome situation for Weedon was getting the men to use the latrines. Weedon's orderly book has many entries on this subject, reiterating Washington's orders which carried threats of harsh penalities.[8]

Enlistments of many of Weedon's troops expired in January. Weedon, however, had some optimism, as he indicated in a letter to Patrick Henry that he expected "most of the old Soldiers will be returning to service." He was

---

[5] 20 January, 1777, *Valley Forge Orderly Book*, 1902: p. 201; Wildes, 1938: p. 199.

[6] 6 and 9 January, 1778, *Valley Forge Orderly Book*, 1902: pp. 184, 186, and 188. Also see 10 and 12 January, 1778, Febiger Orderly Book, Harvard University Library; Stoudt, 1963: pp. 68, 73, and 76.

[7] 19 and 28 January, 1778, *Valley Forge Orderly Book*, 1902: pp. 198 and 212-215.

[8] 19, 28, and 29 January, 18 and 26 February, and 14 April, 1778, *ibid.*, pp. 198-199, 214-216, 242-243, 289 and *passim*.

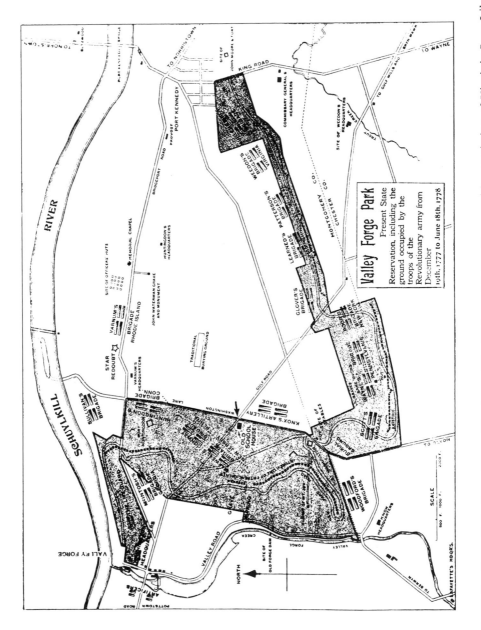

Fig. 5. Valley Forge Park. From Henry Woodman, *The History of Valley Forge*. With permission of Virginia State Library.

disappointed when three hundred of his best men, Pennsylvanians attached to his brigade, and half of the Virginians returned home. For those who remained, although they were short of shoes, blankets "and other Necessaries," at least they were "Comfortably Covered from the weather."[9]

Weedon heard conflicting reports on troops being raised in Virginia. Richard Henry Lee wrote on January 2 that two thousand men were to be drafted "from among the unmarried to fill the Regiments" and that ten regiments of volunteers for six months were soon to be raised.[10] Weedon learned later that the Virginia legislature had defeated a bill for raising 5,000 volunteers for six months, and he wrote Lee hoping that the legislature could reconsider.[11] Thomas Nelson, writing from Williamsburg, gave Weedon some assurance that "the Volunteer plan is not dropt, but will be carried into effect as soon as the Assembly arises."[12]

General Weedon advocated the enlistment of deserters from the British Army. He reminded Washington that "enlisting Deserters and prisoners from an Enemies Army is no new thing in War. It is, however, a measure that has its inconveniences when they are Annexed to troops Operating against their Army." He would be sorry to see the adoption of any measure "Repugnant to the Systematical customs of our Enemy and the known Usage of War." A corps of prisoners and deserters from the enemy who volunteered "might answar every purpose on the Western Waters, and would hereafter be a very great Acquisition to that Country." Most of these "would become Inhabitants after the Troubles ware over, would Settle and protect the Country from Savage invasions, would introduce Agriculture, Trade & Manufactures, and while our unhappy disputes last would serve the Garrison army posts in the interior parts of Country, while the Continental Troops employed in such Service might be drawn into the Field."[13]

Serenity eventually prevailed during the winter at Valley Forge, disturbed only by an occasional alarm or a skirmish a

---

[9] Weedon to Patrick Henry, 4 January, 1778, WL, BUL; Return . . . Virginia Line, February, 1778, Washington Papers, Series 4, Reel 47, LC.

[10] Richard Henry Lee to Weedon, 2 January, 1778, Ballagh, 1911: 1: p. 373.

[11] Weedon to Richard Henry Lee, 1 February, 1778, Lee Papers, UVL.

[12] Thomas Nelson to Weedon, 22 January, 1778, AKF.

[13] Weedon to Washington, 5 February, 1778, WL, BUL.

few miles outside the camp.[14] One event did cause excitement and made good news to report to Virginians back home. Twenty-one-year-old Captain Henry Lee with eight men held off a British detachment of two hundred at Spread Eagle Tavern, about five miles southeast of the Valley Forge encampment. Weedon gave all the details with relish to Richard Henry Lee and John Page. Henry Lee's heroism, Weedon said, "was one of the Gallentest things that has happened this war," and "too many pritty things cannot be said of this Gallent little officer."[15]

One issue which proved most contentious and which vexed Washington unendingly at Valley Forge was dispute over rank. Whether over real or imagined wrongs, by the end of April ninety officers in the Virginia line alone had resigned.[16] On the general officer level, Congress's insistence on appointing generals, often with little consultation or investigation with the military, was the source of the problem. Politicians had their favorite candidates for promotion. Although Congress usually deferred to seniority, this was no easy matter to determine, since original commissions often bore the same date and since officers left and reentered the service.

Appointment of foreign generals over the heads of American officers caused several major crises, which were usually ineffectively resolved by Congress's giving the foreign officer a staff appointment. The promotion of Thomas Conway on December 13 to Major General over twenty-three brigadier generals had tremendous repercussions. Several major generals and nine brigadier generals—including Weedon—protested to Congress and threatened to resign. Again Congress's solution was to assign Conway a staff department.[17]

Brigadier General William Woodford had been pressing Congress to reconsider the rank that Congress (February 21,

[14] E.g., regarding Morgan; see Lord Stirling to Washington, 23 December, 1777, Washington Papers, Series 4, Reel 46, LC. Also an alarm on the twentieth at the artillery part; see Capt. Fleming to Maj. Bauman, 20 January, 1778, Sabastian Bauman Papers, NYHS.

[15] Weedon to Richard Henry Lee, 1 February, 1778, Lee Papers, UVL; Weedon to John Page, 25 January, 1778, WPC, CHS.

[16] Freeman, 1949-: 4: p. 614n.

[17] *Ibid.*, 594n; 19 January, 1778, Ford, 1904-1937: 10: p. 63. The brigadier generals: McIntosh, Knox, Maxwell, Poor, Weedon, Huntington, Scott, Paterson, and Varnum.

1777) had assigned him as last of the four Virginia brigadiers because Woodford had resigned his colonelcy previously. As noted before, Woodford had acquiesced in this decision; but now he had changed his mind. Woodford, like his Virginia neighbor, Weedon, had long military service dating back to the French and Indian War, and had in effect been field commander of the Virginia forces at the beginning of the war. Having served in the northern campaigns, he was an able officer and had been wounded at the Battle of Brandywine, from which he was now on a long furlough recuperating. If without distinction, he seems to have had the respect of his men—but not all—for he appears to have been rather pompous and a dandy. One orderly sergeant entered into his book orders issued by "beau Woodford." The sergeant, perhaps holding a personal grudge, one time put after an order: "Beau Woodford Commander of the Virg. Divis and the Damndest Partial Rascal on this earth without exception."[18]

All that Congress had done on Woodford's request was to vote on August 18 that he had permission to retire and to keep his rank.[19] But in November Congress took up the overall issue of rank once again and reconsidered Woodford's case. The first inkling Weedon had that Congress was bent upon re-ranking Woodford above himself came when he learned the news from Washington on December 2. A Congressional Resolution on November 29, 1777 had been introduced by Joseph Jones, whom Weedon had regarded as a friend. The resolution instructed Washington to "regulate" the rank of Major General Arnold and Brigadier Generals Woodford and Scott according to a resolution of November 12, 1777 which confirmed principles adopted by a board of general officers on August 19 "for the settling the rank and precedence of officers;" commissions of those officers were to be "called in and cancelled, and new commissions granted them in manner aforesaid."[20]

George Weedon knew Congress's action was preliminary to reducing his seniority and placing Woodford as first among the Virginia brigadier generals and hence that Woodford would be first in eligibility for the next opening for major general in the Virginia line. On December 26 Weedon

[18] "Revolutionary Army Orders," 1914: pp. 12-13.

[19] Burnett, 1921-1938: 3: p. 147n.

[20] 29 November, 1777, Ford, 1904-1937: 9: p. 981; Sellers, "Virginia Continental Line," 1968: p. 294.

carefully penned a long letter to Congress in protest. Having second thoughts, he rewrote the letter in more succinct form and dispatched it to Congress on December 29. He began: "I have the honor to address Congress on a late Resolve respecting relitive rank which I Conceive extremely injurious to my honor and reputation as an Officer, and which will in it's consequences involve great part of this Army in unhappy disputes if carried into execution." Weedon explained his claim of rank over Woodford and Scott. Woodford had been out of the service, having resigned his colonelcy, before he was appointed brigadier general the same day as Weedon, February 21, 1776. Scott had not been made brigadier general until April, 1777. Weedon also argued that the regulations adopted by a board of general officers, of which he had been a member, concerned only state and battalion rank and were not intended to apply to general officers appointed by Congress. He had the "highest regard" for Woodford and Scott "not only as particular Acquaintances, but as good and Valuable Officers." He concluded: "the rank and reputation of an Officer is all thats dear to him and till mine is forfeited by misconduct, shall trust in the justness of Congress to permit my holding it, uninterrupted."[21] Weedon's letter was read in Congress on January 3.[22]

On the same day that Weedon wrote Congress (December 29), he sent Washington proposals for reforming regulations on rank at the battalion level. He did not offer suggestions as to his own case, except to observe that the eldest colonel of a state line should be given priority in promotion to brigadier general. Weedon recommended that "the Army should be immediately put on the American Establishment for life, upon Similar principles with the British Army," even allowing the purchase of rank. He said, however, that initial purchase should be limited to that of ensign; later purchase could go as high as Colonel, but any above lieutenant should afford existing lieutenants first option to buy higher rank. "This would be a sure means of always having good and frugal Officers." Weedon also used the opportunity to

---

[21] Weedon to the President of Congress, 29 December, 1777, Reel 178, PCC, NA; the original draft, 26 December, 1777, is in the WC, APS. Also Weedon to Richard Henry Lee, 12 April, 1778, Lee Family Papers, VSL. In reference to Woodford, in the original draft of Weedon's letter, Weedon said he had the "greatest respect" for Woodford and that he was "an intimate Acquaintance." Thus the final draft was slightly more impersonal.

[22] 3 January, 1778, Ford, 1904-1937: **10**: p. 15.

comment that "all titles in the staff of the Army" without commissions in the line should be abolished. Staff appointments, "a nuscence to refined Notions of Rank," have "already proved fatal to the Service," are "nothing more than Sinecures," and "they Impoverish the Magazines, Strip the Country & Debauch the Army, for having nothing to do, and holding Rank at the same time, are the Only Gentlemen of pleasure and Gallantry."[23]

Washington wrote Congress on January 1, calling attention to Weedon's letter to Congress, which "stated his objections to Genl. Woodford's taking Rank of him." Washington informed Congress that Muhlenberg had the same complaint as Weedon and had gone to Virginia. Washington enclosed a letter from General Anthony Wayne supporting Weedon's position, commenting only that Wayne thought Woodford had no claim to seniority of rank. Washington begged Congress to "proceed to the final settlement of the relative Rank of the Brigadiers."[24]

Unable and unwilling to reach a decision itself, Congress sent a Committee of Conference to Valley Forge to settle the dispute over rank. Originally the Committee consisted of all three members of the new Board of War—Gates, Mifflin, and Pickering—and three Congressmen—Francis Dana, Joseph Reed, and Nathaniel Folsom. The members of the Board of War, for whatever reason, did not go to Valley Forge, and three other persons were added—John Harvie, Charles Carroll, and Gouverneur Morris. Carroll also did not join the other members. When the Committee met on January 28, only Folsom, Morris, Dana, Reed, and Harvie were in attendance.[25] As Weedon pointed out, the committee was to arrange every department in the army, to "regulate Rank & fix future promotions on a more permanent and equitable footing, and take into their Consideration every other Matter that will Expedite the Service and promote the Falicity of this Army. I trust their labors will be crowned with Success."[26] Weedon was planning to take a furlough, and Washington

---

[23] Weedon to Washington, 29 December, 1777, WC, APS.

[24] Anthony Wayne to Washington, 28 December, 1777, Washington Papers, Series 4, Reel 46, LC; Washington to the President of Congress, 1 January, 1778, Fitzpatrick, 1931-: 10: p. 246.

[25] Burnett, 1921-1938: 61n. The Congressional resolution establishing the committee was January 10.

[26] Weedon to Richard Henry Lee, 1 February, 1778, Lee Papers, UVL.

told him that the Committee's work on the rank controversy
"ought to be done before you leave Camp."[27]

It was not until February 14, two weeks after their meetings
began, that the Committee considered the brigadier generals'
claims of rank. Woodford (who had just returned to camp),
Weedon, and Scott appeared before the Committee. With the
Committee telling him that they had no further need of him,
Weedon left on furlough. After several more days of
deliberation, the Committee, in Washington's words,
"judging themselves incompetent to the decision," referred
the controversy to a board of general officers.[28] The
Committee of Conference continued at Valley Forge to mid-
March, and only stated general principles for promotion.[29]

Washington ordered the board of all general officers (except
Woodford, in order to avoid a conflict of interest) to meet at
General Stirling's quarters and declared that their decision
would be final. But for some reason the board could not
convene right away, and Washington, therefore, tried again to
have the Committee of Conference reconsider the dispute.[30]
The Committee again insisted that the case be turned over to
the general officers, and it presented on March 2 a
chronological review of the dispute, including both state and
Continental service, with the implication that both should
count in determining seniority. Briefly the review is as
follows:

July 1775	Woodford appointed Colonel of the second Va. State Regiment
September 19, 1775	Woodford received his commission and Scott appointed his Lieutenant Colonel
February 13, 1776	Woodford appointed Colonel of the second Va. Continental Regiment . . . . Weedon, Lieutenant Colonel of the third
April 5, 1776	Fifth Va. Regiment became vacant

---

[27] Washington to Weedon, 10 February, 1778, Fitzpatrick, 1931: 10: p. 469.

[28] Washington to Woodford, 21 February, 1778, *ibid.*, p. 490; Weedon to Richard
Henry Lee, 12 April, 1778, Lee Family Papers, VSL; the Committee of Conference
Minutes, 14 and 16-18 February, 1778, Burnett, 1921-1938: 3: 86 and 89. In a letter to
Washington, Woodford stated he wanted the matter settled as soon as possible and it
would be to his advantage to have a large number of officers on the board. (Woodford
to Washington, 21 February, 1778, Washington Papers, Series 4, Reel 47, LC.)

[29] Committee of Conference Minutes, 19-20 February, 1778, Burnett, 1921-1938: 3:
p. 92.

[30] Washington to Woodford, 21 February, 1778, and Washington to the Committee of Congress, 1 March, 1778, Fitzpatrick, 1931-: 10: p. 490 and 11: p. 1, resp.

June 3, 1776	Third Regiment became vacant and Mercer made brigadier general over Woodford "in which he chearfully acquiesced."
June 9, 1776	Scott appointed Colonel of the fifth and Weedon of the Third. Scott by this appointment claimed rank of Weedon which was accepted by Weedon
September 1776	Stephen appointed brigadier general over Woodford whereupon he resigned
February 21, 1777	Muhlenberg, Weedon, and Woodford appointed brigadier generals, with Congress declaring that their rank should be afterwards settled
February 22, 1777	Congress placed Woodford last by a resolution
April 1, 1777	Scott appointed brigadier general
August 19, 1777	"Upon a Dispute of Rank in the Pennsylvania Line a Board of General Officers determined on the Principle, that Rank & Precedence should be settled among Officers according to the Standing they held in the Army immediately before their present Commissions excepting Promotions for Merit . . . ."
November 12, 1777	Congress by their resolution confirmed this principle
November 29, 1777	Congress directed Washington to regulate the rank of Generals Arnold, Woodford, and Scott according to the resolution of November 12

[the claims of the four Virginia brigadier generals are set forth] . . . .
The within Case and the Claims thereon having been referred to the Committee of Congress they request the Opinion of a Board of General Officers on the forgoing State of Facts which is submitted to them as more properly cognizable by Gentlemen of the Army than those in a civil Line. [Signed] Francis Dana[31]

Meanwhile, Weedon had gone home, as had Muhlenberg some time before. Weedon stopped at York, the temporary

---

[31] Committee at Camp Moore Hall, 2 March, 1778, Reports of the Committees of Conference . . ., PCC, NA.

capital, for two weeks. There he collected back pay in inflated Continental currency[32] and presumably did some lobbying with the Congress. At least Woodford thought Weedon was lobbying in his own behalf and protested to Washington of Weedon's visit to Congress.[33] The President of Congress, Henry Laurens, undoubtedly met with Weedon, as he entrusted with him letters to the governors of Maryland, Virginia, and North Carolina.[34]

All the major and brigadier generals at camp met at General Stirling's quarters on March 4 to consider the dispute, and in a day's time concluded unanimously (at least so thought Washington) that Woodford at the time of his reentering the army should have been restored to his seniority and that Muhlenberg, Scott, and Weedon should rank next in that order. The board made this report to the Committee of Conference, who referred it again to Congress.[35]

Muhlenberg returned from his home in Woodstock, Virginia, about the time of this decision. Belatedly he protested to the Committee of Conference, saying that Woodford had never claimed "preceding over Weedon & myself" until twelve months after he reentered the service and that Woodford had been promoted brigadier general "not on Account of his former Standing in the Army as being senior colonel but merely as a favor for former services done."[36]

Congress had the report of the board of general officers read March 19 and *"Resolved* That General Washington call in and cancel the commissions of Brigadiers Woodford, Muhlenberg, Scott, and Weedon; and that they rank in future agreeable to the following arrangement: Woodford, Muhlenberg, Scott, and Weedon."[37] A final determination had been made. Woodford, previously when he had been passed over,

---

[32] 21 February, 1778, Ford, 1904-1937: **10**: p. 187. Weedon received $2500.

[33] Woodford to Washington, 19 February, 1778, Washington Papers, Series 4, Reel 47, LC.

[34] Henry Laurens to Gov. Henry, to Gov. Johnson (Md.), to Gov. Caswell (N.C.), 1 March, 1778, Letter Books, PCC, NA.

[35] General Orders, 3 March, 1778, Washington to the Board of General Officers, 4 March, 1778, and Washington to Weedon, 15 March, 1778, Fitzpatrick, 1931-: **11**: pp. 19, 21, and 87, resp.; *Valley Forge Orderly Book*, 1902: pp. 248-249. The report was signed by Gen. Sullivan, who himself had earlier threatened to resign over the rank dispute with Conway.

[36] Muhlenberg to the Committee of Congress, 7 March, 1778, PCC, NA.

[37] 19 March, 1778, Ford, 1904-1937: **10**: p. 269.

had threatened to resign. Now it would be seen whether Weedon would leave the army. Muhlenberg would be persuaded by Washington to put country above honor, and would remain in the service. At worst, the whole affair would result in keeping one general and losing another.

Back in Fredericksburg, Weedon assumed direction of forwarding Virginia troops to camp. In addition to Washington's request that he do this, Congressman Richard Henry Lee wrote unofficially that "I am sure you will serve America and honor yourself" in assembling and sending on drafted troops.[38] Governor Henry also relied on Weedon for this task. This time Weedon did not have to worry about inoculation for smallpox, as he did before when on leave; for Washington ordered that the Virginia troops not be vaccinated until they "got near the Vicinity of the Army." Governor Henry, however, directed that the troops be inoculated before leaving Virginia. In this dilemma Weedon chose to follow Washington's orders.[39]

Less than a month after he returned to Fredericksburg, Weedon received a letter from Washington informing him of the action pending in Congress over the settlement of rank and asking Weedon to return immediately to the army.

> The situation of the Army in respect to Gen. Officers at this time, the anxiety of General Woodford to visit his family, and the fast approach of the period for opening the Campaign, urge me to request that you will return to Camp as soon as possible. It is unnecessary for me to enlarge upon this subject. Your precise and accurate knowledge of your circumstances, in this instance, will suggest to you at once, that your presence here is exceedingly material. A great number of Officers are now absent, and many more are pressing for the same purpose and must be indulged.

The commander in chief was sympathetic and offered advice which Weedon could well have heeded.

> I am heartily sorry that there should have been grounds for a dispute of this nature and should be happy if the parties interested would chearfully acquiesce, in whatever determination it may receive. That I have and would still advise, and if it

---

[38] Richard Henry Lee to Weedon, 14 March, 1778, AKF.

[39] For Weedon's comments on his role in directing troops northward, see Weedon to Page, 31 March, 1778, WPC, CHS.

should be against you, I really think, it will be more for your honor and reputation to do it, than to leave the service. The Gentlemen who have had the affair before them, and those who have it now, must be equally indifferent about your claims, and whatever judgement is given upon the occasion should be considered, as the result of an impartial inquiry and founded in justice. I have been told, if the point of precedence is settled in Genl. Woodford, that Genl. Muhlenberg as well as Genl. Scott, will submit to it without hesitation.[40]

Washington again wrote Weedon on March 29, enclosing a copy of the Congressional resolution, reiterating his advice and requesting Weedon's "most expeditious return." But if Weedon were determined not to serve under Woodford and Scott he should inform Washington "as the State of the Virginia Troops . . . will demand another immediate appointment in your room."[41]

Weedon had intended to return to the army until he learned of the action of the board of general officers. In a letter to Washington on March 30, after detailing in length his activities in forwarding troops from Virginia, he stated that he was sorry

> to inform your Excellency that a Continuance of my Service is uncartin, as by a late report of a board of officers, sent to Congress, I am informed they have deranged the Virginia line of General officers, and after my serving so long as second in Command, have given boath Woodford & Scott precedence of me. The instance of General Woodford's pretensions is without Example. Your Excellency knew my determination if that took place long before I left Camp, and I hope you will not look on my adopting the measure so near the approach of a Campaign as incompatable with the Gentleman, and officer. I ask but justice . . . .[42]

Upon receiving Weedon's letter of March 30 implying that he might resign, Washington wrote Congress of his distress over resignations in the Virginia Line, which he attributed to insubstantial pay and rewards.[43] The thought of Weedon's brigade alone reminded him that this brigade had undergone

[40] Washington to Weedon, 15 March, 1778, Fitzpatrick, 1931-: 11: pp. 87-88.

[41] Washington to Weedon, 29 March, 1778, *ibid.*, p. 173.

[42] Weedon to Washington, 30 March, 1778, Washington Papers, Series 4, Reel 48, LC.

[43] Washington to the President of Congress, 10 April, 1778, Fitzpatrick, 1931-: 11: p. 239.

an almost complete turnover, and now its commander was on the verge of resigning. All four of Weedon's colonels had resigned or had been cashiered.[44]

The Congressional resolution of March 19 was a bitter disappointment for George Weedon, although not unexpected. Probably he had thought that if the dispute were referred once more to Congress, he had a chance to win on his position. But such had not been the case. Now the only honorable course was to resign. But perhaps Congress might yet see their error. Should he resolutely accept the decision and resign or make one more attempt to convince Congress of the justice of his claim? Congress had vacillated on the issue, and it might do so again. He had a number of friends and supporters. General Charles Lee was to write his sister several months later that he considered Weedon among his friends and men of honor in the army.[45] Francis Lightfoot Lee wrote Weedon that he had supported him in Congress on the rank issue, and, in sending Weedon a copy of the resolution, commented that the Congressional vote, however, was founded on the "opinion, that the surest way of not injuring the feelings of military Gentlemen was to conform to the ideas of the Gentlemen of the Army . . . and not any preference given the other gentlemen."[46]

Another supporter Weedon could count on was Richard Henry Lee, a congressman like his brother. In a long letter to Lee, who was in Virginia at the time, enclosing the resolution, Weedon revealed a strain of bitterness that would grow even more pronounced.

> I have Coolly and impartially considered every Circumstance attending this extraordinary change. I have advised with many friends on the Subject. I have endeavoured to divert myself of little Punctilios and place it on the most generous Military scale. I possibly can, but cannot with my own feelings as an Officer, or with Coroborating Opinion of my friends pursue any other line of conduct consistent with my honor than to refuse service under those that have been so long my inferior officers, and who have taken such ungenerous steps to obtain precedence of me.

Concerning the board of general officers,

[44] The new colonels: Christian Febiger, John Gibson, John Green, and William Davies. (Sellers, "Virginia Continental Line," 1968: p. 302.

[45] Alden, 1951: pp. 353-354.

[46] Francis Lightfoot Lee to Weedon, 31 March, 1778, Burnett, 1921-1938: 3: p. 147.

I make not the least doubt but those Gentlemen divested themselves of every Vestige of partiality, but what grounds it was taken up on, or what presedent they followed, I cant pretend to say, as I have never had an Opportunity of defending myself in any one instance but before the Committee, who I expected was to determine it. I informed the General, and I also informed the Committee, that I should have no objections to General Scotts taking Command of me, provided all Similar promotions out of the line of Succession was deranged, so as not to make me the only Instance. Indeed I wished it, for the peace & falicity of the Army, but what must the world think when they see me banded about like a foot ball, and tamely subject my reputation to the Command of every Individual. Would they not naturely conclude I am Callus to every speck of honor?

I would ask if Generals Mercer & Stephens ware now in Service, whether General Woodfords relative rank would be ratified & he take precedence of them? If not, why should he of Muhlenburg and myself at this day? The case I apprehend is exactly Similar and carries the same propriety. If he was disgusted by their promotion, why would he Accept again an Appointment under them without declaiming politickly his intentions. And if after so long service as an inferior officer, he has a right to claim his former rank which he publickly laid down and retired into the body of the people, has not every officer who has resigned in consequence of promotions over them the same pretentions? The Absurdity is clair to the meanest Capacity, and the evil spirit of Intrigue was never more stricklingly Obvious . . . . Our Countries Arms, I bless my stars, has never been tarnished under my Command. I have Sacrificed as much prosperity and domestic happiness for the cause we are all engaged in as any one of my Circumstances, and I must have discharged my duty as faithfully. I will chearfully continue to spend my last Shilling & last drop of blood when I can do it with honor, and shall only add that I cannot serve in the present Arrangement, which is opposite to all Milatary Usage and without example in ours, or any other Army on Earth.

Weedon asked Lee to convey to Congress his decision not to serve in the army—interestingly he did not forthrightly say he was resigning: "And that the Service may not suffer, I must request the fav. of you to inform Congress of the same, that they may proceed to the Appointment of some other person to fill my place."[47] Lee on the same day wrote Weedon, saying that he was on Weedon's side and that he did not think

[47] Weedon to Richard Henry Lee, 12 April, 1778, Lee Family Papers, VSL.

Woodford's "Talents superior to yours;" he begged Weedon not to resign.[48] The day after writing his letter to Richard Henry Lee, Weedon wrote Washington of his decision to leave the army.[49]

Still, George Weedon had second thoughts. Perhaps Congress would reverse its resolution. He wrote General Nathanael Greene, the man he most admired in the army next to Washington, and Greene's reply of April 27 placed the blame for the decision over rank upon Congress and not the general officers, among whom, he said, Weedon was held in high esteem. "You mistook the Report of the General Officers respecting your Relative Rank," Greene pointed out. "They carefully avoided saying any thing about the Rank; after the Congress had appointed and Ranked you: but reported how you ought to have been Ranked in the first Instance." Yet Congress had dealt with the matter in

> such a Humiliating manner to the Officers affected, giving no reasons for the change and new arrangement, but only declaritive of their good will and pleasure, and in the Language of the Creator—Let there be light and there was Light . . . . I can give you no further advice upon the Question. I know your value and usefulness in the Army. I feel for you the warm attachment of a faithful Friend and am sorry the Publick should be deprived of your Services, and your Friend of your Society: but I cannot advise how to act. If you feel yourself degraded; I wish you to come to Camp nevertheless, be your determination what it may . . . [50]

Weedon sulked for a few more weeks in Fredericksburg. He wanted very much to return to the army. The next campaign, soon to take place, might well end the war. He had been through the thick of the war thus far and wanted to share in the laurels of victory. For one who had been a military man half his adult life, what other distinction was there? Yet the honor of an officer had to be preserved. Greene's advice had been merely that Weedon must decide on his own conscience. Though still convinced he should leave the army, Weedon felt his case had not been fully aired. A visit to Valley Forge might ease his mind, and perhaps there might be some way he could return with honor.

---

[48] Richard Henry Lee to Weedon, 12 April, 1778, AKF.

[49] Burnett, 1921-1938: 3: p. 89n.

[50] Greene to Weedon, 27 April, 1778, L. W. Smith Collection, Morristown National Historical Park.

Weedon had missed out on the light-hearted activity at Valley Forge during the spring. He heard of the grand entertainment celebrating the French Alliance, the wicket and other ball games among the officers, and the numerous dine and dance parties given by the commander in chief himself.[51]

In late May, George Weedon returned to Valley Forge. He stayed at camp several weeks, consulting with various officers. It was not an opportune time, however, to arouse interest in his case, as the army was readying to pursue Clinton should he abandon Philadelphia. The army was arranged without him, and it was sorrowful to watch his brigade, along with Muhlenberg's now in a division commanded by Stirling, prepare for the march and to find that part of his brigade was assigned to Woodford.[52]

While at Valley Forge, Weedon reaffirmed his decision to follow the course of honor and leave the army. He sent a brief letter, quoted in full below, to Congress, asking permission to retire.

It is with real concern I find myself Arranged in a line of rank which I conceive repugnant to all Military Usage, and without example in Ours or any other Army on Earth, and which (tho' reluctantly) Obliges me to request of Congress leave to retire from Service. The present establishment of the Virginia line, wounds my honor so sensably as to drive me to this disagreeable measure. Give me leave to assure you sir, that triffling Punctilios should by no means have governed my Conduct. The present Occation of my Uneasiness, is of a nature too Capital for any Military Character having Regard for his Rank & Reputation to act under. And constrains me therefore to retire from a service, the Success of which I have much at heart, and in which I trust have hitherto discharged my duty. It is unnecessary to assign Reasons further, since Congress cannot be unacquainted with the causes that gave rise to a dispute between Brigadiers Woodford, Scott, and myself upon the Subject of precedence in the Army.[53]

---

[51] E.g., *Military Journal of Ewing*: pp. 48-51, 6 May, 1778; Capt. Lt. B. Howe to S. Bauman, 23 April and 11 May, 1778, Sebastian Bauman Papers, NYHS.

[52] Arrangement of the Army . . ., 28 May, 1778, Fitzpatrick, 1931-: **11**: p. 465; *Lee Papers*, 1871-: **2**: pp. 410-411; Weekly Return of the Continental Army . . ., 13 June, 1778, Stryker, 1927: p. 277. Presumably Weedon's brigade had a number of Negroes. Later, after re-arrangement of the army, there were 775 Negroes in the army, of which 40 were in Woodford's brigade; 98 in Muhlenberg's; 24 in Scott's. (Return of the Negroes in the Army Brigades, 24 August, 1778, Washington Papers, Series 4, Reel 51, LC.)

[53] Weedon to the President of Congress, 27 May, 1778, Reel 178, PCC, NA.

Weedon's letter was immediately read in Congress, a day after its May 27 date, "whereupon, a motion was made for commitment; and on motion Resolved that the Consideration thereof be postponed."[54] Weedon was not informed that Congress had tabled his request. Two weeks later, he inquired of Richard Henry Lee, who had now returned to Congress at York, what had happened to his request. If Congress had taken no action on the request for permission to retire

> I could wish to know as early as possible what Indulgence they will allow me, as in this Awkward and unprecedented situation I can not Act. Congress I dare say must be satisfied my constant Services since the commencement of the American War, merits a more honorable reward then bestowing my rank on another person, at a period when every thing promises a reward for the hardship, dangers & sufferings which I participated in Obtaining it. And as my uneasiness proceeds intirely from their own resolutions, which in this Instance I humbly conceive not to be founded in justice, I hope they can have no objections to my not Serving in the present Virginia line . . . .[55]

As the army left Valley Forge, Weedon decided to visit Congress himself. He followed Congress to Philadelphia, after the British evacuation.

Weedon took sick—apparently his first prolonged severe attack of the gout. At age forty-three, he was even more heavy-set than before. Because of overindulgence in food and drink, the wearing down of his metabolic constitution from the demands of army life, and the emotional stress that he was going through, Weedon was a prime target for this disabling disease. It is known that he suffered terribly from it towards the end of his life. If such was the case in the summer of 1778, this condition undoubtedly influenced his decision. Although he had determined not to serve under Woodford, it is possible that he might have buried his grudge and have returned to the army— if there was not this added problem of health. Public honor perhaps would have overridden private honor. Weedon regarded himself as a professional soldier, and concerns for duty and patriotism might have substantially weighed in favor of changing his mind. Yet, being sick, the sacrifice in returning to active service would be all the much greater, and the illness made him more prone to rationalize his predica-

---

[54] 28 May, 1778, Ford, 1904-1937: 11: p. 544.
[55] Weedon to Richard Henry Lee, 13 June, 1778, Lee Family Papers, VSL.

ment on the basis of offended honor—public and private.

Still in Philadelphia on August 14 without any notice of
action from Congress on his request, Weedon addressed a
letter to Congress reviewing his reasons for leaving the army.
He cited the resolution of March 19 and the conflicting previous record in the journals of Congress. He was sorry to
trouble Congress, "but my reputation, as well as my disagreeable and expensive Situation, demands something conclusive."
He asked "what every gentleman has a right to demand, and
what I hope you will grant to one that has faithfully served
you." As if seeking to reopen his case, Weedon enclosed
Woodford's letter to him of March 17, 1777, by which
Woodford had relinquished "all pretensions of precedence."
Weedon said he had been deprived of his rank, "which was
taken by regular Succession, and perfectly consistent with the
usage of all Armies . . . . That some mistake has been the
Occation of this injury to me, I cannot doubt." Since Congress
had not reconsidered its resolution of March 19, "I am
induced to make this claim to justify my conduct to my
Country. As in the present arrangement I cannot serve."
Specifically Weedon now requested that should Congress
choose "to continue me in the line till I can take an Active
part again with propriety, I shall whenever that is the case, be
ready and willing to serve."[56]

Congress considered Weedon's request on the eighteenth.
With twenty-one ayes and seven noes (9 of 12 states, aye)
Congress voted:

> Brigadier Weedon be permitted to retire, that he hold his
> present rank in the said armies, and that he be called into
> service whenever, from a change of circumstances, the
> inconveniences he now labors under can be removed; provided
> that during the time of his being retired, he shall not be
> entitled to receive pay or rations, and provided also that unless
> he shall be called into, and remain in service during the war, he
> shall not be entitled to half pay.

Only two Virginians voted: Thomas Adams, no; John Harvie,
aye.[57] Thus Weedon had the unusual arrangement: he could
keep his present rank, without pay or rations, and could
return to active duty in the future.

Weedon was not altogether pleased with this compromise,

---

[56] Weedon to Henry Laurens, 14 August, 1778, WL, BUL.

[57] 18 August, 1778, Ford, 1904-1937: 11: pp. 807-808.

which left him in limbo. He had his title, but was stripped of everything else. It would have been more honorable to have had a complete separation from the army. It seemed likely that he would not be recalled. As John Penn, a congressional delegate from North Carolina, observed, it was unthinkable to permit "any officer to return to the line, a little before the end of the war to entitle him to receive half pay."[58] His illness continuing, Weedon remained in Philadelphia, and did not leave for Fredericksburg until the end of September.

Whatever were the compelling reasons for Weedon's refusal to return to active service, he had simply done what other officers did or threatened to do. At least he had the satisfaction that he had won, if only partially, in his fight to vindicate his honor. As Douglas Southall Freeman aptly put it, Weedon went home and "kept both his complaint and his commission."[59]

---

[58] John Penn to [Wiliam Woodford?], (shortly after 18 August), 1778, Burnett, 1921-1938: 3: p. 396. Wrote Penn: "General Weedon was not well pleased with the determination of Congress; indeed he was quite the reverse as I have been informed."

[59] Freeman, 1949-: 5: p. 79.

VIII. RETIREMENT AND RECALL

For all the change from soldier to civilian, return to domesticity had its rewards. George Weedon welcomed the opportunity to be a real father to the Mercer children. He now had time to give attention to the settlement of the affairs of General Mercer's estate and to check into his own plantation on the Potomac. Weedon renewed old friendships, and he found some diversion in the public and social life of the thriving Fredericksburg community. Yet there were moods of despondency. Having staked so much on the American cause, he had anxiety that now people might consider him a quitter for having left the army. From his own little world he followed every detail of military events, as if he were still a shaper in the destiny of America.

Two days after Weedon returned home to Fredericksburg from Philadelphia in October, 1778, he penned a long letter to General Greene (which he had also done just before leaving Philadelphia). He reflected upon the arts of cabal in regard to Greene and himself.

> My own private opinion wanted nothing to establish your name & worth with me, but I've been a little Surprized at hearing some people say, since the Rhode Island affair, That Greene . . . retrieved his Character. I have Asked when he had lost it, or what rascal had deformed it, and have been Answered that they had heard so & so. Such calumny can never hurt real Merit which will in the end show itself under every disadvantage and finally burst on the heads of the Censorians, to their eternal shame and disgrace . . . I know the delicate feelings of my friend, and how quietly and deservedly he merits the rewards due the brave, the prudent and diligent Soldier.

Weedon again reviewed Congress's settlement of his rank dispute. "Congress, and myself run another heat before I left them," he said. "They got the start of me formerly, and by Turkey keep it. I am not however distanced . . ." Gouverneur Morris "was my particular friend in debate as was many other able Speakers, who condemned the measures that brought on the dispute, and justified the conduct I had pursued in

138

Consequence." Although Weedon's "heart and Soul" was with Greene, he would not be drawn into service again, unless it "shall be honorable." Weedon hoped that "our Correspondence will be permanent." Kitty Weedon sent her "love to you and lady, and if you will please present mine at the same time."[1]

Weedon still held to his view that the war was all but over. One decisive blow, such as could have occurred at Brandywine, would end it. Enthusiasm for the war in northern Virginia had waned. John Taylor, one of many Virginians who shared Weedon's opinion, wrote that "it is not impossible but that this winter may put an end to the war, or at least may see the British troops withdraw."[2] The war had come to a stalemate in the North. Already, however, it was being renewed with vigor in the South. Congress called for 1,000 Virginia militiamen to be sent to Charleston.[3] Should the occasion arise for Weedon to reenter military service, the prospect would be that he would be sent southward; yet for some reason, probably because of the many obstacles for ordered battle and the climate, Weedon always had an aversion to serving in the South.

Weedon wrote General Greene regularly, but for a long time his letters went unanswered. Writing on November 20, Weedon said he had achieved a peace of mind. He assured Greene that he was

> much altered; in so much that I have become a Socrates, and I find for the real ease, and peace of mind (without which life is a burthren). It is absolutely Necessary to imbibe more, or less, of that Sage Old fellow's principles . . . . The Actions of Brandy Wine & Germantown, I have frequently considered . . . .My Ideas co-incide exactly with yours respecting the Gen. Orders, which however did not so forcible strike me, til you Delineated their meaning, and tho' you are the only man I ever complained to—Or ever will—I do say boath you and myself ware differently treated to what Military Characters in Similar Cases have experienced, whose Services ware not more important, or displayed more prudence or firmness.[4]

---

[1] Weedon to Greene, 5 October, 1778, Greene Papers, CL.

[2] John Taylor to William Woodford, 9 October, 1778, Peter Force Transcripts, LC.

[3] Martin Pickett to John Churchill Brooke et al., 28 October, 1778, Martin Pickett Letters, VHS.

[4] Weedon to Greene, 30 November, 1778, Greene Papers, CL.

In March, 1779, Weedon reported, "Our Coast swarms with privateers, Scarcely one Vessel in ten gets in safe, insomuch that our trade is almost totally destroyed." He also noted the runaway inflation in Virginia.[5] Weedon heard from Washington, who asked him to forward a letter to General Scott,[6] and from Baron de Riedesel, a prisoner of war in the Convention army at Charlottesville. Following the example of Jefferson and other prominent Virginians, who were sociable with the captive officers, Weedon gave a warm reply to Riedesel, saying that he would like to make his acquaintance and that he wished that Riedesel could visit Fredericksburg.[7]

Colonel Walter Stewart, commander of a Pennsylvania regiment, stayed with the Weedons for about a week in March, 1779. Stewart and Weedon afterwards kept up an intermittent light-hearted correspondence. Stewart received advice from Weedon on courting the ladies. Kitty once "got a sight of your letter by my carelessness in leaving it on the Table," Weedon wrote, and she "laught heartily" at some of the contents. In the same letter, addressed to Stewart on his way northward to camp at Middlebrook, Weedon afforded some hints of his social life in Fredericksburg.

> I am much mistaken if there is not some of the fair sex in this place that would have readily granted you a longer furlough from a fixed melancoly which I have observed ever since your departure. I rec'd Balls present of the History of the four Kings and this Evening intend having a party. Fitzhugh and lady is set of for the Petersburgh Races. I was the death of an excellent Saddle of Mutton at his house the day before he went away. It was handsomely garnished with Madiera & Claret & succeeded by the damnest hott rubber I ever was concerned in. We continue the Old System in Town as you know our method of Killing Time shall not describe it.[8]

By April, 1779, it seemed that George Weedon still had not become used to sitting out the war. He wondered what course the war might yet take. Writing to Councillor John Page at Williamsburg, Weedon advised of the need for defense

---

[5] Weedon to Greene, 10 March, 1779 *ibid.*

[6] Washington to Weedon, 6 March, 1779, Fitzpatrick, 1931-: 14: p. 205.

[7] Weedon to Maj. Gen. Riedesel, 23 February, 1779, WL, BUL. Riedesel had written Weedon on 17 February.

[8] Weedon to Col. Walter Stewart, 22 March, 1779, Stewart Papers, NYHS; Stewart to Mrs. A. Stewart, 14 March, 1779, Force Transcripts, LC.

preparation in Virginia, the probability of a British invasion and its likely form (in which he was remarkably prophetic), the proper arrangement of the militia, and his own interest in being placed in charge of Virginia military security. On the latter point he anticipated the creation of the office of Commissioner of War, which the state would eventually establish. But to say that Weedon was angling only for a Virginia military appointment does him injustice. He seemed a bit despondent:

> so reduced and Debilitated was I, by a long Spell of sickness which I contracted at Valley Forge, that for some months after I returned from the Northward, I had not Spirit to do any thing. Nor can I boast of one days perfect Health from last June, till very lately. I thank god I am so far recovered now as to injoy life again with some degree of Satisfaction, and promise myself the happiness of seeing you Next Month . . . . An inactive life at this time when our Country Calls for the exertions of every Individual, is of all things the most Irksome to me, but till Congress can employ me in a line that I am justly intitled to, must content myself, unless my own Country should want my Service.[9]

Weedon's prediction of a British invasion was borne out in part by the Matthew-Collier raid a month later. Although the British landing was of only several days duration, causing destruction from Portsmouth to Suffolk, Weedon feared that the British expeditionary force of over 2,000 would establish a permanent base in Virginia. As Weedon reported to Colonel Stewart:

> I was led to believe at first that it was only a plundering expedition set on foot by that noted Rascal Goutridge [Goodrich] who is among them, and who a few days ago paid a visit to Smithfield . . . . I now begin to think they mean to hold a post amongst us, as they have ships in the mouth of Rappahannock, and in James River; and an Account this moment received says that Twenty Sail have gone up the Bay. We are doing every thing in our power to make head against them, but I am sorry to say that after so long a War we are by no means adequate to proper opposition. We have men enough, but nothing else. I hope this will rouse the knowing ones from their lethargy and teach them to be better prepared in future . . . .[10]

---

[9] Weedon to John Page, 12 April, 1779, WC, CHS.

[10] Weedon to Walter Stewart, 18 May, 1779, Stewart Papers, NYHS.

Contrary to Weedon's expectations, the British force soon embarked and returned to New York. What the British did not do at this time they would do a year and a half later, when they would engage in a full invasion and establish a permanent post in Virginia, as Weedon anticipated.

Settling various items pertaining to General Mercer's estate required some attention throughout 1779 and early 1780. Weedon managed the Stafford County plantation (or as he called it, the "Plantation over the River"), and paid Mrs. Mercer rent. He presided over repairs, and he had the plantation, which Mercer had bought from George Washington, surveyed. In May, 1779, Weedon went to Alexandria to arrange further payment to Washington for Mercer's land on Four Mile Run in Fairfax County.[11] Early next year he was attempting to sell Mercer's "Yohogania Land."[12] As an executor of Mercer's estate, along with John Tennent of Caroline County and Isabella Mercer (the widow), Weedon had the responsibility of keeping the accounts for the estate. Weedon was also involved in an effort to prevent the establishment of a new ferry on the Rappahannock, which would compete with a ferry at Hugh Mercer's property. He, along with James Hunter and James Hunter, Jr., successfully petitioned the Virginia Assembly not to grant permission for the rival ferry.[13]

Weedon conducted several real estate transactions during his "retirement." Weedon's and Mercer's lot #203 in Fredericksburg (purchased jointly from Roger Dixon in 1764) was sold to Samuel Selden of Stafford County on April 28, 1779.[14] On the same day lots #240 and 250 (where the Sentry Box would be built), which also had been obtained from Dixon in 1764, were conveyed to James Mercer, attorney-at-law, and in turn were purchased by Weedon for £600 currency from Mercer on May 5, 1779 (but not recorded until 1782).[15] On March 1, 1780, George and Catharine Weedon sold to Jacob Whittier of Fredericksburg for $2,664 two hundred

---

[11] Ledger Book #2, VSL.; Washington to Lund Washington, 17 and 18 December, 1779, Fitzpatrick, 1931-: 17: pp. 409 and 424.

[12] Ledger Book #2, VSL.

[13] 15 May, 1779 and Petition of James Hunter, James Hunter, Jr., and George Weedon, 18 May, 1779, Legislative Petitions, Fredericksburg, VSL; 23 October, 1779, Legislative Petitions, Spotsylvania County, VSL; Quinn, 1908: p. 171.

[14] 28 April, 1779, Crozier, 1905: p. 368.

[15] Ibid.; Embrey's Index . . ., Fredericksburg City, Grantee, H-Z, VSL; King, "General Weedon and his Home 'The Sentry Box,'" mimeograph.

twenty-two acres in St. George's parish, Spotsylvania County
—land conveyed by deed from Margaret Gordon (Catharine's
mother) in 1772.[16]

For a while, Weedon occasionally took supper and/or club
at his former tavern, still leased to William Smith. But the
relationship between landlord and tenant progressively
worsened, as Smith stopped making rent payments. The only
return Weedon was getting on his tavern property (except for
use of the slaughterhouse) was credit for the few supplies
obtained from Smith. Smith continued to default on the rent,
and Weedon eventually stayed away from the tavern; he would
in the future have to take Smith to court.[17]

In late summer, 1779, the Weedons vacationed at Bath. The
town, located at the "Health Springs" in the Valley in
Berkeley County, had become a very popular resort, attracting
as many as four hundred people at a time from a cross-section
of the aristocracy and frontiersmen of Virginia and
Maryland.[18] When Weedon returned on September 19 he
found a letter from General Greene (September 6) awaiting
him, and he was delighted at long last that Greene was willing
to renew their friendship. "Its very true," Weedon wrote, "I
really did begin to think you either wanting in respect, or very
lazy, as I had wrote several times without receiving in return a
single scrap of a pen. Your pleading guilty restores you
however to favour and affection." As to how he had been
spending his time, Weedon told Greene that "Major Forsythe
was not far out, in saying I preferred an Active life in the
Service of my Country, to that of a Gallant which I have
personated ever since my expedition to Bath, where I have had
every amusement, in the small way that heart could wish,"
namely the balls, "Routs, Fishing parties, card parties, &c
&c—of which that place abounds during the season." But
"there was a something wanting of a more manly nature."
The vacation had not lifted him from his despondency.

> The dirty Acts of mankind as you observe have given me such a
> disgust to the world, that its a mean matter of difference to me
> how long I continue an Inhabitant of it. I am pleased however
> to hear I have friends where all the Virtue of the Continent
> Centers, and that my conduct respecting a retired life, in

---

[16] 1 March, 1780, Crozier, 1905: p. 352.

[17] Fredericksburg District Court Papers and excerpts from ledger of accounts with
Smith (xerox copy supplied by G. H. S. King).

[18] Bridenbaugh, 1965: pp. 179-180.

Consequence of degradation offered my Military Character, is approved by them. And I publickly declair that I am ready & willing to stand or fall with my Country in any Service that dose not Subject me to the Command of General Woodford . . . .
Faction and party during the National Counsell of this continent, has sunk them beneath Scandle, nor can I talk, or think, of their measures with any degree of patience. You must however my good friend, make allowances, & consider how much depends on able and Active Men.

Upon Greene's Quartermaster Department "depends the Salvation of America." Good and honest men are hard to find.

. . . . perjury and trechery has become as common as Indian Corn, and few there is that looks a day further than his own private emoluments. It is not enough to drive a man distracted, to think that after so long a war, we shd. only be in a situation to act on the defensive? When there has been more money spent in triffling projects, and Cabal, that would have enabled the Genl. had it been properly dispersed to [have] anihilated the British Army long ago . . . .

Wayne's and Lee's "enterprises add great lustre to our Arms . . . . It must prove to the world what General Washington would do, was he properly supported." Weedon said that he longed to hear "some official Accounts from Genl. Sullivan. He is truly a Child of misfortune, however there is one thing in his favour in the Expedition [against the Iroquois and Tories], that is, he has no Brackish Water to Cross or should dread the consequence."[19]

The revival of correspondence with Greene seemed to give Weedon a lift. He enjoyed the exchange in news and military gossip. When he wrote Greene on October 12 he said he was happy to learn of the acquittal of Henry Lee, "my much Esteemed friend," in his court martial trial for his conduct at Paulus Hook in August, 1779. Nothing more "astonished" Weedon than to hear that Colonel Nathaniel Gist of Virginia had preferred charges against Lee. "For the Lords sake what could induce that head of the Wrongheads to Calumniate so Splendid, so Gallant, so brave and Officerlike conduct as that little Hero displayed in that affair. For which he ought to be loved, Honored, and adored, instead of being Arraigned and brought to Trial. I am sorry for the Colo., as it must hurt him in the Oppinion of all good men."

---

[19] Weedon to Greene, 20 September, 1779, Greene Papers, CL.

On other matters, Weedon observed, concerning news of the arrival of a French fleet in America under Admiral d'Estaing, that "Poor England. Its over with you indeed. The Asylum of Villainy, Disapation, pride, Cruelty, Sunk . . . despised, Contemn'd & set at Nought." Weedon mentioned a letter from his friend, William Fitzhugh, a delegate at Congress, which told of two hundred Hessians "who were bound for Halifax" but "mistook their way" and arrived in Philadelphia. Weedon inquired of "the long talked of Imbarkation going on at N. York"; he feared the British were headed for Virginia, "and some Circumstance which I am informed of by a member of Our Political Wheel, confirms me in my Opinion." With the Convention army at Charlottesville, Weedon considered this all the more a possiblity. As he had advocated before, he wished the prisoners could be sent beyond the Blue Ridge. Weedon also inquired of Greene; "Pray where is Sullivan: I have never yet been able to find out his real Object. I hope Niagara is not part of it," as the British had too strong a fort there. But if Sullivan is only "to chastize Mr. [John] Butler and his Banditti, he is fully Adequate to that Service," provided he sets up "ambuscades in his Advance" and secures a safe retreat. Weedon also informed Greene that Robert Forsyth "is returned with an Appointment in the Commissaries Department, which will Bake his Cake. I am much pleased at it. He is a deserving little fellow, and will I am sure Discharge his Duty with Fidelity and Punctuality which in these depraved days is a bold word."[20]

Weedon continued in the hopes of a military appointment in Virginia. As noted before, he had stated to John Page his desire to be placed in charge of the defense of Virginia, particularly to command the militia within the state. Back in June, according to one of Woodford's supporters, Edmund Pendleton, Weedon had been "disappointed," and "much Chargreened" by not being named to the new Virginia Board of War.[21] Weedon increasingly spoke out on the need for state defense preparations. Even though he had an eye on military preferment in the state, he was sincerely motivated in that he could not sit idly by when there was so much to be done.

Probably unknown to George Weedon, in September, Henry Laurens of South Carolina nominated him in Congress to fill the vacancy on the Board of War. For whatever reason,

---

[20] Weedon to Greene, 12 October, 1779, *ibid.*; Greene to Weedon, 6 September, 1779, AKF.

[21] Edmund Pendleton to William Woodford, 21 June, 1779, Mays, 1967: 1: p. 291.

Weedon's nomination was not pursued, and Jesse Root was named to the Board two weeks later. When another vacancy occurred soon thereafter, Laurens nominated Colonel William Malcolm.[22] The old matter of rank, however, was again brought up in Congress in December when it heard a report from the Board of War on a memorial from Muhlenberg protesting the same resolution of March 19, 1778 that Weedon had. Deciding that an "explanatory resolution" was necessary Congress resolved that it had "the most favorable opinion of the merit and characters of the gentlemen" mentioned in the resolution of March 19, 1778 and "That the arrangement made therein was founded upon principles not affecting the personal characters or comparative merits of those officers."[23]

Perhaps George Weedon had an occasional visit with Colonel Alexander Spotswood, who had been retired from the army in similar fashion himself. Spotswood, proprietor of "Nottingham" in Spotsylvania County and one of the largest landholders in Virginia, unlike Weedon, seemed to lose any inclination to return to the army. Weedon might well have profited from Spotswood's example on how to put the military life out of his mind, as indicated in a letter of Spotswood to Colonel Stewart in November, 1779. Spotswood was now the "compleat country Squire" and

> all thoughts of entering the Army again are banished—and now confine myself to the Following Divisions—In the Summer, I attend my Farm—in the Fall my running horses—and in the winter, Fox hunting and a Rubber passes away time—I shall be all over Pennsylvania next spring—not merely for pleasure but to collect a Number of Grass seeds, and to gain a little more knowledge in the Culture of it. I am now preparing Elegant Stables in Town for the Reception of my Friends horses.[24]

With horseracing returning—Virginians had denied themselves this pleasure long enough because of the war— George Weedon could have taken a cue from Spotswood and revived the Jockey Club. But this was such a bother before, and besides promoting horseracing would now be below his dignity as a general still nominally in service.

---

[22] 4 and 26 September, 19 October, and 26 November, 1779, Ford, 1904-1937; 15: pp. 1027, 1109, 1187, 1384, resp.

[23] 29 December, 1779, *ibid.*, pp. 1418-1419.

[24] Alexander Spotswood to Col. Walter Stewart, 20 November, 1779, Force Transcripts, LC.

In February, 1780, Weedon noted the burning of Spotswood's house; but Spotswood "was fortunate enough to save most of his effects." Many fires happened in the Fredericksburg neighborhood during the winter, occasioned by what Weedon regarded as "one of the most Intence Winters that ever was known. It is Seven Weeks this day [February 15] that the whole Surface of the Earth has been one continued Sheet of Ice."[25]

The "Virginia line" came for a while in February to Fredericksburg, "and a pretty figure they Cut for Sixteen Batns."[26] The thrill of the sight of the veteran Continentals, soon to be furloughed before being regrouped to march to Charleston, stirred the martial zeal in Weedon, although he probably had few words, if any, with General William Woodford, commander of this "division." Two months later Woodford would collect the troops who had rejoined the service along with new volunteers into a brigade of twelve hundred "effectives,"[27] which Woodford would lead southward. Yet Weedon was as disillusioned as ever over the neglect of the war effort. As he wrote Greene on February 15, "but Heavens! how I am alarmed at many reports respecting provisions, for godsake what is the meaning of it? Is the finances of America exausted or has Congress been playing their Old Game? . . . . I hope in god the want is over as we have not heard of your Disbanding which many reports led us believe would be the case." As for Virginia,

> I really am ashamed of the Dominion for believe there never was such a relaxation known. Indeed they have no excuse as their never was a better time for Recruiting men. Sure I am that with the Bounty allowed I could recruit a Thousand men myself in a very short time and yet so shamefully is that Service Neglected that I do not believe their is a man Inlisted in a month. We ought all of us to pray for peace, and hope in god it is not far of, but I perfectly agree with you in being fully prepared for war, as the surest way of Obtaining it.[28]

Celebration of Washington's birthday provided the leading social event of the winter in Fredericksburg. As was Washington's custom himself, the birthday was observed under the Old Style date—February 11. Two Virginia

---

[25] Weedon to Greene, 15 February, 1780, Greene Papers, CL.

[26] *Ibid.*

[27] Weedon to Greene, 16 May, 1780, *ibid.*

[28] Weedon to Greene, 15 February, 1780, *ibid.*

Continental regiments in Fredericksburg "added much to the
rejoicings of that day." At noon, "a grand salute of 13 pieces
of cannon were discharged, succeeded by a feu-de-joye, fired
by the troops," who presented "a very Martial appearance,
and went through their firings with the greatest regularity and
good order. In the evening the Weedons attended "an elegant
ball at the coffee-house."[29] Weedon reported the event to
Greene: "I wish I could have had you boath [including Mrs.
Greene] hear on his Excellencies birth Night. Mrs. Green
should have seen what her Dancing Genl. could do."[30]

Fredericksburg was now one of several recruiting stations in
Virginia for the Southern army. General Muhlenberg, placed
in charge of recruiting in Virginia, himself stayed about a
week in the town during early May, and Weedon had a chance
to renew an old acquaintance.[31] Colonel Christian Febiger
("Old Denmark"), whom Weedon had known as a commander of a Virginia regiment at the battles of Brandywine
and Germantown, assumed the duties of recruitment in
Fredericksburg.[32]

Weedon, like other Virginians, waited anxiously in May for
news of the outcome of the British siege of Charleston. His
own estimate was that, although all communication was cut
off from Charleston, the American force and supplies were
sufficient to withstand the siege.[33] Ironically, shortly before
word arrived in northern Virginia of the surrender of the
American army at Charleston—and hence Woodford's
capture—Weedon applied for a position in the Northern
army, providing that he not serve under Woodford. Weedon
wrote Colonel William Grayson, formerly a delegate to
Congress and now a member of the Board of War, of this
intention. Grayson showed Weedon's letter to Joseph Jones.
As Jones reported to Washington, Weedon desired "to serve
in the northern Army if any employm't can be carved out for
him." Jones's letter to Washington explains how far Jones,
who was now a co-proprietor of the Fredericksburg brewery

---

[29] *Virginia Gazette* (Dixon and Nicholson), 26 February, 1780.

[30] Weedon to Greene, 15 February, 1780, Greene Papers, CL.

[31] Boyd, 1950: 3: 363n. and 371n. Muhlenberg had been appointed by the Board of
War in late 1779 to take command of collecting men and supplies in Virginia for the
Southern theater. But he did not set out from Philadelphia until 10 March, 1780,
Muhlenberg, 1849: pp. 181-184.

[32] 23 May-30 May, 1780, and *passim*, Febiger Letter Book, 1779-1780, VSL.

[33] Weedon to Greene, 16 May, 1780, Greene Papers, CL.

as well as Congressman, was willing to go to help Weedon, even though Weedon blamed Jones as an instigator of the change in rank seniority.

> This Gentleman for whom, as an Officer, I entertain a regard, has attributed the regulation of his Rank, wch. has occasioned his retiring, in great part to me; tho. God knows I did no more in the matter than was my Duty by moving in Congress that the dispute be ref'd to a Board of G. Officers. He has ever since his return kept himself aloof from me. Abt. this I have no concern. I promised Col. Grayson I wo'd mention the proposal to you and had no doubt if a place could be found for him you wo'd call him into service. His only objection it seems is his serving under Woodford. If you shall find an opening for Genl. Weedon, I believe it will be agreeable and convenient to him but I request it may not be known to him that I had any concern in the business . . . .[34]

Washington, in reply to Jones, expressed surprise that Weedon was still in the army on inactive status. "I thought General Weedon had actually resigned his Commission," he said, "but be this as it may, I see no possibility of giving him any command out of the line of his own State. He certainly knows that every state that has Troops enough to form a Brigade claims, and has exercised, uniformly, the previledge of having them commanded by a Brigr. of its own, nor is it in my power to depart from this system without convulsing the Army; which at all times is hurtful, and may be ruinous in this."[35]

Recovering from the shock of Lincoln's surrender at Charleston, Congress ordered the creation of a new Southern army to counteract the overall British offensive now developing in the South. An act of Congress conferred upon General Gates the command of the Southern army on June 13.[36]

It was now appropriate to call back into active duty Weedon and Daniel Morgan. The Continental Board of War considered Weedon's status, and on June 16 reported to Congress that Weedon by resolution of Congress of August 18, 1778 had been permitted to retire, on condition that he hold his rank and that he could "be called into service whenever from a change of circumstances the difficulties he then

---

[34] Joseph Jones to Washington, 23 May, 1780, Burnett, 1921-1938: 5: pp. 163-164.

[35] Washington to Joseph Jones, 31 May, 1780, Fitzpatrick, 1931-: 18: pp. 453-454.

[36] President of Congress to Washington, 13 June, 1780, Burnett, 1921-1938: 5: p. 213.

laboured under should be removed, that time seems now to be arrived, and he is desirous of serving again." Congress, without delay, acted on the recommendation, and ordered that Brigadier General Weedon "be called into service, and employed in the southern department as Major General Gates shall direct." The same action was taken with Morgan, who was promoted to brigadier general.[37]

President Huntington immediately wrote Washington, Gates, Weedon, and Morgan of the resolutions. Weedon was informed, with the resolution of June 16 enclosed, that "it is the Pleasure of Congress that you be employed in the Service in the southern Department as Major General Gates shall direct."[38]

In his acceptance, Weedon cited "the train of misfortunes that has Attended our Operations in the South, and the total deranged Situation of our Affairs in that Quarter" as "Sufficient Motives for my ready Obedience to this your Excellencies Order . . . . tho' my feelings as an Officer have been much wounded by unfortunate Arrangements." Weedon briefly reminded Congress of the details of his "Degradation." Then he added: "but your Excellency can be no Stranger to my former Services. And Notwithstanding what has happened; Shall Cheerfully afford my small Exertions in defence of my Country, so long as I can do it with propriety, And hope my future Conduct will speak for itself. Congress may therefore consider me in their Service, And shall always be happy to Execute any particular Orders that they may in the Course of the war find Necessary to Direct."[39]

Summer, 1780, appears to have been a time of even less communication between Congress and the commander in chief than before. Washington learned after the fact of the appointment of Gates as commander of the Southern army and of the recall of Weedon and Morgan. On the same day that Weedon wrote the President of Congress of his acceptance he addressed a long letter to Washington telling him of Congress's action, reviewing for the forgetful commander in chief the circumstances of his having left the army, and expressing his willingness to serve conditionally.

---

[37] 16 June, 1780, Ford, 1904-1937: **17**: pp. 518-519.

[38] Samuel Huntington to Gen. Gates, 16 June, 1780; to Brig. Gen. Weedon, 18 June, 1780; to Washington, 18 June, 1780, Letters of Samuel Huntington, PCC, NA.

[39] Weedon to the President of Congress, 30 June, 1780, Reel 178, *ibid.*

. . . . I never expected to take Service in the Continental line again. The train of misfortunes attending our Operations to the Southward, has Occationed in some measure a Change of Circumstances. And the Gloomy Situation of our affairs in that Question induced me to express a willingness to participate with my Counting the Danger that threatened us. . . . I take the Earliest Opportunity of informing your Excellency of my Obedience to this Call and tho' there are Circumstances that will make Service in the Southern Department not altogether agreeable, yet I shall Submit till other Service offers. But must at the same time inform you that as Subjecting myself to my Friends Woodfords Order was the reason of my first withdrawing, so will it Operate in all future cases if ever in the Course of duty we should come to act together. It may also be necessary to assure your Excellency that this proceeds intirely from what I conceive to be Military, and from no private peek or Contempt of his Abilities as an Officer. On the Contrary I have ever had a high Opinion of him as a Soldier and have for a Number of years lived with him in the Strickest Friendship; but enough of this. I hope it's unnecessary to assure your Excellency of my strict Adherence to your Orders and of the Happiness I shall have in Executing any Commands you may from time to time have for me.[40]

Weedon also heard from John Walker, a Virginia member of Congress. The appointment, said Walker,

I am sure will be agreeable to you, and may you render your country that service she stands in need of and that which I know you wish to do. . . . Our resources are undoubtedly sufficient and we want but exertions to work out our salvation. We are now roused and I hope the work will be finished before we fall into another fit of the lethargy. . . . This [Pennsylvania] and the neighbouring States are straining every nerve to bring the present campaign to a happy conclusion; let it not be said that Virginia was exceeded either in zeal or in exertions by any one of them . . . .[41]

The next several months Walker kept Weedon posted on news pertaining to the American forces and intelligence. "The tories in Carolina have had a gentle currying," he said. "Thank God for small mercies. I hope this is but a trifling

---

[40] Weedon to Washington, 30 June, 1780, Washington Papers, Series 4, Reel 67, LC.

[41] John Walker to Weedon, 27 June, 1780, Burnett, 1921-1938: 5: p. 239.

prelude to some adagio that is to come. I speak in musical terms to a musical man."[42]

On June 17 Congress passed a resolution directing the Virginia executive to order five thousand militia to the Southern army and to hold an additional three thousand in readiness. The Virginia government complied immediately to the extent of sending more than two thousand men southward.[43] This was at the time when Weedon received notice of his recall, and hence it was too early for him to be associated with any troop movement. In July, the Virginia General Assembly called up 3,000 men for eighteen months.[44] Weedon gave his assistance to the raising of these troops. He found so many prospective recruits had been declared deserters and were therefore ineligible for enlistment that he inquired of Washington whether it would be a "good idea" for the commander in chief to issue a proclamation offering a "free pardon" to all deserters surrendering themselves up by a given day. This would "be a means of getting some hundreds more men, for knowing they can no longer Secrete themselves, would make a Virtue of Necessity and Deliver themselves up."[45]

It was not clear to George Weedon what would be his assignment. He could expect to lead a Virginia force to Gates's army in the South. Or perhaps Gates would direct him to supervise defenses and recruitment in Virginia. But before a decision could be made, Gates suffered a disastrous defeat at Camden, and once again a new Southern army would have to be constructed under a different commander. Meanwhile Weedon would be left to act on his own the best he could in raising and organizing troops in Virginia.

Weedon's honor as an officer and gentleman had been vindicated by his recall by Congress. He could for the time being expect to serve within the bounds of his country, Virginia—his first allegiance. Now it was to be his duty that would be most exasperating; it would be vague and perplexing, and he would have to search it out.

---

[42] John Walker to Weedon, 11 and 25 July and 15 August, 1780, *ibid.*, pp. 256, 295, and 330, resp.

[43] Joseph Jones to Washington, 19 June, 1780, *ibid.*, p. 228; Boyd, 1950-: 3: p. 457n.

[44] Febiger to Col. William Grayson, 18 June, 1780, Febiger Letter Book 1779-1780, VSL. Febiger remained at Fredericksburg until about 1 September on recruiting assignment and then left for Philadelphia.

[45] Weedon to Washington, 24 August, 1780, WC, APS.

IX. VIRGINIA INVADED

Although assigned to the Southern army, George Weedon had no orders as to what to do or where he should be; so he assumed that he should assist General Muhlenberg, who was also left in Virginia, as best he could in collecting troops and materiél for Gates's army. Muhlenberg was the senior officer in the Virginia Continental line, and Weedon had no qualms about the rank of Muhlenberg, who originally had been placed ahead of him and had retained seniority by the settlement of March, 1778. Weedon could function now in a relatively unstructured situation, unlike his previous service as brigade commander in Washington's army. His judgment and decisions would count for something. This would give him added incentive, not to mention that for the time being he could expect not to be too far from home.

Weedon busied himself in assembling troops at Fredericksburg. He was most concerned with the question of deserters. As Weedon and others had recommended, a "free pardon" for deserters surrendering themselves was granted by Washington, and Weedon instructed the various officers to follow this policy in recruiting. But those deserters who did not come forward he sought to have apprehended.[1] Weedon directed arms and accoutrements, some being obtained from the gun factory near Fredericksburg, to places of rendezvous— Fredericksburg, Winchester, and Alexandria—and on to Richmond, where Muhlenberg sent them on to various points.[2]

At Fredericksburg, Weedon formed a committee of officers which inspected provisions and stores.[3] He made arrangements with Colonel William Grayson in Philadelphia, who was now assisted by Christian Febiger in forwarding clothing and tents for the Southern army.[4] Weedon directed some men

---

[1] Weedon to Sgt. Jones, 28 August, 1780 and Weedon to Capt. James Wood, 28 August, 1780, WC, APS.

[2] S. K. Bradford to Weedon, 28 and 31 August, 1780 and Weedon to Muhlenberg, 28 and 31 August, 1780, *ibid.*

[3] Weedon to Capt. James Wood, 28 August, 1780, *ibid.*

[4] Weedon to Col. William Grayson [Sep.-Oct, 1780], *ibid.*

and supplies, under instructions from General Gates, to the Continental depot at Chesterfield Court House, where Colonel William Davies then took charge in forwarding them to "the advanced army." In Fredericksburg, Weedon had the assistance of Richard Young, quartermaster for the Spotsylvania County militia. Hampering Weedon's work was a shortage of money; he applied to Colonel William Finnie, DQMG for the Southern department, for money, and also urged Gates to issue a money draft on the Virginia treasury for supplies.[5]

The news of the victory at King's Mountain on October 7 was conveyed by express from Muhlenberg to Weedon. Weedon reported to Greene his impressions.[6] This British defeat provided a needed morale boost after the debacle at Camden in August. Weedon soon learned also that Washington had appointed General Greene to head the Southern army (October 5 and approved by Congress October 30) and that Major General Baron von Steuben would be sent to Virginia.[7]

Leslie's Invasion

As the war heated up in the Carolinas, the British allowed an invasion of Virginia as part of their southern strategy. On the night of October 19, a British fleet of sixty sail, carrying an expeditionary force of twenty-five hundred men under General Alexander Leslie, anchored off Cape Henry. Leslie had been given the options of invading Virginia to cut off supplies being sent to the American troops in the Carolinas or to sail further southward and join Cornwallis. Governor Jefferson received word on Sunday, October 22, that the enemy had begun debarkation in the vicinity of Portsmouth. Immediately the governor informed George Weedon, "we have taken Measures for assembling a force to oppose them and are to beg the favor of you to come immediately on to aid in the command of them." General Muhlenberg and militia generals Thomas Nelson and Edward Stevens "are also called

[5] Weedon to Gates, 16 September, 1780, *ibid.*; Weedon to Richard Young, 2 October, 1780, Richard Young Papers, VSL.

[6] Weedon to Greene, 17 October, 1780, Greene Papers, CL; Joseph Jones to James Madison, 24 October, 1780, Ford, 1889: p. 38.

[7] In Congress, 30 October, 1780 and Huntington to Steuben, 31 October, 1780, Steuben Papers, NYHS.

to lend their Assistance."[8] Jefferson wrote President Huntington of Congress, asking that "Congress will please to consider whether these [Virginia generals] can be aided by any other Officer of higher Rank and of approved Abilities and Trust." He also said that the lack of arms "prevents every hope of effectual Opposition."[9] It seems that Jefferson intended that each Virginia general would command respectively forces that he could collect, until a commander in chief of all Virginia forces could be appointed. General Edward Stevens had joined Gates's army, and thus, for the present, command in Virginia was left to Muhlenberg, Weedon, and Nelson. As Joseph Jones noted, Weedon "is now under marching orders."[10]

Nelson did what he could to assemble militia at Williamsburg. Muhlenburg, in Richmond, found he was so "destitute for officers" that he put ninety men in a company, and asked Weedon to send down all officers in Fredericksburg.[11] Muhlenberg marched towards Portsmouth with about 800 men, most of whom had been collected at Chesterfield Court House originally for the purpose of reinforcing the Southern army. Muhlenberg suggested that Weedon go to Richmond and stay there a few days to organize troops as they came in, hopefully into two "battalions." He asked Weedon, "pray what can I do without some Cavalry & Cannon?"[12] It was understood that if a large number of troops could be raised Muhlenberg would command the first brigade, and Weedon the second.[13] As a precautionary measure, the Virginia government ordered the removal of the Saratoga prisoners from Charlottesville to Frederick, Maryland, with Congress concurring, "that we may have our hands clear for these new Guests."[14]

Weedon had various matters to attend to in Richmond. He made a list of supernumerary and resigned officers, which he sent to General Nelson, along with recommendations for

---

[8] Jefferson to Weedon, 22 October, 1780 and Jefferson to Washington, 22 October, 1780, Boyd, 1950-: 4: pp. 38n. and 60-61.

[9] Jefferson to Samuel Huntington, 22 October, 1780, *ibid.*, p. 58.

[10] Joseph Jones to Madison, 24 October, 1780, Ford, 1889: p. 38.

[11] Muhlenberg to Weedon, 22 October, 1780, WC, APS.

[12] Muhlenberg to Weedon, 27 and 28 October, 1780, *ibid.*

[13] Joseph Jones to Madison, 24 October, 1780, Ford, 1889: p. 38.

[14] Jefferson to Gates, 28 October, 1780; Jefferson to James Wood, 16 November, 1780; and Cont. Board of War to Jefferson, 6 December, 1780, Boyd, 1950-: 4: pp. 78, 120 and 181, resp.

arranging troops and for opening communications between Nelson and Muhlenberg.[15] Weedon organized a "light Company" of 350 men, commanded by Captain Abraham Kirkpatrick, which he sent on to Nelson. "Indeed I fully intended joining you myself before this," he wrote the Virginia militia general, "but the Total Deranged Situation of Military Matters in this Quarter will keep me here, a few days longer."[16] Weedon's work in Richmond included supervision of the assemblage of flat-bottomed boats at Hood's Point for the purpose of transporting troops back and forth across the James[17] and making arrangements for hospital supplies and patients.[18] Weedon complained to Jefferson that, as the militia "are now coming in fast" to Richmond, "we shall be much distressed to feed them unless steps are taken previous to their Assembling."[19]

The law for impressing wagons and provisions had expired, but Weedon had authority to use the "invasion law," which gave "a standing power," as Jefferson put it, "to the commanding Officer to authorize any Commissioned Officer to impress every kind of necessary." Jefferson even went so far as to tell Weedon that if he could not find enough commissioned officers for this duty "we will give them Militia Commissions to make their proceedings strictly legal." Jefferson sent Weedon a draft of £125 "new money equal to £5,000 old, there being none but the new which can be issued from the treasury."[20] To what extent Weedon had to resort to the impressment power at this time, if at all, is not known. Jefferson did give Weedon a militia commission for a Mr. Triplett, which may have been in connection with Jefferson's impressment policy.[21]

Among his other duties in Richmond, Weedon noted: "I have been obliged in the eyes of the Assembly, to have arms repaired, swords mounted, artillery found, with not only fixed ammunition, but spunges, Ladles, screws, drag ropes &c—and in short every other Article, in most branches of Military Defence."[22]

[15] Weedon to Gen. Thomas Nelson, 2 November, 1780, WC, APS.

[16] Weedon to Nelson, 29 and 30 October, 1780, *ibid.*

[17] Weedon to Major Cooke, 31 October, 1780, Boyd, 1950-: 4: p. 81n.

[18] Charles Mortimer to Weedon, 30 October, 1780, WC, APS.

[19] Weedon to Jefferson, 3 November, 1780, Boyd, 1950-: 4: p. 94.

[20] Jefferson to Weedon, 6 and 7 November, 1780, *ibid.*, pp. 97 and 100.

[21] Jefferson to Weedon, 7 November, 1780, *ibid.*, p. 100.

[22] Weedon to William Grayson, 29 October, 1780, Sparks MSS, Harvard University Library.

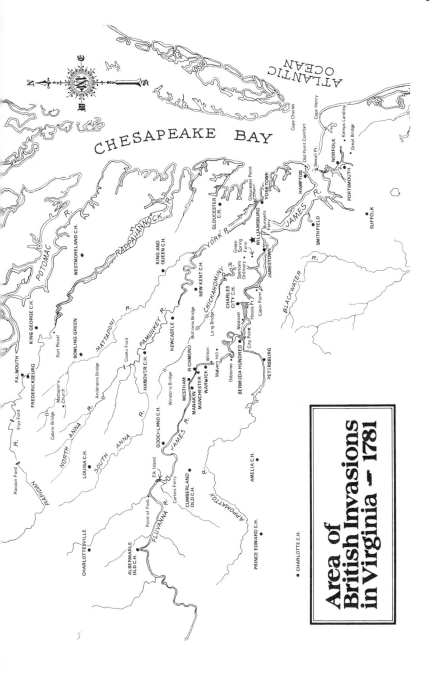

Map 4. Area of British Invasions in Virginia, 1781. Drawing by Paul Nickerson, Richmond City Planning Commission.

Weedon found time to send an account of the invasion and his activities to Colonel Grayson. To the details, he added that the enemy "have visited us at a time that I always wished they might; to wit, the Sitting of the Assembly. Now we are invaded, not a single Department but what is found totally deranged. There never was such a spirit as is burst forth with the people of the Big Knife. Had we but means to put in their hands, we could bid defiance to Sir Henry Clinton and his whole Army."[23] Weedon also reported to General Gates on November 2, and mentioned that 300 Maryland Continentals had arrived in Richmond and were being forwarded to the Southern army.[24]

The invasion force held a "position" from Portsmouth to Sleepy Hole on the Nansemond River. Seven thousand Virginia militia had been called out, but since none of the counties had yet resorted to a draft, the men in the field were volunteers. Muhlenberg's army of nearly a thousand men, operating on the southside of the James, had moved to Stoners Mill at the head of Pagan Creek about six miles from Smithfield. Since he had mostly raw troops and no horses, Muhlenberg informed Weedon that he would "risk nothing material;"[25] the reinforcements were "so trifling that I am oblig'd to stand aloof." He asked Weedon: "when will You be able to Join us?"[26] Two days later he wrote Weedon that "if you move down I wish you to take the nearest rout for this place."[27] Weedon wrote Muhlenberg on November 3 that he had "a prospect of getting togather a strong Brigade in a day or two with whom I shall march."[28] It was a good feeling for George Weedon to be about to lead men in the field again. He felt himself physically fit for an outing.

While Nelson was sending several hundred troops from Williamsburg to the vicinity of Yorktown, Weedon left Richmond (about November 10) with a force of nearly 1,000 men. On his way to join Muhlenberg, Weedon visited Williamsburg to inspect the defense preparations there, while his brigade, under Colonel (Charles?) Harrison, continued directly on to Muhlenberg's camp. Weedon and Nelson left

---

[23] *Ibid.*

[24] Weedon to Gates, 2 November, 1780, WC, APS.

[25] Muhlenberg to Weedon, 29 and 31 October, 1780 (2 letters), *ibid.*; Weedon to Grayson, 29 October, 1780, Sparks MSS, Harvard University Library.

[26] Muhlenberg to Weedon, 3 November, 1780, WC, APS.

[27] Muhlenberg to Weedon, 5 November, 1780, *ibid.*

[28] Weedon to Muhlenberg, 3 November, 1780, *ibid.*

Williamsburg on the twelfth, and, overtaking Colonel
Harrison and the militia brigade, arrived on the thirteenth at
Muhlenberg's headquarters at Stoners Mill. The fourteenth
"was spent in reconnoitering, Arranging," and "moddling
our Troops while a light Corpse of 300 men under the command of Colo. [Josiah] Parker was pushed down to Suffolk, to
lay within Striking distance of the Enemy, till we ware in
proper condition to give their Advanced post a blow." The
enemy "however saved us the Trouble by evacuating their
ground" that evening, "retreating to Portsmouth where they
continued their Embarkation;" at 2 a.m. they completed it
"with Signs of the greatest precipitation." The enemy left
behind captured vessels and most of the Negroes they had
seized or who had gone over to the British. General Weedon
had only praise for the Virginia citizen soldiers. He cited their
"ready Obedience . . . in Organizing, their Alacrity in duty,
their perseverance in exceeding hard Service," and "their
rapid Progress in Discipline."[29]
     For several days it was a guessing game where Leslie's force
was next headed. The enemy on November 15–16 moved
down to Sewells Point (on Hampton Roads). Muhlenberg's
and Weedon's troops then took a position at Warrasqueak
Bay, ten miles up the James on high ground overlooking
Newport News. This was "the most convenient" place to
"oppose" the enemy should they sail up the James. Nelson
commanded a body of troops dispersed at Yorktown, Rich
Neck, the "Half way House," and Hampton. Colonel Parker
had a small detachment close to the enemy's fleet, and had
orders to report "the Earliest Intelligence."[30]
     Weedon heard from General Gates, who thought American
forces should now be concentrated in the southern theater. "In
my Opinion," he said, "it is High Time General Washington,

---

[29] Weedon to Col. William Fleming, 19 November, 1780, Emmett Collection,
#8418, NYPL; Jefferson to Edward Stevens, 10 November, 1780, Boyd, 1950-: 4: p. 111
Before leaving Richmond, Weedon filed with the Virginia government a "Treasury
Receipt" for £1200 "for additional Military Claims." (Virginia Land Office, French
and Indian Bounty Warrants, Cert. #676-681, Auditor's Office, 10 November, 1780,
VSL.) Muhlenberg wrote Weedon: "I had formed a plan to surprize the Enemy's post
at Doctor Mills to Morrow night but as you are so near I shall put it off but take notice
you are to be here on Monday night, if not, you pay for the Supper." (1 November,
1780 (11 p.m.), WC, APS.

[30] Weedon to Richard Henry Lee, 18 November, 1780, Lee Family Papers, VSL;
Weedon to Greene, 19 November, 1780, Greene Papers, CL; Nelson to Weedon, 22
November, 1780, WC, APS; Joseph Jones to James Madison, 18 November, 1780,
Hutchinson and Rachal, 1963: 3: p. 184.

and Five Thousand of Our best Troops, were in full March from the Head of Elk, for James River! I say General Washington, because his Influence, Authority, and Support, are to the Full as much wanted as His Abilities."[31]

On November 23, Weedon was at "Col. Cocks," sixteen miles from Muhlenberg's force. He wrote Colonel William Davies to send down from the Richmond area more militia and tents.[32] But extra aid was unnecessary. Leslie's fleet set sail November 23 southward, and would reach Charleston on December 16.

While Weedon was in the field, the new commander in chief of the Southern army, accompanied by Steuben and others, passed through Fredericksburg. Mrs. Weedon cordially welcomed the military group, and Greene stayed at the Weedons' house. Writing to General Weedon on the twenty-first from Richmond, he commented on Mrs. Weedon's "great politeness," and observed that he "was very sorry" to find her "exceedingly unhappy at your going into service again." He had "left Mrs. Green equally unhappy at my going to the Southward; and I am not certain whether she will not follow me as far as Virginia; but as her constitution is slender, and the journey long and fatiguing, I hope she will not. If she should, I have advised her to take lodging in your neighbourhood."[33]

Weedon wrote Greene on the nineteenth that he was sorry to have missed him in Fredericksburg, and hoped to see him in Richmond.[34] But Greene spent only several days at the capital, and Weedon's letter was delivered to Major General Baron von Steuben. The Baron informed Weedon that Greene had left him in Richmond "to endeavour to arrange the Military Department of this State." Both Muhlenberg and Weedon were now under Steuben's command. Steuben assured Weedon that "I reckon much on your advice & Assistance," and said he would be "extremely happy" to confer with Weedon "as soon as you can with propriety leave your command."[35]

With the enemy having departed, Weedon could afford to leave the field, and Muhlenberg would take complete charge

---

[31] Gates to Weedon, 14 November, 1780, AKF.

[32] Weedon to William Davies, 23 November, 1780, WC, APS.

[33] Greene to Weedon, 21 November, 1780, Balch, 1857: p. 131; Thane, 1972: pp. 180-182; Thayer, 1960: p. 287.

[34] Weedon to Greene, 19 November, 1780, Greene Papers, CL.

[35] Steuben to Weedon, 23 November, 1780, WC, APS.

of the dwindling militia force south of the James. While Muhlenberg moved the militia army up the James to Cabin Point, Weedon headed for Richmond, where on November 24 he met with Steuben. The two generals decided on arrangements for sending to Greene in Carolina 800 infantry, including Major Henry Lee's corps, due to arrive in Richmond at any time. In all a reinforcement of 1,200 men was planned.[36]

For a full week Weedon stayed in Richmond attending to military business. He decided that he preferred military service in Virginia rather than being given a command in the South, and so wrote Greene two letters to this effect. There were two reasons: "to Mitigate as far as possible the feelings" of his "affectionate Family," and "in doing which I cant think but the Service will at the same time be fully Answered by directing my Attentions to the Military Operations of this State." Weedon hoped that Greene would see "no impropriety" in this request, which "hurts me . . . when I reflect on the happiness I should have in being with you, and the desire I ever had of Acting under your immediate direction." He did not rule out serving in the Southern army if Greene should so direct, but "you will Oblige me Exceedingly by Announcing your Orders as soon as possible." Weedon suggested that the first Virginia general officer that should be ordered "forward" should be "the Eldest in Command," meaning, of course, Muhlenberg! "It was Obvious" one Virginia general should remain in the state "until further Orders." Troops had to be raised, regimented, and officered before they could go into the field. "The State is also Subject to Invasion." Weedon also advised Greene to send the military hospital "northward" from North Carolina and to place a Virginia surgeon, Matthew Pope, in charge of it.[37] Pope, however, never received a Continental appointment.

In replying, Greene said he was "exceeding unhappy of Mrs Weadons being rendered so miserable by your entering service again," and for the time being Weedon would stay in Virginia to assist Steuben.[38]

After returning to Fredericksburg, Weedon in several weeks was back in Richmond "on the Business of Arranging the Virginia line." But he found this could not be done until all

---

[36] Steuben to Washington, 24 November, 1780, Steuben Papers, NYHS; Muhlenberg to Steuben, 26 November, 1780, in Muhlenberg, 1849: p. 379.

[37] Weedon to Greene, 30 November, 1780, Greene Papers, CL.

[38] Greene to Weedon, 26 December, 1780, Weedon Letters, HL.

"the dispersed Officers" were given "proper Notice" to return to duty. Writing to Greene from Richmond on December 21, Weedon recommended a field command in the Southern army for Major Alexander Dick of Fredericksburg, who was then serving as an aide to Muhlenberg.[39] Dick had an unusual career in the Revolution thus far, having served as a marine officer with John Paul Jones, with whom he quarreled, and having escaped from a British prison. He would soon lead a little militia force in the defense of Richmond against Arnold's invasion. Weedon brought Richard Claiborne from Fredericksburg to Richmond with him and, unable to secure for him an appointment in the Virginia line because no new arrangement had been made "got him Appointed" quartermaster for the state.[40]

Arnold's Invasion

Scarcely had George Weedon returned again to Fredericksburg from Richmond when he learned of Benedict Arnold's invasion. Arnold had set out from New York on December 20 with twenty-seven ships carrying an expeditionary force, consisting mainly of the loyalist Queen's Rangers and New York volunteers. The turncoat general carried the same instructions as Leslie to cut off munitions and materiél that could be used by the Southern army. In addition, Arnold was to establish a strong post at Portsmouth. After plying a stormy sea for better than a week, Arnold's fleet and 1,600 man force reached Hampton Roads on the thirtieth. With his usual penchant for swift action, Arnold gave orders to sail immediately up the James. The next day the British captured some twenty-odd Virginia sloops in the river, and these were used to transport Arnold and some 800 men further up the James. In the evening the invasion party stopped at Hood's Point, where Colonel John Graves Simcoe dispersed a small militia band. On January 4 the enemy disembarked at Westover, and began an advance towards Richmond, about twenty-five miles away. Arnold occupied Richmond for a day, during which time Simcoe went to Westham, eight miles west of the town, and destroyed the foundry. Arnold faced only small groups of militia, and at no time was a shot fired on the

---

[39] Weedon to Greene, 21 December, 1780, Greene Papers, CL.
[40] Weedon to Greene, 23 January, 1781, *ibid.*

enemy. Back at Westover, Arnold stayed at the house of his cousin-in-law, Mrs. Byrd, for three days, awaiting favorable winds; during which time Simcoe, with several dozen Rangers, routed a small militia band at Charles City Court House. The rapid advance on Richmond caught the Virginia government totally unprepared. Nelson moved some militia up from Williamsburg to the Chickahominy River, and Steuben was trying to collect militia in Chesterfield County. Militia eventually turned out in large numbers, but it was too late. Arnold was soon back in Portsmouth.

Steuben sent an express to Weedon on January 2, ordering him immediately to Richmond.[41] But Weedon had to take a little time to collect militia. Weedon learned of the occupation of Richmond on January 6, the day that Arnold evacuated the town, although he claimed it was not until several days later that he "was officially inform'd of their having Carried Richmond by a Coupe de Main." Weedon itemized the depredations at Richmond to Greene, and added that the enemy made "a safe retreat to their Camp at Westover & Barkley [Berkeley] without firing a shot. This you'll say is pritty late to tell two or three Visits of this fiend"; perhaps now this would "open the Eyes of our wise heads."[42]

Weedon took upon himself to order colonels of ten neighboring counties to call out militia and to assemble at Bowling Green "with all available arms and equipment." He went to Caroline County to "assemble what men I can." Weedon informed Steuben of his actions, and said that militia from other counties would join him unless "you please to direct it otherwise."[43] When, on January 8, Weedon received word that the enemy had evacuated Richmond and were presumed heading down the James, he countermanded his orders "for fear they should point up the Potowmack," but cautioned the militia commanders to keep their men "Arranged," so as not to be caught off guard.[44] Excepted from these orders were the Stafford, Spotsylvania, and Caroline militia. On January 10, Jefferson wrote Weedon, saying "I have heard you have embodied a number of men to join Genl

---

[41] Steuben to Weedon, 2 January, 1781, Steuben Papers, NYHS.

[42] Weedon to Greene, 23 January, 1781, Greene Papers, CL.

[43] Circular Letter [Weedon] to the Commanding Officers of Militia, 7 January, 1781 and Weedon to Steuben, 7 January, 1781, WL, BUL. The ten counties in the militia call were: King George, Loudoun, Orange, Spotsylvania, Stafford, Caroline, Prince William, Culpeper, Fairfax, and Fauquier.

[44] Countermanding Orders to the Militia, 8 January, 1781, WL, BUL.

Nelson. Under this situation I am really at a loss what to direct, and must leave you to act according to your discretion." If Weedon thought that Hunter's iron works just outside of Fredericksburg were adequately protected, Jefferson said, he wished Weedon would join Nelson, as his force was insufficient to defend Williamsburg and the tidewater area south of the James.[45]

Taking one hundred fifty Stafford militia southward, Weedon stopped at Hanover Court House on the eleventh, where he was joined by two hundred Spotsylvania militia. He had to do without the Caroline militia because for the seven hundred men he had assembled, there had been only fifty muskets. Weedon decided to remain at Hanover Court House until further orders from Steuben or Jefferson.[46] He sent out another circular, citing authority from Governor Jefferson, to county lieutenants of counties in the vicinity of Fredericksburg to "embody every man you Can Arm and hold them ready for further Orders." He added that "a small Corps of well found Horses would be of the greatest utility."[47]

Fearing that the enemy would next move up the Potomac, Steuben ordered Weedon back to Fredericksburg. Jefferson considered enemy raids up the Rappahannock a real possibility, and directed Colonel Sampson Mathews and nine hundred militiamen coming down from Rockbridge, Augusta, Rockingham, and Shenandoah Counties to join Weedon at Fredericksburg.[48]

After his return to Fredericksburg on the thirteenth, Weedon, now acting on a specific request from Jefferson, called upon the county lieutenants of fourteen counties to have every man who could be armed and equipped to be on ready alert for marching. Collecting 1,100 men for "the defence of the Potomack," and with seven hundred of these stationed at posts between Fredericksburg and the Potomac, Weedon felt he was "fully prepared for Mr. Arnold's reception." Other preparations included having all the lead in

---

[45] Jefferson to Weedon, 10 January, 1781, Boyd, 1950-: 4: pp. 335-336.

[46] Weedon to Jefferson, 11 January, 1781, WL, BUL.

[47] Circular Letter to the Commanding Officers of Militia, 11 January, 1781, *ibid.*; Weedon to Steuben, 11 January, 1781, Steuben Papers, NYHS.

[48] Weedon to Greene, 23 January, 1781, Greene Papers, CL; Weedon to Jefferson, 12 January, 1781; Jefferson to Sampson Mathews, to Steuben, to Weedon, 12 January, 1781; and to Charles Dick, 15 January, 1781, Boyd, 1950-: 4: pp. 343-344, 346-347 and 364.

Fredericksburg "run into Ball," putting a "fatigue party" to the task of making cartridges, having an engineer inspect the area around Hunter's works, and equipping "a Cour" of forty horse.[49] Weedon asked Jefferson for money for recruiting and for a supply of lead to be sent to Fredericksburg.[50] For a few days Weedon had the company of "my friend Genl. Muhlenberg," who arrived in Fredericksburg on the eleventh to confer with Weedon on the northern Virginia defense. The two generals rode with General William Smallwood, who was on his way to Maryland, to inspect Hunter's works, which all three agreed "could not be Fortified to advantage."[51]

The fear that the enemy would invade northern Virginia mounted. Weedon heard from John Augustine Washington (at Bushfield) that some British ships had advanced up the Rappahannock, and Richard Henry Lee had ridden down and seen them. Lee and Washington met with the field officers of Lancaster and Northumberland Counties at Northumberland Court House to make arrangements to set up posts at the mouth and along the river and also at the mouth of the Potomac.[52]

Weedon had all kinds of requests from the local militia commanders. Colonel John Skinker of King George County wrote that he had "formed the Young Men of the County into three Companies," but was waiting "for the Rum, you promised to send for the Militia of this County."[53]

Besides local preparations, Virginia defense now consisted of three collections of forces: one under Weedon at Fredericksburg; another under Nelson at and near Williamsburg; and the third under Steuben (who was filling in for Muhlenberg) at Cabin Point—thirty seven hundred in all.[54]

On the sixteenth, Steuben, having intelligence that the whole enemy army was heading for Smithfield, ordered Weedon to march for Williamsburg with whatever militia he had.[55] A few hours before receiving Steuben's orders on the

---

[49] Weedon to Steuben, 15 January, 1781, Steuben Papers, NYHS; Weedon to Greene, 23 January, 1781, Greene Papers, CL; Weedon to Jefferson, 15 January, 1781, Boyd, 1950-: 4: pp. 376-377.

[50] Weedon to Jefferson, 16 January, 1781, WL, BUL.

[51] Muhlenberg to Steuben, 12 January, 1781 and Weedon to Steuben, 15 and 19 January, 1781, Steuben Papers, NYHS.

[52] John Augustine Washington to Weedon, 17 January, 1781, AKF.

[53] Col. John Skinker to Weedon, [18?] January, 1781, ibid.

[54] Jefferson to Virginia Delegates in Congress, 18 January, 1781, Hutchinson and Rachal, 1963: 2: pp. 292-293.

[55] Steuben to Weedon, 16 January, 1781, AKF.

nineteenth, Weedon sent off a report to the Baron describing his reconnaissance (January 16–18) of the area from Fredericksburg to the Potomac and down the river thirty miles and his strategic placement of local militia units. Weedon thought that the immediate threat was that the enemy might attempt only a "diversion, to prevent us from Succouring the Southern Army." Arnold would be disappointed, "for we have Virtue enough amongst ourselves to oppose such a set of Ravages." The best way to offset the enemy's naval advantage, according to Weedon, was to keep a sizable proportion of the militia embodied: "the Executive would find it much the frugalist way in the End." Also money should be used to bring in volunteers "to make up deficiencies in the Continental Quota," for "there is not a day but fine young fellows are Offering themselves to me."[56]

As soon as he received Steuben's orders, Weedon wrote Steuben that five hundred riflemen were "detached" and were marching southward; and he said he would call up a similar number from various counties to take their places. Meanwhile, Weedon added, "I shall consider myself under Marching Orders & be assured no time shall be lost after your further pleasure is known."[57] Actually, in Jefferson's view, these riflemen from the western counties that formed the "detached" troops were not intended to be kept in the field, since their tours of duty were short and they would have to be discharged.[58]

Trying to put militia into defensive positions along the Potomac and Rappahannock Rivers, sending reinforcements southward, and then keeping track of them was a baffling experience for George Weedon. If it could be figured out when and where the British invaders would next strike, then there could be clear action. George Weedon must have felt much as General Charles Lee did at the beginning of the war when Lee was in charge of setting up defenses for the whole southern coast line against a British invasion that could occur almost anywhere—"like a Dog in a dancing school."

Steuben changed his mind about bringing Weedon to Williamsburg, and on January 20 ordered him to stay put, as "we must not intirely lose sight of the Defence of Fredericksburg." All the militia in the counties near Fredericksburg

---

[56] Weedon to Steuben, 19 January, 1781, Steuben Papers, NYHS (Letter #1).

[57] *Ibid.* (Letter #2).

[58] Jefferson to Steuben, 19 January, 1781, Boyd, 1950-: 4: p. 412.

should be discharged but still be on the alert in case the enemy came that way. General Muhlenberg was to lead the other militia to Williamsburg. Weedon would have the "essential Service in making the necessary arrangements, & embodying the Militia when call'd out."[59]

Conflicting orders, a many-headed militia system to deal with, a Virginia government without energy or resolve, lack of funds, a people apathetic during the invasion of their country, and the anxiety over where the enemy might strike next, all sorely put George Weedon to the test. It was also a test of American character. To Greene he wrote: "You judge right when you say we are strong. Nothing is wanting but prudent Measures to make us Independent. A wise Nation after Six years war would Certainly be prepared with the Means of defence, but so far has private gratification predominated over public Security that at this day we are found without any Military arrangement worthy the Attention of a petty people." If "we have not Virtue enough remaining in the body of the people to Oppose a set of Ragamuffins, headed by the greatest Rascal on Earth, let us Suffer rather than loose sight of the grand Object."[60]

---

[59] Steuben to Washington, 20 January, 1781, AKF.

[60] Weedon to Greene, 23 January, 1781, Greene Papers, CL.

X. DEFENSIVE NIGHTMARE

As long as Arnold commanded the invasion army anything was possible. His raid on Richmond was a brilliant feat in a war marked by overcaution. George Weedon was determined that should Arnold invade Northern Virginia there would be an "army of the Potomac" awaiting him. He would also, if necessary, take to the field to join other Virginia forces, with possible aid of Continental troops and French naval units, to entrap Arnold at Portsmouth.

"Your arrangements for the defence of Potomac and Rappahanoc appear to have been judicious," Jefferson wrote Weedon on January 31.[1] For the next month and a half George Weedon continued to supervise all aspects of militia mobilization in the Northern Neck and Fredericksburg area—organizational, logistical, and operational. The problems were almost insurmountable. Weedon persuaded provision commissioners in the counties to act, although their powers under the law were in question.[2] Since the money press in Richmond was broken, he could not pay the bounty of $2,000 for enlistment in the Continental service. Jefferson informed him that the lead supply in Richmond was depleted, having been sent to the northern and southern armies.[3] Workingmen walked off the job at both James Hunter's iron works and Charles Dick's gun repair factory. To recondition arms received from the northern counties and three hundred fifty stand of arms sent by Steuben to Fredericksburg, Weedon had artisans in the militia pressed into service as repairmen. He endeavored to establish a small magazine of arms and ammunition in Fredericksburg and put Richard Young in

---

[1] Jefferson to Weedon, 31 January, 1781, Boyd, 1950-: 4: p. 491.

[2] *Ibid.*

[3] Jefferson to Weedon, 21 January, 1781, *ibid.*, p. 423; Weedon to Jefferson, 23 January, 1781, WL, BUL; Weedon to Steuben, 4 February, 1781, Steuben Papers, NYHS.

charge. An effort to have county lieutenants to forward public arms of discharged persons to the depot only met with partial success.[4]

Intelligence of the enemy was a critical matter. Possessing formidable naval power, they could move swiftly up the navigable waterways and strike at will. The American forces in the field kept watch at Cabin Point under Steuben and Muhlenberg and at Williamsburg under Nelson.[5] But at any time the enemy could as easily shift to an expedition up the Potomac or Rappahannock. Weedon established an intelligence network with the militia commanders in the counties along the lower Potomac and Rappahannock. There were several alarms that indeed the British were making the Potomac an invasion route, but at worst seven enemy ships moved fifteen miles up the river.[6]

In early February, Arnold sent 400 men to the edge of the Dismal Swamp, on the road leading from Suffolk to Portsmouth. The enemy destroyed all American works at Great Bridge and then withdrew. Arnold then called all his troops into Portsmouth, and it seemed that another large offensive by the enemy would soon begin.[7] About February 12, the French fleet was sighted, and Muhlenberg's troops moved to within one and a half miles of the enemy encampment to prevent their foraging.[8] The stalemate continued while the Virginians waited to see what support there would be from the French and whether regular troops would be sent down from Washington's army.

Weedon arranged for militia of six counties to be on alert to march with two days' notice, and called for three hundred of

---

[4] Weedon to Steuben, 23 January, 1781, Weedon to Steuben, 29 January, 1781, and Steuben to Board of War, 29 January, 1781, Steuben Papers, NYHS; Weedon to Steuben, 30 January, 1781 and Weedon to Col. Skinker, 28 January, 1781, WL, BUL; Steuben to Weedon, 1 February, 1781, AKF; James Hunter to Jefferson, 25 January, 1781, Boyd, 1950-: 4: p. 448.

[5] Steuben to Board of War, 29 January, 1781, Steuben Papers, NYHS; "Extract of a letter from a gentleman in Virginia, 22 January, 1781" from *The Connecticut Courant and Weekly Intelligencer* (Hartford, Conn.), 13 February, 1781, in "Notes and Queries," 1955: p. 265.

[6] Weedon to Thomas Gaskins, 24 January, 1781, to Col. John Gordon, 24 January, 1781, and to the Commanding Officer of Militia . . . [Cols. J. H. Brooke, Peyton, Skinker, Garrrard, Waggener, and to Richard Henry Lee], 28 January, 1781, and to Gen. Nelson, 29 January, 1781, WL, BUL; Weedon to Gaskins, 22 January, 1781, AKF; Weedon to Steuben, 29 January, 1781, Steuben Papers, NYHS. Intelligence was to be passed through a chain of the militia commanders to Weedon.

[7] Muhlenberg to Steuben, 9 February, 1781, in Muhlenberg, 1849: pp. 382-383.

[8] Muhlenberg to Steuben, 18 February, 1781, *ibid.*, pp. 384-385.

the best riflemen from Frederick, Berkeley, and Shenandoah Counties to join him. Rockbridge and Augusta riflemen were detached to Williamsburg. Weedon wrote Steuben that should he "want Strengthening" more men would be forwarded.[9] Weedon considered that 2,000 militia "constantly embodied" could protect the Northern Neck and the James River "from Sudden Descents; a "Coup de Main" would cost ten times as much as the cost of such a militia force, "as we have been taught by sad Experience."[10] Weedon now began to feel that at last Virginia citizens were becoming aroused to support the war effort. The cooperation of the militia in turning out was heartening, but there was a gap between the people and the government, and "the means of defence is by no means Adequate to the Spirit of the people."[11]

As Weedon himself was only too well aware of, there were not enough funds to maintain large numbers of militia in service. Steuben, under pressure from the Virginia government, ordered Weedon to discharge the militia from Spotsylvania, Caroline, Stafford, King George, Orange, and Essex Counties.[12] Weedon wrote Jefferson saying that he would act according to Steuben's order, but asked, would it "not be prudent to keep up a defence here?"[13] He thought it necessary to keep militia embodied because of the sightings of the enemy in the Potomac.[14] Nevertheless he discharged the King George and Stafford militia on January 27, retaining the Spotsylvania and Orange militia until definite confirmation that the enemy had left the Potomac. This miffed Steuben. "I believe you have mistaken my meaning with respect to the Militia," he wrote. Steuben insisted that all militia in and near Fredericksburg and all under Weedon's command "be immediately discharged in such a manner tht they may be called together at a Minutes warning, as the expense which the State is put to on Account of the militia is enormous." If the British should advance towards Fredericksburg, then the militia should be called out, and General Nelson's force would also be sent to Fredericksburg.[15] Weedon discharged the

[9] Weedon to Anthony Thornton, 21 January, 1781, to Col. Henry Lee, 28 January, 1781, to Jefferson, 23 January, 1781, and to Col. Skinker, 26 and 28 January, 1781, WL, BUL; Weedon to Steuben, 23 January, 1781, Steuben Papers, NYHS.

[10] Weedon to Steuben, 29 January, 1781, Steuben Papers, NYHS.

[11] Weedon to Richard Henry Lee, 28 January, 1781, WL, BUL.

[12] Weedon to Gen. Thomas Nelson, 29 January 1781, *ibid.*

[13] Weedon to Jefferson, 23 January, 1781, *ibid.*

[14] Weedon to Richard Henry Lee, 28 January, 1781, *ibid.*

[15] Steuben to Weedon, 28 January, 1781, AKF.

Spotsylvania militia on the thirtieth, and presumably shortly afterwards, acting on further orders from Steuben, did the same with the Orange militia.[16] One problem in discharging the drafted militia (usually one-tenth of those enrolled) was that the same men could not be called back into service until the other nine-tenths had seen active duty.[17]

General Nelson complained of the haphazard coming and going of the militia at Williamsburg and that he could not keep an accurate tab on them. About 1,400 militia, many of them sick, under Colonels Robert Lawson and Josiah Parker, in Muhlenberg's command, were still in the field south of the James. Nelson decided to attend the Virginia Assembly as a delegate and suggested to Steuben "the Propriety of ordering Genl. Weedon" to take over his command at Williamsburg.[18]

Arranging the Virginia Line

Meanwhile there was a matter that was to prove irritable to George Weedon, to say the least. The old issue of his having foregone his obligations to duty and country was brought out again at the very time that he was doing his utmost to serve his country as an officer and soldier.

At long last there was to be a meeting of the field officers to arrange the Virginia Continental line. Steuben, who issued the call, was eager to get many of the Continental officers back into active service. Weedon wondered whether it would be possible to have officers already in the field to leave their posts and attend, although he himself promised Steuben he would leave to "joine the moment I am able to ride if you think it prudent."[19] All officers, according to a proclamation by Steuben, not attending before February 18, "shall be adjudged superseded or Subject to a Court of Inquiry," unless specifically excused. Steuben asked Weedon and Muhlenberg to get together to resolve any problems that might arise during the meeting.[20]

---

[16] Steuben to Weedon, 1 February, 1781 (copy), *ibid.*; Weedon to Col. Winslow, 30 January, 1781, WL, BUL.

[17] Weedon to Steuben, 30 January, 1781, Steuben Papers, NYHS.

[18] Thomas Nelson to Steuben, 2 February, 1781, *ibid.*; Muhlenberg to Steuben, 31 January, 1781, in Muhlenberg, 1849: p. 381.

[19] Weedon to Steuben, 4 February, 1781, Steuben Papers, NYHS.

[20] Arrangement of the Virginia Line, February 1781, MS, VSL; Steuben to Muhlenberg, 18 February, 1781, in Muhlenberg, 1849: pp. 383-384.

The officers met on February 10 at Chesterfield Court House. George Weedon missed the opening session, but, with Steuben insisting "Your presence will be absolutely necessary," Weedon showed up on the seventeenth. Thirteen field officers formed the board, with four others who were prisoners of war on parole present. Muhlenberg did not attend, and Weedon immediately found that the mood of the field officers was so hostile that he left.[21]

George Weedon had looked forward to an arrangement of the Virginia Continental line, but little had he anticipated that there would be a concentrated effort to have him ousted from the Continental service. William Davies, son of the Great Awakening divine, Samuel Davies, was the instigator. Davies had stuck it out in the northern theater after Valley Forge, and not only resented Weedon's leaving the service, but also seems to have been a very ambitious officer, for he himself was angling for a promotion to brigadier general. Colonel Davies, who had already demonstrated his administrative ability as commander of the Continental depot at Chesterfield Court House, would soon be named Virginia's Commissioner of War, replacing the rather incompetent George Muter, the first appointee to the office.

The officers drew up a most extraordinary document, condemning Weedon's reentry into the service as a brigadier general in the Continental line. It is interesting to note that Steuben was also resented by the officers,on different grounds, but the officers delicately avoided confrontation with a general operating under direct orders from Congress, Washington, and Greene. Although four of the thirteen officers sitting on the board, who originally attended the meeting, were absent when the protest document against Weedon was signed on the eighteenth, Davies regarded it as representing a unanimous decision. Eight reasons were given why General Weedon should not be included in the Virginia Continental line: (1) Weedon was absent almost three years from the service (actually less than two years, from summer, 1778 to summer, 1780); (2) his retirement was "unjustifiable"; (3) it was unfair to readmit him when other officers had

---

[21] At a Board of Field Officers begun at Chesterfield, 10 February, 1781 by order of ... Steuben, Arrangement of the Virginia Line, February, 1781, MS, VSL; Field Officers of the Virginia Line to Steuben, 18 February, 1781, Letters Addressed to Congress, PCC, NA; Steuben to Weedon, 11 February, 1781, Steuben Papers, NYHS; Weedon to Greene, 17 February, 1781, Greene Papers, CL.

endured the hardships of the war; (4) it was "absurd" that Weedon should now be entitled "to great indulgences," especially since he had been considered as not belonging to the Virginia line; (5) the resolution of Congress for Weedon's retirement was merely an *ex parte* arrangement without a hearing before other officers; (6) Weedon only returned because of Woodford's captivity; (7) if Weedon were allowed to return, then the claims of other officers in similar circumstances should be acknowledged; and (8) rank and command should "be the rewards of constant and faithful service."[22] The officers were undoubtedly also jealous over what they regarded as Weedon's personal assumption of command and the forceful and energetic way in which he exercised it during the invasion crisis.

The representation against Weedon was submitted by Davies to Steuben, the President of Congress, and Washington. Steuben, perhaps wishing to play down the dissension, did not send Washington a copy until April 15.[23] To Steuben, Davies wrote: "I am instructed to assure you our opposition to the return of General Weedon is not founded upon any personal pique towards him, but that we can never consent to serve in an army, where our rights as officers are so essentially injured.[24] To the President of Congress:

> We are persuaded Congress will disapprove of General Weedon's attempt to place himself over our heads after so long an absence, during a period the most instructive of any since the commencement of the war. I am, however, directed to assure Congress of our high respect for them, and determination to submit the event to their wisdom and justice, trusting that the high rank of General Weedon, so far from authorizing such irregularities will rather operate against the propriety of admitting so dissatisfactory a precedent.[25]

Washington, who always kept aloof as possible from quarrels involving officers' seniority, discreetly took himself

---

[22] Field Officers of the Virginia Line to Steuben, 18 February, 1781, Letters Addressed to Congress, PCC, NA. This letter was enclosed in a letter of William Davies to Samuel Huntington, President of Congress, 20 February, 1781. Interestingly, Davies, the leader of the protest against Weedon, appears sixth in the list of signatures.

[23] Fitzpatrick, 1931-: **21**: p. 367n.

[24] Davies to Steuben, 20 February, 1781, Steuben Papers, NYHS.

[25] Davies to Samuel Huntington, President of Congress, 20 February, 1781, Letters Addressed to Congress, PCC, NA.

out of the controversy. To Davies he wrote: "Being a stranger to the transaction which took place at the time General Weedon was thought to have retired from service, I can give no decided opinion upon the propriety of his assertion of his rank or your objections to it." Only Congress could decide, as Weedon's retirement "was founded upon a special Resolve, which, if there was such a one, was never communicated to me."[26] Davies wrote other Virginia officers, who were on active duty and could not be present at the Chesterfield meeting, and seems not to have received much favorable response.[27]

Nothing came of the officers' protest. Writing to Meriwether "Fiddlehead" Smith, a Virginia member of Congress, Weedon enclosed copies of "the remonstrance from the Board of Field Officers at Chesterfield." He said he had "heard no more of that matter since, nor Cannot think they mean to Carry it further, but for fear they should, I beg your interposition at the National board."[28]

Brigade Commander at Williamsburg

General Weedon and Governor Jefferson conferred in Richmond on February 15 concerning Greene's request for reinforcements. "I took the Occation to strongly Urge the necessity," Weedon said, of reinforcing Greene "immediately from the Counties most Contiguous" to North Carolina. As a result, over a thousand militia from Botetourt, Montgomery, Washington, Pittsylvania, and Henry Counties were ordered to march to Greene's army. Weedon advised Greene that Steuben would soon be sending on a force gathering at Chesterfield Court House and that it was better to yield ground to the enemy than to risk defeat.[29]

Weedon returned to Fredericksburg with orders from the Virginia executive for the counties of Fauquier, Prince William, Loudoun, and Fairfax to send one fourth of their militia (estimated at 1,090) to Fredericksburg to be placed

---

[26] Washington to William Davies, 24 March, 1781 and to Steuben, 1 May, 1781, Fitzpatrick, 1931-: **21**: p. 367 and **22**: p. 19, resp. Washington informed Steuben that the matter of Weedon serving in the Continental Line was entirely up to Congress.

[27] E.g., Febiger Letter Book, 1781-1782, note 1 April, 1781, VSL.

[28] Weedon to Col. M. Smith, 9 March, 1781, WL, BUL; Evans, 1975: p. 57.

[29] Weedon to Greene, 17 February, 1781, Greene Papers, CL.

under General Weedon's command. Steuben instructed Weedon to take these troops to Williamsburg, to supplement Nelson's force, now having dwindled to four hundred.[30] Weedon would take over from Nelson at Williamsburg; Muhlenberg would stay at Suffolk, and Colonel James Innes at Cabin Point. Steuben had marched five hundred Continentals and an equal number of militia from Chesterfield Court House to Dinwiddie Court House and expected to lead this force personally to reinforce Greene.[31]

Forming the new militia army was beset with difficulty. Militiamen deserted to avoid service in the field.[32] The delay of the Fauquier and Loudoun militia in coming into Fredericksburg caused Weedon to postpone his march by a few days.[33] Weedon made one "good" regiment of Grayson's Prince William militia and a "battalion" of the rest.[34] He wanted Governor Jefferson to "draw out the Delinquents."[35] No wonder he lamented, "Sure I am if an Officer order'd to superintend and expedite Militia Movements does not in that Service loose his Reputation, he may risque it on all other occations."[36]

The troops that Weedon commanded were "sadly Arm'd," and he pressed Jefferson to send cartridge boxes and arms to Hanover Court House. The governor said there were none to be had; yet he urged Weedon to march anyway: "For God's sake lose not a moment."[37] Weedon sent several officers to Bowling Green to procure supplies from the provision commissioners, according to the invasion law, but they were

---

[30] Robert Andrews to Weedon, 27 February, 1781, AKF; Weedon to Col. Wagener, to Commanding Officer of Fauquier County (J. H. Brooke), and to Col. Henry Lee, 21 February, 1781, WL, BUL; Steuben to Jefferson, 21 February, 1781 and Jefferson to Thomas Nelson, 22 February, 1781, Boyd, 1950-: 4: pp. 680 and 687. The militia expected: Fairfax, 200; Fauquier, 270; Prince William, 185; and Loudoun, 400—total, 1,055, and with officers, 1,090.

[31] Steuben to Weedon, 22 February, 1781, AKF; Steuben to Jefferson 24 February, 1781, Boyd, 1950-: 4: p. 701.

[32] Francis Peyton to Weedon, 24 February, 1781, AKF.

[33] Weedon to Richard Henry Lee, 3 March, 1781, Lee Family Papers, VSL; Weedon to Jefferson, 3 March, 1781, Boyd, 1950-:5: p. 54.

[34] Weedon to Steuben, 9 March, 1781, WL, BUL. Grayson planned to join Weedon in Williamsburg and to command a regiment.

[35] Weedon to Jefferson, 4 March, 1781, ibid., Jefferson to Steuben, 5 March, 1781, Boyd, 1950-: 5: p. 65.

[36] Weedon to Steuben, 8 March, 1781, Steuben Papers, NYHS.

[37] Weedon to Steuben, 28 February, 1781, ibid., Weedon to Jefferson, 28 February, 1781, WL, BUL; Jefferson to Weedon, 5 March, 1781 and Weedon to Jefferson, 9 March, 1781, Boyd, 1950-: 5: pp. 70-71 and 109, resp.

to make sure "provisions are to be levied as equitably as possible from the inhabitants, in exchange for certificates."[38]

Weedon was now aware of the grand design that was in the making. Lafayette was on his way to Virginia with a detachment of the elite light infantry from Washington's army. Admiral Destouches, commander of a French squadron at Rhode Island, agreed to assist in an effort to capture Arnold's army at Portsmouth.

Before marching from Fredericksburg with the 650–700 men he had collected, Weedon sought to instill some martial zeal.[39] In spite of the deficiencies in arms, General Weedon thought that otherwise his men were "tolerable equip," as there was a camp kettle to every eight men, two axes to each company, and a sufficient supply of rum. Weedon distributed tents evenly among all the militia, even denying some troops the tents they had brought with them.[40]

Leaving the camp near Fredericksburg at 8 p.m. on March 6, Weedon's militia took nearly a week to get to Williamsburg.[41] Upon arriving at the capital, General Weedon was perturbed at "the deranged situation of our defence in this Quarter." He thought it necessary to call more men from the northern counties. Steuben concurred. Weedon, therefore, requested Jefferson to have one-fourth of the Culpeper militia under Colonel James Barbour sent to Williamsburg, and, assuming the governor would go along with this request, he notified the Culpeper commander.[42] But confusion followed. The drafts for militia and for Continental troops were held the same day in Culpeper, and some of the officers doubted Weedon's authority to call up a militia draft.[43] Jefferson took note of the situation. An order in council stated that it was necessary during Arnold's invasion "to entrust a General Officer with Authority to call for militia; however, as it produces some

---

[38] Weedon to Mr. Wily Ray, 4 March, 1781 and Marching Orders for Col. Churchill, 5 March, 1781 and Major Cox, 7 March, 1781, WL, BUL.

[39] John Piper Orderly and Account Book, 1781, Orders Issued by Gen. Weedon During the Campaign, 4 March, 1781, LC.

[40] *Ibid.*, Weedon to M. Smith, 9 March, 1781, WL, BUL; Jefferson to Steuben, 7 March, 1781, Boyd, 1950-: 5: p. 89.

[41] 6-12 March, 1781, Piper Orderly Book, LC; Weedon to Steuben, 8 March, 1781, Steuben Papers, NYHS; Acomb, 1958: p. 178.

[42] Weedon to Cols. Barber [Barbour] and William Thornton, 10 and 11 March, 1781, WL, BUL; Weedon to Jefferson, 10 March, 1781, Boyd, 1950-: 5: p. 122.

[43] James Barbour to Jefferson, 27 March, 1781, Boyd, 1950-: 5: pp. 251-252.

Confusions in the rotation of Duty which we wish to make as equal as we can on all the Counties, these Calls in the interior parts of the Country especially will go hereafter from the Executive except where Circumstances require an application from one County Lieutenant to another as provided in the Invasion Law."[44]

Jefferson at first had considered the Culpeper militia "too distant," and had summoned the Hanover, Caroline, Spotsylvania, and King William militia, as part of a call from eighteen counties for 2,190 "originally called in" and 1,031 "supplementary" militia—3,221 in all.[45] Since Weedon had already called out the Culpeper militia, Jefferson directed that the 351 men from Culpeper be marched to Williamsburg.[46] Actually the Culpeper militia marched only three miles out of the county and considered this "as a Tour" of duty.[47]

Weedon led a reconnaissance mission between York and Hampton for a week, and upon returning to Williamsburg on March 19 he forwarded intelligence to Governor Jefferson.[48]

Lafayette had now arrived and had joined Muhlenberg and Steuben at Suffolk, on the south side of the James. Steuben had decided for the time being to hold back from leading a reinforcement to Greene. Weedon commented on the eve of Lafayette's arrival that Virginians did not need Lafayette's troops and that the young general should go southward to help Greene, "for surely we are able to manage Benedic by our own Exertions."[49]

Lafayette was impatient and disappointed. He complained to Weedon that the militiamen lacked ammunition, and hence he could not "push" the enemy. Lafayette's troops had a "Trifling Scarmish" with a patrol of Hessians. The Marquis asked Weedon to give "Succour of provisions &c" to a French detachment of sailors at York.[50] Weedon attempted to set up communications with the French fleet.[51] But soon it was learned that on March 16 the French naval force was turned

---

[44] Jefferson to the County Lieutenant of Culpeper, 22 March, 1781, *ibid.*, p. 204.

[45] Jefferson to Weedon, 13 March, 1781, *ibid.*, p. 141.

[46] Jefferson to The County Lieutenant of Culpeper, 22 March, 1781, *ibid.*, p. 204.

[47] French Strother to the Governor, 28 March, 1781, Executive Papers, VSL.

[48] Weedon to Jefferson, 19 March, 1781, Boyd, 1950-: 5: p. 185.

[49] Weedon to Greene, 9 March, 1781, Greene Papers, CL.

[50] Lafayette to Weedon, 20 March, 1781, AKF; Gottschalk, 1942: p. 203.

[51] Weedon to the Officer Commanding the French Fleet, 21 March, 1781 and Weedon to Lafayette, 21 March, 1781, WL, BUL; Weedon to Jefferson, 21 March, 1781, Boyd, 1950-: 5: p. 203.

back at the entrance of Chesapeake Bay by a British fleet under Admiral Arbuthnot.[52]

Besides commanding his militia force at Williamsburg, General Weedon had local naval responsibility. Five hundred watermen were needed to man patrol boats and armed river vessels (a defense suggestive of Jefferson's later reliance on "gunboats"). He applied to the county lieutenant of Gloucester for watermen,[53] and asked John Page, who was at his plantation, Rosewell, in Gloucester, to send over all the watermen from Kingston.[54] A similar appeal was made to the militia commander at York.[55] Major Mordecai Throckmorton of the Gloucester militia drafted all the watermen he could, but these were only a handful, as some were already in service and others deserted.[56] Weedon kept a boat patrol as low as Mulberry Island near Warrasqueak Bay, and he also posted observers along the shores to gather intelligence. A three-gun signal meant the approach of the enemy "in the direction of the James River."[57] Weedon gave Captain Thomas Chandler of the *Patriot* elaborate instructions and ordered him "not to risque an Action on any Account." But "this great Sea officer Mr. Chandler" disobeyed "my orders in every respect" and was captured.[58]

Troops on the north side of the James were "drawn to a point" at Williamsburg and placed in a brigade under Weedon's command. Militiamen serving from the first of the invasion were discharged.[59] Weedon's brigade consisted of three regiments: the first, commanded by Colonel Charles Dabney; the second, Colonel William Brent; and the third, Colonel [Thomas?] Mathews.

The brigadier general wasted no time in putting his fledgling brigade under regular organization and discipline.

---

[52] Riley, 1949: p. 39.

[53] Weedon to the County Lieutenant of Gloster [Gloucester], 19 March, 1781, WL, BUL; John Walker to Steuben, 20 March, 1781, Steuben Papers, NYHS.

[54] Weedon to Col. John Page, 19 March, 1781, WL, BUL; John Page to Weedon, 20 March, 1781, AKF.

[55] Weedon to Officer Commanding at York, 19 March, 1781, WL, BUL.

[56] Weedon to Mordecai Throckmorton, 22 March, 1781, *ibid*; Mordecai Throckmorton to Weedon, 20 March (2 letters) and 23 March, 1781 and Edward Travis to Weedon, 22 March, 1781, AKF.

[57] Weedon to Capt. Chandler, to Capt. Saunders, and to Capt. Humphreys, 28 March, 1781, WL, BUL.

[58] Weedon to Steuben, 9 April, 1781, Steuben Papers, NYHS; James Maxwell to Jefferson, 4 April, 1781, Boyd, 1950-: 5: p. 334. Chandler died in captivity.

[59] Weedon to Jefferson, 28 March, 1781, Palmer, 1875-1886: 1: p. 603.

He appointed George Lee Turbeville, deputy adjutant general; Richard Littlepage, orderly deputy; and Major Thomas Armistead, brigade inspector. On March 26, the first day of the existence of the new brigade, General Weedon issued general orders. It was like old times again, and Weedon rose to the occasion. He set a tough line, and tried to excite an esprit de corps by giving a diatribe on the villainy of Arnold and lauding the "victory" of Greene at Guilford Court House.[60]

Despite the commotion in Virginia, it seemed that all the action was taking place with Greene's army in North Carolina. But Greene was desperate for reinforcements, especially for a replacement for Virginia militia serving with the Southern army whose terms had expired. General Steuben proposed to the Virginia executive to march the 2,000 militia stationed on the south side of the James to Halifax to join Greene's army. Weedon met with Lafayette and his commandant of engineers, Colonel Jean-Baptiste Gouvion, as a "board of officers," and endorsed Steuben's plan. Nelson, now back in Williamsburg, was also to have been a member of the board, but was ill.[61]   General Weedon wrote Governor Jefferson that Steuben's plan would "in a great measure terminate the War." He believed "it the best Policy in this State to keep the War abroad. In doing that we must make our Objects at a distance. One fixed Maxim in all Military operations is to support the grand contending Parties: as all other objects are thrown out merely to bring on a diversion . . . ."[62]

Weedon agreed with Steuben's assumption that Arnold, even with the arrival of a British reinforcement, would not conduct a real invasion of occupation in Virginia. "It was ever my opinion they would endeavour to succour Ld Cornwallis by penetrating N. Carolina; holding at the same time a strong Post in the lower parts of Virginia to keep us diverted," he wrote Steuben on April 3.[63] In a similarly worded letter to Jefferson of the same date, reiterating what he also said to Steuben, Weedon recognized the dilemma:

---

[60] 26-28 March, 1781, Piper Orderly Book, 1781, LC. Excerpts of these orders were published in the *Virginia Gazette* (Dixon and Nicolson), 31 March, 1781.

[61] Weedon to Steuben, 29 March, 1781, Steuben Papers, NYHS.

[62] Weedon to Jefferson, 27 March, 1781, Boyd, 1950-: 5: p. 267.

[63] Weedon to Steuben, 3 April, 1781, Steuben Papers, NYHS.

And whether it would be more political to support *power-fully*, Genl. Green, with our Regular Troops as well as the Militia from those Counties most contiguous to Him and to act here totally on the defensive, till the event of our operations in that Quarter are known, I leave to your Excellency to determine. If we are successful there, the Work here will be easy. If on the contrary we should suffer a superiority in that Quarter, we shall be most sadly pressed in Virginia.

Weedon offered his opinion that fifteen hundred new Continental levies that Jefferson depended upon for the defense of Virginia should be sent to Greene.[64] But Weedon did have some hesitancy over Steuben's plan, as he confided to Muhlenberg: "should they think this part of the Country and our two little Armies an Object worthy their Attention, it will be a bad excuse for us to say 'who'd have thought it.' "[65] Such would be the case with the invasions of Phillips and Cornwallis.

The Virginia Council rejected Steuben's plan.[66] Jefferson summed it up to Weedon: "thus pushed for men, the Baron's proposition was not acceded to as exposing the Country too much."[67] Attempting to console Steuben, Weedon wrote: "I was fearful our Scheme would be rejected by the Executive who has not an Idea beyond Local Security. We Must therefore content ourselves till a force is raised which they will have nothing to do in point of direction."[68]

Lafayette with his light infantry departed from Williamsburg on March 28 and headed for Annapolis, hoping that Washington would send him to the Southern army. Before he left, he helped Weedon implement the concentration of the troops north of the James in Williamsburg—leaving only small guards at Toe's Point on the York River, Newport News, Point Comfort, and Mulberry Island.[69] At least General Weedon felt it was "Exceedingly judicious" that the troops were drawn "from below at the time we did," as "the Enemy

---

[64] Weedon to Jefferson, 3 April, 1781, Boyd, 1950-: 5: p. 338.

[65] Weedon to Muhlenberg, 4 April, 1781, WC, APS.

[66] Steuben to Weedon, 29 March, 1781, AKF; In Council, 29 March, 1781, Boyd, 1950-: 5: pp. 275-276.

[67] Jefferson to Weedon, 31 March, 1781, *ibid.*, p. 309.

[68] Weedon to Steuben, 1 April, 1781, Steuben Papers, NYHS.

[69] Weedon to Col. Dabney, 24 March, 1781, WL, BUL; Nolan, 1934: p. 163.

GENERAL BENEDICT ARNOLD IN 1778.

FIG. 6.   General Benedict Arnold. From: H. C. Lodge, *Story of the Revolution*, Vol. 2, p. 148. With permission of Virginia State Library.

Certainly meant to strike some part of our dispersed line, which they would have easily affected, before they were drawn to a point."[70]

Thus, instead of pressing for an entrapment of Arnold, the Virginia forces were in a defensive posture. As Lafayette was taking his leave, the war in Virginia was to assume a new dimension. General William Phillips, already familiar with Virginia as a prisoner of war in the Convention army and recently exchanged, arrived at Lynnhaven Bay on Sunday, March 25, with twenty-three transports carrying an expeditionary army, accompanied by four ships of the line and four frigates.[71] Although he had discounted the idea, George Weedon well knew that if Phillips stayed to reinforce Arnold a full-scale invasion of Virginia was a probability.

Phillips, the conqueror of Ticonderoga and whom Jefferson regarded as "the proudest Briton of them all," assumed command from Arnold at Portsmouth. The combined British force of about 4,500 was capable of a full offensive. But Phillips was cautious, and planned no major operations in Virginia until Portsmouth was made secure. Immediately opposing the British were Muhlenberg's thousand man force at Suffolk.[72] George Weedon had about the same number at Williamsburg.

Steuben was certain that the enemy would only send out foraging parties and that soon most of the British force would be sent to Cornwallis's army. Thus Steuben, at Chesterfield Court House, made ready, as he did before, to lead a detachment of new Continentals to reinforce Greene. He notified Weedon that "the movements of the Troops under you will be entirely under your direction. I would only recommend it to you to keep up a correspondence with Genl Muhlenberg that you may act in concert."[73] Weedon wrote Muhlenberg to this effect, mentioning that Steuben and Lafayette had "left me here to shift for myself."[74]

If George Weedon did not completely share Steuben's view that the enemy would not remain in full strength in Virginia, he thought that at least it would be a while before the British would launch an invasion into the interior of the state. He

[70] Weedon to Steuben, 1 April, 1781, Steuben Papers, NYHS.

[71] Weedon to Jefferson, 29 March, 1781, Boyd, 1950-: 5: pp. 283-284.

[72] Lafayette to Washington, 18 April, 1781, Gottschalk, 1944: p. 186; Hocker, 1936: pp. 112 and 115.

[73] Steuben to Weedon, 1 April, 1781, Steuben Papers, NYHS.

[74] Weedon to Muhlenberg, 4 April, 1781, WC, APS.

applied to Steuben for a few days' leave to visit Fredericksburg to help his family move to a different house. The Weedons had to be out by April 12. There had been some disagreement with the landlord, James Duncanson, who claimed that rent for 1778 was still due. Duncanson had already leased the house to a new tenant.[75]

But permission for a brief leave was not immediately forthcoming, and Weedon continued to attend to military affairs at Williamsburg. He found his role as a commander of a militia brigade an impossible task. Militiamen were constantly returning home upon the expiration of their brief tours of duty, and some even before. Of the various counties called upon to supply militia to Weedon at Williamsburg, Weedon complained to Governor Jefferson that only Caroline and Spotsylvania had sent any men. "How inadequate the Strength of the Troops under my Command must be to the Service Expected from them," he told Jefferson. Like Steuben and Lafayette, his patience with the Virginia government was growing thinner: "Indeed I cannot see how the Country is to be defended, when a Call of the Executive is paid as little regard to as it would be from those noways in Authority. And even those few that come into the field, only remain as long as they please, and then go back, some with their officers at their heads, without consulting the Service or the Officer commanding."[76]

Weedon established a "floating Magazine" up the James River at Sandy Point, where arms were supposed to be collected and given to troops on both sides of the James. But few arms were obtained. In addition to the problem of the scarcity of arms in the state, the Continental ordnance depot, previously located at the Westham foundry, which had been destroyed by Arnold, had been removed by Captain Nathaniel Irish to the more distant Prince Edward County.[77]

To maintain even a semblance of discipline among the raw militia troops at Williamsburg was difficult. Weedon's orders for April 5 stated that soldiers firing muskets and destroying fences, palings, and the like were to be "instantly" punished. The troops were paraded at five in the morning and three in the afternoon, and inspection of arms and accoutrements was held morning and evening. The men were restless because

[75] Weedon to Steuben, 1 April, 1781 and John Meals to Weedon, 30 October, 1780, *ibid.*

[76] Weedon to Jefferson, 28 March, 1781, Boyd, 1950-: 5: p. 273.

[77] Major Pryor to Weedon, 9 April, 1781, WC, APS.

they thought they should be discharged as long as there was no emergency, but Weedon strictly held that no one could be discharged until he had served a full tour of duty. "The defence of their Country," he said, should be "sufficient reasons to stimulate the Troops to a persurverance Becoming a Free & Independent People" until they were properly relieved.[78]

With the pullback of troops north of the James to Williamsburg, the people of the lower tidewater area "murmer Exceedingly, and threaten to make their terms with the Enemy." Weedon, therefore, sent a detachment under Captain William Davenport to Newport News "for the sake of Contentment, but it will not afford Cover to the Country, or render any Security more than Giving Countenance to the people." Davenport was ordered to change his position frequently and "to Act as a party of Observation." Weedon informed the county lieutenants involved that he sent the detachment "below to Co-operate with your Militia in Protecting your defenceless Counties. I do not mean by this to draw your farmers & Planters into the field in force, but would wish you to Ascertain your Defenses, and so Arrange them as to Act in force on the shortest Notice."[79]

For several weeks Weedon got enmeshed in the complexities of prisoner exchange. He sent out a number of flags of truce to General Phillips, keeping Jefferson and Steuben informed of developments. Besides exchanging particular individuals, Weedon attempted to bring about a general exchange, involving militia captured by the British and an assortment of marines, pickets, and "pirates" who had fallen into American hands during the invasion period. Arrangements bogged down over disagreement as to categories of prisoners, conflicting jurisdictions of Continental and state authority, and Steuben's resentment of Weedon acting on his own. Also, as the negotiations seemed about to bear some fruit, Weedon would return to Fredericksburg and would not receive Phillips's letter, which proposed a definite exchange (within a two week deadline), until the deadline was ready to expire and the British army had taken to the field and hence were not disposed to further negotiation.[80]

---

[78] 5, 7, 8, and 10 April, 1781, Piper Orderly Book, 1781, LC.

[79] Weedon to Steuben, 1 April, 1781 (2 letters), Steuben Papers, NYHS; William Davenport to Weedon, 8 April, 1781, "Letters . . . Weedon," 1927: p. 257.

[80] See Weedon correspondence pertaining to this subject in Boyd, 1950: 5: pp. 283, 297, 324, 352, 364-365, 402, and 555-556; Balch, 1857: 133, 136-142, and 144-145; also

Phillips's Invasion

It was known to Weedon several weeks before the event that Phillips's army at Portsmouth was "making great preparations for a Move." Weedon "conjectured" on April 8 that Phillips would form a junction with Cornwallis by way of the "Great Bridge, Cape Fear, or up James River & by Petersburg." At least "Genl Philips is honest enough to confess he is coming out, but leaves us to Judge to what Quarter he means to point." British troops were embarked, but the ships remained in the Elizabeth River. This hesitation Weedon interpreted to mean the enemy was planning to sail to Cape Fear.[81]

But Weedon had to revise his prediction when he received a report on April 10 from Major Turberville that a small fleet of fifteen enemy vessels had entered the Potomac River. This afforded an excuse for Weedon to repeat his request to Steuben for permission "to ride up to Fredericksburg for a few days to remove my family." While in Fredericksburg he would provide for the defense of Hunter's works and the arms factory. Weedon asked that some troops be sent back for the defense of Fredericksburg, which request was vetoed by both Steuben and Jefferson, even though the report of an enemy flotilla in the Potomac was all too true and there were to be raids along both sides of the river.[82]

Consent for Weedon to go to Fredericksburg was granted by Steuben. Weedon promised he would send the baron a report on the British operations in the Potomac and American defenses in the Northern Neck.[83] Before he left Williamsburg, Weedon took time to write a long letter to Greene, congratulating him on his "exertions" in the South and reviewing the military situation in Virginia for the past month. On a general theme, he said:

The events of war are uncertain and turns on so nice a pivit

Weedon to Jefferson, April, 1781 and Weedon to Steuben, 26 April, 1781, WC, APS; Weedon to Steuben, 8 and 15 April, 1781, Steuben Papers, NYHS; Weedon to Capt. Doswell, 29 March, 1781, WL, BUL. Also see Carson, 1965: p. 134 and Herndon, 1969: pp. 320-321.

[81] Weedon to Steuben, 8 April, 1781, Steuben Papers, NYHS.

[82] Weedon to Steuben, 10 April, 1781 and Lt. Col. Oliver Towles to Steuben, 14 April, 1781, *ibid.*; Weedon to Washington, 11 April, 1781, WC, APS; Weedon to Jefferson, 21 April, 1781, Dreer Collection, HSP; Edmund Read to Jefferson, 10 April, 1781 and Jefferson to Weedon, 17 April, 1781, Boyd, 1950-: 5: pp. 399 and 483-484, resp.; Matthews, "Lee," 1939: pp. 376-377.

[83] Weedon to Steuben, 15 April, 1781, Steuben Papers, NYHS.

that we are often disappointed of our golden hopes in the moment of sanguine expectation, and we find changes of the most triffling nature give a Turn to matters of the utmost national consequence. Had these Cursed N. of Militia done their duty the head of the Serpent in the south would have been loped off. The tail might have quivered a while but our work boath in that Quarter and this would afterward been easy.

Alluding to Steuben's plan, which had been rejected by the Virginia government, Weedon gave the impression that he, too, had intended to march to Greene's aid: "The plan was to have taken the most choicest part of the men under Muhlenberg and myself and by forced & rapid marches thrown ourselves into your Neighbourhood, struck his Lordship a Coup de grace and returned immediately . . . ." Referring to the attempt to capture Arnold, Weedon said that "part of the time passed in great expectations of Glory being alloted to the Command on the Norfolk side," but when a fleet arrived in the Bay "instead of Mons de touche [Admiral Destouches] it turned out to be Arbuthnot from Gardners Bay!" On the personal side, Weedon asked, "why will you discountenance Mrs Green from paying us a Visit?" He had written Mrs. Greene "by all means to come as far as Fredericksburg; this I did before I knew you was against it." If she did make the journey, "Mrs. Weedon will make her as happy as your Absence will Admit of—she would have an Opportunity of hearing from you more often and while with us would be at home. Do change your mind and recommend it."[84]

Weedon left Williamsburg on April 15, and placed Colonel James Innes in temporary command until General Nelson should arrive. With the invasion soon underway and Phillips moving up the James, Innes would take the militia brigade, on April 20, along New Kent road up the James and would keep his men near Richmond.[85] From Williamsburg, Weedon "pushed across the Country into the Northern Neck," and arrived in Fredericksburg on April 20, whereupon he made his report to Steuben, as promised.[86]

With the embarkation of 2,500 men at Portsmouth on April

---

[84] Weedon to Greene, 14 April, 1781, Greene Papers, CL.

[85] Weedon to Steuben, 15 April, 1781 and James Innes to Steuben, 18 and 19 April, 1781, Steuben Papers, NYHS; Innes to Jefferson, 20 and 23 April, 1781, Boyd, 1950-: 5: pp. 505 and 539-554, resp.

[86] Weedon to Steuben, 21 April, 1781, Steuben Papers, NYHS; Weedon to Jefferson, 21 April, 1781, Dreer Collection, HSP.

18, the British invasion began in force along the James. The immediate objective was to disperse militia assembled at Williamsburg and to destroy American stores on the south side of the James untouched by Arnold's raid. The expeditionary force consisted of light infantry, Queen's Rangers, Jägers, and the American legion. On April 20 it split into several units: Abercromby went to the Chickahominy, Dundas to the north of that river, and Simcoe along the York. Phillips and Arnold went ahead to Burwell's Ferry and debarked to occupy Williamsburg. By the twenty-second all British units had rejoined. Leaving Williamsburg, the British force touched at City Point on April 24. Muhlenberg had followed the British Army up the James and now united with a few Continentals and militia under Steuben at Petersburg. The British marched towards Petersburg on the twenty-fifth, and were met by Steuben's and Muhlenberg's force, highly buoyed on rum commandeered by Steuben in Petersburg, in a hotly contested battle on the Appomattox River, east of the town. The American force crossed the river and retreated to Chesterfield Court House, and were pursued by Phillips. Arnold, in the meantime, split off from Phillips and went to Osborne's, on the James River halfway between Petersburg and Richmond, and there in a kind of comic opera destroyed the capital ships of the Virginia navy. Steuben retreated to Falling Creek, near Richmond. Phillips burned the barracks and destroyed other property at Chesterfield Court House, and then marched laterally to rejoin Arnold at Osborne's; from there the reunited British army marched towards Richmond. Steuben and Muhlenberg crossed to Richmond to await the expected arrival of a Continental detachment under Lafayette. On the twenty-ninth Phillips's army reached Manchester, on the banks of the James, opposite Richmond.[87]

With Phillips's invasion, General Weedon took emergency measures at Fredericksburg. He ordered powder that had been sent from Philadelphia for Greene's army to stay in Fredericksburg, and he sent wagons destined for Greene to Carter's Ferry, which he considered a safer route than through Richmond.[88]

Lafayette, after nearly a month in Maryland, on April 14 started his Continentals for Virginia. At Susquehanna Ferry,

[87] Arnold to Clinton, 12 May, 1781, Tarleton, 1787: pp. 334-336; Jefferson to the President of Congress and Washington, 23 April, 1781, Boyd, 1950-: 5: pp. 538-539; Stedman, 1794: 2: p. 383.

[88] Weedon to Jefferson, 23 April, 1781, WL, BUL.

FIG. 7. General William Phillips. Photo No. 111-SC-92594 in the National Archives.

he declared, "I am on my way and the Susquehana has been my Rubicon; I am going to run after General Phillips but I do not hope to catch him." He would either take over the command in Virginia or form a junction with General Greene.[89] The Marquis reached Fredericksburg on April 25, and stayed two days, during which time he conferred with Weedon. Weedon made arrangements for backcountry riflemen, new militia, Continental recruits, light dragoons (recently returned from guarding the Saratoga prisoners), and the remnant cavalry of Charles Armand's famous "legion," who were in the Fredericksburg vicinity, to join Lafayette's army.[90]

Lafayette's troops reached Richmond at dusk on April 29. Opposite across the river was Phillips's army. Early the next morning, as the British soldiers boarded boats to cross the James, the skyline on the hills of Richmond was silhouetted with some 3,300 American soldiers—1,200 Lafayette's Continentals, 2,000 militia (Steuben, Muhlenberg, Nelson), and sixty dragoons. General Phillips had second thoughts, and, as Lafayette said later, this display "put these cowardly plunderers underway down the River." The British army destroyed property at Manchester and also Warwick, five miles to the south. On May 1 they embarked at Osborne's, and on May 9 they entered Petersburg, where Phillips awaited the arrival of Cornwallis's army.[91]

Weedon reported to Lafayette on May 1 that he was getting sixty new levies, a reinforcement which he was sending to the latter, and that he was trying to collect horses. "After seeing all in motion from hence [I] shall come myself unless you direct otherwise," Weedon said. He calculated that "If Mr. Philips does not penetrate N. Carolina his intentions is to knock up the Trade of this State in which Case he will visit all our Rivers."[92]

[89] Lafayette to Luzerne, 14 April, 1781, Leland and Burnett, 1915: p. 598; Nolan, 1934: pp. 164-167.

[90] Lafayette to Weedon, 27 April, 1781, Weedon to Steuben, 26 April, 1781, Weedon to Gen. Spotswood, 27 April, 1781, and Weedon to Capt. Reede, 27 April, 1781, WC, APS; Weedon to Major Willis, 2 May, 1781 and Orders from Weedon to Col. Towles, 3 May, 1781, WL, BUL; Jefferson to Lafayette, 28 March, 1781, Boyd, 1950-: 5: p. 271; Nolan, 1934: pp. 167-169.

[91] John Banister to Theodorick Bland, 16 May, 1781, Campbell, 1843: 2: p. 69; Lafayette to Washington, 4 May, 1781, Gottschalk, 1944: p. 189; Arnold to Clinton, 12 May, 1781, Tarleton, 1787: pp. 337-338; "Journal . . . Wild," 1890: p. 137; Gottschalk, 1942: pp. 218-219; Nolan, 1934: pp. 169-170.

[92] Weedon to Lafayette, 1 May, 1781, WL, BUL.

Lafayette, from Bottom's Bridge, sixteen miles southeast of Richmond, wrote Weedon on May 3 that the enemy "having been frustrated" at Richmond would probably move against Fredericksburg. For this reason Weedon should stay in Fredericksburg and continue to assemble "Good Riflemen" and mounted militia. Lafayette did not want any men "to Be taken from the fields" or any alarm given. Rather, Weedon should form "a well appointed Corps" of about eight hundred "Men Horse and foot," who would be ready to take the field whenever the enemy would be sighted at the mouth of the Potomac. If this should happen, Lafayette would join Weedon. Meanwhile Weedon should also select advantageous positions for fighting the enemy, and he should have all public stores ready to be moved.[93] In writing to Washington of his plans, Lafayette regarded Hunter's works as "the only support of our operations in the Southward."[94] Lafayette had gauged correctly the difficulty of getting militiamen any distance from their farms during planting season; as Colonel James Hendricks wrote Weedon, "at this season" it would take a dozen counties to furnish a thousand men.[95]

Persuaded by Lafayette that the "next Visit" of the enemy would be either in the Rappahannock or Potomac Rivers, Weedon asked militia commanders of seven Northern Neck counties to have their men and provisions ready "that at the Shortest Notice you may be able to Act as Service may point." They should also have "young Gentlemen" form "into a Corps of light Dragoons," and a "chain of expresses" should be established among the county commanders.[96] Later Weedon also requested that Culpeper and Orange militia be placed on the "minute plan."[97]

Weedon had his own ideas about a defense strategy. Should Phillips move below Williamsburg, Weedon advised Lafayette to send troops to Hanover Court House, which would be in striking distance to both the Potomac and the James. If Lafayette advanced north to the "Protection of this Country," a column of light infantry should cross at Port

[93] Weedon to the Colonels of Frederick, Barkley [Berkeley], and Shenandoah Counties, 7 May, 1781, ibid.; Lafayette to Weedon, 3 May, 1781, AKF; Gottschalk, 1942: pp. 224-225.

[94] Lafayette to Washington, 4 May, 1781, Gottschalk, 1944: p. 190.

[95] Col. James Hendricks to Weedon, 9 May, 1781, AKF.

[96] Weedon to Col. Leroy Peachy, to Col. J. A. Washington, and to Col. Gaskins, 4 May, 1781, WL, BUL; Harry Lee to Weedon, 18 May, 1781, AKF.

[97] Weedon to Cols. James Barber [Barbour] and Burnley, 22 May, 1781, WL, BUL; Col. James Barbour to Weedon, 15 May, 1781, AKF.

Royal, twenty-two miles below Fredericksburg, and the rest, with all the baggage and artillery, should cross at Fredericksburg, where there were boats large enough to transport wagons. Weedon called attention to Boyd's Hole, twenty miles below Fredericksburg on the Potomac, as the best landing; the most advantageous place to take a position was the heights near the head of Potomac Creek, seven miles from Hunter's works and six miles from Boyd's Hole. Weedon had reconnoitered the area from Boyd's Hole, as Lafayette had asked him to do; he was planning to do so again and would stop at Port Royal to make sure boats were ready. Phillips, Weedon pointed out, with "the Command of the water," would be satisfied to conduct a war of harassment, "with a View of destroying the Trade by burning our Tobacco (the Staple Commodity) of the Country, our Shipping, our public workes, & finally taking away our Negroes"; this would also serve the purpose of diverting aid from Greene. "We had better suffer his Depredations than Neglect that grand Object, as one is only a partial Evil, the other permanent."[98]

Backcountry riflemen coming into Fredericksburg were disappointingly few and poorly armed. Sixty of an expected 217 came from Shenandoah; 123 of 267 from Frederick; and none from Berkeley and Hampshire. Weedon took the county lieutenants to task for their men being held back "at this important Crisis."[99] Lafayette wanted the riflemen to be formed into battalions of two hundred each so that they could be "Annexed to Legions I Have formed under Continental Majors."[100] Fortunately, out of nowhere, Weedon wrote Lafayette, he "had just found" a small regiment of two hundred eighty men under Colonel Edmondson (perhaps William Edmondson and the Washington County militia), which he was sending on.[101];

Most disconcerting was the shortage of arms. Of the riflemen from the backcountry, one of six was without arms. The militia of counties around Fredericksburg, Weedon informed Jefferson, were totally unarmed.[102] Two large shipments of arms from Philadelphia, which Weedon had expected to receive for arming local militia, went to

---

[98] Weedon to Lafayette, 5 May, 1781, WL BUL.

[99] Weedon to Cols. of Frederick, Barkley [Berkeley], and Shenandoah Counties, 7 May, 1781, *ibid.*

[100] Lafayette to Weedon, 16 May, 1781, Gratz Collection, HSP.

[101] Weedon to Lafayette [7-8?] May, 1781, Dreer Collection, HSP.

[102] Weedon to Jefferson, 9 May, 1781, WL, BUL.

Lafayette's and Steuben's troops.[103] Weedon had a "fatigue party" repairing what few arms there were in Fredericksburg.[104] Lafayette still pressured Weedon for horses: "Unless we have a respectable body of horse . . . Simcoe and Tarleton will run the country."[105]

Lafayette's letter to Weedon of the sixteenth bore startling news: "Gen. Phillips is dead and Arnold now is in command." Cornwallis had crossed the Roanoke River and was on his way to join the British army at Petersburg.[106] Phillips died on May 13 or 14 at Petersburg after a two-week illness of what is generally thought to have been yellow fever. His grave was left unmarked in the Blandford Churchyard so that Americans could not desecrate it. It was perhaps fitting that the pudgy gunner general, scarcely fifty years old, was laid to rest in a land that he had come to first as a prisoner and then had returned to subdue.

George Weedon heard the same news from General Muhlenberg. The latter, writing from Lafayette's headquarters at Wilton, added a light touch: "It is almost an Age since I heard from you last; so that I begin to think nothing will go down with you but Major Generals."[107]

Weedon had word that General Anthony Wayne and a detachment of Pennsylvania Continentals were on the way to Virginia, but there were conflicting reports about Wayne's actually having started. George Weedon would do everything he could to support Lafayette, but he had "to lament that the means are not adequate to my desire of doing it."

It occurred to him that he might be stuck in Fredericksburg while important battles were fought elsewhere in Virginia—a strong possibility given additional aid of Continental troops. If he could have a preference, "Indeed I wish rather to partake of the Field than to be so disappointed in Succouring the Operating Army."[108]

---

[103] Weedon to Lafayette, 14 May, 1781, *ibid.*; William Grayson to Weedon, 1, 8, and 14 May, 1781, AKF.

[104] Weedon to Lafayette, 5 May, 1781, WL, BUL.

[105] Lafayette to Weedon, 16 May, 1781, Gratz Collection, HSP.

[106] *ibid.*

[107] Muhlenberg to Weedon, 16 May, 1781, AKF.

[108] Weedon to Lafayette, 19 May, 1781, WL, BUL.

XI. A RECEPTION FOR CORNWALLIS

George Weedon could rightly expect that there would be
real action in Virginia. Cornwallis's junction with the
invasion army of Virginia made for one of the largest field
concentrations of British forces during the war. Including a
reinforcement arriving at Portsmouth under General Leslie,
Cornwallis commanded over 7,000 troops. Leaving Petersburg
on May 24 and picking up several regiments sent up by Leslie,
Cornwallis, with nearly 6,000 men, was on his way to complete the invasion of Virginia. Arnold, meanwhile, had
returned to New York, taking with him claims to his share of
the booty from his campaigns in Virginia.

The new commander of British forces in Virginia had free
rein, although he understood that Clinton might soon order
him to invade Pennsylvania or to return to the Portsmouth
garrison and send most of his troops to New York. What
needed to be done in Virginia would not take long.
Cornwallis had three goals: to "dislodge" Lafayette from
Richmond and perhaps defeat him in battle; to destroy
American stores and property along the rivers; and,
specifically, to destroy the gun factory and iron works at
Fredericksburg. Opposing Cornwallis was Lafayette's little
army, numbering in late May about 3,200, half of which were
militia under General Muhlenberg.[1] The size and effectiveness
of Lafayette's army would depend appreciably upon Weedon's
ability to raise men and supplies in the Northern Neck and
vicinity of Fredericksburg. Also it was Weedon's responsibility to provide a defense of Fredericksburg and along the
Rappahannock and Potomac in general.

From City Point, Cornwallis crossed the James to Westover,
and on May 28 his army camped sixteen miles from
Richmond at Bottom's Bridge. Much as in the New Jersey
campaign of the winter of 1776–1777, Cornwallis expected to

---

[1] Return of the Troops under the Command of Brig. Gen. Muhlenberg, 1 June,
1781, Cornwallis Papers, Intercepted Letters, Pub. Records Office, 30/11/105, micro.,
VSL.

bag the fox. Lafayette "cannot escape me," he was heard to say. As the British army moved towards Richmond, Lafayette pulled out and marched along "the upper road towards Fredericksburg." To avoid delay, Cornwallis's army swung around Richmond to the east. Lafayette was able to keep his distance "upon a parallel line with the Enemy keeping the upper part of the Country."[2] At Hanover Court House, on May 28, Lafayette asked Weedon to send more militia. He also noted, in response to Weedon's request for a blanket authority to command the local militia that, in case of "an Alarm," Weedon should make "demands in the Name of the Executive" as if he had received orders from the governor. Lafayette justified this action to Governor Jefferson on grounds that Weedon had no powers from the executive.[3]

Cornwallis was unable to catch Lafayette, and, as the Marquis wrote Weedon on the twenty-ninth, "the Enemy seem to have abandoned their projects against this Army" and were headed for Fredericksburg. Lafayette was going to march to Fredericksburg "as fast as possible," and he requested Weedon to evacuate all supplies and military stores from the Fredericksburg vicinity. Weedon was asked "to call out every Militia Man that can be collected & armed" and to "prevail upon the Gentlemen to mount & equip themselves as Volunteer Dragoons." Lafayette ordered all militia that might be on the road to return to Weedon's command. All boats and bridges below Fredericksburg should be destroyed.[4] From Davenport's Ford, on May 31, Lafayette directed Weedon to join forces with him the next day at Mattaponi Church, in Spotsylvania County fifteen miles south of Fredericksburg. Should General Wayne arrive with his detachment "our inferiority will not be quite so alarming," Lafayette pointed out. Cornwallis "is going from his Friends, and we are going to meet ours."[5]

With so much to do all at once, Weedon informed Lafayette that he could not join him on June 1. He was busy rounding up the stores, equipment, and livestock belonging to the

---

[2] Lafayette to Jefferson, 28 May, 1781, Boyd, 1950-: **6**: p. 26.

[3] *Ibid.*, Lafayette to Weedon, 28 May, 1781, WC, APS; Weedon to Lafayette, 22 May, 1781, WL, BUL.

[4] Lafayette to Weedon, 29 May, 1781, WC, APS.

[5] Lafayette to Steuben, 31 May, 1781, Cornwallis Papers, Intercepted Letters, Pub. Records Office, 30/11/105, micro., VSL; Lafayette to Jefferson, 31 May, 1781, Boyd, 1950-: **6**: p. 52.

government and sending these on to Albemarle Old Court House. He was trying to "disperse the tobacco." Acknowledging Lafayette's concern for Mrs. Washington and others of the commander in chief's family, Weedon assured Lafayette most of the ladies had been sent to safe places. Weedon explained that he had risked Lafayette's censure, "well knowing that few men added to your operating force, could have but small weight in any thing decisive, whereas their assistance in getting out of the way of the enemy such stores and other articles" as the British "now make an object of, might retard" the enemy's

> movements, and prove the salvation of this town. I hope I have not displeased you, when I add that the Stafford and King George militia are assembling on the Heights at Hunter's works, no one to arrange or dispose of them, no one to direct the supplies for Genl. Wayne, no one to transact the smallest piece of business here but myself. Surrounded with calls of every nature, and under the applications of every denomination, I have trusted to your candor til I hear from you again.[6]

Besides seeing to it that the militia in counties north of the Rappahannock "ware Arranged and held on the Minute plan," General Weedon called out into the field Prince William, King George, Stafford, and Spotsylvania militia and established camp, during the emergency, at "Heights near Hunter's," at Falmouth across from Fredericksburg. Four hundred militia arrived; the two hundred fifty King George and Stafford militia, however, went home after ten days contrary to Weedon's "request." Weedon called out one-half of the militia of the lower counties of the Northern Neck, who were to rendezvous to King George Court House, twenty-five miles from Fredericksburg. He ordered the Prince William militia to join Lafayette. Acting on a request by Lafayette, Weedon sent Charles Dick out to contact General Wayne and hurry him on.[7] Weedon also made arrangements for boats for Wayne to cross at Norman's Ford, on the upper Rappahannock, and prepared himself to join Lafayette with his militia.[8]

---

[6] Weedon to Lafayette, 31 May, 1781, WL, BUL; Weedon to Lafayette, 1 June, 1781, Balch, 1857: p. 147.

[7] Weedon to Lafayette, 22 and 31 May, 1781 and Circular [to county commanders], 30 May, 1781, WL, BUL; William Grayson to Weedon, 29 May and 5 June, 1781 and Jesse Ewell to Weedon, 13 June, 1781, WC, APS; Weedon to Lafayette, 4 June, 1781, Balch, 1857: p. 148.

[8] Weedon to Capt. Lewis, 2 June, 1781, WC, APS; Weedon to Wayne, 3 June, 1781, Wayne Papers, HSP.

On June 1 Cornwallis concluded that nothing could be gained from close pursuit of the elusive Lafayette or from going directly to Fredericksburg. He heard of the evacuation of the town and that Hunter's works were in disrepair; this objective "did not appear of so much importance as the stores on the other side of the country," he reported to Clinton. Nor did he think he could prevent a junction between Lafayette and Wayne. Instead he aimed at the destruction of stores at Albemarle Old Court House and Point of Fork, both on the upper James.[9] But Cornwallis's change of plans was not known to Lafayette. When the enemy shifted temporarily to the right, Lafayette interpreted this as an attempt to intercept Wayne's detachment, and he thought it "almost an even bet" that the enemy would head straight for Fredericksburg. With this in mind, he asked Weedon to send all militia to rendezvous at Orange County Court House, where Lafayette would soon join them.[10]

Cornwallis made an oblique retreat back to the James. He detached from the main army Tarleton's dragoons to Albemarle Old Court House and Charlottesville (to disrupt the Virginia Assembly) and Simcoe and his rangers to Point of Fork, where Steuben's little band of Continentals, expecting to march off to Greene's army, was guarding the other collection of stores. George Weedon learned from Captain Presly Thornton that the enemy began their retreat at 2 a.m. on June 3, going from Cook's Ford to Nagrow Ford, where they left two of their soldiers "hanging on the Limb of a Tree."[11]

Weedon visited Lafayette's camp at Raccoon Ford, on the "South Branch of Rappahannock" (the Rapidan), on June 7. Lafayette had taken this position the day before to await the arrival of Wayne. In reporting on the conference Weedon said that since Cornwallis "points towards our Stores in the Southern Communication," Lafayette "inclines to hang on his rear till his hands are Strengthened with Cavalry & Infantry;"[12] and he "had Ordered me to stand fast till the Designs of the Enemy can be Ascertained."[13] Wayne joined

---

[9] Cornwallis to Clinton, 30 June, 1781, in Tarleton, 1781: pp. 348-349.

[10] Lafayette to Weedon, 2 June, 1781, WC, APS.

[11] Capt. [Presly] Thornton to Weedon, 3 June, 1781, *ibid.*

[12] Weedon to Col. Blackburn, 8 June, 1781, *ibid.*, Lafayette to Weedon, 8 June, 1781, Sol Feinstone Collection, APS.

[13] Weedon to William Grayson, 8 June, 1781, WC, APS.

Lafayette on June 10, and the American army followed at a safe distance the British retreat southward to the James.

When Weedon returned to camp at Hunter's Heights, he had intelligence from Richard Henry Lee that the enemy was sighted in the Potomac. Weedon immediately ordered a halt of the Northern Neck militia that were "in motion," and sent Colonel William Nelson to command them. If the enemy were really in the Potomac, Nelson was to see to it that the rest of the militia were embodied and the whole militia force was then to "form a junction" with Weedon.[14]

Should there be no hostile presence in the Potomac, Weedon expected to join Lafayette, if Lafayette approved. The cause of the alarm turned out to be a British ship under a flag of truce in the Potomac to deliver supplies for the convention prisoners.[15] Weedon, however, also learned that a British marauding party had plundered Urbanna, at the mouth of the Rappahannock, and had "done some mischief in Northumberland."[16] So there was just enough provocation in the two rivers to keep Weedon from joining Lafayette. That the enemy still meant to operate in the Potomac and Rappahannock was very much a possibility. Many of the inhabitants, heeding Weedon's advice, moved their livestock, Negroes, and families away from the shores of the rivers.[17]

It looked as if George Weedon would perpetually be on a sort of glorified guard duty of the Northern Neck. Since he had assumed the chief responsibility in defending this area, he found himself stereotyped in the unrewarding role of coordinator and supporter. While he dealt with potential danger, the action was elsewhere. Again a familiar order came from Lafayette, at Mechunk's Creek: "Request you will Superintend and direct the distribution of the troops north of Rappaonak while the Enemy Have Nothing But plundering parties"; if a large enemy force should appear Weedon should collect all the militia at one place and "attack or retreat."[18] A week later, Lafayette hastily wrote: "Your exertions have been of infinite Service, and although I wish you with us, yet we

[14] Weedon to Nelson, 9 June, 1781, Weedon to Col. J. A. Washington, 8 June, 1781, and Weedon to Lafayette, 9 June, 1781, *ibid.*

[15] J. A. Washington to Weedon, 9 June, 1781, *ibid.*

[16] Weedon to Lafayette, 11 June, 1781, *ibid.*

[17] Richard Henry Lee to Weedon, 1 June, 1781, *ibid.*, Weedon to [Richard Henry Lee], 31 May, 1781, WL, BUL; Richard Henry Lee to Arthur Lee, 4 June, 1781, Ballagh, 1914: 2: pp. 229-230.

[18] Lafayette to Weedon, 13 June, 1781, AKF.

FIG. 8.   General Charles Cornwallis. From J. S. Copley, "The Most Noble Charles Marquis Cornwallis . . . . Major General of the Ordnance, Lt. General of his Majesty's Kingdom of Ireland." Engraved by Benjamin Smith (London). pub. 1798. With permission of Virginia State Library.

must suffer greatly should we lose the assistance to be derived from your remaining a little longer where you are .... To-morrow perhaps we may know where he [Cornwallis] is going .... If he looks towards Potomack, you will of course take your measures.''[19]

George Weedon at least was not having the misfortunes of the former commander in chief of Virginia forces. To Major General Baron von Steuben, service in Virginia had been most humiliating. He had been unceremoniously replaced by Lafayette in the supreme command. He had alienated the Virginia government by his blunt remarks on the state's war effort. Since Lafayette arrived, Steuben was in a kind of limbo, detached with a reinforcement to march to join Greene—but the Southern commander had told him to stay in Virginia for the time being.[20] Lafayette ignored him. At Point of Fork, about forty-five miles above Richmond, on June 5 Simcoe and his Queen's Rangers came upon Steuben and his five-hundred-man force. By Simcoe performing a ruse of lighted campfires and dispersing his men, Steuben thought he was up against an advance of the whole British army. Steuben pre-cipitously headed southward towards North Carolina; but on reconsideration, he halted, and then changed directions and delivered his troops to Lafayette. Steuben took sick leave at Charlottesville before rejoining the American army for the siege of Yorktown. "The conduct of the Baron," Lafayette wrote Washington, "is to me unintelligible—every man woman and child in Virginia is roused against him. They dispute even on his courage ...."[21]

No one thus far accused Weedon of cowardice. Yet, it is interesting to note, fifty-two years later, a seventy-three-year-old man, in filing a pension claim, said he had served under "genl. Joseph Weden" at Williamsburg and had fought in a skirmish at Stony Point (on the James), in which the militia were defeated and driven away owing "to the cowardice of Genl. Wedens command."[22] The applicant, Zachariah

[19] Lafayette to Weedon, 21 June, 1781, *ibid.*

[20] Steuben to Weedon, 12 June, 1781, *ibid.*

[21] Lafayette to Washington, 18 June, 1781, Gottschalk, 1944: pp. 201-202. When Steuben took his sick leave, Lafayette commented: "I am glad he goes as the hatred of the Virginians to him was truly hurtful to the service." (Lafayette to Hamilton, 6 August, 1781, Syrett, 1961: **2**: p. 644.)

[22] Zachariah Wharton and Sarah, his widow, claim application, 27 May, 1833, Morgan County Court, Revolutionary War Pension Applications, #S-6487, NA. Wharton was born in 1760, and died in 1835. He had fourteen children. He was drafted from the militia of Spotsylvania County, where he lived during the war.

Wharton, having his facts jumbled and perhaps being a little senile, may have, after the many years, confused the reputations of Weedon and Steuben among Virginians.

George Weedon continued to provide logistical support for Lafayette's army. Informed of shipments from Philadelphia ahead of time, he had to attend to the last link in the route by seeing to proper crossings, prevention of pilfering, finding wagons, and the like. He kept an officer at Noland's Ferry to give directions to the supply trains.[23] Richard Young still assisted as quartermaster in Fredericksburg.[24] William Grayson, a commissioner of the Board of War in Philadelphia, frequently corresponded. Grayson was responsible for sending shipments of arms, ammunition, clothing, and other supplies to Weedon at Fredericksburg. Grayson's letters to Weedon always included advice on military tactics in Virginia, usually pointing out that it was better to skirmish rather than risk a general action.[25] Writing to Weedon, Grayson said, "Pray inform me what you want. Everything shall be done that can be done"; but "as to the credit of the State I dont believe any body would trust her for half a crown."[26] A month later he changed his tune: "Your credit has risen here to a very considerable height: It is no longer a disgrace to be a Virginian."[27] Grayson regularly sent shipments of two to three hundred stand of arms to Weedon, who then forwarded them to Lafayette or to Continental stores. From April through early July four thousand stand of arms from Philadelphia were sent via Weedon.[28]

Weedon tried to convince William Davies, Commissioner of War for Virginia, that he should retain eight hundred to a thousand stand of arms for the magazine in Fredericksburg. "The Marquis thinks the security of this place & the defence of Potomac of so much importance to the public," he wrote Davies, "that he will not suffer me to joine him and must

[23] Weedon to — Price, 16 June, 1781, Balch, 1857: pp. 155-156; Simon Sommers to Weedon, 24 July, 1781, AKF.

[24] Weedon had Richard Young, the quartermaster, shoe three of his own horses. (Weedon to Young, 28 May, 1781, Richard Young Papers, VSL.)

[25] William Grayson to Weedon, 5 June (2 letters), 12 June, and 26 June, 1781 and Weedon to Lafayette, 12 June, 1781, WC, APS; William Grayson to Steuben, — June, 1781, Steuben Papers, NYHS.

[26] William Grayson to Weedon, 29 May, 1781, WC, APS.

[27] William Grayson to Weedon, 3 July, 1781, AKF.

[28] Weedon to Lafayette, 22 May, 1781 and to Col. Davies, 7 July, 1781, WL, BUL; Weedon to Major Pryor, 28 May, 1781, Cornwallis Papers, Intercepted Letters, Pub. Records Office, 30/11/105, micro., VSL.

therefore insist upon having as many Arms as may be Necessary for that Service."[29] Davies finally consented to Weedon's keeping one thousand stand provided there was strict accountability.[30]

What seems trivial, nevertheless, took up a great deal of Weedon's time. One such matter was to arrange for hilts for swords to be made at Dumfries; but the work was delayed when the artisans demanded "ready money." Weedon did not feel that he could use the "public tobacco." To keep down costs, he had "rolled iron" substituted for brass in the hilts.[31]

Finding shoes for Lafayette's troops in the Fredericksburg area was impossible as "all the stores & Factories" were sent away "on the first of the Enemies Advance." Weedon pressed the Continental Board of War to supply shoes, and he sent an express to General Daniel Morgan to seize shoes from the various "factories" in the back counties and to send them on immediately. The quartermaster in Alexandria, Colonel Hendricks, was also told to use impressment for shoes and other commodities.[32] Weedon contacted the officials of thirteen counties for the procurement of supplies.[33]

There was also a shortage of provisions. Lafayette was in great need of bacon, salt fish, rum, whisky or brandy, and vinegar. Especially he sought from Weedon spiritous liquors as "the Water of this Country is very unhealthy to Northern soldiers"—a large supply of vinegar and rum "wou'd be very welcome."[34] Weedon found that the vinegar in the Northern Neck was of poor quality—"composed of cyder."[35] He asked officials in the counties to collect provisions under the "specifics tax" law, and if this was not sufficient to use "reasonable purchases"; as a last resort there could be military impressment, "without injuring individuals materially which your good judgment will direct."[36] Cooperation in the local area was gratifying. One county alone provided sixty barrels

---

[29] Weedon to Davies, 16 July, 1781, WL, BUL; Weedon to Gov. Nelson, 16 July, 1781, Dreer Collection, HSP.

[30] Davies to Weedon, 3 August, 1781, AKF.

[31] Richard Graham to Weedon, 14 June, 1781, and Weedon to Richard Graham, 17 June, 1781, WC, APS; Weedon to Richard Graham, 20 June, 1781, WL, BUL.

[32] Weedon to Lafayette, 17 June, 1781 and Weedon to Col. Hendricks, 17 June, 1781, WC, APS.

[33] Weedon to Mr. Graham, 8 July, 1781, WL, BUL.

[34] Lafayette to Weedon, 16 June, 1781, WC, APS.

[35] James Hendricks to Weedon, 22 July, 1781, AKF.

[36] Weedon to Lafayette, inclosing circular letters (10 counties), 18 June, 1781, Balch, 1857: p. 158.

of bread and twelve hundred gallons of vinegar.[37] With only six wagons, Weedon sent to Lafayette on June 20 seven hundred gallons of whisky and three hundred gallons of vinegar.[38] "With Spirited Aid," Weedon wrote Richard Graham, the pun unintended, "we might have signaliz'd Virginia with a Cornwalliad." He asked Graham, at Dumfries, to throw in a "Quarter Cask of Wine for our good Marquis."[39]

It was difficult to obtain wagons, as farmers kept them out of sight, especially after Lafayette had broadly used his impressment powers on his return march to Virginia. Weedon gave Captain Sommers at Noland's Ferry and Richard Young at Fredericksburg authority to impress wagons.[40] Grayson complained to Weedon in July that arms were held up in Philadelphia because wagoners "heard that one of their fraternity got taken by the Enemy."[41] From time to time, Weedon made up a "brigade of wagons" from those he could secure in the local area and from the few that were retained in the Continental service.[42]

Weedon "used every method in my power" to get flat bottom boats built—four in Alexandria, on which "I pledged my own estate," and two at Fredericksburg. But still "the Credit of the Country being so very low it is utterly impossible to engage the most trifling Article upon trust," he wrote Commissioner Davies. Even after the boats were built, Weedon had trouble obtaining carriages because of lack of money. He probably used his own property as collateral again, though he inquired of Davies if the carriages could be paid for out of the "public tobacco."[43]

Weedon appointed Dr. John Julian to replace Dr. Charles Mortimer, who resigned, as the "Director" of the "hospital department" at Fredericksburg. Julian, though holding only a state commission as an army surgeon, presumably would serve under Dr. Thomas Tucker, director-general of the

[37] Weedon to Lafayette, 27 July, 1781, WL, BUL.

[38] Weedon to Lafayette, 20 June, 1781, WC, APS.

[39] Weedon to Richard Graham, 17 June, 1781, *ibid.*

[40] *Ibid.*, Weedon to Capt. Sommers, 3 July, to Mr. Graham, 8 July, and to Lafayette, 8 July, 1781, WL, BUL.

[41] William Grayson to Weedon, 18 June, 1781, WC, APS.

[42] Weedon to Lafayette, 18 June, 1781, Balch, 1857: p. 158; Weedon to Lafayette, 2 July, 1781, WL, BUL.

[43] Weedon to Lafayette, 22 and 31 May, 1781 and Weedon to Davies, 7 and 16 July, 1781, WL, BUL; James Hendricks to Weedon, 14 July, 1781, AKF.

hospitals for the Southern army. Mortimer had resigned in exasperation over lack of medical supplies. Although only "one diseased negro fellow" required care at the time, a "convenient house" in Fredericksburg was needed "to prevent any pestilential disorders among the inhabitants" and to isolate "the patients from drunken and riotous Company."[44]

While Lafayette followed Cornwallis, militiamen in the Northern Neck were given a brief respite from the draft and allowed to attend to their fields, although single men without families were subject to immediate call.[45] Lafayette's army, nevertheless, had swelled to 4,565 men, with 2,240 militia still in the field and with the addition of Wayne's and Steuben's Continentals. Since the army was not strong enough to do battle with Cornwallis's veterans, unless from an exceptional position, Lafayette's force continued to tag alongside the British army in a parallel line.[46] Simcoe and Tarleton rejoined Cornwallis, and on June 15 the British Army headed towards Richmond from Elk Hill on the James. Cornwallis occupied Richmond June 16–21, and then moved down the James towards Williamsburg, with Lafayette following at a safe distance. The British occupied Williamsburg and made camp on Jamestown Island.[47] Of the clash at Spencer's Ordinary on June 26 between units under Butler and Simcoe, Weedon wrote Lafayette that "a few more such stroaks will sink his L'ships reinforcement."[48] Apparently this was in reference to knowledge that General Clinton had ordered Cornwallis to send several thousand of his troops to New York.

From intercepted letters, Sir Henry Clinton knew that Lafayette would not attack even a reduced British force in Virginia. Clinton thought "it probable that the Season may have put an End to all Operations in Chesapeak, except by

---

[44] Dr. Mortimer to Weedon, 18 June, 1781 and Weedon to Dr. Julian, 20 June, 1781, Balch, 1857: pp. 157 and 159; Col. James Innes to Gov. Nelson, 24 July, 1781, Palmer, 1875-: 2: p. 243.

[45] William Nelson to the County Clerk of —, 16 June, 1781, WC, APS; Weedon to Col. Skinker, 15 June, 1781, Balch, 1857: pp. 154-155.

[46] Col. Febiger to Col. Theodorick Bland, 3 July, 1781, Campbell, 1843: 2: p. 71; Lafayette to Washington, 28 June, 1781, Gottschalk, 1944: p. 203.

[47] Cornwallis to Maj. Gen. Leslie, 19 June, 1781 and Major Alexander Ross to Lt. George Pattison ADC, 20 June, 1781, Cornwallis Papers, 30/11/87, Pub. Records Office, micro., VSL; Simcoe, 1844: p. 225; "Journal of Wild," 1890: pp. 142-143; "Yorktown Campaign . . . John Davis," 1881: pp. 294-295.

[48] Weedon to Lafayette, 2 July, 1781, WL, BUL; James McHenry to Weedon, 26 June, 1781, WC, APS.

Water."[49] With only an "effective force" of 10,931, he needed more men to withstand a siege of New York.[50] As Weedon heard from William Grayson, "The affair at N. York is meant to be serious, it will either be taken, or the Enemy will be compelled to withdraw their troops from the Southward."[51] Washington and Rochambeau, Grayson also reported, were moving their forces towards New York, which he said would require the sending of a detachment from Cornwallis, and "will make matters perfectly easy in Virginia." The "general talk" in Philadelphia "is about the siege of N. York." The "Yankey levies are coming in fast."[52] With Cornwallis pulling down the James and with the probability that he would send part of his army to New York, Weedon was all the more confident that the British Army in Virginia could be contained: "I would not doubt but the Old *Dominion* will extricate herself with equal honor notwithstanding her Neighbors have set with folded Arms while she was so Cruelly pressed; but whose Afraid, the more Danger the more honor. Stedy and Spirited Exertions for a few months longer will do our Business."[53]

Cornwallis was also ordered to establish a new base of operations. Before crossing the James to move southward, his rear guard decoyed a detachment under General Wayne into battle on July 6 at Green Spring, on Jamestown Ford. An old friend, Colonel Walter Stewart of Wayne's Pennsylvanians, wrote Weedon of the bloody encounter: "The Idea of my being Wounded arose from my being almost Cover'd with Blood by riding a Wounded Horse . . . . It was Certainly the Warmest and most severe fire I was ever in, and I think we very fortunately escap'd as we did."[54]

The British Army crossed the James to the south side, and by the fourteenth was in the vicinity of Portsmouth. Tarleton, from July 9 to 24, was dispatched to raid American stores and horses as far as one hundred fifty miles into the backcountry. Covering thirty to forty miles a day, Tarleton's dragoons

---

[49] Henry Clinton to Maj. Gen. Leslie, 23 June, 1781, Cornwallis Papers, 30/11/97, Pub. Records Office, micro., VSL.

[50] Extract of a letter from Sir Henry Clinton to Earl Cornwallis, 11 June, 1781, in Lee, 1869: pp. 440-441.

[51] William Grayson to Weedon, 17 July, 1781, AKF.

[52] William Grayson to Weedon, 10 July, 1781, *ibid*.

[53] Weedon to Davies, 7 July, 1781, WL, BUL.

[54] Col. Walter Stewart to Weedon, 27 July, 1781, AKF.

could not be overtaken by General Wayne's men who went after them. With Cornwallis setting up headquarters at Suffolk, Lafayette withdrew to Malvern Hill, sixteen miles south of Richmond on the James, and then to Hanover County to wait and see what the Earl's next actions might be.[55] "In case there is no appearance of a move of the enemy and no propriety in our going toward Portsmouth, I intend reconnoitring the grounds about Fredericksburg," he wrote Washington.[56] Lafayette permitted many of the militia to go home, but defections were so great that he was again asking Weedon for reinforcements. At the end of July Weedon sent down three hundred Hampshire and Frederick riflemen, who had been delayed in Fredericksburg while their rifles were being repaired. Some drafted militia were also sent to Lafayette's camp.[57]

Weedon kept an eye on the lower Northern Neck for any signs of hostile movements by the enemy. In late July he made an inspection tour along the Potomac, and found "all things are peaceable in that Quarter." Writing to Lafayette, he said that Cornwallis "at present cutts a dispicable figure Cooped up in his fastings at Portsmouth. We must expect he will move some where shortly, as he cant keep his hands long from Picking & Stealing."[58]

Indeed, as there now seemed to be no immediate threat of invasion up the Potomac and Rappahannock Rivers or Cornwallis heading again towards the Fredericksburg area, Weedon found time to comment on events for his friend, General Greene, who, like Weedon had been too occupied the past several months to renew their correspondence. "Your old Friend Earl Cornwallis has paid us a kind of Civil Visit," said Weedon,

> as all he has done in a Military view only serves to compleat his ruin and forever blast his Military reputation. He has left a Country he had been two years fighting for to be over run and his Garrisons struck in every Quarter by your Victorious Troops. And for what? The Question is easily Answered. To steal Negroes and burn a few hhds Tobacco. He Vauntingly

[55] G. Damer to Lord George Germain, 29 July, 1781, *Report . . . Drayton House*, 1910: 2: pp. 210-211; Simcoe, 1844: p. 239; Gottschalk, 1942: pp. 264-267; Wright, 1905: pp. 262-264.

[56] Lafayette to Washington, 20 July, 1781, Sparks, 1853: 3: p. 363.

[57] Lafayette to Weedon, 1 July, 1781, AKF; Weedon to Lafayette, 27 July, 1781, WL, BUL.

[58] Weedon to Lafayette, 27 July, 1781, WL, BUL.

penetrated with much pomp and Military display as far as Charlotte Ville before the Marquis's hands were so strengthened as to look him in the face. When he found the Gallant little Nobleman no longer attached to the Fabian Game, from being in Condition to look at him, he blushed like a maid of sixteen and footed it back to Williamsburg where no doubt he meant to set up his Government, but finding the reins was likely to be warmly contest'd thought it ware prudent to get into his fastings at Portsmouth by throwing himself over James River at James Town after being much insulted in two encounters, And passing down the South side of James River where he had not a man to oppose him. This ended his Virginia Expedition, at least as it now stands: His Converts ware for Viz—A Lawyer and his son, a Barber and his wife, a Tailor, a Doctr, a Master Grinder, and two Irish lads. The Serious preparations which are making at N York will unquestionably produce such Detachments as will make Matters perfectly easy in these Southern States or give us possession of that Garrison. The Foederal Army have joined and are moving down. It is true Sr. Harry [Clinton] may decamp by Water but then our whole force will Operate Southerly.

Cornwallis, "as in many other things," had been "out Generaled, and now cuts a most dispicable figuar cooped up in his lines at Portsmouth from whence I expect he will shortly Curs us, and quit us." Weedon commented on Greene's activities: "your disappointment at Ninety six must no doubt have tried your Military Philosophy if soldiers possess any, however, those are events in War that will happen." Somewhat exaggerating what he felt to be the truth and simply paraphrasing remarks by William Grayson, Weedon said the exertion in Virginia during the invasion "has been wonderful, and it is no longer a disgrace to be call'd a Virginian even in the Coffee House at the Metropolis of Pennsylvania. And be it remembered that hard as we ware pressed in the first of it, not a man was sent from any of our Sister States to aid us, tho' we ware at the same time so much Engaged in the Southern Operations. It was thought harde of and I dair say you will think with me, not without reason."[59]

The British reinforcement for New York weighed anchor on July 31, but only proceeded about forty miles up Chesapeake Bay.[60] As so many times before, there was again at least a

---

[59] Weedon to Greene, 27 July, 1781, Greene Papers, CL.

[60] James McHenry to Weedon, 1 July [August 1], 1781, AKF.

possibility of a British expedition up the Potomac. Richard Henry Lee had "a string of lookouts" from one end of Westmoreland County to the other, and he was ready to report any intelligence to General Weedon,[61] who himself, however, felt that the British ships would sail up the Bay.[62] Indeed, in Philadelphia, Congress learned from an intercepted letter of Lord Germain to Clinton that Cornwallis was to aid in an invasion of the middle states.[63] Lafayette, back at Malvern Hill, could only guess at the destination of this British force. He wrote Weedon: "upon you I depend for the first disposition and the earliest information." If the enemy set sail up the Potomac, Lafayette said, "I will move there with the greatest rapidity as my present situation is as nearly calculated to protect the different posts of the State as possible."[64]

Lafayette felt that his troops were disposed to meet any emergency. Wayne was at Goode's Bridge near Malvern Hill on the north side of the James with the Pennsylvania and Virginia Continentals and "looks towards Roanoke or Portsmouth"; Muhlenberg and a detachment of light infantry, some riflemen, and cavalry had "an intermediary position "between me and Suffolk," with Colonel Parker's militia in the "neighborhood;" and "General Weedon is in person at Fredericksburg and, the moment a fleet appears, will call out the militia."[65]

But Cornwallis received orders from Clinton to call back the reinforcement and to establish a base at Old Point Comfort or Yorktown, either one with a harbor big enough for Clinton's ships. Finding Old Point Comfort too unreliable for defense, Cornwallis elected to take his army to Yorktown. On July 29, the British commander embarked his army from Portsmouth, leaving Brigadier General Charles O'Hara to come on later after destroying the garrison. Because of contrary winds it took four days for the British to land at Yorktown and at Gloucester, on the other side of the York River. Immediately fortifications were begun at both places. As to Yorktown, Cornwallis admitted, "the position is bad, and of course we want more troops." He was also "not easy about my post at

---

[61] Richard Henry Lee to Weedon, 1 August, 1781, *ibid.*

[62] Weedon to Richard Henry Lee, 31 July, 1781, WL, BUL.

[63] President of Congress to President of Pennsylvania, 7 August, 1781, Burnett, 1921-1938: **6**: p. 168.

[64] Lafayette to Weedon, 27 July, 1781, AKF.

[65] Lafayette to Washington, 30 July, 1781, Sparks, 1853: **3**: p. 365.

Gloucester" and needed more Negroes because his soldiers could not work in the intense heat.[66]

Weedon kept in close touch with Lafayette, who moved from Malvern Hill to Hanover County to collect the various parts of his army and new militia and supplies. With the enemy now confined narrowly to bases at Yorktown and Gloucester, the opportunity presented itself for concentrating American troops in Virginia in a siege position about these posts. It seemed that at last the enemy had been convinced of the futility of invading Virginia by the major rivers. Cornwallis, knowing the risk of his position, expected soon to join forces with Clinton and bid farewell to Virginia. George Weedon, with a sigh of relief, considered that he might not any longer have the worries of the "protection of the Potomac." Hopefully he could now join Lafayette in the field. Yet as long as the British remained in Virginia, the Northern Neck was vulnerable. Weedon still faced the old dilemma, even if to a lesser degree, of whether to continue to look after the defense of Northern Virginia and to support Lafayette or to get into the field himself. The British could stay put, or, at any time, Cornwallis might take a roundabout route northward by way of the Northern Neck and, without effective American naval power, British raiding parties could still go up the rivers. There would be a brief period of watchful waiting.

---

[66] Earl Cornwallis to Brig.-Gen. O'Hara, 2 August, 1781 and Cornwallis to Clinton, 12 August, 1781, Ross, 1859: 1: pp. 112-113.

XII. SEALING
CORNWALLIS'S FATE

George Weedon had to wait a little while longer for a field command. If Lafayette moved to check the British at Yorktown, a militia force would be needed to do the same at Gloucester. Meanwhile Weedon continued to direct the "succouring" of Lafayette's army and the readying of the militia.

During the second week in August, Lafayette took his army from Hanover County down to the forks of the York River (the junction of the Pamunkey and Mattaponi Rivers), where he could keep a close watch on the British at Yorktown and Gloucester.

For the time being, Cornwallis could easily escape and return to the Carolinas or march northward, but expecting the arrival of a fleet from New York, he went ahead with fortifications. Lieutenant Colonel Thomas Dundas received charge of the British force at Gloucester, which consisted of Simcoe's rangers, a regiment of Hessians, companies from the twenty-third and eighty-second regiments, the Jägers, and North Carolina volunteers. From Gloucester, a little more than a half mile acoss the York River from Yorktown, the British could protect their shipping, prevent the passage of enemy ships, keep open an escape route, and collect forage and supplies.[1]

In Fredericksburg Weedon sent on to Lafayette the few men who straggled in from the back counties.[2] He forwarded to Lafayette some of the arms and military stores that had come his way, but allowed the rest to be detained at several of the county court houses.[3] Weedon was glad that Commissioner Davies did not insist upon all military equipment being sent down. "Indeed could you Establish every County in the form

---

[1] Hatch, 1940: p. 268; Wickwire, 1970: p. 372.

[2] Weedon to Col. Triplit, 18 August, 1781, WL, BUL.

[3] Weedon to Col. Hendricks, 8 August, 1781, *ibid.*; Simon Sommers to Weedon, 12 August, 1781, Davies to Weedon, 21 August, 1781, and Weedon to Davies, 25 August, 1781, AKF; Weedon to Davies, 26 August, 1781, Society Collections, HSP; Weedon to Davies, 29 August, 1781, Dreer Collection, HSP.

of a little republic," he wrote Davies, "it would be means of making us formidable in the Eyes of the world . . . . The Enemy knowing us prepared to receive them would not be so lavish of their Visits."[4]

Lafayette's army still lacked sufficient provisions, and Weedon continued to do what he could to collect various articles of food and drink. Especially he sought flour, which was the greatest scarcity in the army.[5] From August 8 to 18 he made a tour of five lower counties of the Northern Neck and took a detailed inventory. Among the items he reported were 36,000 head of cattle. He also inventoried the arms and ammunition.

On this trip General Weedon got a first-hand look into the situation of the militia. He found there were 2,250 militia in the five counties. Weedon conferred with Richard Henry Lee, and the two men "formed a plan of defence." Half the militia (1,100) were to be in readiness and well armed and should be sent to a camp to be "formed hereabouts." Weedon and Lee spoke of a "legionary corps," but it is not clear whether this meant that the militia of each county should be a legion, that there should be one elite unit, or that this principle should be applied to the militia at camp. The "legionary corps" would provide its own equipment, except when "a misfortune in service" should occur and then "reasonable Allowances" would be expected.[6] Both Weedon and Lee wrote Governor Nelson and Commissioner Davies on the subject. Davies responded: "I like the systematic plans of defence, which the gentlemen of that part of the country seem disposed to adopt"; but as to a "legionary corps . . . I am fearful they will not be oeconomical enough in their draughts of Supplies," and the government would not allow impressment of horses, "as the Country groans under the abuses."[7]

It was reported erroneously that Cornwallis was bringing all of his army to Gloucester. Accepting the report at face value, General Weedon considered that this "drawing to a point" was a "sure presage of Mischief" and that it indicated

---

[4] Weedon to Davies, 25 August, 1781, AKF.

[5] Lafayette to Weedon, 29 August, 1781, *ibid*.; Thomas Towles to Thomas Clayton, 9 August, 1781, Richard Young Papers, VSL; Lafayette to Gov. Nelson, 11 September, 1781, Chinard, 1928: p. 59.

[6] Richard Henry Lee to Weedon, 23 August, 1781, and Weedon to Davies, 25 August, 1781, AKF; Weedon to Davies, 18 August, 1781, WL, BUL. The five counties: King George, Westmoreland, Richmond, Lancaster, and Northumberland.

[7] Davies to Weedon, 21 August, 1781, AKF.

"a general Move which no doubt will be up the Rappahannock." He therefore recommended to the governor that a camp be formed on "high ground" in Caroline County of Culpeper, Orange, Spotsylvania, Caroline, Essex, and Hanover militia, which would be a "Second line of defence for the Southside of Rappahannock." If "nothing serious Appear in Potowmack," the King George, Stafford, Prince William, and Fairfax militia could also join the camp. Weedon informed Governor Nelson that he ordered the commanding officers of the four lower counties of the Northern Neck (Westmoreland, Richmond, Lancaster, and Northumberland) "to attend to the motions of the Enemy," and if the "enemy penetrate Gloucester" the militia of these counties were "directed to move to keep abreast of them." Should the governor order out the militia to Gloucester Neck, Weedon declared, "I shall instantly take the Field with them."[8]

Although the report that Cornwallis had moved his force across the York River proved false, the Gloucester post was retained. George Weedon now considered that a large militia force should be stationed outside of Gloucester. He asked Colonel Davies to consult with Governor Nelson on the "propriety" of establishing a militia "camp below," where troops from the Northern Neck could be "easily thrown across" the Rappahannock at Hobb's Hole or Leedstown. In writing to Davies, Weedon also mentioned that "Gen. Depotil [Louis Le Bégue de Presle Duportail] the chief Engineer beat up my Quarters the other Night riding Express" on his way to Lafayette's army.[9]

Events were now shaping to bring on a showdown with Lord Cornwallis. Washington and Rochambeau joined forces and headed for Virginia. On August 29, Weedon learned that a French fleet under Admiral De Grasse was "hourly expected in Chesapeake." Governor Nelson wrote him on September 3 that indeed twenty-eight "Line of battleships" and six frigates had arrived outside of Hampton Roads.[10] De Grasse stayed a few days to debark 3,000 men under the Marquis Saint-Simon, who were sent as a reinforcement to Lafayette. On September 5, the French ships sailed out of the Bay and engaged a British

[8] Weedon to Gov. Nelson, 21 August, 1781, Dreer Collection, HSP; Circular Letter to the County Lieutenants, 20 August, 1781, WL, BUL; Weedon to Richard Henry Lee, 20 August, 1781, Lee Papers, UVL, VSL micro.

[9] Weedon to Davies, 29 August, 1781, Dreer Collection, HSP.

[10] *Ibid.*; Gov. Nelson to Weedon, 3 September, 1781, and Lafayette to Weedon, 1 September, 1781, AKF.

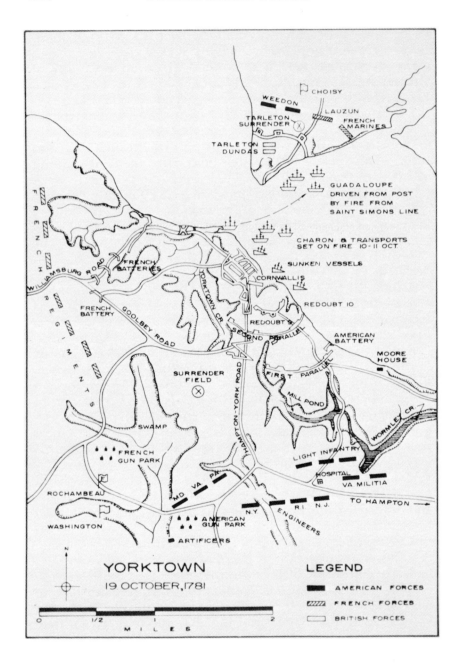

Map 5.   Yorktown and Gloucester. From T. Triplett Russell and John K. Gott, *Fauquier County in the Revolution* (Warrentown, Va., 1975). With permission of the authors.

fleet under Admiral Thomas Graves, after which Graves returned to New York and De Grasse's fleet entered Chesapeake Bay and joined with Admiral de Barras's naval force arriving from Newport. The French would now effectively blockade Yorktown and Gloucester. British frigates, however, in the York River, the *Charon* and *Guadeloupe,* and smaller ships, *Fowey, Bonetta,* and *Vulcan,* kept the river blocked to French vessels and still allowed communications between Yorktown and Gloucester.[11]

As George Weedon waited for more news, he suffered from "a very high fever." While recuperating, he wrote General Greene of the latest intelligence of the French fleet and of the allied army on the way from the north. Of the newfound naval power, he said, "I think my dear fellow there is little risque of our ever being the Juniors at Sea again." Also "New York will Certainly be ours before Xmas. The Business with his Lordship in this State will very soon be at an End, for suppose you know eer this, that we have got him handsomely in a pudding bag."

To Greene an account was given of Weedon's recent activities. "The Situation of this place; and Potowmack River becoming an Object; have been fixed here for its Protection, and have made a little republic of ten Counties that ware under my immediate Command. We now geting a Decided Superiority of the Bay & Rivers removes every fear." Still embittered by the recommendation of the board of officers in February, he wrote: "[I] shall Instantly joine the Army and the first Oportunity, shall bring the Officer refusing my Orders to a Court Martial. It will then be known whether Congress or a board of Officers takes precedence." As to the protest of the board of officers to his staying in the service, Weedon added, "I have never heard any thing of that Extraordinary Affair since the Birth of it, And dont believe either Congress or the Commander in Chief will ever give it an Answer."

Yet George Weedon was exuberant: "I am all on Fire—by the Great God of War. I think we may all hang up our Swords by the last of the year in perfect peace and Security." Apologizing for not writing more, Weedon gave Greene a bit of fantasizing: if the fever had not been so great he would "have taken you first to the Marquis and Count De Grasse looking into affairs then to have Whiped you over into the

---

[11] Lewis, 1945: pp. 180-182; Ward, 1952: 2: p. 885. For the disposition of De Grasse's ships, see Moore, 1860: p. 538.

State of New York, Nay to have Dined you with Genl W & Count Rochambeau; then just touching at the West Indies; to have Introduced you to Ryder Alley Kan in the East, and then to have Delivered you safe over the Guards at high hills of Santee"; but this was "a work too much for a sick one."[12]

One fourth of the militia from counties of the Northern Neck and on the north side of the James were ordered into active duty for three months. Militia from counties above the York were to form outside Gloucester, the others, at Williamsburg.[13] Disappointedly, George Weedon did not receive orders from the governor to command the militia at the Gloucester camp. It seems that Governor Nelson favored Colonel James Innes for this appointment, as Innes already commanded militia in the area. Weedon did not even learn of the militia draft until after the call was issued. All that the governor asked Weedon to do was to assist the staff departments in securing supplies for Washington's army, which was expected to come overland (actually most of the army went by way of Chesapeake Bay).[14]

Weedon was quite miffed. He replied, on September 5, to Governor Nelson's letter that while he stayed in Fredericksburg he could "pay strict attention to what you request." But he had sent his aide de camp to Lafayette's headquarters for orders and expected to be in the field in several days. Since

> I understand Directions are gone to draught the Counties of the Northern Neck, my continuing here without a man, not even being advised of what was done, with those Counties whom I have so long Superintended; makes it Necessary for my own reputation, particularly at a time like the present, to seek more Active & respectable Service.[15]

George Weedon had no intention of being excluded from the Yorktown campaign. Fortunately, just as he was about to set out on his own he received a letter from Lafayette, dated September 11, informing him of the militia build-up at Gloucester, "which I would be happy if you were to command."[16] Weedon had already had his "baggage waggon

---

[12] Weedon to Greene, 5 September, 1781, Miscellaneous Letters, The Pierpont Morgan Library.

[13] Davies to Richard Henry Lee, 31 August, 1781, Lee Papers, UVL, micro., VSL; 5 September, 1781, MacMaster, 1971: p. 415; "Shepherdson, David," in McAllister, 1913: p. 122.

[14] Thomas Nelson to Weedon, 3 September, 1781, AKF.

[15] Weedon to Gov. Nelson, 5 September, 1781, U.S. Army Box, 1781, NYPL.

[16] Lafayette to Weedon, 11 September, 1781, AKF.

horses" shod and was ready to go.[17] He departed as soon as he received Lafayette's letter (if not before). A factor that may have hastened Weedon's departure was a letter he received from Washington, dated September 10 at Mount Vernon. The commander in chief said that he, Rochambeau, the Chevalier de Chastellux, and other French officers were starting out for Fredericksburg. Washington asked Weedon to instruct county lieutenants of the counties enroute to keep roads open and also to have "french horses" or carriages ready for the French officers. Washington and his entourage stopped over at Fredericksburg, September 11–13.[18] George Weedon must have missed seeing Washington by hours or perhaps a day. He may not have received Washington's letter in time; but understandably he did not want the commander in chief to find a Continental brigadier general languishing, without any authority, in Fredericksburg.

Some militia joined Weedon at White House Ferry on his way to Gloucester.[19] On the thirteenth, he was at the camp forming at Hubbards Heights (also Hubbards Fields), about ten miles above the British encampment.[20] Among Weedon's first actions in taking "Command of the cooperating Army on the North Side of York River" was to send Major Hunter, "a Volunteer Aide de Camp," to the "allied Fleet" to determine De Grasse's "pleasure" concerning "movements" for Weedon to make.[21] When approached by local citizens to grant flags of truce in order to get Negroes and other property back from the British, Weedon refused on grounds that these were matters for the Virginia government.[22]

---

[17] Richard Young to Mr. Dickinson, 10 September, 1781, Richard Young Papers, VSL.

[18] Preeson Bowdoin to James Hunter, Jr., 15 September, 1781, James Hunter Papers, UVL; Washington to Weedon or Alexander Spotswood, 10 September, 1781, Fitzpatrick, 1931-: 23: pp. 110-111 and 113n.; MacMaster, 1971: p. 417.

[19] "Breedon, Enoch," in McAllister, 1913: p. 169.

[20] Weedon to Washington, 18 September, 1781, Washington Papers, Series 4, Reel 81, LC.

[21] Weedon to His Excellency The Count de Grasse or the Commander in Chief of his Most Christian Majestys Fleet, 15 September, 1781, WL, BUL.

[22] There were a number of complications involved. See Weedon to Officer of the Flag at Urbanna, 15 September, 1781, ibid.; Weedon to Ralph Wormeley, 17 September, 1781, Ralph Wormeley to Weedon, 17 September, 1781, and Warner Lewis to Weedon, 20 September, 1781, AKF; Ralph Wormeley, Jr. to Weedon, 21 September, 1781; Gov. Nelson to Col. Innes, 18 September, 1781 and Robert Andrews to Weedon, 26 September, 1781, McIlwaine, 1929: 3: pp. 55-56 and 68; Lt. Col. John Taylor to Lafayette, 5 September, 1781, Petition (7 persons, including Ralph Wormeley and Ralph Wormeley, Jr.), 8 September, 1781, and Gov. Nelson to Ralph Wormeley, Jr., 14 September, 1781, Palmer 1875-: 2: pp. 343-344, 404-405, and 421, resp.

Of 2,000 militia expected to come to Weedon's camp, eventually about 1,500 did, with no more than 1,200 present at a given time. Governor Nelson, himself in the field at Williamsburg and hence the overall commander of the militia, asked Weedon to continue Colonel Innes in command of the "brigade" of several hundred militia that Innes had already brought into the area.[23] General Weedon complained of the slowness of militia coming into camp, to which Governor Nelson pointed out that the "Gloucester Army" was to receive only militia from north of the Pamunkey River, with the exception of those from King and Queen County. But he assured Weedon, "I shall take care that your Force be made so respectable, as to enable you to awe the Enemy on your Side & to act an offensive Part."[24] Nelson insisted that Weedon send him reports on the militia—numbers, where they came from, equipment, and other information.[25] Weedon contacted various local county provisions commissioners asking for supplies. Governor Nelson gave him impressment authority in King and Queen and Middlesex Counties.[26]

One of Washington's first orders at Williamsburg was to instruct Weedon to enlarge the "magazine of Grain" on the Gloucester side and to make all commanding officers responsible for "waste" and "destruction" of arms and ammunition. He also requested that Weedon put a stop to Simcoe's foraging parties that had ranged ten to twelve miles from the British post.[27] Weedon replied on the eighteenth that he was honored to hear from Washington, and he offered his "warmest congratulations to your Excellency on your safe returning once more to your own Country." Most of the stored grain had already been seized by the enemy. Weedon accounted for his disposition of troops. "My greatest apprehensions," he said, "are the Enemies throwing up a Body by water which may Land in our Rear, but every

---

[23] Thomas Nelson to Weedon, 17 September, 1781, AKF.

[24] Gov. Nelson to Weedon, 19 September, 1781, Palmer, 1875-: 2: p. 462.

[25] Richard Clough Anderson to Weedon, 23 September, 1781, AKF.

[26] Nelson to Weedon, 24 and 27 September, 1781, AKF; Weedon to Mr. Tunning, Commissioner of Middlesex County, 14 September, 1781, Weedon to Commissioner, Accomack and Northampton Counties, 14 September, 1781, and Weedon to Thomas Nelson, 27 September, 1781, WL, BUL. Weedon issued an impressment warrant for King and Queen County. (Weedon to ---, 27 September, 1781, Hill Family Papers, Charles Ryland Collection, xerox, VSL.)

[27] Washington to Weedon, 15 September, 1781, AKF.

precaution & care shall be taken to gain Intelligence of their movements."[28]

This letter was delivered to Lafayette, who was acting commander in chief while Washington and Rochambeau were away conferring with De Grasse. Replying on September 19, Lafayette said: "I will not add any thing on a subject you appear to have at heart, the restraining the enemy within bounds, or confining them as near as possible to their lines."[29]

As Weedon had experienced so often before, it was not an easy task to organize and to make proper disposition of the militia. Finding the militia so "totally deranged and badly Supplied with Arms & Ammunition," Weedon made his "first Object" to assemble regiments, battalions, and companies and to form a "Partizan Legion" of four hundred men under Lieutenant Colonel John Webb. On the seventeenth Weedon sent Webb and his men down to Ware Church and the court house, six miles below Weedon's camp and four miles from the enemy's lines. He also ordered Colonel John Page with four hundred men to Poplar Springs Church to support Webb, to "protect" the inhabitants, and to guard against British foraging parties. Both Webb and Page were to secure their right flanks and maintain communication with each other.[30]

Weedon's hands were tied, however. Not only was he without artillery and sufficient arms and ammunition, but also he saw the number of his militia dwindle. On the eighteenth, he had to discharge militia from the counties of Fluvanna, Goochland, Henrico, Chesterfield, King and Queen, and Louisa because their tours of duty had expired.[31] Weedon complained to Governor Nelson. On September 24, Nelson wrote Weedon that he was "sorry to hear that your force is still so inconsiderable. I shall take care that you be properly reinforced."[32] Two days later, the governor ordered four to five hundred Loudoun militia on their way to Williamsburg to join Weedon's army.[33]

[28] Weedon to Washington, 18 September, 1781, Washington Papers, Series 4, Reel 81, LC.

[29] Lafayette to Weedon, 19 September, 1781, L. W. Smith Collection, Morristown National Hist. Park, micro., VSL.

[30] Weedon to Col. John Page, 17 September, 1781 and Weedon to Col. Webb, Commanding the Partizan Legion, n.d. [ca. 15 September, 1781], WL, BUL.

[31] Weedon to Gov. Nelson, 18 September, 1781, ibid.

[32] Thomas Nelson to Weedon, 24 September, 1781, AKF.

[33] Robert Andrews to Weedon, 26 September, 1781, McIlwaine, 1929: 3: p. 68.

News from Washington, on September 20 after he had returned to Williamsburg, aroused mixed feelings in Weedon. The commander in chief had persuaded Rochambeau to send the Duc de Lauzun's legion of infantry and cavalry to join "the Troops under your Command in Gloucester County, to aid in restraining the Enemy, and preventing their Collection of Provisions and Stores from the Country. This Service, if you are the Seniour Officer, you will endeavour to perform, with all your Diligence, without precipitating your Troops into too great Danger." Lauzun "is an Officer of Rank and long Standing in the Service of his Most Christian Majesty, a Brigadier General in the Army now under Command of the Count de Rochambeau," and, therefore, "you will be pleased to show him all that Respect and Attention, that his Rank and Services justly demand." In reference to Weedon's letter of the eighteenth, Washington added: "I am very sensible of your Attention, and am sorry for the Embarrassments you meet with. I hope they will soon be removed."[34]

Washington's instructions to Weedon implied that both brigadier generals, Weedon and Lauzun, would act in conjunction, with neither commanding the other. It is interesting to note, however, that Rochambeau, in his *Memoirs*, said that he sent Lauzun's Legion "to take up a position on the road to Glocester, and place itself at the disposition of Brigadier-General Voueden [Weedon]."[35]

Relations between Weedon and Lauzun would be strained even before the two men met. Some of the Duke's cavalry, before being sent to Gloucester, had stopped at West Point, at the forks of the York River, and apparently had engaged in some pilfering of the countryside. George Weedon lost no time in calling to the attention of Lauzun the misconduct of his men. "The repeated complaints made by the Inhabitants of Depredations committed on their property," wrote Weedon,

> by the French Troops induces me my dear Sir to request your Interposition in stoping a measure which adds Distress, to the Distressed, and may be the means of discontent among the Citizens who we no doubt should protect & defend. I am sure those things have never reached your Ears, but believe me the

---

[34] Washington to Weedon, 20 September, 1781, Fitzpatrick, 1931-: **23**: pp. 126-127 and 130.

[35] Wright, 1838: p. 66.

Sufferings of the peaceable, and well disposed Country men are great, and alarming. And I do not see how it is to be prevented, but by a total stop being put to the Troops rambling out of Camp.[36]

Weedon's letter undoubtedly offended the surly Frenchman, and may have been one reason for the contempt that Lauzun would have for the American militia commander.

On the surface, at first, both men gave appearances of good will. Lauzun told Washington that if General Weedon were placed under his orders, "I should certainly make him obey;" but he had "not the least objection to serve under him" if Washington thought this best, and Washington could "depend on my maintaining the most friendly relations with him."[37] A day before Lauzun arrived to join the militia force at Gloucester, Weedon wrote Washington: "I shall pay the most pointed attention to this distinguished Character & shall embrace every opportunity of improving his advice so far as relates to the Service on this Side."[38]

Hearing that the enemy "intended a grand Forage," Weedon sent Webb's detachment before dawn of September 22 to a position near Abdington Church, "covering all the Roads leading from Gloster Town." Weedon himself led "three small Battalions" to Ware Church as support. As he reported to Washington,

Our patrols of Horse were below the Mile Stone. We remained till near 12 OClock. Whether the Enemy got Intelligence of our being out, or whether my Information was not so perfect will not undertake to say. They however eluded us by coming half a Mile up the Road from Town & turning down on the Right Hand headed for Sarys [Sarah's] Creek about 2 miles from Town and made a small Forage in little Guinea, a Circumstance not known to us till after our Return. The Garrison at Gloster are I understand exceedingly Sickly. They act very cautious when they came out generally a day previous to their moving. They give out among the Inhabitants their design of foraging a different part of the Country to what they really go

---

[36] Weedon to the Duke de Lauzun, 20 September, 1781, WL, BUL; Sturgill, 1970: p. 59.

[37] "Narrative . . . Lauzun," in Stevens, 1881: p. 52.

[38] Weedon to Washington, 26 September, 1781, Washington Papers, Series 4, Reel 81, LC.

to. My weak Situation has obliged me to lay further down them than I could have wished. This Militia Service is perplexing. One third of the Men that I found in this Quarter when I took the Command have Since been discharged, & no reinforcement joined. I shall however attempt another Forage tomorrow. Our Appearing in the lower country frequently has had the good effect of Keeping the Enemy from coming far abroad.[39]

Just before noon, September 24, Count D'Arat with Lauzun's cavalry arrived at Weedon's camp. Weedon sent his aide de camp, Major Hunter, "in search of the Infantry of the Dukes Corps," but Hunter returned a day later "without being able to gain any Intelligence of them." With the cavalry reinforcement, Weedon announced to Washington that he planned to take a position on September 25, at Dixon's Mills, close to the enemy lines.[40] But, after having the area further reconnoitered and finding "a Neck on Tongue of Land accesable almost in every part by Water intersected by roads leading to every point," Weedon, with the unanimous consent of the field officers, decided against the move until the army was stronger and Lauzun's infantry should arrive. He also thought it best to await knowledge of the movements of Washington's army, which was about to invest Yorktown. Weedon apologized to the commander in chief for misleading him as to his plans: "I am sorry I gave your Excellency reason to believe we had advanced which certainly would have been the case, but for the above causes which did not so forcable weigh with me at first." He expected in a day or two to advance; in the meantime, being about four miles from the enemy lines, he reported, "we shall dispute with them for our Share" of forage.[41]

Lauzun came in at the head of his infantry on September 27. Officially Weedon wrote Washington: "I am . . . exceedingly happy in the society and Support of the Duke de Lauzun and his corps, a perfect Harmony Subsists and shall make it my Study to improve it."[42] But actually the two men had an instant dislike for each other. Lauzun viewed Weedon as a boorish leader of a peasant army, while Weedon considered the dandyish aristocrat, who had obtained rank by purchase and infuence at the French royal court, as nothing more than

---

[39] Weedon to Washington, 23 September, 1781, *ibid*.

[40] Weedon to Washington, 25 September, 1781, *ibid*.

[41] Weedon to Washington, 26 September, 1781, *ibid*.

[42] Weedon to Washington, 29 September, 1781, *ibid*.

a snob. Although attracted to military professionalism, Weedon believed in an army founded on democratic principles. Let the French Army stay on the Yorktown side. Weedon and his Virginians could do the job required at Gloucester. Send more militia, not foreigners. This was to be Weedon's last chance for glory, and he knew it; understandably he did not want to share it with an interloper. Yet he would do his duty.

In all, the French Legion amounted to about three hundred cavalry and three hundred infantry. Weedon accompanied Lauzun and his officers to reconnoiter the ground between Dixon's and Burwell's Mills. Weedon convinced Lauzun that it was too "hazardous" to move up to the Gloucester lines for the time being. On the twenty-seventh, Weedon reported an "Operating Strength" of 1,134 militia. Innes commanded "the Advanced Brigade" of three battalions of infantry and one of "Granidears." Webb was now at the head of a fifty man "Corps of Horse"; the rest of Weedon's force consisted of two regiments, one each commanded by Colonels Page and Griffin.[43]

Washington moved his army down to lay siege of Yorktown on September 28. Before he left Williamsburg, however, he had Rochambeau send the Marquis De Choisy to De Grasse to request a detachment of marines to reinforce Lauzun. De Grasse gave General De Choisy 800 marines. Washington wrote Weedon on the twenty-seventh, notifying him of the reinforcement and of a general senior to Lauzun accompanying them.[44] Weedon replied that he would be glad to serve under any senior general that Washington might appoint. Sending Major General De Choisy to Gloucester was the best way to insure against any dispute between the two brigadier generals, Weedon and Lauzun, from getting out of hand.

On September 28 Weedon and Lauzun went with a foraging party to Abdington Church for oats and barley belonging to Colonel Warner Lewis "by the owner's desire." Providing cover, three battalions of militia infantry, one hundred of Lauzun's cavalry, and thirty militia dragoons advanced southward to Seawell's Ordinary. While the wagons were loading, Weedon and Lauzun rode to within one mile of the

---

[43] Weedon to Nelson, 27 September, 1781, AKF; 27 September, 1781, Bourg, 1880: p. 445; Hutchinson and Rachal, 1963: 3: p. 253n.

[44] Washington to Weedon, 27 September, 1781, AKF; Washington to de Grasse, 27 September, 1781, Fitzpatrick, 1931-: 23: p. 144; Sturgill, 1970: p. 53.

British post. The enemy also had come out with a foraging party; they fired "a few pieces" and "went home with only a small quantity of corn . . . not chusing to Venture a single yard after Mr. Simcoe reconnoitred us with his Glass who swore to his people, 'our Rifle men ware as thick as the stalks in the Corn Field.'" Weedon observed that he saw no one at work on fortifications at Gloucester and that British deserters whom he picked up said that nothing had been done for "some days."

In making his report, on the twenty-ninth, to Washington, General Weedon said he wanted "to push on a regular Approach against Gloster," but he had "not a single Entrenching Tool of any sort nor do I believe it possible to get any in this Country." He felt, however, a siege might not be necessary, "for am well Assured when your Approaches commence, the post at Gloster will either be Evacuated, or a rapid push made by all the British Horse to punctuate thro this country, turn your left and throw themselves into North Carolina. This would be Hazardous, but what will they not attempt in their present Situation."[45]

General Choisy and the marines arrived on October 1. Weedon was informed by Washington several days later that "As Genl Choisey is an Officer immediately under the command of the Count Rochambeau, my Orders in future will pass thro' the Count."[46] The allied forces before Gloucester now consisted of nearly 3,000 troops (Lauzun's Legion of 600; French marines, 800; and 1,200–1,500 militia under Weedon). With this build-up on the north side of the York, Cornwallis sent Tarleton, in the evening of October 2, over to Gloucester Point with one thousand "legion cavalry and mounted infantry."[47]

Washington several times advised Weedon that Cornwallis might try to escape across the York. Weedon kept Washington posted on the defensive measures he had taken, and the commander in chief commended Weedon for his diligence.[48] Weedon's emphasis on caution was in direct accordance to Washington's orders, as Douglas S. Freeman has pointed out.[49]

[45] Weedon to Washington, 29 September, 1781, Washington Papers, Series 4, Reel 81, LC.

[46] Washington to Weedon, 3 October, 1781, Fitzpatrick, 1931-: **23**: p. 169; Acomb, 1958: p. 142.

[47] Tarleton, 1787: p. 376; Hatch, 1940: p. 273.

[48] Washington to Weedon, 30 September, 1781, Fitzpatrick, 1931-: **23**: pp. 155-156.

[49] Freeman, 1949-: **5**: p. 342.

"To make our Co-operation as defensive as possible," Weedon informed Washington, he had Innes's brigade and Webb's horse "with the polite approbation of the Duke annexed to his Legion"; the rest of the militia either made up the left wing of Choisy's force or were "in camp in a Line . . . under my Command." With the enemy from boats plundering twenty miles "in our rear," Weedon detached a band of militia "to protect & cover the Country, & if possible strike them."[50]

Choisy decided to move the allied troops closer to Gloucester. On the morning of October 3, he led the marines, legion, and some militia down Severn Road towards Gloucester Point. The militia grenadiers under Colonel John Mercer went by way of the York River Road. The two parts of the army united where the two roads came together to form a long lane, with an open plain on the right and woods on the left. At daybreak of the same day, Lieutenant Colonel Dundas took out most of the British garrison down the Gloucester Road on "a grand forage." Tarleton led the covering party of four hundred horse and two hundred infantry.[51]

At Ware Church, Weedon planned to bring up the remainder of the militia, but was delayed because of a shortage of wagons. Lauzun sent a note to Weedon on the day of the advance: "I will be much obliged to you Dear General to inform me what time you intend to march yourself. I will be happy if we would have some things to do with Tarleton and Simcoe. I wish very much to make farther acquaintance with those Gentlemen. I intend to command myself the legion."[52] Weedon planned to join the left wing of the advanced force the next morning, using wagons that would have been returned from "the first division." One worry that he also had was that the Loudoun militia, who arrived on the second, were "not more than half Armed."[53]

Three miles from the Gloucester post, the British foraging party loaded wagons and "bat-horses" with Indian corn. At 10 a.m. they headed back to the garrison. Part of the covering body entered one end of the lane at the same time the allies appeared at the other end. Tarleton took his force into the woods and advanced; Lauzun's hussars charged down the

[50] Weedon to Washington, 3 October, 1781, Washington Papers, Series 4, Reel 81, LC.

[51] Wright, 1838: p. 68.

[52] Lauzun to Weedon, 3 October, 1781, AKF.

[53] Weedon to Nelson, 3 October, 1781, WL, BUL. Weedon referred to Innes's troops as "Innis's Bloody Advance."

lane. Tarleton came over to open ground and a hot skirmish ensued. Lauzun and Tarleton were about to engage in hand-to-hand combat, when Tarleton's horse careened and over-threw its rider. Getting upon a strange horse, Tarleton again led an advance. This time he was met by Mercer's grenadiers, mostly old veterans, who put up a steady fire. Lauzun re-formed his Legion in Mercer's rear. Unable to break through the allied line, the British withdrew to their garrison. During the encounter, fifty British soldiers were killed or wounded; of the allies, three killed and eleven wounded (including three officers). After the British retreat, the allied army made camp on the field of the skirmish, one-and-one-half miles from the Gloucester post.[54] For several nights thereafter patrols met and exchanged fire.[55]

Weedon, in his report to Washington, praised the "Gallant conduct of that distinguished Officer," Lauzun, who with Mercer "totally routed the Enemy."[56] Washington wrote Weedon that he was very pleased at "the Advantage obtained over the Enemy as it gives a noble Instance of that Bravery & Ardor in Spirit in the Allied Troops,"[57] and in his general orders commended Lauzun's legion and Mercer's grenadiers.

Not as gracious as Weedon, Lauzun complained virulently that he had not had Weedon's cooperation at any time.

> I joined General Wiedon's corps with my regiment. He blockaded Gloucester in a drole way; he was more than fifteen miles from the enemy's posts, frightened to death, and did not dare to send a patrol half a mile from his army. He was the best man alive and all that he desired was to take no responsibility. I proposed to him to approach Gloucester and to make next morning a reconnoisance near to the English posts; he consented and we went out with fifty huzzars. When we were within seven or eight miles of the enemy he said to me that it was useless to go any further and we should see nothing more; I so urged him that he could not refuse to follow me. I drove in the enemy's posts and went far enough to obtain a precise idea of their position. My General was in despair; he told me that he would not go with me again; as he had no desire to be killed.[58]

---

[54] Comte de Choisy to Weedon, 3 October, 1781, *Correspondence*, Senate Document, 1931: p. 73; Green, 1868: pp. 137-138; Balch, 1876: p. 145; Bass, 1957: p. 184; Tarleton, 1787: pp. 387-389; Hatch, 1940: pp. 275-277; Johnston, 1881: pp.128-129.

[55] 4 October, 1781, Bourg, 1880: p. 446.

[56] Weedon to Washington, 3 October, 1781, Washington Papers, Series 4, Reel 81, LC.

[57] Washington to Weedon 4 October, 1781, Fitzpatrick, 1931-: **23**: pp. 173-174.

[58] "Narrative of Lauzun," in Stevens, 1881: pp. 52-53.

Lauzun also called Weedon "a coward and a sloth."[59] Lauzun was as contemptuous of the Virginia militia:

> I reported to M. de Rochambeau what I had seen; I informed him that no reliance could be placed on the American militia and that it was indispensable that he should send me at least two more battalions of French infantry . . . [Choisy] began by ridding himself of General Wiedon and the entire militia, telling them they were all cowards, and in five minutes they were almost as much afraid of him as of the English, which is certainly a great deal to say. The next day he wished to occupy the camp I had reconnoitered. General Wiedon preferred to move a day later and remained behind with about six hundred men of his division.
> Just as we reached the Gloucester plain some Virginia State Dragoons came up in great fright and told us that they had seen the English dragoons out and that for fear of accident they had hurried to us at full speed without stopping to see anything more.

Lauzun seems to have had a habit of maligning fellow commanding officers. Of his immediate superior, he said, "M. de Choisy is an excellent and worthy man, absurdly violent in temper, constantly in a rage, quarrelling with everybody, and without common sense."[60]

The charges against Weedon by Lauzun were entirely unjustified. He was ignorant of Washington's directions to Weedon, the problems faced by Weedon, and the measures that Weedon had already taken. Weedon had to keep in mind the overall situation, including the British raids at his rear. Without wagons and with many of his men unarmed, a delay by one day in advancing his men was not a mistake.

For the next two weeks, as Washington tightened the vise at Yorktown, George Weedon had various concerns. He sought arms and medical supplies from Governor Nelson.[61] The governor was able to get two hundred fifty of the four hundred stand of arms that Weedon needed, but he did not know "what can be done for you in a medical Way." Nelson requested that Weedon countersign all vouchers presented by French officers for supplies.[62] Three King William companies were

[59] Quoted in Hughes, 1926-1930: 3: p. 661.

[60] "Narrative of Lauzun," in Stevens, 1881: pp. 52-53. Lauzun went on to become commandant of Corsica and a general of the French Army. Falling out with the Committee of Public Safety, he was guillotined on 31 December, 1793. (Hatch, 1940: p. 272n.)

[61] Weedon to Nelson, 5 October, 1781, Palmer, 1875-: 2: p. 525.

[62] Nelson to Weedon 8 and 14 October, 1781, AKF.

discharged from Weedon's force, and the Gloucester militia went "home to remain." As a result, Weedon estimated that the whole allied force was down to two thousand men. "Indeed," he wrote Washington, "I wish your Excellency may not suppose us much Stronger than we really are."[63]

To be prepared in the event that Cornwallis tried to cross the York, Washington sent Weedon looking for boats "within his reach." This Weedon did, bringing boats from Cumberland and Frazier's ferries and putting them in a creek on the Gloucester side. Weedon also secured watermen, with the aid of impressment powers which Governor Nelson gave him.[64] George Weedon, it seemed, was again being relegated to the thankless but very important role of supervising logistics. In a letter to Washington, in which he excused himself for having to write "on an Old trunk in the pines," Weedon also noted that he and General Choisy had worked out a better system of communications with Washington's camp.[65]

Anticipating an attempt by the British to retreat across Gloucester Neck, Weedon, acting under directions from Washington, ordered the county lieutenants of the area to have axmen and groups of "Armed Men" in readiness. If Cornwallis should "force a passage thro' the Defences of this Camp, he may meet with opposition at every defile in your County by your throwing down Trees, breaking up Roads & Bridges, and exposing him wherever you can taking care to drive off all your Stock of every Kind upon the first knowledge you have of his advance."[66] General Choisy, thinking of siege operations, ordered Weedon to "use every means in your power to obtain by Empress or otherwise" axes, picks, shovels, and other entrenching tools.[67] Weedon undoubtedly still thought that a real siege was unnecessary, as the British would either surrender or attempt to escape. On the twelfth, he wrote Richard Henry Lee: "They keep a pretty strong Garrison at

[63] Weedon to Washington, 13 October, 1781, Washington Papers, Series 4, Reel 81, LC; Jonathan Trumbull ["from Gen. Washington"] to Weedon, 8 October, 1781, AKF; Washington to Comte de Grasse, 16 October, 1781, Fitzpatrick, 1931-: **23**: p. 225; McAllister, 1913: p. 169.

[64] Weedon to Washington, 13 October, 1781, Washington Papers, Series 4, Reel 81, LC; Nelson to Weedon, 14 October, 1781, AKF.

[65] Weedon to Washington, 8 October, 1781, Washington Papers, Series 4, Reel 81, LC.

[66] Circular Letter to the County Lieutenants, 12 October, 1781, WL, BUL.

[67] Claude Gabriel de Choisy to Weedon, 7 October, 1781, AKF.

Gloster Town. We however Answar every purpose by keeping them compleatly Circumscribed, as they must share the fate of their Master."[68]

On October 10, the British landed eighteen flat boats with troops on the Gloucester side and were met by fire from Choisy's artillery. On the sixteenth, Cornwallis made the long-expected effort to escape by way of Gloucester. A "principal part" of his troops were sent over, but a "violent storm" prevented the rest from crossing; and the first division returned to the York side. The next day Weedon learned in a dispatch from Jonathan Trumbull, Washington's aide, that Cornwallis called for a twenty-four-hour truce and that representatives from both sides were meeting at the Moore House, outside of Yorktown, to discuss "a Cessation of Hostilities."[69]

The negotiations resulted in surrender. At 1 p.m. on October 19, one hour before the capitulation at Yorktown began, two of the Gloucester redoubts were delivered, one each to the French and Americans. At 3 p.m., to the sounds of trumpets and drums playing "a british or German march," the Gloucester garrison—the British infantry with shouldered arms and cavalry with swords drawn—marched between two columns of the allied army. The vanquished soldiers laid down their arms in stacks, were received by General Choisy at the end of the line, and were paraded back to the post. Because Tarleton feared his own "Tarleton's quarter" from Virginia militiamen, with long memories of the slaughter at the Waxhaws, Choisy allowed only Colonel Mercer's grenadiers to participate with the French troops at this stage of the surrender.[70]

Washington had asked Choisy to inform Weedon of the arrangements of the surrender. With his own militia excluded from the surrender ceremony, it is likely that General Weedon absented himself from this dramatic occasion. In the hour of victory, so George Weedon must have felt, it was as if the French, as cowbirds, had snatched the glory for themselves.

---

[68] Weedon to Richard Henry Lee, 12 October, 1781, Lee Family Papers, micro., VSL.

[69] Jonathan Trumbull to Weedon, 17 October, 1781, AKF; Simcoe, 1844: pp. 252-253; Hatch, 1940: pp. 278-279.

[70] Washington to Choisy, 19 October, 1781, Washington Papers, Series 4, Reel 81, LC; Bass, 1957: p. 4; Hatch, 1940: p. 282. According to a French officer, 1850 (including 750 sailors) were surrendered at Gloucester. (Gallatin, 1931: p. 27).

Fig. 9.   General Banastre Tarleton. Line etching from the painting by Sir Joshua Reynolds, pub. H. P. Johnson, *The Yorktown Campaign and the Surrender of Cornwallis, 1781*. With permission of Virginia State Library.

To George Weedon, who thought the war had already lasted far too long, the victory at Yorktown and Gloucester left no doubt that it would soon be over. Before returning to civilian life, General Weedon, in accordance with orders from Washington, Choisy, and Governor Nelson, took charge of all British prisoners and equipment on the Gloucester side until proper disposition could be made.[71] Refugees were to be paroled, except for "notorious offenders." Governor Nelson asked Weedon to "oblige the least atrocious offenders to appear before the Governor & Council" at Richmond on November 20 and "then set them at Liberty."[72]

Prisoners of war from Gloucester were to be marched to Fredericksburg, where they would be joined by those from Yorktown and placed under the charge of General Robert Lawson. From Fredericksburg, the prisoners would be sent to Winchester, Virginia, Frederick, Maryland, and Carlisle, Pennsylvania.[73] On October 21, Weedon sent off all the Gloucester prisoners able to march, conducted by Colonel West's regiment from Fairfax County; thirteen hundred sick and wounded, including those from Yorktown, were left behind in Gloucester.[74]

Weedon spent a few more days at Gloucester and then went to Richmond. On October 31, he was at the capital making arrangements for the collection of a "Fleet of Flat bottom Boats" at Hood's Point on the James.[75]

Meanwhile Washington had come to an understanding with Governor Nelson that the "British sick, left in Gloucester" should be sent to Fredericksburg. On November 3, under guard of a New York regiment commanded by Colonel Phillip Van Cortlandt, 467 "Convalescent British prisoners" started out for Fredericksburg. Having returned to Fredericksburg himself, Weedon wondered where the invalid prisoners

[71] Washington to Choisy, 20 and 22 October, 1781, Choisy to Washington, 20 and 22 October, 1781, and Weedon to Washington, 21 October, 1781, Washington Papers, Series 4, Reel 81, LC; Arthur St. Clair to Weedon, 21 October, 1781, AKF; Washington to Weedon, 20 October, 1781, Fitzpatrick, 1931-: **23**: p. 251; Nelson to Weedon, 21 October, 1781, McIlwaine, 1929: **3**: p. 90.

[72] Nelson to Weedon, 21 October, 1781, McIlwaine, 1929: **3**: p. 90.

[73] Nelson to Weedon, 20 October, 1781 and Arthur St. Clair to Weedon, 21 October, 1781, AKF; MacMaster, 1971: p. 423.

[74] Weedon to Washington, 21 October, 1781, Washington Papers, Series 4, Reel 81, LC; Washington to Nelson, 3 November, 1781, Fitzpatrick, 1931-: **23**: p. 305; Weedon to Nelson, 20 October, 1781 and Nelson to the Commandant at Fredericksburg, 21 October, 1781, Palmer, 1875-: **2**: pp. 560 and 564, resp.

[75] Weedon to Thomas Russel, 31 October, 1781, WL, BUL.

of war could be put up. He wrote the governor that there were no unoccupied houses and the old barracks were now "totally Demolished;" hence it would be utterly impossible to Accomodate them here." The local quartermaster had no authority to provide wood and straw, and there was no money to purchase any thing.[76]

Fortunately, neither the main body of prisoners of war or the invalids paused very long at Fredericksburg, although a few of the sick were left for awhile in the so-called hospital there.[77] In any event, Weedon was exasperated over the whole business of receiving prisoners of war. Militia guards went home immediately upon arriving in Fredericksburg, although Weedon did obtain a guard of Stafford militia to accompany some of the prisoners of war to Winchester. He pleaded to Governor Nelson and Commissioner Davies to grant provisions,[78] but otherwise Weedon had the good sense to refuse taking any further responsibility for the prisoners coming in and out of Fredericksburg.

At last, with the enemy cleared out of Virginia and the war definitely winding down elsewhere, George Weedon could relax with family and friends. It had been a busy and frustrating year. Making preparations for defense of the Northern Neck and Fredericksburg during the three British invasions, collecting and supervising militia and supplies, twice serving in the field as the commander of Virginia militia first at Williamsburg and then at Gloucester, and performing a host of other administrative tasks, Weedon was exhausted. Except for a brief sickness, he had enjoyed good health, although occasionally there were the warning pains of encroaching gout. Probably no one worked harder or sacrificed as much as he did in the defense of Virginia. If there was not the glory that he often spoke of and which always seemed to elude him, there was a heroism of sorts. He had the full respect of his countrymen, and the old animosities from his brother officers subsided. He had given full measure to his country.

[76] Weedon to Nelson, 7 November, 1781, Dreer Collection, HSP; Robert Andrews to Weedon, 6 November, 1781, McIlwaine, 1929: 3: p. 95; Washington to Gov. Nelson, 3 November, 1781, Fitzpatrick, 1931-: 23: p. 324.

[77] Memorial of Charles Mortimer to Congress, 2 February, 1783 and Accounts Continental Hospital in Fredericksburg, 10 February, 1783, Memorials Addressed to Congress, PCC, NA.

[78] Weedon to Young . . . vouchers, 12 and 14 December, 1781, Richard Young Papers, VSL; Weedon to Davies, 22 December, 1781, Gratz Collection, HSP. For disproving the persistent legend that there was a grand peace ball in Fredericksburg, with Washington attending, shortly after Yorktown, see Matteson, 1941: pp. 152-156.

XIII. A VETERAN AT HEART
(1782-1786)

It was refreshing not to have the cares of war. Although George Weedon was realistic enough to recognize that further military "exertion" might be needed, otherwise the enemy might "recover and fatal consequences may follow," he did not fully expect to return to the army, even though this was a possibility as he intended to keep his commission until the war's definite end. Weedon believed that Americans should still pay attention to national security, and hence he did not approve of Congress's reducing the army to "Twenty odd Regiments" after Yorktown. Nevertheless, with a reduction in the army and a standstill, even in the Southern theater, in all likelihood Weedon had come home to stay.

Weedon found everyone in Fredericksburg congenial, and he was happy that prosperity was returning. Trade began "to raise its Drooping Head once more," he noticed, and there was a "small Jingle of the Harde stuff."[1] Weedon would become active in community life, and, as he discovered, there were many loose ends to attend to relating to military matters.

It was a delightful time for the Weedons when in mid-February, 1782, Catherine (Kitty) Greene stayed with them during a stopover on her trip to join her husband in South Carolina. After Mrs. Greene finally arrived at Greene's headquarters, the commander of the Southern army good-humoredly took Weedon to task for having detained his wife. "Pray how come you to use compulsion and detain Mrs. Greene with you near a week?" queried Greene. "It is well for you my power of punishing is not equal to my will. Perhaps if it was, you might be sent to the promontory of Moses: and from thence to Thrashing noses." But

> as Mrs. Greene arrived in much better health and spirits than I expected I take upon me the power of the Pope and grant you a pardon . . . . She says you was very polite to her but this was to be expected from a Gentleman who had been serving a

---

[1] Weedon to Greene, 12 December, 1781, Greene Papers, CL.

Campaign with the French Army. Have you learnt to bow properly? I have been so long in the Woods & Mrs. Greene says that I have the graces to study anew . . . you see after all my labours I am under petticoat Government still.[2]

Mrs. Greene herself wrote Weedon that she wished "to return again to the country of rosy cheeks, and to throw off the yellow masks, for every body wears one here . . . . Remember, I engage you for a partner to dance with on my return which must be next spring."[3]

To Greene's letter of April 22, Weedon replied in June. Referring to Greene's comment on Mrs. Greene being detained by the Weedons on her way south, Weedon pointed out that "her short stay in Fredericksburg only served to interest a small Circle of Acquantances in her future happiness, rest her Horses, and shew her patriotism by joining in Celebrating the Birth Night of our Christ [Washington]." Again noting Greene's contentiousness over Mrs. Greene's visiting in Fredericksburg, Weedon said,

> for this my Nose is to be Exposed to a Bandy legged Drummer, a Trumpetters wife &c. My Politeness has been so talked of lately by Burnet and others that I begin to think myself the Punch of the Army, heavens knows where it came from. If empty Pockets, Constitutes and Quakifies a man for the Business, I am at present, and have been for a long time perfect in Bowing, Shruging, Dancing &c. But should that misfortune come in Contact with the Chesterfieldian Ideas [Chesterfield Court House, officers' protest against Weedon, February 1781], the Graces and Your humble Servent, are total Strangers.[4]

Two letters from General Greene in late 1782 further indicate Greene's growing friendship with Weedon. The first, written October 1, several months after the evacuation of Savannah, and the second, on December 21, a week after the British pulled out of Charleston, reveal Greene in a relaxed mood. In the letter of October he mentioned that Mrs. Greene had been a month at one of the sea islands and that "she often mentions you and Mrs. Weedon with great regard and intends to have a good frolick at Fredericksburgh on our way to the Northward. Prepare accordingly."[5] In his letter of December,

[2] Greene to Weedon, 22 April, 1782, WC, APS; Thayer, 1960: p. 399.

[3] Mrs. Greene to Weedon, n.d. (1782?), Balch, 1857: p. 98.

[4] Weedon to Greene, 12 June, 1782, Greene Papers, CL; Preeson Bowdoin to James Hunter, Jr., 12 February, 1782, James Hunter Papers, UVL.

[5] Greene to Weedon, 1 October, 1782, WC, APS.

Greene wrote, "I am sorry I am not likely to have the happiness of commencing an attack upon the two gun battery of Fredericksburg. Congress has anchored me here for the winter at least. Mrs. Greene is anxious to see you, but thinks you will want more than one season to recruit, so as to hold out to accomplish a dance, if you have her for a partner." Greene had an idea for a dancing assembly. "What think you of a room eighty feet long and forty wide, with an arched roof and gallery for the music. . . . I wish you and Mrs. Weedon were with us, as we cannot be with you. But you would be obliged to promise not to fail in the middle of a dance."[6]

Peace

George Weedon eagerly kept abreast of news of peace developments. To General Gates, in February 1782, he passed on the latest intelligence. He referred to "Big George's Speech" in the English House of Commons, in which the king

> Confesses to them, that his Army in Virga has been unfortunate but holds out a desire of further Bloudshed. Master William [Prince William, who was in New York city at the time of the battle of Yorktown] has returned to England Safe, and was in Condolance with his Daddy [George III] on the Misfortune of the Noble Earl [Cornwallis], and the prospect their Affairs in General wore, in America, the West Indies and other parts of the World.[7]

Throughout the remainder of 1782 Weedon received bits of information concerning negotiations for peace. At last news of the signing of the Preliminary Articles of Peace (November 30, 1782 and dispatched to America in mid-December) reached Virginia sometime in late January, 1783. George Weedon expressed his exuberance to Greene.

> Ten thousand congratulations attend You on having compleated the Object of Your Operations with so much honor to Your self and little Army. And ten times ten Thousand to all the Gallant Continentals under Your command on the prospect of Peace. We have at last brought

---

[6] Greene to Weedon, 21 December, 1782 and Maj. Burnet to Weedon, 7 January, 1783, Balch, 1857; pp. 200-201.

[7] Weedon to Gates, 26 February 1782, AKF.

that Grimmy throat fellow *George* to acknowledge us Free and
Independent States . . . . The Terms have not yet transpired
further than Independence. It is however certain that a General
Pacification has taken place. We must therefore sing, "Oh be
joyful in the lord all ye Lands," &c . . . .
I shall have more pleasure in taking you by the hand now more
than ever . . . . As we have now Peace you can better afford Mrs
Green a pair of shoes extraordinary to celebrate the joyful
tidings in, but I beg her ladyship may not over do the matter, as
I am now in training against she Arrives in Virginia.
Praying my love to Genl Wayne & all my old Brother Soldiers.[8]

Twenty-four-year-old John Francis Mercer, who had served
as a militia colonel under Weedon at Gloucester and was now
a freshman Congressman in Philadelphia, informed Weedon
frequently on the progress of peace.[9] But there was a moment
that Weedon doubted the authenticity of a real peace. In
March, 1783, he wrote Mercer that he heard from a Mr. Tilton,
captain of a ship that sailed up the Rappahannock, that the
peace negotiations had broken off. "This Week has appeared
the longest and most tedious I can remember to have spent,"
he said. "Peace and war have Ultimately changed with the day
tho without the smallest reason from any good Authority. I
have been a strong Advocate for the former and back my
Opinion with a Bever Hatt which I fear another person will
ware." Tilton's information was that the British were holding
out for "all the Islands in the West Indies to be returned her
And Holland a full Restitution for the St. Eustatia affair."
Weedon was confident, however, that "surely another week
will clair up our doubts, one way or the other." Weedon added
revealingly that "I continue Exceedingly fat in person and
Extremely poor in purse."[10]

There was at least one unmistakable sign of British
intentions for peace, Weedon pointed out to Mercer: "One
thing . . . gives me hopes they are such as we wish, and that is,
we are scarcely one hour without private Expresses from the
Northern Merchts to their Tobacco Agents in Virga." Weedon

---

[8] Weedon to Greene, 25 February, 1783, Weedon Letters, HL.

[9] Some of Mercer's letters to Weedon are printed in Balch, 1857; pp. 203-209 and
223: 4 and 18 March, 1, 11 and 29 April, and 20 September, 1783. Also Theodorick
Bland reported to Weedon the Congressional Proclamation of Peace. (Bland to
Weedon, 11 April, 1783, *ibid.*, p. 207.) On Mercer's career at the time, see Garnet, 1907:
pp. 200-202.

[10] Weedon to John F. Mercer, 11 March, 1783, L. W. Smith Collection, Morristown
National Hist. Park, Micro., VSL.

hoped that Mercer's next letter would bring something definite. "How will it elevate me to be informed of peace," he said.[11] Although he had nothing to complain of concerning what he had heard of the Preliminary Articles of Peace, Weedon, in writing to Greene, said he did not like the use of the word "Provincial" in the articles. Weedon still thought there was value in "an Old saying" that was "worthy of Attention in these days of uncertainty"—"fore warned, fore Armed." But "upon the whole," Weedon had "little fears of a General end to Our Warfare troubles in America."

Weedon added a personal note to Greene:

> You tell me Mrs Green is unwell and low Spirited. I am sorry from my soul to hear it. If she has lost her Spirits it is low with her indeed. Had You recd My last letter, covering one to her, I could in some measure Accounted for it. In that I have Accepted her Challange to dance down 40 Couples as her partner, on her way Northwardly, And unguardedly told her of the Great improvement I had made in that Science, and that upon a Certain Occation (which Originated in the South) I had sent off four *Bell Hoops* in one Evening, wadling like lame Ducks. I wish she was with us, We would Nurse, and laugh her well in a few days or I am Mistaken. Tell me do You mean to Pitch Your Tent in the South or not? I think You are in some measure Contracted for, in the Most Honorable way. If the Climate agrees with You, and Mrs. Green, You ought to reside among your reclaimed Friends who have so Generously afforded proofs of their Attachment. This however Your Constitution must decide.[12]

In a few days Weedon heard from both Mercer and Bland of the signing of treaties between England and France and England and Spain (January 20).[13] Congress's proclamation for the cessation of hostilities on April 11 was immediately transmitted to Weedon. Referring to the Congressional proclamation, Weedon wrote Mercer that "this looks like what we Military men call a Coup-de-Grace or finishing stroak to the War and happy I am it has terminated so favourable to America." In commenting on the loyalists, Weedon said they were the

---

[11] Weedon to John F. Mercer, 18 March, 1783, Gratz Collection, HSP.

[12] Weedon to Greene, 28 March, 1781, Greene Papers, CL; In the postscript: "Kitty [Mrs. Weedon] joins me in our love to Mrs. Greene and often wishes to be with her."

[13] John F. Mercer to Weedon, 24 March, 1783 and Theodorick Bland, Jr. to Weedon, 25 March, 1783, WC, APS.

cause of much Altercation in the House of commons, but I Observe some of the principle Speakers think as we do, that Congress may recommend restitution, but unless we are also restored, our Negroes, Plate, Town Houses & &c or an adequate compensation for them, the different legislators will scarcely be so much influenced by the recommendation [in the Treaty] as to return confiscated property to those kind of Cattle.

A great celebration of the peace was to be held the next day, April 23, in Fredericksburg. At twelve noon there was to be "a grand Salute" to the "Sovereign States in Congress"; the firing was to take place under "a display of the 13 Stripes, riged to a 40 foot Pole on the Top of the Market House," followed by a "public" dinner and a toast "proper on the Occation, with 13 rounds to each." In the evening there was to be "a general illumination, and on Friday Evening a Brilliant Assembly." Weedon boasted that there was not a Tory in Fredericksburg: "A Stick dose not rise to a Horizontal line." As

for my own part I am so transplanted with an honorable end being put to our Warfar troubles, and a full Attainment of the Object for which they ware commenced, that I Anticipate with joy the flow of plenty which must soon follow. And as Your Brother James's song says, "forgeting all wrong in a cup & a song," &c that I sit down with contentment, without a Dollar in my pocket, waiting a more plentiful Circulation. N. B. All Friends well and as gay as larks. No Deaths except Old Hopson who has been long troubled with a whiskey fever.[14]

Weedon's mood and feelings about the times is seen in a letter he wrote James Hunter, Jr. in July—a reply to Hunter's of a month before. Hunter, younger cousin of James Hunter, Sr., who ran the iron works, had come to Fredericksburg from Philadelphia in 1774, and was a good friend of the Weedons. He had made a considerable profit in trade with the West Indies during the war, and, now in Norfolk, was about broadening his shipping interests, which would later take him to England as a leading trade promoter. An excerpt from Weedon's letter also indicates the relationship between the two men.

---

[14] Weedon to John F. Mercer, 22 April, 1783, Etting Collection, Revolutionary War Papers, HSP.

Your movements are so rappad and Sudden that it would take
an Argus to find You out, and a . . . Anchor to fix You at
Moorings a fortnight at a time. I wish my dear Fellow I had it
in my power to plan you a Campaign in which Interest &
honor ware blended happy should I be in Communicating it.
And ware the Peruvian, and Brazilian Banks mine, they and
my personal Aid should be at Your command to carry it into
full Execution. The Rascally part so far out number the
Virtuous that unless a Strict Dicipline is introduced shortly I
shall fear it will come to Tanta ta-Bara Rogues all. Oh that I
had but the mustering of a certain sett, they should know what
martial law was. I'll promise You, the honest mariner should
no longer be tosed [tossed] too & frow on the waves of
Adversity, while they lay basking in smooth waters. We have
peace now however, and a large Field opens for all kinds of
Speculation. Besides this the advantage of Castle Building is
emence. Mine do Tumble now and then, but this . . . with a
few materials will carry us thro this troublesome world. Some
laws last Session with a late Proclamation will I fear Operate
against . . . Interest. A discrimination in a certain sett should
and no doubt will be made or I pronounce us impolitic. We
jogg on here pritty much in the old way as to Society but our
Fare is greatly altered for the Better. Chester Double & Single
Gloster, and Samon, Cheeses, Porter, Punch, and wine are
common, and we some times draw up in Aray to Sanctify a
Calapash. I should like much to wage War against Your
Trouts, and have it in contemlation [sic] to reconnoitre some
of their strong grounds near Norfolk this fall. In that case shall
Forrage on You. . . . Mrs. Weedon begs to joine in affectionate
compliments to You & Mrs. Hunter. Believe dear Jimmy with
much Esteem.[15]

At last the war was over. The final peace treaty was signed
in September. The army, already having vanished, would be
officially disbanded in November; only a handful of soldiers
would be kept at West Point. Weedon, as was expected of the
Continental officers, himself had resigned his commission on
July 11, 1783.[16] For George Weedon, seeming to punctuate the
end of the war and the beginning of peace was General
Greene's visit to Fredericksburg on September 11–12, on his
return from the South. Greene was greeted "with open arms"
by the Weedons. The city of Fredericksburg gave Greene and
his aides a public dinner, and presented the general with "a
very polite address." This was to be the last time that George

[15] Weedon to James Hunter, Jr., 24 July, 1783, James Hunter Papers, UVL;
Coakley, "Virginia Commerce," 1949: pp. 304, 317, and 342.

[16] Fitzpatrick, 1931-: **6**: p. 43n.

Weedon would see his hero, who showed signs of a declining health that was always, at best, frail. It had been a friendship that had begun early in the northern campaigns, and had grown through years of correspondence—although admittedly there was a good deal of fantasizing as to the friendship on Weedon's part. But Weedon had early taken the mettle of Greene, and he had never been ashamed, nor did he have much cause to be, of his unstinting adulation. Greene's response to the "hearty welcome" of the citizens of Fredericksburg stirred in Weedon a certain pride himself. "Happy in your assurances," said Greene, "I shall feel myself amply rewarded, if I have but the good wishes of my Country."[17]

Veteran Affairs

Virginia Continental officers were anxious to secure bounty lands promised by the state as well as to exchange their five year commutation certificates voted by Congress for lands. The state had provided for lands on the Cumberland and Tennessee Rivers, and the Act of Cession in 1781 had said that if more lands were needed, military lands could also be opened up between the Scioto and Little Miami Rivers in the Ohio Country. Thwarting Virginia claims along the Ohio were efforts being made by Continental officers from other states that Congress establish federal military lands north of the Ohio.[18]

General Steuben asked that Weedon look into the grant of fifteen thousand acres of land which the state of Virginia had awarded him, and he authorized Weedon to locate the tract. Weedon wrote Steuben, in April, 1782, that no warrants would be issued by Virginia until the end of the war, but he would pay "strict attention" to Steuben's interests, "and if I get any thing for myself You will have Yours also."[19]

For ten days in June, 1782, Weedon and other officers of the Virginia line tried to get the General Assembly to take definite action, favoring state grants of the Ohio lands, but they

---

[17] 12 September, 1783, FCCM; Thayer, 1960: pp. 427-428. The letter to Greene was signed by Charles Mortimer, chairman of the reception committee.

[18] Boyd, 1950-: 6: pp. 572-573.

[19] Davies to Steuben, 8 March, 1782 and Weedon to Steuben, 7 April, 1782, Steuben Papers, NYHS; Steuben to Weedon, 20 February, 1783, Balch, 1857: p. 202.

accomplished nothing because the Assembly "has been taken up with Political matters, between this State and Congress."[20] Almost a year passed, and Weedon was still waiting for some action by the Virginia Assembly. To Theodorick Bland, Jr., in Congress, Weedon reported in April, 1783, that he expected the next session of the legislature to have "a plan of adopting something" on the land bounties, "and rest assured I shall particularly attend to your interest in this business." Virginia land grants along "with our five years full pay, will enable us poor Continentals to tell our stories and drink our Cyder with a cheerful mind." He asked, "what becomes of the land Congress promised us? We have a demand on that honorable body . . . . If any thing is done, or will be done in it, be so Obliging as to Advise me, and act for me there." Weedon also had loan office certificates, issued in 1776 and 1777, at the value of 1,600 dollars, and he wanted to know if any means had been "adopted to liquidate them."[21]

Weedon hoped to exchange his bounty warrants for land in the Ohio Country. Commenting on another lobbying effort, Weedon wrote Steuben on May 5, 1783 that the "line of Officers" would assemble in Fredericksburg on May 12, "for the purpose of adopting some mode for the Location & Surveying our lands," which "will be laid before the assembly with some other requisitions . . . ." In "the mean while," Weedon continued,

> Let me hint to you that the Bear-skin You once made me laugh about will in a few Years be exceedingly Valuable, and will answer as a Corps-de-reserve to old Age or a Young Generation. If you will look into [Thomas] Hutchins's map you will see a Delightful track of Country on the North side of Ohio between the Rivers Sioto and Great Miami, in Rocky River. From every Account I can get . . . this is certainly the land of promise and Garden of America.[22]

The legislature considered the memorial of the officers, which asked the state to place all of the Virginia military lands north of the Ohio and to pay for surveying. Wrote Joseph Jones: "This report was so repugnant to the cession to Congress and to the remonstrance in 1779, whereby the legislature promised to furnish lands beyond the Ohio to the

[20] Weedon to Greene, 12 June, 1782, Greene Papers, CL.

[21] Weedon to Theodorick Bland, Jr., 1 April, 1783, Weedon Letters, HL.

[22] Weedon to Steuben, 5 May, 1783, Miscellaneous Collection—Weedon, NYPI.

States wanting lands for their lines;" therefore the legislature gave "it a check for the present."[23] Nevertheless, the officers went ahead with a plan they had adopted in their May meeting for surveying, on their own, land north of the Ohio. Colonel Richard Anderson, "an officer of skill & Integrity," was employed as an "agent for the whole" and as surveyor. Weedon notified some absentee officers of the plan and pointed out that for Anderson to look after one's claims, he needed a surveying fee in advance—"in the proportion of £8.16 for 10,000 Acres"— and also a fee for chain carriers.[24]

But Weedon was optimistic that the assembly would insist on using lands north of the Ohio to satisfy the Virginia bounty claims. To Steuben, in June, 1783, he wrote: "[I] have connected your Interest with mine in the Land Business and hope we shall be Neighborly on the banks of the Scioto. My fish Trap and hunting ground shall be at your Service, but no man except those who can give a good account of himself shall have the same privilege."[25]

Further complications ensued in working out an interpretation of the terms of the Virginia cession acceptable to both Congress and the state. In October, 1783, the Virginia Assembly agreed to a compromise, as Weedon later explained to Steuben:

> Everything that could be done for us with propriety was granted, but there were so many Interests to reconcile and some of them of a National Nature that we the Deputation from our line were Oblige to Compromise Matters in the best Manner we could, and by the Laws as they now stand must begin our Surveys on the Cumberland and Tenesee Rivers and go to Scioto for Deficiencies.

The officers were allowed to appoint their own surveyor and superintendent "to see strict justice done as well to the absent officer as those on the spot; with a Covering party of 100 Men, and as many Deputy Surveyors as we might think proper to employ."[26] But actually receiving and locating specific grants would be a long process in the future.

---

[23] Joseph Jones to Madison, 8 June, 1783, Ford, 1889; p. 113.

[24] Weedon to Capt. ——, 22 June, 1783, Etting Collection, Revolutionary War Papers, HSP; James Mercer to John Francis Mercer, 26 June, 1783, Jennings, 1951: p. 187; Cad. Jones to Gen. Muhlenberg, to the care of Genl. Weedon, 9 December, 1782, "Correspondence . . . Wood," 1921: p. 40. The Virginia line had been called together by General Muhlenberg.

[25] Weedon to Steuben, 24 June, 1783, quoted in Boyd, 1950-: 6: p. 573.

[26] Weedon to Steuben, 24 February, 1784, Weedon Letters, Sparks MSS, Harvard University Library; Jones to Jefferson, 29 December, 1783, Ford, 1889: p. 135.

The Virginia legislature awarded General Weedon 10,000 acres of military lands "in Consideration of his services" as a brigadier general in the Continental line. Unlike Muhlenberg, who went down the Ohio to make his own inspection,[27] Weedon showed little interest in the quality of his lands, which were located in Kentucky "on the head Waters of the first large Creek [Deer Creek] running into the Ohio above the mouth of Kentucky [River]." By the close of 1785, 4,000 acres of Weedon's lands had been surveyed in Kentucky. His tract bordered that of George Lewis and Gustavus B. Wallace. In 1786 Weedon assigned 2,000 acres to James Mercer.[28] Available land in Kentucky was running out, and Virginia military lands had to be found north of the Ohio. The confirmation of Virginia military lands in the Ohio country would not be made until by an act of Congress on August 10, 1790 (with a supplementary act of June 9, 1794). The remaining 6,000 acres Weedon was entitled to would eventually be located between the Little Miami and Scioto Rivers, along "Darby's creek."[29]

An unpleasant situation developed when commissioners settling military accounts in Virginia reported that Weedon had drawn back pay, after he had re-entered active service, for the time of his "retirement," 1778–1780. He was served a writ by the state to make restitution for the pay drawn in arrears. Weedon was furious. He knew that other general officers, especially Putnam, Gates, Sumner, and Morgan, had received pay for the periods of their long absences from the army, without being held to account. Weedon raised the issue with the Secretary at War, General Henry Knox, who endorsed what Weedon had done. Said Knox:

> I remember I felt in common with your brother officers the extreme hardship of your case which irresistably impelled you to conform to the point of honor held sacred in the army never to endure being superseded in rank. I should hope that under these circumstances which were inevitable on your part that

---

[27] Muhlenberg to Weedon, 15 February, 1784, WC, APS.

[28] Virginia State Land Office Surveys, #19, 404, and 540-541. Four thousand acres in Fayette County were entered as surveyed, 20 December, 1785, signed Richard Anderson *et al.* (Virginia State Land Office Military Bounty Warrants, #1, Land-Office Warrant #91, VSL.) In April, 1786,Weedon paid £52 4s. 6d. to have lands of William Mercer (Hugh Mercer's land grants) surveyed. (Ledger Book #3, VSL.)

[29] James Madison, President of the U.S., ..., 27 July, 1810, AKF; " ... from Numerical Abstract of Virginia Land Warrants, #91" (Weedon's), J. K. Martin Pension Papers, VSL; "Land Warrant ...," 25 March, 1808, fascimile, Rising Sun Tavern, Fredericksburg.

you would be entitled to the Same treatment of Generals
Putnam Sumner and a variety of other cases some of them
perhaps not so cogent as yours in the mind at least of a military
man. These have received pay and emoluments during very
long recesses from the field.[30]

Weedon sent a blistering letter to Governor Patrick Henry
and also one to a Virginia colonel—most likely John F.
Mercer—asking him to take his case to the assembly. Weedon
conceded that, according to the Congressional resolution of
1778, he could not draw pay and rations "or be intitled to half
pay unless called into the field again." But his return to
service changed all that. He told Governor Henry that his case
was "a continental matter altogether" and that he wished "it
to be referred to Congress with whom it Originated, and who
must Ultimately decide upon the case and whose decision I
shall strictly conform to." To the colonel, whom Weedon
asked to state his case to the legislature, he also pointed out
that Congress should decide. "I am in hopes," he said, that
"You and my other Friends will be able to Explain the matter
so as to remove all Suspicions, as on the Scale of justice I am
sure it's right and the usages of the Army in Similar Instances
confirm my Opinion."[31] It seems that Weedon was
convincing, and there were no further attempts to have him
make reimbursement for pay drawn for the period of his
inactive service.

Only briefly did George Weedon reflect on the possibility of
obtaining some position in a postwar military establishment.
Unlike many of his brother officers, he would not harass the
Confederation government or, later, Washington's Administration with applications for a job. In September, 1783, he
did sound out, however, on John F. Mercer, in Congress, the
idea of federal military employment.

I observe You are now Arranging Your Peace Establishment
which will require deep and serious Deliberations, but having
the Aid of His Excellency have not a doubt but all will be right.
I was thinking that an officer in each State should be retained
in Service as an Adjutant Genl. whose Business it should be

[30] Henry Knox to Major General Weedon, 3 March, 1785, War Office, AKF.

[31] Weedon to Gov. Henry, 2 April, 1786, WL, BUL; Weedon to Col. ---, n.d.
[probably to John F. Mercer, late March to 2 April, 1786], MS #19732, VSL. Mercer
delivered Weedon's letter of 2 April to Gov. Henry, as indicated on that letter, and the
unaddressed and undated letter bears instructions on the same subject.

not only to Inspect the Militia of the State but also the Posts and Magazines and to make Report thereof every Quarter or half Year. No doubt however but the General will think of every thing proper, and if any snug post or place in the Peace Establishment should offer where I can be of Service You will particularly Oblige me in proposing me. I am rather of the wrong side of life to look far forward in Business, and wish to be Employ'd the remainder of my days in some way that I am more Acquainted with.[32]

Weedon, in fall, 1783, was a founder of the Society of the Cincinnati in Virginia. The parent organization had been formed in May by a group of officers meeting at General Steuben's quarters at the Verplanck mansion in Fishkill, New York. Washington was elected the national president. The Virginia chapter emerged from a meeting called by General Muhlenberg at the Fredericksburg Town House, October 6–9. About 300 officers were enrolled, which was done without the officers having to attend. Actually only about forty were present, and this number was decided upon as a quorum. Next to Gates, Weedon was ranked as the senior general, followed by Muhlenberg, Scott, and Morgan, in that order. Gates was elected president; Muhlenberg, vice-president; Carrington, treasurer; and Towles, secretary.[33]

It is not known exactly how Weedon felt about the society. Most likely he saw that its advantages were that it provided opportunity for old comrades-in-arms to get together and that it was a means for officers to concert actions in reference to veteran benefits. Within a year of its founding, the society, nationally, had aroused immense criticism because of its hereditary feature and its potentiality for use as a lobby for Continental army officers. As public ire mounted, Washington, who reluctantly supported the society, considered advocating its abolishment, and refrained from doing so only because of the involvement of foreign officers and the society's charitable activity on behalf of war orphans and widows.[34] George Weedon, surely like Washington, did not favor the hereditary requirement, as he had no children or collateral relatives who could succeed him.

---

[32] Weedon to John F. Mercer, 9 September, 1783, Duke University Library.

[33] Weedon to Washington, 15 November, 1783, Dreer Collection HSP; Hume, 1934: pp. 103-108; "Roster" in Hume, 1938: pp. 3-7.

[34] Freeman, 1949-: **6**: pp. 11-12 and 45.

Washington declared against the hereditary requirement, and the issue was hotly debated at the general meeting of the society in Philadelphia, May 4–8, 1784, at which Weedon was a member of the Virginia delegation, along with Colonels William Heth, "Light Horse Harry" Lee, and James Wood. The national assembly voted to abolish the hereditary requirement, and adopted the "Altered and Amended Institution of the Society of the Cincinnati." The abolition of the hereditary rule, however, never went into effect nationally because a unanimous consent of the thirteen state societies was required, and some remained opposed. At the meeting of the Virginia Society, October 5–7, 1784, at the Town House in Fredericksburg, the members voted to do away with the hereditary basis for membership—which rule on the local level was to last until the late nineteenth century. At the October, 1784 meeting Weedon was elected president.[35]

Probably some officers, such as William Davies, refused to attend meetings of the Virginia Society because Weedon was president. But overall there was not much enthusiasm. Many officers wanted the meetings advertised and held in Richmond. When the society next met on July 4–5, 1785, there was no quorum, and no business was accomplished. Weedon advertised an October meeting,[36] but again there was probably the difficulty in gaining a quorum, and no record of the meeting exists. It was the same problem when a few of the old officers convened on July 4–5, 1786, when Weedon was elected president pro tem. At last the society moved its meetings to Richmond. At a session in Richmond, November 15–18, 1786, Weedon was elected president. Because of the low attendance, the number for a quorum was lowered to thirty. A letter from Washington was read, stating that he did not want to be re-elected president-general of the national society.[37]

---

[35] See "Minutes," 5-7 October, 1784, Hume, 1938: pp. 12-14; Hume, 1934: pp. 200-201.

[36] Muhlenberg to Gates, 27 March, 1785, Gates Papers, NYHS; Weedon to Gates, 26 July, 1785, Emmet Collection #5997, NYPL.

[37] T. Meriwether to Gates, 22 November, 1786, Gates Papers, NYHS; "Minutes," 1784-1786, Hume, 1938: pp. 14-31. Gen. Gates, who was ill much of 1785-1786, remained the honorary head of the Virginia Cincinnati. Weedon kept in touch with him in arranging and advertising for the meetings of the Society. (Weedon to Gates, 20 May, 1786, Emmet Collection #15030, NYPL; Richard Carson, Jr. to Gates, 20 May, 1786, Gates Papers, NYHS.)

Community Affairs

Now that the war was over, George Weedon could again take an active part in community life. He ran in the councilmanic election of March, 18, 1782, the first to be held under the new charter which incorporated Fredericksburg as a city, and, although not winning quite enough votes to become an alderman (four from the top six in the voting), he was elected a councilman. The first meeting of the new city fathers was held at the coffee house on Friday, March 22. During his first year in office, Weedon served on a committee of five to draw up a petition "and remonstrance" to the General Assembly, asking for amendments to the act of incorporation of the city for an enlargement of boundaries. He was also one of a committee of three to draw up articles for a fire company, and he visited Fredericksburg residents in order to get their signatures for the document.[38]

In subsequent elections, through 1786, Weedon won fifth place in 1783 (by which he became an alderman and therefore also a justice on the Hustings Court); first in 1784 (named recorder); third in 1785 (appointed mayor); and tied for first in 1786.[39] He served only the single term as mayor. Weedon and the council spent many hours on the routine business of governing the town. Serving on the Hustings Court was also time consuming: discharging administrative duties, trying civil suits, and sitting on "examiner's courts," which heard criminal cases and, often through what would be called plea bargaining today, meted out punishment. With defendants accepting a verdict, presentment and a regular trial were avoided.[40] Weedon was one of four directors of the public buildings, an examiner of the clerk's records, and a trustee for the Market House. He also continued to be involved in various committee work of the council.[41]

[38] 22 March, 1782, HCOB-A; 27 and 30 March, 20 April, 2 and 13 May, 1782 and 8 January and 14 February, 1783, FCCM. It may be noted that Weedon's friend, Col. William Daingerfield of Belvidera, Spotsylvania County, committed suicide on 15 January, 1783. (Wyllie, 1966: p. 458n.)

[39] 17 March, 1783, 15 March, 1784, 16 March and 4 April, 1785, and 20 March, 1786, FCCM.

[40] 29 December, 1783, 7 and 26 June, 1784, 3 January, 16, 20, and 28 April, 3, 23, and 28 May, and 5 July, 1785, 6 November, 1786, and 1783-1785 *passim*, HCOB-A. The other four justices, when Weedon was mayor and presiding justice, were James Somerville, William McWilliams, John Julian, and Thomas Miller. A suit, *Weedon v. Thomas Aitkin*, was dismissed, and another suit, *Weedon v. Clarke*, was "discontinued." Cause for the litigation is not known.

[41] 31 May and 24 June, 1784, FCCM. E.g., committees: surveying property boundaries; regulating merchants' supplies of gunpowder.

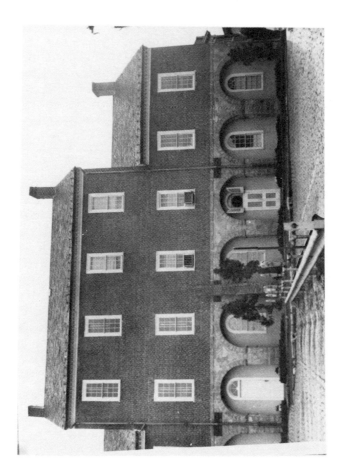

FIG. 10.   Market House, Fredericksburg. With permission of Richmond Times Dispatch.

Besides serving in many capacities as a city official George Weedon had other involvement in the community. He participated in a protest meeting of fifty merchants to denounce Great Britain's closing trade with the British West Indies to American vessels, and he signed the petition to the legislature, which concluded that "Commerce can only be maintained on the grounds of reciprocity."[42] There was a growing feeling that commercial advantages could be better attained through a stronger national government. Weedon may have been thinking along the lines of Mann Page and other prominent Virginians, who were calling for Congress to recommend to the states the holding of a convention to amend the Articles of Confederation.[43] Weedon was also one of sixty-five persons in the Fredericksburg area to petition the House of Delegates against a state law of May, 1784, which excluded foreign vessels from certain ports, including Fredericksburg.[44]

In 1786 Weedon was elected one of six trustees whose task was to raise money for the building of a new St. George's Episcopal Church. One of their methods was through a lottery.[45] As a matter of fact, Weedon had an attraction to lotteries of any kind and could not resist buying lottery tickets. In 1784 he won a lot in Richmond, which he sold to Henry Banks.[46] When he could, he got tickets in the lottery in Philadelphia. Once Muhlenberg wrote Weedon that he had inquired "at the Lottery Office" and found that "a Light Waggon will be unnecessary to carry off the prize money."[47] There appears to have been competition in obtaining lottery tickets from Philadelphia. Charles Mortimer admonished his son, Jack, in that city: "I told you to get a ticket in the third Class of the lottery, and Mr. Barclay to pay for it that you may be thereby entitled to a ticket in the 4th Class. Have no partnership in it with any person. Its my desire you would not mention your having any ticket to General Weedon."[48]

[42] To the Speaker and Gent. of the Assembly, 2 December, 1784, Legislative Petitions, Fredericksburg, VSL.

[43] Mann Page to Richard Henry Lee, 14 December, 1784, Lee Papers, micro., VSL.

[44] To the House of Delegates, 28 November, 1785; re-submittal of the same petition, 17 November, 1786 and 26 October, 1787, Legislative Petitions, Fredericksburg, VSL. Eighty-two persons signed the 1787 petition; 101 that of 1786.

[45] Petition of William Fitzhugh, George Weedon, Charles Mortimer, Eliazar Callender, John Lewis, and Francis Thornton [trustees] to the Speaker of the House of Delegates, 17 November, 1786, ibid.

[46] Ledger Book #4, 1784, UVL.

[47] Muhlenberg to Weedon, 18 July, 1786, WC, APS.

[48] Charles Mortimer to John Mortimer at Messrs. Barclay, Brown, and Co.,— July, 1786, Minor Family Papers, VHS.

Weedon became a trustee of the Fredericksburg Academy. In 1782 the legislature had permitted the defunct gun factory to be converted into an academy supported by subscriptions. In 1786 Weedon and the other nine trustees petitioned the General Assembly to sell "part of the land, which is low, sunken and in its present situation very noxious to the health of the scholars" and also to sell the powder magazine, which, though empty, "ought not to be near Youth." The petition was granted.[49]

Along with other civic leaders, George Weedon continued to be active in the Masonic Lodge. In September, 1783, the members of the Lodge moved from a room at Richard Kenney's house back "to our Old Sanctom Sanctorom," as Weedon wrote to James Hunter, Jr., thanking him for a bell that Hunter had presented to the Lodge. With the return to the old hall, "we form us Working Masons, and repare a Principal Arch under our old Lodge room . . . . After our Work is over we take refreshment at Bensons in the Usual way."[50] In April, 1784, the Lodge bought from James Somerville for £40 a lot, which was to be used for a Masonic cemetery. Weedon was one of ten Lodge members providing security for the purchase[51] of what is now called the "Old Masonic Burying Ground," one of the quaint attractions of historic Fredericksburg.

Domesticity

With peace, wartime restrictions upon entertainment were relaxed. George Weedon welcomed the re-opening of the Fredericksburg races in October, 1783, and the biannual fair. The new feeling of levity was evident in Weedon's letter to James Hunter, Jr. in September, 1783.

> Dont you mean to give us the pleasure of Your Company at our Races? I will promise You great Sport, and free Quarters if You can find time to partake. Travelling from the Wilderness [just west of Fredericksburg] three days ago in a

---

[49] 2 November, 1786, Legislative Petitions, Fredericksburg, VSL; May session, 1783, and October session, 1786, Hening, 1820-: 11: p. 204 and 12: p. 372, resp. The trustees in 1786 were: James Mercer, Charles Carter, William Fitzhugh, Thomas Lomax, Alexander Spotswood, Francis Thornton, George Weedon, French Strother, Mann Page, and John Dawson.

[50] Weedon to James Hunter, Jr., 9 September, 1783, James Hunter Papers, UVL.

[51] 6 April, 1784, Fredericksburg City Hustings Deed Book, A, VSL.

deep Revene, who should I Meet joging along the road like an old Speculator as full of Thought as an Egg is of Meat, but Your ribb [wife]. It was the first of my knowing she was in this part of the World, Not having Recd. Your letter. After Shaking hands & making some Domistic inquiries . . . my dear Madam where are You rambling. "I am going up to Orange & Culpeper to see all Your Old Acquaintances I suppose. No really, My Old man sends me there to do some Business for him. He is unwell and cant turn out himself so he has sent me. Good by, my Compliments to the Ladies. I'll give You a Call when I return." She was as hearty as a buck, and expect her down in a day or two.[52]

Weedon enjoyed meeting old friends and comrades, who came from afar for the races and fairs and with whom he could pass a convivial evening with the best food and drink. If his overindulgence was adding a few more pounds to his already corpulent frame, it was worth it, as Weedon believed that life was to be enjoyed.

The Weedons—presumably the whole extended family, including Isabella Mercer (Hugh's widow and Weedon's sister-in-law), her five children, and Mrs. Margaret Gordon (Kitty Weedon's mother)—all moved into Weedon's tavern, probably early in 1782. Leasing the tavern to William Smith had only caused headaches. During the entire five years from April, 1776 to April, 1781, Smith had defaulted on the rent: £580, with interest. He had also neglected keeping up the property. Weedon charged that 115 panes of glass had been broken (£20 damages); windows and other wood work had become "decayed & ruinous;" two locks were missing; the stairs to the cellar and the plastering along the stairs had been pulled down (£30); weather boards and floors of the stable had been "pulled down and destroyed" (£30); and Weedon's precious billiard table had been in "want of due care & repairing, greatly defaced & Injured" (£30). The damages were attested to by Edward Carter, Stephen Lacorte, and Mann Page upon the termination of the lease in 1781. Weedon took his time, but eventually brought suit against Smith for £500. The case was tried in the Hustings Court in 1784, with the charge of "Trespass on the Case" being deleted. The court

---

[52] Weedon to James Hunter, Jr., 9 September, 1783, James Hunter Papers, UVL. A year later, to Col. Fitzgerald of Alexandria, Weedon wrote: "will you come to our Races. Tell me You will & shall keep a Matress for You." (Weedon to Col. Fitzgerald, 17 August 1784, Gratz Collection, HSP.)

awarded Weedon £200 and ordered Smith to provide two good locks, clean out the cellars and the yard, repair the stable, furnish plank to lay one-third of the loft over the saddle room, plaster the ceiling of the cellar, and repair the stairs of the cellar.[53]

There was too much hustle and bustle, however, in living in the former tavern. Although Weedon did not operate a public tavern, many of the old patrons did not care about the difference and were always dropping around. "Our monthly Balls, Jockey Club, Fairs—and other Amusements & Societies, I have been principally Concerned in Establishing" drew so many people to his place, Weedon complained, that "indeed my House is already so much like a public House that I can stand it no longer." He decided to move out and lease the property to someone who would run it as a tavern. At the end of 1783 or early 1784, the Weedons rented a house from Alexander Dick that had been the residence of Charles Dick, his father, before he died two years before. Weedon advertised for rental of the tavern, and contacted James Hunter, Jr., in Norfolk, to try to find a suitable tenant. Weedon said that "any Active man" might "make a Fortune in it in a very few Years." He wanted £280 annual rent

> which as Houses now rent is Cheaper than any in Town in proportion to the Conveniencies and advantages it has over any other. It being so convenient to the Market House would insure the Business of all Public amusements, My Stables, and the Established Credt. of the House would at all times command Custom sufficient provided it was kept in a Genteel manner. If I do not rent it, I would willingly become a partner in opening it on a Company Account, and proposed it to You to be concerned with me. I think a thousd. pounds would Accomodate it Genteely & Your living below would have at all times an Oportunity of laying in the best of Liqr on good terms. I suppose a prudent & honest man, and woman might be got for £100 pr. Year, and my living on the spot could have an Oportunity on this matter, and If You like to be concerned write me fully by post, as there is no time to be lost.[54]

---

[53] Miscellaneous papers, including indenture between Smith and Weedon, 17 February, 1786, Fredericksburg District Court Papers, xerox supplied by G. H. S. King; 1 November, 1784, HCOB; Ledger Book #4, account William Smith, 1 January, 1786, UVL.

[54] Weedon to James Hunter, Jr., 6 January, 1784, James Hunter Papers, UVL.

Weedon succeeded in renting the tavern building to Nathaniel Twining in 1784, with John Legg having the use of the stable.[55]

In Fredericksburg, in 1784, Weedon had two improved lots and seven slaves, four of whom were under age sixteen.[56] The Negroes may have been taken from the Crab Cove plantation on the Potomac, which Weedon may have decided not to operate, as at this time he was advertising for its sale. Some of the slaves he may have used on the Mercer plantation, across the river, which, as an executor of Mercer's estate, he had the responsibility of managing. Or perhaps Weedon leased out several of the slaves in the Fredericksburg area; the extant ledger books, however, do not reveal this.

Operating the Crab Cove plantation had been too much trouble, especially for an absentee owner. The slaves came and went as they pleased. A cruel overseer had resigned in 1781, giving as a reason that he could not take care of both Weedon's and Major Stoddart's plantations at the same time, and Weedon had difficulty in finding a replacement. There was hardly any more pork and beef produced than to satisfy the needs of the plantation and an overseer. The best of Weedon's beef had been "taken . . . for the army," and as a result only "the young and poor" cattle were left.[57]

After the races in October, 1783, George Weedon took Billy Mercer to Philadelphia, where Weedon's eighteen-year-old nephew would study painting with the renowned Charles Willson Peale. Weedon had "adopted" the Mercer children and was bringing them up, as Hugh, Billy's younger brother, was to say many years later, "as a most tender & anxious father"[58] Billy was a sensitive and timid youth, and, like his brother George, deaf and dumb. George Weedon had tried

---

[55] Ledger Book #4, account Capt. John Legg, April, 1784, and account Nathaniel Twining, 30 September, 1784-1 December, 1785, UVL; Ledger Book #3, account Nathaniel Twining, May, 1784-December, 1785, VSL.

[56] 26 June, 1784 and 20 September, 1785, FCCM.

[57] Charles Tooke to Weedon, 27 August, 1781, Balch, 1857: pp. 95-97. For Weedon's claims for public reimbursement of beef and pork, see King George County Public Service Claims Certificates, 1781-1782, #156, n.d., Public Service Claims Certificates, photostats, VSL; 11 and 31 December, 1783, Westmoreland County Court, and 23 December, 1783, King George County Court, pp. 226, 228 and 245, resp., Public Service Claims Commissioners Book, VSL.

[58] Hugh Mercer, Jr. to Col. John Trumbull, 18 May, 1838. Hugh Mercer, Jr. was to be educated at the expense of the national government. For Weedon's application for this assistance, see 21 June, 1783, Ford, 1904-1937: 24: p. 50. Weedon and Billy left sometime after 17 October.

unsuccesfully to have the Virginia legislature appoint him as the legal "agent" for Billy in the disposition of the military lands, which he had inherited as the oldest son of General Mercer.[59] Having failed in this appointment, Weedon nevertheless looked after Billy's interests in all respects.

Peale accepted Billy as part of the family. Billy learned a passing craftsmanship at portraiture. Later he became best known for a painting of the Battle of Princeton, now at the Historical Society of Pennsylvania. His miniature of Edmund Pendleton may be seen in the Virginia Historical Society. Undoubtedly some of his paintings, probably unidentifiable, hang in the homes of old Virginia families today. A painting of George and Catharine Weedon, attributed to William Mercer, once was known to exist, but currently cannot be located.[60] Helping to keep an eye on young William Mercer in Philadelphia was the son of Weedon's friend Dr. Charles Mortimer, Jack, who was an apprentice in a counting house in the city.[61]

Although Billy worked hard and even got his heel frostbitten while painting in a room in the State House which Peale used as a studio,[62] he could be stubborn. On one occasion Billy even refused an assignment by Peale, but it seems he was soon straightened out by the painter's fatherly advice.[63]

In February, 1784, George Washington came to Fredericksburg to visit his mother, and the city council gave him a warm welcome, including a gala dinner,[64] which the Weedons undoubtedly attended. Weedon seems to have kept in contact with Washington's mother and sister Betty, widow of Fielding

---

[59] Petition of George Weedon to the Speaker and House of Delegates, 12 June, 1783, Legislative Petitions, Fredericksburg, VSL.

[60] See Groce and Wallace, 1957. The dates given in this volume for William Mercer, 1773-1850, are inaccurate; the dates should be 1765-1839. See also Lynnes, 1970: pp. 13ff. The author wishes to acknowledge gratitude to George H. S. King, who has given copies to the author of his correspondence in attempting to locate the William Mercer painting of the Weedons.

[61] Charles Mortimer to John Mortimer, 20 December, 1785 and 15 January, 1786, Minor Family Papers, VHS. Jack Mortimer was an apprentice to Barclay, Brown and Co.

[62] Sellers, 1947: 1: pp. 223-224 and 230-234.

[63] *Ibid.*, pp. 242-245; Peale to William Mercer, 21 February, 1784, Charles Willson Peale Letter Book, APS.

[64] Washington to the Mayor and Commonalty of Fredericksurg, 14 February, 1784, Fitzpatrick, 1931: 27: p. 332.

Lewis. Curiously Weedon wrote Washington in August, 1785: "The old lady your mother talks of paying you a visit in Sept. I mean doing myself the honor of escorting her."[65]

Weedon maintained close ties with John Francis Mercer, who had now returned from Congress. In February, 1785, Mercer married Sophia Sprigg of Cedar Park in Anne Arundel County, Maryland, and gave indication of settling down to the life of a planter. Weedon visited Mercer at Marlborough, in Stafford County, and on one occasion mentioned one of Mercer's new in-laws, "a young Sprig who Dines with me today." To James Monroe, who was in Congress at New York, Weedon wrote that Mercer "& Family ware doing well. The lady complains indeed, but I fancy it is only the effects of a Conjugal transaction." Weedon went on to observe "how great a Farmer" Mercer was becoming. Weedon would soon lose touch with his friend, as Mercer moved to his wife's estate in Maryland, where he again entered politics and eventually became governor of the estate.[66]

James Monroe and Weedon were soon to be neighbors. Upon leaving Congress, Monroe moved from Albemarle County to Fredericksburg, where there seemed to be more opportunity for practicing law and where Monroe thought he would have a better base for his political ambitions. Monroe planned his move for more than a year. He had Weedon take care of some of his business transactions in Fredericksburg and help him find a house in which to live. As Weedon had already begun building what he called the Sentry Box, or at least improving a house that may have been on lot #250, he tried to interest Monroe in buying the uncompleted building for £400 and £100 for the lot.[67] Monroe decided against the "snugg Sentry Box," and instead set up residence in a house belonging to his uncle, Judge Joseph Jones of King George County, on Caroline Street a block and a half from the Sentry

[65] Weedon to Washington, 10 August, 1785, Washington Papers, Series 4, Reel 95, LC.

[66] Weedon to James Monroe, 26 July, 1785, Monroe Papers, Series 2, Reel 9, LC; Weedon to James Monroe, 2 August, 1785, James Monroe Papers in Virginia Repositories, micro., VSL; Garnett, 1909: pp. 202-203.

[67] Weedon to Monroe, 30 May, 1785 and 26 July, 1785, Monroe Papers, Series 2, Additional MSS, Reel 9, LC; James Monroe to Jacquelin Ambler, with "Warrant payable to order of Gen. Weedon," 20 June, 1785 and Weedon to Monroe, 2 August, 1785, James Monroe Papers in Virginia Repositories, micro., VSL; Cresson, 1946: pp. 92-93.

Box.[68] Weedon himself was so attracted to the Sentry Box, which he described as "secluded on the Hill and where I call a plesent place," that he went ahead with work on it so that he could move his large "family" there. Overlooking the Rappahannock, the Sentry Box commanded a broad view, which had been familiar to the youthful George Washington when he was growing up on the opposite bank at Ferry Farm, which for many years had been the Weedon administered property of the heirs of Hugh Mercer.

---

[68] Brown, 1959: p. 49; Cresson, 1946: p. 93 and 97; Ammon, 1971: p. 63. Monroe's law office was on Charles Street.

XIV. HOME AND HEARTH
(1786-1793)

George Weedon supervised diligently the completion of the Sentry Box. His ledger books indicate the variety of work that had to be done. Weedon had accounts with merchants and tradesmen of Fredericksburg for posts, nails, underpinning, plank, brickwork, painting, digging, shingles, chimneys, steps, shutters, plastering, and iron work. Andrew Kerg and Thomas Grant were hired as carpenters, along with George McCutchen's slave, Phil. A cornice for the house was obtained from John Hardy. Richard Garner put up the cornice, did the "plaining and Jointing" of 2,432 feet of flooring planks, and built the kitchen shed. William Spearman assisted in erecting a stable of one hundred forty feet fron hewn timber; he also worked on the cellar window frames, the "Cellar Porches," and the "framing" for the "Necessary House."[1]

The Sentry Box was fifty-one feet long, twenty feet wide, and two stories high. The roof consisted of wooden shingles. The cellar went the whole length. Besides the main house, there was a one-story "study," twenty-eight feet wide; an ice house, fifteen feet square; a kitchen, twenty-eight feet long and forty feet wide; and a meat house, fifteen feet square. These buildings, like the residence, had wooden sidings. The nearest neighbors to the Sentry Box, at least at a later date, were John Hardie and the widow of Henry Armistead.[2] About October, 1786, the Weedons and the Mercers moved into the Sentry Box.[3]

Weedon sold his Crab Cove plantation, on the Potomac River at Rosier's Creek, to Thacker Washington in October,

---

[1] Ledger Book #4, UVL.

[2] Mutual Assurance Society of Virginia, Declarations, Catharine Weedon, 31 March, 1796, micro., VSL. The Mutual Assurance Society was established 26 December, 1795.

[3] The first letter extant written from the Sentry Box is Weedon to Oliver Towles, 12 October, 1786, Miscellaneous Weedon Letters, NYHS. For a recent article on the Sentry Box and the changes made by its current owner, see *Richmond Times-Dispatch*, 18 march, 1976, Sec. H.

Fig. 11. Sentry Box Today. Photo courtesy of Historic Fredericksburg Foundation, Inc.

1786. The 535 acres brought £2,800[4] Although Weedon had neglected the plantation, it was an attractive property. Three hundred sixty acres had been cleared and were "well adapted to the cultivation of all kinds of grain." Sixty acres were in a salt marsh. In advertising the property three years before, Weedon had stated that the location was a "most noted place for all kinds of fish and fowl." It had a large barn, stable, "corn houses," slave quarters, and a residence (two rooms upstairs and four below). There were "admirable springs close to the door" and plenty of apple and peach trees.[5]

Weedon still supervised Hugh Mercer's farm. When Mercer had bought it from George Washington, he had the intention of laying it out in lots for a town. Mercer was killed, however, before he could petition the Assembly for this purpose. Nearly ten years later, the executors of Mercer's estate—Weedon, Isabella Mercer, and John Tennent—petitioned the legislature that seventy-one acres of the property (in Stafford County) be allowed for town development.[6] The House of Delegates seems to have tabled the petition.

By 1788 Weedon had a farm of 629 acres at Fall Hill, in Spotsylvania County just outside of Fredericksburg, to which he had brought his slaves from the Crab Cove plantation. Even though the new plantation was close at hand and Weedon could keep an eye on it, apparently, judging from Weedon's accounts, the farm was never much more than self-sustaining. One can only speculate how Weedon had acquired this land. The 150 acres he had purchased from his mother-in-law, Margaret Gordon, in St. George's Parish of Spotsylvania County, March 1774, may have served as the nucleus for this farm. On January 19, 1793 Weedon attached a "memorandum" to Mrs. Gordon's account, noting a final payment to her of £300 (which could, however, also have been part or full final payment for the Weedon tavern. He conveyed "interest warrants" to her in 1786 and successively thereafter, a fact which may also indicate that he purchased the Fall Hill land from Mrs. Gordon at the time Weedon sold his plantation on the Potomac.[7]

[4] 4 October, 1786, King George County Deed Book, #7, VSL. The property was now in King George County instead of Westmoreland; the county line was redrawn by act of the legislature in 1778. (Eaton, 1942: p. 2.)

[5] *Maryland Journal and Baltimore Advertiser*, 5 August, 1783, Weedon's advertisement of 29 July, 1783, Maryland Historical Society.

[6] To the Speaker and Gen. of the House of Delegates, 9 December, 1785, Legislative Petitions, Fredericksburg, VSL.

[7] 24 March, 1774, Crozier, 1950: 1: p. 310; Weedon to Spotsylvania Sheriff, 1790 (tax on the Fall Hill farm £1 16s. 5d.) and Weedon to Edward Herndon, Deputy Sheriff of

The Fall Hill farm kept the Weedons in a supply of produce and meat. Weedon did not get along with his illiterate overseer, George Fletcher. He deducted from Fletcher's wages the value of "4 head of Cattle lost in the woods for want of looking after."[8] Fletcher quit. Jessey Hayden was hired on as Weedon's new overseer in January, 1792, for £22 10s. a year "with an allowance of five Barrells of Corn & 350 lbs of meat."[9]

There were other property interests and transactions. Weedon, until at least 1787, was renting warehouse space.[10] In March, 1787, he bought two hundred ninety acres in St. George's Parish in Spotsylvania County from James Mercer, which was part of the estate, first of Charles Dick and then his son and heir, Alexander Dick, who had died March 17, 1785. But Weedon, "finding it inconvenient to meet the payments," re-conveyed the land back to Mercer after only a month of possession.[11]

In addition to the lot where the Sentry Box was located (#250), George Weedon also owned lot #240 (across Caroline Street from the Sentry Box), #239 (joining #240 on the west), and #260 (facing towards the river from the Sentry Box), which had been purchased from William Fitzhugh of Chatham and William Fitzhugh of Marmion, and #259 (towards the river next to #260), acquired from Roger Dixon; and he leased from Philip Roots lots #230 and 231 (back to back across Caroline Street and next to #240). Weedon's final acquisition was lot #251, adjacent to the Sentry Box on Caroline Street, purchasd from Dr. Charles Mortimer on December 20, 1792 for £100 currency.[12]

On lot #26, at the south end of Weedon's tavern property, there was a residential house which he rented to Walter

---

Spotsylvania County, 1791, Personal Accounts—Weedon, VSL; Weedon's Will, Fredericksburg Hustings Court Will Book, A, VSL; Ledger Book #4, account Mrs. Margaret Gordon, UVL.

[8] 13 May, 1792, account George Fletcher, Ledger Book #4, UVL. Fletcher signed his name with an "X."

[9] January and 27 November, 1792, account Jessey Hayden, *ibid*. Several "Buildings" on Weedon's farm were rented to John Shelton. (June, 1793, account John Shelton, Ledger Book #3, VSL.)

[10] E.g., rented from Jacob Kuhn (1784) and Messrs. Lilly and Fisher (to September, 1787), Ledger Book #4, UVL.

[11] Crozier, 1905: 1: pp. 404-405.

[12] *Ibid*.; 25 November, 1791, HCOB-C.

Gregory as early as 1786, if not before. Gregory was still the occupant at the time of Weedon's death in 1793, but Walter Scott was living in the house at the time of Catharine Weedon's death in 1797. This property at the later date included a one-story "store," a meat house, and a combination store house and kitchen. Gregory paid an annual rent of £12 18s. Thomas Clark, in 1786, was a tenant of Weedon's, but it is not clear what property was involved.[13] John Legg, from 1787 to 1792, had a five-year lease from Weedon for part of lot #26; whether he had use of any of the buildings or kept his stabling privileges at the tavern next door is not known. Legg paid only £11 5s. 9d. per annum.[14]

James Pottinger succeeded Nathaniel Twining as proprietor of the Weedon tavern, on the corner of Caroline and William Streets (#25). Pottinger paid an annual rent of £270, and he also leased Weedon's billard table at £50 a year. Pottinger let the tavern deteriorate, and repairs of £22 7s. had to be made when John Benson leased the tavern at the end of 1788. Weedon rented a stable to Gustavus B. Wallace for £20 a year in 1789—probably at the tavern property. Weedon seldom patronized the tavern when Pottinger had it, preferring instead to take a "Club" at Mrs. Hackley's or Thomas Clark's taverns. But when Benson took over, Weedon again frequently visited his old tavern, charging expenses against the rent.[15]

Family and Friends

Being a fond parent to the Mercer children, George Weedon took a personal interest in their education and training. John (b. 1772) and Hugh (b. 1776) studied at the Fredericksburg Academy, which was presided over by the Reverend Thomas Ryan. Since the Mercer family lived with the Weedons at the Sentry Box, a year's tuition for John and Hugh at the Academy was only £4 4s. each. Weedon seems to have been an indulgent uncle, as he frequently ordered new clothes for

---

[13] Mutual Assurance Society, Declarations, 3, #7, 1 April, 1796, micro., VLS; Gregory and Clarke accounts, Ledger Book #4, UVL.

[14] Fredericksburg City Hustings Court Deed Book, A; Ledger Book #4, UVL.

[15] 15 December, 1792 and 10 July, 1793, account John Benson, and *passim*, Ledger Book #3, VSL; 17 November, and 15 and 22 December, 1792, account John Benson, and *passim*, Ledger Book #4, UVL.

John and Hugh from Walter Gregory's tailor shop.[16] Ann Gordon Mercer's education included tutelage from Bartholomew Fuller, who instructed John and Hugh in mathematics at the Fredericksburg Academy. It is assumed John finished his schooling at the academy in 1790 when he turned eighteen years old.

Congress had pledged to educate the youngest son of General Hugh Mercer and the eldest son of Dr. Joseph Warren, who was killed at the battle of Bunker Hill. In July, 1789, Weedon wrote John Page that Congress was in arrears for the tuition and books for Hugh. He inquired of Page that "when you and my friend [James] Madison find a convenient & proper Oportunity of asking for a years Support . . . you will much oblige the Family of our late Friend Genl. Mercer by doing it."[17] Hugh, who would complete his studies at the academy about 1793, would then enter West Point, from which he would graduate.

Of the two deaf and dumb nephews, only Billy had the advantage of study away from home. Little is known of George. While Billy was in Philadelphia learning to be a painter, a great deal of correspondence passed between Weedon and Billy's teacher, Charles Willson Peale. Peale at one time wrote Weedon that "William Mercer is treated as our Son, and Mrs. Peale never Cuts an Apple or Orange without giving him part of it. I trust he will love us as long as life lasts." Occasionally Peale had to remind Weedon that he was in arrears in financial support for Billy. Billy came home in April, 1786, and returned to Philadelphia late next year to complete the picture that he had begun on General Mercer at the Battle of Princeton. "The Tragic Scene of the Death of Billy's Father," Weedon wrote Peale, "I am very Anxious to have . . . . I wish you would look at it when he returns and if any touches be found Necessary make him do it. He is the very picture of his father himself, was he made to be about 40

---

[16] Receipts for 23 June, 18 and 31 October, and 20 December, 1791, 11 February, April, 20, and 23 June, 1792, and *passim*, VLS; accounts Rev. Thomas Ryan, 1789-1791 and 1793, *passim*, Ledger Book #3, VLS; 31 October, 1791, account James Southall, Ledger Book #4, UVL. For two letters pertaining to Weedon's order for two paintings from John Trumbull—apparently never paid for by Weedon and hence not completed by Trumbull—see John Trumbull to Hugh Mercer, 4 December, 1827, and Hugh Mercer to col. John Trumbull, 18 May, 1838, Gratz Collection, HSP. Hugh died 4 August, 1853 (age 77); John Mercer died in 1817; accounts Walter Gregory, *passim*, Personal Accounts-Weedon, 1790-1792, VSL.

[17] Weedon to John Page, 23 July, 1789, WPC, CHS. George Weedon Mercer, deaf and dumb like William, died unmarried. For subsequent progeny of the other Mercer children, see Goolrick, 1906: pp. 105-108.

or 45 Years Old . . . . He and his Family may Never forget the man who taught him a profession so admired by all men of Science, and by which he is to get his Bread . . . "[18]

After his return home for good in 1788, Billy Mercer established himself as a "Limner," and he made a modest living for himself. An obituary at his death many years later at the age of eighty-four reveals something of his personality. William Mercer was "amiable and tractable," of a "quiet and gentle disposition," and had a "retiring and unobtrusive diffidence and pure benevolence"; he was "endowed with much perspicuity and quickness of discernment and of information," especially on any subject relating to the American Revolution.[19]

Isabella Gordon Mercer, Weedon's sister-in-law, died in the fall of 1791. The Hustings Court named Weedon guardian of the two minor children at the time, Hugh (age 15) and Ann (16 or 17 years old), with Weedon posting bond of £600. French S. Gray, James Dykes, and Beverly Chew were named executors for Mrs. Mercer's estate, with Weedon as administrator. Gustavus B. Wallace served as Weedon's security.[20]

Besides old acquaintances, Weedon's circle of friends widened among civic leaders, new merchants in town,[21] and war veterans. From time to time the Weedons were hosts to Revolutionary War officers passing through Fredericksburg. One such visitor was Colonel William Heth, who stopped over at the Weedons for several days in February, 1788, on his way to New York as a state commissioner to liquidate the state

---

[18] Peale to Weedon, 18 December, 1785, 21 February, 7 March, 3 and 13 April, 1786, Peale Letter Book, APS; Weedon to Peale, 20 September, 1786, AKF; Charles Mortimer to John Mortimer, 9 April, 1786 and 21 April, 1788, Minor Family Papers, VHS; Ledger Book #4, UVL. At the time Billy left, the Peales had a daughter, born April, 1786, named Sophonispa. (Sellers, 1947: 1: p. 248.) Jack Mortimer accompanied Billy Mercer to and from Philadelphia.

[19] *Fredericksburg Political Arena*, 27 August, 1839, VHS. William Mercer died 20 August, 1839 "after a protracted sickness." He had continued to paint until his fatal illness. It is unfortunate that, except for the Pendleton miniature (VHS) and the picture of the Battle of Princeton, his other paintings have not been located or identified for the general public.

[20] 25 November, 1791, HCOB-C; 25 November, 1791 and 24 February, 1792, Fredericksburg City Bond Book, A, 1782-1832.

[21] E.g., as evident in writing letters of introduction for Robert Patton, Charles Urquhart, and Jack Mortimer in seeking out "commercial connections" in the north. (Weedon to John Page, 23 July, 1789, WPC, CHS; Weedon to Gen. Benjamin Lincoln,—July, 1789, collection of Charles McDaniel, Fredericksburg; Weedon to Henry Knox, 20 April, 1789, Knox Papers, Massachusetts Historical Society.)

military debts with John Pierce, the United States commissioner of army accounts. The old colonel had lost an eye in the
war and was now as stout as Weedon himself. Other dinner
guests of the Weedons during Heth's stay at the Sentry Box
were Colonel (Burgess?) Ball, Dr. Charles Mortimer, the
Reverend Thomas Ryan, and Captain John Enys, a British
officer touring the United States. Heth was startled to find
that Enys had been the commander of the guard when Heth
had been a prisoner in Canada during the war.[22]

Washington visited his mother in Fredericksburg several
times during this period, and George Weedon had a chance to
meet with him. The former commander in chief stayed with
his sister, Betty Lewis, at whose home Weedon joined
Washington for dinner on April 28, 1787. The other guests
were Colonel Charles Carter, Judge Mercer, and John Lewis.
For two days in June, 1788, Washington was again in Fredericksburg. On June 12, William Fitzhugh held a small dinner
party for Washington; Colonels Charles Carter and Francis
Willis "and their Ladies" and General Weedon (mentioned in
that order) also attended. Probably Catharine Weedon did not
accompany her husband at either of the two dinners. Two
months before he would set out for his inauguration as president, Washington made his last visit to his mother in February, 1789, and possibly George Weedon called on the soon to
be President-Elect.[23] During his southern tour in 1791, President Washington stayed in Fredericksburg, April 8-10, and
George Weedon, as a council member, president of the Society
of the Cincinnati and a veteran general, must surely have been
received by Washington.[24]

George Weedon enjoyed his life of ease and pleasure, as if
there were no tomorrow. He became more susceptible to
gambling than he used to be. Frequent purchases of lottery
tickets and presumably some addiction to cards proved costly
to him.[25] A "Memorandum" to Weedon's account with
Thomas Brumfield, covering the period 1785–1790 is reveal-
ing: "The above enormous a/c [£163] was in consequence of

[22] Heth, 1892: pp. 323, 325, and 329; Cometti, 1976: p. 253.

[23] Weedon to Henry Knox, 17 June, 1788, Fitzpatrick, 1931-: **29**: p. 517; 10-13 June, 1788, Fitzpatrick, 1925: **2**: p. 366; Duke, 1949: pp. 155-156.

[24] Washington to Jefferson, Alexander Hamilton, and Henry Knox, 4 April, 1791 and William Harvey "to the President of the U.S.A.," 11 April, 1791, Washington Papers, Series 4, Reel 100, LC.

[25] Receipt, 1 February, 1792, for six "packs of cards," account James Blair, Personal Accounts-Weedon, VSL. In all of Weedon's ledger books, purchase of lottery tickets is a recurring item.

disipation, and unguarded conduct and will I hope be a lesson to those who follow me."[26]

As ever, Weedon was inclined to overindulgence in food and drink. His cellar was amply stocked with wine and ale, indicating perhaps that he no longer preferred the rum punches of the old days.[27] An interesting allusion to Weedon's drinking is contained in a document prepared by President Washington in the winter of 1791–1792. After the defeat of General St. Clair's army in the Northwest Territory on November 4, 1791, the President and Congress were looking for a new commander in chief of the army. The "Opinion of the General Officers," intended as a reference guide for discussions on the appointment in the Cabinet, mentioned twenty generals and gave capsule character evaluations of sixteen generals "now living, and in this Country . . . ." Omitted in the evaluations were "those who it is conjectured would not, from age, want of health, and other circumstances come forward by any inducements . . . and such as ought not to be named for the important trust of Commander in Chief." Weedon was one of the generals considered:

> Majr. Genl. (by Brevet) Weedon
> Not supposed to be an Officer of much resource though not deficient in a competent share of understanding; rather addicted to ease and pleasure; and no enemy it is said to the bottle; never has had his name brot. forward on this acct.[28]

The highlight of social activity at the Sentry box was the splendid Christmas festivity. Hugh Tennent Weedon Mercer fondly recalled in 1837:

> For many years after the Revolution my uncle celebrated at 'The Sentry Box' (his residence, and now mine) the capture of the Hessians, by a great festival—a jubilee dinner, if I may so express myself—at which the Revolutionary officers then living here and in our vicinity, besides others of our friends, were always present. It was an annual feast, a day or so after Christmas Day, and the same guests always attended. . . . I

---

[26] Ledger Book #3, account Thomas Brumfield, VSL. Except for lottery tickets, other items of Weedon's indebtedness in this account are omitted. There is cash "paid you at sundry times."

[27] Receipts, 1790-1792, Personal Accounts-Weedon, VSL. Weedon's purchases were almost exclusively wine and ale.

[28] "Opinion of the General Officers" (considered in the Cabinet), 9 March, 1792, Fitzpatrick, 1931-: **31**: pp. 509-515; "Washington's Opinion of his General Officers," 1879: #2: p. 81. The document is also printed on pp. 82-87.

was young, and a little fellow, and was always drawn up at the table to sing 'Christmas Day in '76.'

Two young servant boys he was bringing up as waiters in the family were posted at the door as sentinels, in military costumes, with wooden muskets on their shoulders; one he called Corporal Killbuck and the other Corporal Killdee. It was always a joyous holiday at 'The Sentry Box.'

Hugh still had a copy of the words of George Weedon's song, "Christmas Day in '76."

On Christmas Day in seventy-six
Our ragged troops, with bayonets fixed,
   For Trenton marched away.
The Delaware ice, the boats below,
The light obscured by hail and snow,
   But no signs of dismay.
Our object was the Hessian band
That dare invade fair Freedom's land,
   At quarter in that place.
Great Washington, he led us on,
With ensigns steaming with renown,
   Which ne'er had known disgrace.
In silent march we spent the night
Each soldier panting for the fight,
   Though quite benumbed with frost.
Greene on the left at six began,
The right was with brave Sullivan,
   Who in battle no time lost.
Their pickets stormed; the alarm was spread;
The rebels, risen from the dead,
   Were marching into town.
Some scampered here, some scampered there,
And some for action did prepare;
   But soon their arms laid down.
Twelve hundred servile miscreants,
With all their colors, guns, and tents,
   Were trophies of the day.
The frolic o'er, the bright canteen
In center, front, and rear, was seen,
   Driving fatigue away.
And, brothers of the cause, let's sing
Our safe deliverance from a king
   Who strove to extend his sway.
And life, you know, is but a span;
Let's touch the tankard while we can,
   In memory of the day.[29]

[29] Hugh T. W. Mercer to the "grandfather of Judge Beverly Wellford, of Richmond," 8 February, 1837, quoted in Goolrick, 1906: pp. 84-87.

Community and Government

George Weedon continued to be active in civic affairs, and his popularity was evident. He won the most votes in the 1787 councilmanic election; he came in third in 1788 and 1789, first in 1790, fourth in 1791, and second in 1792. When, in March, 1788, Fredericksburg was divided into three wards, Weedon was one of four councilmen assigned to represent the first ward. His special duties during the period included serving as one of four "fire wards" and on a committee for leasing the "public Wharf."[30] As an alderman, Weedon still sat on the bench of the Hustings Court. With attacks of gout becoming more severe, beginning late 1788, Weedon's attendance at the monthly sessions of the Hustings Court became increasingly irregular. Occasionally he sat on examining courts that dealt with felonies and on special sessions as courts of oyer and terminer to try slave offenses.[31]

Weedon became more active at St. George's Church, and was elected a vestryman in 1789. He held military certificates for the church until they were sold eventually by the church treasurer. In addition to tithes, Weedon contributed to subscriptions for a new bell and the building of a wing to the church, which would give the church a cruciform appearance. As assigned by lottery among the "subscribers," the Weedons' pew was number twelve.[32]

Being a trustee of the Fredericksburg Academy (sixty students, fifteen of whom were boarded) took some of Weedon's time, in attending the semi-annual meetings, in visiting classes once in a while to "hear the several scholars rehearse their lesson," and, with all the trustees in attendance, conducting a "public examination" of the students.[33] Weedon

---

[30] 17 March and 11 July, 1787, 7 and 12 March and 10 April, 1788, 16 March and 6 July, 1789, FCCM.

[31] 15 January, 1787 and 29 March, 1788, and 1789 *passim*, FCCM; 6 August and 3 September, 1787, 4 August and 1 September, 1788, and October 1788-January 1789 *passim*, 23 October, 27 November, and 25 December, 1789 *passim*, 23 October, 27 November *passim*, 23 October, 27 November, and 25 December, 1789, HCOB-C; Weedon to Washington, 2 December, 1788, Washington Papers, Series 4, Reel 98, LC; 20 November, 1788, Legislative Petitions, Fredericksburg, VSL.

[32] 8 September and 26 November, 1787, 7 June, 1788, and 17 October, 1789, St. George's Parish Vestry Book, 1746-1817, micro., VSL; Quenzal, 1951: pp. 20-22 and 91; Slaughter, 1847: p. 26.

[33] Meeting of the Trustees . . ., *Virginia Herald and Fredericksburg Advertiser*, 17 May and 12 June, 1788 and 6 and 30 July and 26 November, 1789; Meeting of the Trustees . . ., 2 November, 1789, Legislative Petitions, Fredericksburg, VSL. Other trustees besides Weedon in 1789 were: James Mercer, President; Mann Page, Vice President; William Fitzhugh; Charles Carter, Jr.; Lawrence Brooke; and John Minor.

and the other trustees, all of whom had personally underwritten the debts of the academy, had difficulty in getting persons who owed the academy to pay up, and even petitioned the Virginia Assembly to bring suit against the debtors. Some money was raised by lotteries.[34]

Strangely there is no indication of George Weedon's reaction to the government of the United States receiving a "new roof." Unquestionably he favored a stronger national government of one sort or another, as did most former Continental Army officers. He had made it clear in earlier years that he supported the idea of a permanent military establishment. He probably echoed the current sentiment of his Cincinnati brethren and various nationalists of a need for "a hoop to the barrel." Whatever comments he may have made on the Constitutional Convention, the Virginia Ratifying Convention, and simply the launching of the new ship of state have not survived, however. The Fredericksburg area was sharply divided between Antifederalists and "Federalists." If George Weedon was not an outright nationalist, it may nevertheless be assumed that he did not put much stock in neighbor James Monroe's Antifederalism, which advocated a Bill of Rights and opposed the treaty making power in the Constitution.[35]

As Weedon seemed to lack interest in the forming of a new central government under the Constitution, he also showed no inclination at all in soliciting a military command. After all, he was too old, in his fifties, and suffering from gout. There were plenty of younger men, who, having served in the Revolution in the lower ranks as Weedon had done in the French and Indian War, were now staying in military service or wanted to return to it. Weedon had not been excited by Congress's call for an army of 2,040 men,[36] ostensibly to fight the western Indians but actually to quell Shays's Rebellion. Nor was Weedon one of the many veterans who plied Washington with applications for patronage jobs.

The gunfactory property—the land and the "ruinous buildings"—had been purchased for £863 16s. and only £637 3s. 8d. had been paid; therefore the trustees had involved themselves for the remainder—£188 8s. 3d., "a dear loss."

[34] Meeting of the Trustees . . ., 2 November, 1789, Legislative Petitions, Fredericksburg, VSL; *Virginia Herald and Fredericksburg Advertiser*, 14 August, 1789.

[35] For Monroe's part in the Virginia Ratifying Convention, see Cresson, 1946: pp. 96-102.

[36] 10 October, 1786, Ford, 1904-1937: **31**: pp. 892-893.

Cincinnatus

The Society of the Cincinnati provided a means for Weedon to keep in contact with officers whom he had known during the war and gave him an opportunity to correspond with General Gates, who was acting president of the national organization after Washington's resignation, as well as Washington himself. One time Weedon sent Washington some "Jerusalem Artichoke" which he had received from "Mr. [John or Mann] Page." Washington, however, returned the gift because a Captain Grymes had already sent him five bushels of the sunflower seed, which he considered "sufficient to make the experiment I had in contemplation." Washington did say that he would follow Weedon's directions in planting, and he asked Weedon whether the seeds should be planted in hills or "in drills" and at what distance.[37]

George Weedon relived war experiences with the veteran officers whenever the Society of the Cincinnati met. He worked hard to keep the Virginia chapter of the society a going concern, despite so many officers' refusing to take an active part. Weedon presided at meetings held in Richmond on March 20 and April 24, 1787. But he absented himself from the July meeting because of "Business of the utmost importance."[38] Weedon was re-elected president of the state society when the chapter convened in Anderson's Tavern in Richmond on November 10, 1787.[39] In forwarding the November, 1787, proceedings to Washington, Weedon asked that Washington send him some cuttings of the yellow or golden willow trees. Washington complied by sending fifty cuttings and advised Weedon that the best time for planting them was in the spring.[40]

Meetings of the Virginia Society of the Cincinnati were held July 4 and November 13, 1788, again at Anderson's Tavern. Only twenty-four members appeared for the November session, when Weedon was re-elected president. On Friday, November 15, the society members lined up in procession to

---

[37] Washington to Weedon, 25 March, 1787, Fitzpatrick, 1931-: **29**: p. 182; Weedon to Gates, 23 February, 1787, Emmet Collection, #8258, NYPL.

[38] Weedon to Col. Meriwether, 4 July, 1787, Hume, 1938: pp. 31-33 and 167n.

[39] "Minutes," *ibid.*, pp. 34-35.

[40] Washington to Weedon, 3 and 17 December, 1787, Fitzpatrick, 1931-: **29**: pp. 328-340.

accompany the body of a cohort, Dr. Alexander Skinner, to the cemetery.[41] Weedon transmitted the minutes of this meeting to Washington, adding that "a very severe fit of the gout which crippled me for three months deprived me the pleasure of visiting you at Mount Vernon this fall agreeable to promise."[42] Whether the society met throughout 1789 is not known, although there was a special meeting in August, 1789 to vote a sum of money to pay for costs of an eagle made by Major L'Enfant for the state branch.[43] At the end of the year, the society met at the Eagle Tavern in Richmond, and Weedon was re-elected president.[44]

Weedon presided over the annual meeting at the Eagle Tavern in Richmond in October, 1790. With only twenty-one members present, Weedon was re-elected president. It was a bad year for the Virginia chapter, which was one of seven state branches not to be represented at the general meeting in Philadelphia in May.

Curiously Weedon and Colonel William Davies represented the Virginia society at an extra general meeting in Philadelphia in May, 1791. The two men probably had little to say to each other. Weedon could not forget how Davies had tried to have him dismissed from the Virginia Continental line in 1781, and Davies still refused to attend meetings of the society in Virginia as long as Weedon was president. The local society performed a charitable function in distributing modest annuities for widows and children of deceased officers in need. Although Weedon advertised the October, 1791 meeting of the Virginia society in the Fredericksburg newspaper, only twenty-two showed up for the annual get-together in Richmond. In order to keep the society going, a standing committee was appointed to conduct routine business.[45]

By 1792 Weedon considered the presidency of the Virginia chapter of he Cincinnati with travel to Richmond each year for the annual meeting too much of a physical strain. He

---

[41] 13-14 March, 1788, Proceedings of the Cincinnati of Virginia, Washington Papers, Series 4, Reel 98, LC.

[42] Weedon to Washington, 2 December, 1788, *ibid*.

[43] "Minutes" and Weedon to Col. Theo. Meriwether, 11 August, 1789, Hume, 1938: pp. 167 and 179, resp.

[44] Hume, 1938: pp. 36-37.

[45] "Minutes" and Extract from the Journal . . . Cincinnati of the State of Virginia, 27 October, 1790, *ibid*.; pp. 40-42, 180, and 411; *Virginia Herald and Fredericksburg Advertiser*, 22 September, 1791 (item: 30 August, 1791).

wrote his vice-president, James Wood, on October 1, 1792, submitting his resignation. He said that he had been in hopes of laying the "inclosed papers" before the October meeting, "but my declining state of health has deprived me of that Satisfaction, and of the pleasure of meeting my field companions this October. Indeed I see little hopes of a change for the better in any short time, that I am induced to resign that honorable station of President to which my friends have so frequently called me assuring them that I shall ever retain a grateful remembrance of their attention, and to the last moment of life a prayer for their prosperity."[46]

The Last Year

Hardly able to get up and about in early 1793, George Weedon abandoned his civic respnsibilities. His last attendance on the Hustings Court was January 25, 1793, and he refused to be a candidate in the March councilmanic election,[47] thus capping a decade of municipal service. When he ventured out it was most likely to visit the Rising Sun Tavern, which was several blocks down Caroline Street from the Sentry Box and which his friend, Gustavus Brown Wallace, had purchased in April, 1792.[48]

Perhaps Weedon's last public appearance was to attend the Fourth of July festivities. In addition to the fire works, a large public banquet was held at 2 p.m. in the Market House, where "the Cap of Liberty" was "placed in the center of the table; after which 15 truly federal toasts were drank, accompanied by a discharge of cannon." Probably the Weedons, for the first time, passed up the gala ball in the evening, sponsored by the "Daughters of Freedom" at Mrs. Hackley's tavern.[49]

From the seclusion of the Sentry Box, George Weedon was as avid a reader of newspapers as he had always been. He rejoiced at President Washington's re-election and the news that the Virginia electors voted unanimously for him, but he

---

[46] Weedon to James Wood, 1 October, 1792, Society of the Cincinnati Papers, NYPL.

[47] 25 January and 18 March, 1793, HCOB-C.

[48] License to keep tavern to Lt. John Frazer, 22 March, 1793, Rising Sun Tavern, Fredericksburg; *Virginia Herald and Fredericksburg Advertiser*, 22 November, 1793. Wallace leased the tavern to Lt. John Frazer in March, 1793; Frazer died in November, a month before Weedon's death.

[49] *Virginia Herald and Fredericksburg Advertiser*, 4 and 11 July, 1793.

must have disapproved of the Virginia electors casting all their votes for George Clinton, who had been an Antifederalist, for vice-president. For Weedon there were too many Antifederalists (would-be Jeffersonians) who condemned what they regarded as the government's preferential treatment of veteran and speculative interests.

It would be interesting to know Weedon's thoughts on the announcement in the Fredericksburg newspaper on December 12 of the appointment of new Virginia militia general officers—the four major generals being Samuel Hopkins, Jonathan Clarke, Daniel Morgan, and Henry Lee.[50] Earlier in the year he had the satisfaction to learn that Thomas Posey, for whom he had given a strong recommendation, had been appointed a brigadier general in the western army.[51]

The fall of 1793 was a gloomy one in Fredericksburg. Ships from Philadelphia were not allowed into the port, and were detained at Hazel Run for fear of the spread of the yellow fever epidemic from the capital city.[52] Weedon was irritated by hunters who were invading his farm. The last two weeks in October, 1793, he published notice in the Fredericksburg newspaper: "I HEREBY forewarn all persons from hunting, shooting, or in any Manner trespassing on my Lands on the Fall-Hill, as I shall prosecute all those found so doing. GEORGE WEEDON."[53]

One last measure of happiness for George Weedon, shortly before he died, was to witness the marriage of his only niece. Sometime in 1793 (before November 25) Ann Mercer married George Weedon's friend, Robert Patton, who was many years her senior. Although practically on his deathbed, Weedon undoubtedly was able to attend and give the bride away. Observed Elizabeth Thornton Dunbar in a letter to her sister:

> But if I go on so fast I will not have time to tell you about Miss Ann Mercer's wedding. Well, Polly and myself were drawn forth in our best airs on the occasion, last Thursday . . . and saw Miss M. give her hand to the delighted Mr. Patton. You

[50] *Ibid.*, 12 December, 1793.

[51] *Ibid.*, 14 March, 1793; Herndon, 1943: pp. 179-180. Posey applied in June, 1791; Weedon's endorsement is noted, 5 June, 1792.

[52] 16 September, 1793, FCCM; Fontaine Maury, Mayor, to the Governor, 17 September, 1793, Palmer, 1875-: **6**: pp. 536-537.

[53] *Virginia Herald and Fredericksburg Advertiser*, 24 and 31 October, 1793.

may be sure she looked infinitely lovely; her dress was white satin and muslin; her necklace, earrings and bracelets were very brilliant.[54]

Two days before Christmas, 1793, George Weedon died. The *Virginia Gazette and General Advertiser* in Richmond duly reported on December 25: "On Monday evening last departed this life, in Fredericksburg, GEORGE WEEDON, Esq. late Major-General in the army of the United States. The death of this valuable citizen will be long lamented, not only by his relatives, but by all who had the pleasure of his acquaintance."[55] Tradition has it that he was buried in the northwest corner of the Masonic Cemetery in Fredericksburg.[56]

A month before his death, George Weedon made out a long will. It was probated January 24, 1794. Robert Patton and John Mercer were named executors, with William Glassell and Robert Dunbar putting their names on the bond of £15,000 to the Hustings Court.[57] The inventory and appraisement of the estate were returned and recorded April 25, 1794.[58] Hugh Tennent Weedon Mercer, the only minor of the Mercer children, made choice of his brother-in-law, Robert Patton, as guardian.[59] Weedon left Catharine all the Fredericksburg property, except, by a codicil, lot #250 to John

---

[54] Goolrick, 1906: pp. 105-107. Letter of Mrs. (Elizabeth Gregory Thornton) Dunbar to Mrs. Frances Thronton, n.d., quoted on p. 106. Robert Patton lived nearby on Caroline Street. (Mutual Assurance Society of Virginia, 8 July, 1797, #168, micro., VSL.)

[55] *Virginia Gazette and General Advertiser* (Richmond), 25 December, 1793.

[56] George H. S. King to the author, 14 November, 1974. Of the Weedon-Mercer-Patton connection only the graves of the infant son and daughter of Robert and Ann Mercer Patton are identified. It is logical that the Weedons were buried in the cemetery. Mr. King has discussed the matter with Fredericksburg oldsters. This was the contention, for example, of Sallie I. Forbes (1854-1952), great-granddaughter of Robert and Ann Mercer Patton. Most prominent men in the civic life of Fredericksburg and friends of Weedon are buried there, with many of the tombstones still extant. From the inspection of the cemetery, the author considers that the northwest part of the cemetery (as Mr. King believes) is the likely burial place (the Fredericksburg Masonic Lodge placed a headstone at this site marking Weedon's alleged grave, in June, 1978, with a dedication ceremony being held), but still admitting the possibility of St. George's Churchyard and, even more remotely, the grounds toward the river of the Sentry Box. For a list and brief biographies of persons known to be buried in the Masonic cemetery, see Cajett, 1928.

[57] 24 January, 1794, HCOB-C; 24 January, 1794, Fredericksburg City Bond Book, A, VSL.

[58] 25 April, 1794, HCOB-C; the inventory was returned 1 April, 1794. (Fredericksburg City Hustings Court Will Book, A, VSL.)

[59] 23 May, 1794, HCOB-C. Robert Dunbar underwrote the bond of £6,000.

Mercer and lots #231 and #240 to Hugh Mercer. The land at Fall Hill, with slaves and other plantation property, he divided equally between John and Hugh. William Mercer received no mention, and for George there was only the amount still due on the Crab Cove plantation owed by Thacker Washington. One moeity each was assigned to Catharine Weedon on one part and Hugh and John on the other of Weedon's "Six per Cent Stock" registered at the Virginia Loan Office, the total of which was presumably represented by 1,666 2/3 acres of land in Ohio at a later time. George Gray was to receive 3,000 acres in Kentucky. Two thousand acres each were assigned to William Strother, Weedon's half-brother, and Samuel Roddy in Fayette (later Gallatin) County, Kentucky. The house servants were left to Catharine. His "faithful Servant Bob" was to be freed upon the death of Catharine, and if the laws of Virginia at that time prevented this, a petition to the assembly was to be made or "other means" were to be used as his executors "may deem most expedient."[60] Catharine Weedon died in March, 1797,[61] and the two nephews, according to various stipulations in George Weedon's will, succeeded to Catharine's share of the estate.

No mindless statues are mounted in any public place as a reminder of George Weedon. But the portly ex-tavern-keeper made a significant contribution to the winning of independence. He distinguished himself as a field commander in many important battles and operations. He had a major role in the direction of defense preparations in Virginia that thwarted the British invasions. Weedon's insistence on honor, which resulted in temporary leave from the service from early 1778 until summer 1780, without his anticipating it, really worked to his advantage. With all southern Continentals

---

[60] Weedon's Will, Fredericksburg Hustings Court Will Book, A, VSL. For the Ohio lands of Weedon (to John and Hugh Mercer), see ". . . Recorded in Office of the Department of State, 27 July, 1810, pursuant to Acts of Congress, 10 August, 1790 and 9 June, 1794 . . . lands granted to Daniel Call, Devisee of Robert Meares . . . assignee of John and Hugh Mercer," AKF. William Strother died before final determination of the Kentucky land grant. For insurance purposes, the Sentry Box and out buildings were evaluated at $4,950 (based on estimate of $6,200 to build). The value of the tavern property was $4,900. A storehouse on the tavern property, occupied by a Mr. Jackson, was valued at $300.00. (31 March and 1 April, 1796, Mutual Assurance Society Declarations, 3, micro., VSL.)

[61] *Fredericksburg Republican Citizen and Farmers and Planters Chronicle*, 29 March, 1797, Harvard University Library.

being sent to the Southern theater, he could only have met the misfortune of his friend and antagonist, William Woodford— captivity after the siege of Charleston; if by circumstance he had met the next encounter, it would have been disaster at Camden; and, if still surviving, there would have been either the unrewarding exasperation of fitting into Greene's Fabian tactics in the Carolinas or his being given the same responsi- bility in Virginia as he was to exercise anyway upon returning to the army. Undeniably Weedon was the patriot, and he gave his best for his country. As a professional soldier, he also retained his honor. He was gregarious and worldly, but few men had his realism and dedication; as much as anyone he saw the war as it actually was.

BIBLIOGRAPHY

MANUSCRIPTS

County and other local records are mainly available in photostats and microfilm at the Virginia State Library. Those collections from various depositories in microfilm copy at the Virginia State Library and used at the Library are designated by an asterisk. Microfilm collections of selected or miscellaneous items at the Virginia State Library are listed under that heading rather than the original depositories. Collections in microfilm edition, obtained through interlibrary loan, have a double asterisk. Other microfilm and photoduplication made available to the author are identified by a triple asterisk.

American Philosophical Society, Philadelphia
Correspondence of General George Weedon (153 items)***
Correspondence of General Nathanael Greene, 1777-1780
Sol Feinstone Revolutionary War Collection
Charles Willson Peale Letter Book

Brown University Library
Letters of General George Weedon (119 items; many are copies)***

Chicago Historical Society
George Weedon-John Page Correspondence (90 pp.)***

William L. Clements Library, Ann Arbor, Michigan
Nathanael Greene Papers (Weedon Correspondence)***

Duke University Library
Letter of Weedon to John F. Mercer, 9 September, 1783

Historial Society of Pennsylvania, Philadelphia
Anthony Wayne Papers***
Simon Gratz Collection
Etting Collection: Revolutionary War Papers
Dreer Collection: Letters of the Generals of the American Revolution
Society Collections: Revolutionary War Generals
Muhlenberg Orderly Book (Muhlenberg Papers)

Harvard University Library
Sparks MSS (Weedon Letters)***
Febiger Letter Books, 1778-1782*

Henry E. Huntington Library, San Marino, California
Letters of George Weedon ***

Library of Congress
Miscellaneous Collection (Revolution)
Peter Force Transcripts (Letters of Col. Walter Stewart)
John Piper Orderly and Account Book, 1781 (Orders Issued by General Weedon During the Campaign)
Washington Weedon, 17 December, 1787, photostat (Washington photostats)
Peter Force Historical MSS (Orderly Book, 8 September-October, 1776)
Adam Stephen Papers
James Monroe Papers: Additional Correspondence, 1780-1836*
Papers of George Washington: Series 4, 5, 6, and 7*
Diary of Dr. Robert Honeyman*

274

Massachusetts Historical Society, Boston
Henry Knox Papers**

Mills College Library, Oakland, California
Weedon to Hames Hunter, Jr., 4 August, 1776***

Minnesota Historical Society, St. Paul, Minnesota
Allyn K. Ford Collection*** (Includes 133 Weedon items, mostly to Weedon)

Morristown National Historical Park, New Jersey
Lloyd W. Smith Collection*

National Archives
Return of the Officers who have served in the third Virginia Regiment, 1 January,
    1776-28 August, 1778: Revolutionary War Rolls-NA 246
Revolutionary War Pensions and Bounty Land Warrants: Application Files
Orderly Books: 21 August-4 October, 1777 (#853-2); 23 May, 1777-20 October, 1778
    (#853-3); 11 June, 1777-25 April, 1778 (#853-3); 1 February-14 March, 1778 (#853-3)
Military Statements Certificates—M859, reels 52-54
Service Record (Weedon)
Papers of the Continental Congress (247): reels 16, 23-24, 40, 50-52, 68, 78, 96, 175-178,
    and 195.

New-York Historical Society
Steuben Papers**
Gates Papers**
Sebastian Bauman Papers
Walter Stewart Papers
Weedon Miscellaneous MSS

New York Public Library
Emmet Collection
Society of the Cincinnati Papers
U.S. Army Box
Miscellaneous Collection-Weedon
Myers Collection (Heth to Morgan, 30 September, 1777)

Pierpont Morgan Library, New York City
Miscellaneous Letters

Private Collections
Fredericksburg District Court Papers (xerox), G. H. S. King, Fredericksburg
Letter Fascimiles, Charles McDaniel, Sentry Box, Fredericksburg
Hill Family Papers, Charles Ryland Collection, Warsaw, Virginia*

Public Record Office, Great Britain, Virginia Records Project*
Cornwallis Papers, 30/11

Rising Sun Tavern, Fredericksburg
License for tavern-Lt. John Frazer, 22 March, 1793
Land Warrant-Weedon (1808)

University of Virginia, Alderman Library
[Ledger Book #4] Weedon Account Book, 1783-1793, #2525
Miscellaneous Weedon Letters
Lewis Family Papers
James Hunter Papers
Wallace Papers
Lee Papers*
Charles Yates Letter Book

Virginia Historical Society
Thom Family Papers
Hugh B. Grigsby Papers, notes, Section 70
Continental Congress Resolution, 22 February, 1777 and Extract from the Minutes

John Chilton Letters and Diary (3 January-8 September, 1777)
David Griffith Papers: Revolutionary War Letters, 1776-1778
Hugh Mercer's Will, 22 March, 1776, photograph
Martin Pickett Letters
James Hunter's Lease to Nathaniel [sic] Greene, 10 September, 1784
The Minor Family Papers, Section 35: Copies of Letters by Charles Mortimer to John Mortimer

Virginia State Library
Personal Accounts of George Weedon 1790-1792—Receipts (Stack 7, B-14)
John K. Martin Pension Papers
James Monroe Papers in Virginia Repositories*
Lee Family Papers from Various Depositories*
Revolutionary War Records: U.S. War Department, pertaining to Virginia (NA), reels 42-46*
Mutual Assurance Society of Virginia, Declarations*
[Ledger Book #2] Weedon Account Book, 1765, 1773-1785, 1791, from Clerk's Office, Fredericksburg*
[Ledger Book #3] Weedon Account Book, 1784-1793, #21354
Public Service Claims: King George County, (a) Lists and (b) Court Booklet; Certificates; and Commissioners's Book 5
Fredericksburg City Bond Book A, 1782-1832*
Fredericksburg City Hustings Court Order Book: (A) 1782-1785; (B) 1782-1787; (C)1787-1800
Fredericksburg City Common Council Minutes, 1782-1801*
Fredericksburg City Hustings Court Deed Book: (A) 1782-1787 and (B) 1787-1794*
Fredericksburg City Hustings Court Will Book: (A) 1782-1817*
William Allason Letter Book, 1770-1789*
William Allason Papers*
William Allason Ledgers: A through H
Bounty Warrants, Weedon to Col. —, 30 May, 1785, #21058*
Richard Young Papers
Weedon to [J. F. Mercer], n.d., #19732
Legislative Petitions: Fredericksburg; Spotsylvania County
Virginia Land Office—Revolutionary War Military Bounty Warrant Books 1-3
Bounty Warrants (Thornton Papers)
Land Office—Bounty Certificates: French and Indian War Warrants
Virginia State Land Office—Surveys, #19
Draper Collection, Virginia Papers, ZZ, 4*
Virginia Militia Records 1754-1758, #20317*
War MSS: War Office Journal, 18 January-31 December, 1781, #53; List of Officers of the Army and Navy which received Lands from Virginia for Revolutionary Services (10 September, 1833), #43
Executive Papers
Westmoreland County: Court Orders; Deeds and Wills; Records and Inventories
King George County Deed Book, #7
Stafford County Deed Books
Arrangement of the Virginia Line, February 1781-1782
St. George Parish Vestry Book, 1746-1817*
Fredericksburg Lodge A. F. A. M. Record Book, September, 1752-December, 1771, Lodge #4*
Statement showing the value of certain houses in Fredericksburg as assessed for insurance in 1796 and 1822
Executive Communications
Spotsylvania County Committee Resolves, 14-15 December, 1774, #22871
James Hunter Papers

College of William and Mary
[Ledger Book #1] Weedon Account Book, 1772-1773 (meat accounts)***

NEWSPAPERS

Fredericksburg Republican Citizen and Farmers and Planters Chronicle, 1796-1797, Harvard University Library
Fredericksburg Political Arena, 1839, VHS
Virginia Gazette (Rind); (Dixon and Nicolson); (Dixon and Hunter); (Purdie and Dixon); (Hunter); (Purdie)
Virginia Gazette and General Advertiser (Richmond)
Virginia Herald and Fredericksburg Advertiser, 1788-1793
Maryland Journal and Baltimore Advertiser, 1783, Maryland Historical Society

UNPUBLISHED WORKS

Benson, Dale E. 1970. "Wealth and Power in Virginia, 1774-1776: A Study of the Organization of Revolt," dissertation, University of Maine.
Caley, Percy b. 1939. "Dunmore: Colonial Governor of New York and Virginia, 1770-1782," dissertation, University of Pittsburgh.
Coakley, Robert W. 1949. "Virginia Commerce During the American Revolution," dissertation, University of Virginia.
Embrey's Index of Records, Stafford County, (1) Grantees and (2) Grantors (typescript, microfilm, VSL).
Embrey's Fredericksburg City General Index to Deeds, Wills . . ., (1) Grantees and (2) Grantors (typescript, microfilm, VSL).
King, George H. S. "Weedon Family of Westmoreland County, Virginia, Genealogical Chart" (typescript).
————. "George Weedon and his Sentry Box" (mimeographed).
Konigsberg, Charles. 1966. "Edward Carrington, 1748-1810: Child of the Revolution . . .," dissertation, Princeton University.
Matthews, John C. 1939. "Richard Henry Lee and the American Revolution," dissertation, University of Virginia.
Sellers, John R. 1968. "The Virginia Continental Line, 1775-1780," dissertation, Tulane University.

PUBLISHED CONTEMPORARY SOURCES

ACOMB, EVELYN M., ed. 1958. *The Revolutionary Journal of Baron Ludwig von Closen, 1780-1783* (Chapel Hill).
ANDERSON, D. R., ed. 1915. "The Woodford, Howe, and Lee Letters." *Richmond College Historical Papers* 1: pp. 96-163.
————. 1917. "The Letters of William Allason, Merchant of Falmouth, Virginia." *Richmond College Historical Papers* 2: pp. 118-175.
The Aspinwall Papers. 1871. *Collections of the Mass. Hist. Soc.*, ser. 4, **9** (Boston).
BALCH, THOMAS, ed. 1876. *The Journal of Claude Blanchard, 1780-1783* (Albany).
————. 1857. *Papers Relating Chiefly to the Maryland Line During the Revolution* (Philadelphia).
BALLAGH, JAMES C., ed. 1911 and 1914. *The Letters of Richard Henry Lee* (2 v., New York).
BOURG, BARON CRONOT DU. 1880. "Diary of a French Officer 1781." *Magazine of Amer. Hist.* 4: pp. 376-385 and 441-449.
BOYD, JULIAN P., ed. 1950-. *The Papers of Thomas Jefferson* (18 v., Princeton).
BROCK, R. A., ed. 1883 and 1885. *The Official Records of Robert Dinwiddie* (2 v., Richmond).
————. 1892. "Orderly Book of Major William Heth, with excerpt from diary of 1788." *Va. Hist. Soc. Collections*, new ser., **11**: pp. 317-376.
BROOKE, FRANCIS T. 1849. *Narrative of My Life* (Richmond).
BROWN, JOSEPH, ed. "A Book of General Orders for the Year 1777." [Kirkwood, Captain Robert]. *Papers of the Hist. Soc. of Del.* 1910. **56**, 2: pp. 48-277.
BROWN, STUART G., ed. 1959. *The Autobiography of James Monroe* (Syracuse, New York).

BURNABY, ANDREW. 1904. *Travels Through the Middle Settlements in North America
. . . 1759 and 1760* (3rd ed., New York).

BURNETT, EDMUND C., ed. 1921-1938. *Letters of Members of the Continental Congress*
(8 v., Washington, D.C.).

BYRD, WILLIAM. 1966. "A Progress to the Mines," in Louis B. Wright, ed. *The Prose
Works of William Byrd of Westover* (Cambridge, Mass.), pp. 339-378.

CAMPBELL, CHARLES, ed. 1840 and 1843. *The Bland Papers . . . Manuscripts of
Colonel Theodorick Bland, Jr.* (2 v., Petersburg, Va.).

―――――. 1860. *The Orderly Book . . . American Army . . . Williamsburg . . .
General Andrew Lewis from March 18th, 1776 to August 28th, 1776* (Richmond).

CHASTELLUX, MARQUIS DE. 1828. *Travels in North-America in the Years 1780-1782*
(New York).

CHINARD, GILBERT, ed. 1928. *Lafayette in America: Unpublished Letters* (Baltimore).

CLARK, WALTER, ed. 1895 and 1904-1907. *The State Records of North Carolina* (v. 11
and 22-25, Winston and Goldsboro).

COMETTI, ELIZABETH, ed. 1976. *The American Journals of Lt. John Enys* (Syracuse,
New York).

"Correspondence of Col. James Wood." 1921. *Tyler's Quarterly*. **3**: pp. 28-44.

*Correspondence of General Washington and Comte de Grasse, 17 August-4 Novem-
ber, 1781*. 1931 71st Congress, 2nd Session, Senate Document #211 (Washington,
D.C.).

"Correspondence of Leven Powell." 1901-1902. *The John P. Branch Historical
Papers of Randolph-Macon College*. **1**: pp. 24-53 and **2**: pp. 111-138.

CROZIER, WILLIAM A., ed. 1905. *Virginia County Records: Spotsylvania County,
1721-1800* (v. 1, New York).

―――――. 1962. *Westmoreland County Wills and Deeds* Vol. 1 of *Va. County
Records Publications* (Baltimore).

[DAVIS]. 1881. "The Yorktown Campaign: Journal of Captain John Davis of the
Pennsylvania Line." *Pa. Mag. Hist. and Biog.* **5**: pp. 290-310.

"Diary of Lieutenant James McMichael of the Pennsylvania Line, 1776-1778." 1892.
Pa. Mag. Hist. and Biog. **16**: pp. 129-159.

"The Diary of Robert Morton." 1877. *Pa. Mag. Hist. and Biog.* **1**: pp. 1-39.

DORMAN, JOHN F., abstractor. 1973-1974. *Westmoreland County, Virginia Deeds,
Patents, 1665-1677*. Parts 1-3 (Washington, D.C.).

―――――. 1970 and 1972. *Westmoreland County Records, 1658-1661* and *1661-
1664* (Washington, D.C.).

―――――. 1967. *Westmoreland County Deeds and Wills.* #3, 1701-1707 (Washington, D.C.).

―――――. 1962-1964. *Westmoreland County Order Book* (3 parts, Washington,
D.C.).

DUANE, WILLIAM, ed. 1877. *Extracts from the Diary of Christopher Marshall . . .,
1774-1781* (Albany).

"Extracts of a letter from a gentleman in Virginia, 22 January, 1781 . . ., in "Notes
and Queries." 1955. *VHMB*. **63**: p. 262.

EWING, JOSEPH S., ed. 1965. "The Correspondence of Archibald McCall and George
McCall, 1777-1783." *VMHB*. **73**: pp. 312-353 and 425-454.

FARISH, HUNTER D., ed. 1957. *Journal and Letters of Philip Vickers Fithian, 1773-
1774* (Williamsburg, Va.).

FITZPATRICK, JOHN C., ed 1925. *The Diaries of George Washington, 1748-1799*
(4 v., Boston).

―――――. 1931-1944. *The Writings of George Washington, 1745-1799* (39 v.,
Washington, D.C.).

FORCE, PETER, ed. 1837-1853. *American Archives* (ser. 4, 6 v. and ser. 5, 3v., Washington, D.C.).

FORD, WORTHINGTON C., ed. 1894. "Defences of Philadelphia 1777." *Pa. Mag. Hist.
and Biog.* **18**: pp. 1-19, 163-184, 329-353, and 463-495.

―――――. 1904-1937. *Journals of the Continental Congress* (34 v., Washington,
D.C.).

_____ . 1889. *Letters of Joseph Jones of Virginia, 1777-1787* (Washington, D.C.).

FOTHERGILL, AUGUST B., compiler, 1925. *Wills of Westmoreland County, Virginia, 1654-1800.*

FRIEND, MRS. J. B., and ELIZABETH V. GAINES, eds. 1931. "Letters of Charles Moile Talbot to Charles Talbot." *WMQ*, ser. 2, **11**: pp. 315-318.

"From Brandywine to Philadelphia: Extract from the Journal of Sergeant Thomas Sullivan . . ." 1910. *Pa. Mag. Hist. and Biog.* **34**: pp. 229-232.

GALLATIN, GASPARD DE. 1931. *Journal of the Siege of York-Town in 1781* (Washington, D.C.).

GOTTSCHALK, LOUIS, ed. 1944. *The Letters of Lafayette to Washington, 1777-1799* (New York).

GREEN, SAMUEL A., ed. 1868. *My Campaigns in America: A Journal Kept by Count William de Deux-Ponts, 1780-1781* (Boston).

GREENE, JACK P., ed. 1965. *The Diary of Landon Carter of Sabine Hall, 1752-1778* (2 v., Charlottesville).

HALL, WILMER, ed. 1966. *Executive Journals of the Council of Colonial Virginia* (v. **5**, Richmond).

HAMILTON, STANILAUS M., ed. 1898-1902. *Letters to Washington and Accompanying Papers* (5 v., Boston and New York).

_____ . 1898. *Writings of James Monroe* (v. **1**, New York).

HAMMOND, OTIS G., ed. 1930-1939. *Letters and Papers of Major-General John Sullivan. Collections of the New Hampshire Hist. Soc.* (3 v. [**13-15**], Concord, N.H.).

HASTINGS, HUGH and J. A. HOLDEN, eds. 1900-1914. *Public Papers of George Clinton.* (10 v., Albany).

HENING, WILLIAM W., ed. 1820-1823. *The Statutes at Large: Being a Collection of All the Laws of Virginia* (v. **4-11**, Richmond).

HILLMAN, BENJAMIN J., ed. 1966. *Executive Journals of the Council of Colonial Virginia* (v. **6**, Richmond).

HUME, EDGAR E., ed. 1938. *Papers of the Society of the Cincinnati in the State of Virginia, 1783-1824* (Richmond).

HUTCHINSON, WILLIAM T., and WILLIAM M. E. RACHAL, eds. 1962-1963. *The Papers of James Madison* (v. **2-3**, Chicago).

JACKSON, DONALD, ed. 1976. *The Diaries of George Washington* (v. **1-2**, Charlottesville).

JAMES, ALFRED P., ed. 1938. *Writings of General John Forbes* (Menasha, Wisc.).

JENNINGS, JOHN M., ed. 1951. "Letters of James Mercer to John Francis Mercer." *VMHB.* **59**: pp. 184-194.

"Journal of Captain Charles Lewis, 10 October to 10 December, 1755." 1892. *Va. Hist. Soc. Collections.* **11**: pp. 203-218.

"Journal of a French Traveller in the Colonies." 1921. *Amer. Hist. Review.* **26**: pp. 726-747.

Journal of the House of Delegates. 1827-1828. October Session, 1776 (Williamsburg, 1776). Subsequent sessions, to 1793, published individually but bound in several volumes (Richmond).

KENNEDY, JOHN P., ed. 1905. *Journal of the House of Burgesses of Virginia, 1773-1776, Including the Records of the Committee of Correspondence* (Richmond).

The Lee [Charles Lee] *Papers.* 1871-1874. *Collections of the NYHS.* **4-7** (4 v., New York).

LELAND, W. G., and E. C. BURNETT, eds. 1915. "Letters from Lafayette to Luzerne, 1780-1782." *Amer. Hist. Review.* **20**: pp. 341-376 and 577-612. Assistance in translation by Mrs. W. H. Pursley of Richmond.

"Letters of Col. Lewis Willis to Charles Yates, 19 June-10 July, 1777." 1894. *VMHB.* **2**: pp. 214-215 and 429-430.

"Letters of General Weedon." 1927. *Tyler's Quarterly.* **8**: pp. 257-258.

LODGE, HENRY C., ed. 1903. *An Authentic Record of the Movements and Engagements of the British Army in America, June 1777 to November 1778*, by Major John André (2 v., Boston).

LYDENBERG, HARRY M., ed. 1930. *Archibald Robertson, Lt.-Gen., Royal Engineers: His Diaries and Sketches in America, 1762-1780* (New York).
Diary of Frederick MacKenzie. 1930. (2 v., Cambridge Mass.).
MACMASTER, RICHARD K., ed. 1971. "News of the Yorktown Campaign: The Journal of Dr. Robert Honyman [Honeyman], 17 April-23 November, 1781." *VMHB.* **79**: pp.. 387-426.
MCILWAINE, H. R., ed. 1928. *Journal of the House of Delegates of Virginia.* March 1781 session. *Bulletin of the VSL.* **17**, no. 1 (Richmond).
————. 1927-1929. *Official Letters of the Governors of the State of Virginia* (3 v., Richmond).
MAYS, DAVID J., ed. 1967. *The Letters and Papers of Edmund Pendleton* (2 v., Charlottesville).
Memoir of Lieut. Col. Tench Tilghman with . . . Revolutionary Journals and Letters. 1876. (Albany).
The Military Journal of George Ewing, a Soldier at Valley Forge, 1754-1824. 1928. (Yonkers, N.Y.).
MOORE, FRANK, compiler. 1967. *The Diary of the American Revolution, 1775-1781.* Abridged and edited by Scott, John A. (New York).
MORTON, LOUIS, ed. 1960. "The Daybook of Robert Wormeley Carter of Sabine Hall, 1768." *VMHB.* **68**: pp. 301-316.
"Narrative of the Duke de Lauzun." 1881. *Mag. of Amer. Hist.* **6**: pp. 51-53.
NICKLIN, JOHN B. C. 1943. "Genealogical Notes and Queries." (Extracts of the Westmoreland County Order Book, 1675/6-1688/9.) *WMQ.* ser. 2, **28**: pp. 525-530.
NOLAN, J. BENNETT. 1934. *Lafayette in America Day by Day* (Baltimore).
NUGENT, NELL M., abstractor. 1963. *Cavaliers and Pioneers: Abstracts of Virginia Land Patents and Grants, 1623-1666* (Baltimore).
"Orderly Book of George Stubblefield." 1887. *Va. Hist. Soc. Collections.* **6**: pp. 141-191.
"Occupation of New York City by the British, 1776: Extracts from the Diary of the Moravian Congregation." 1877. *Pa. Mag. Hist. Biol.* **1**: pp. 133-148 and 250-262.
"Orderly Book of Gen. John Peter Gabriel Muhlenberg, 26 March-20 December, 1777." 1910. *Pa. Mag. Hist. and Biog.* **24**: pp. 21-40, 166-189, 336-360, and 438-477.
PALMER, WILLIAM P., ed. 1875-1886. *Calendar of Virginia State Papers* (6 v., Richmond).
"Papers, Military and Political, 1775-1778 of George Gilmer, M.D." 1887. *Va. Hist. Soc. Collections.* **6**: pp. 69-140.
PARGELLIS, STANLEY, ed. 1936. *Military Affairs in North America, 1748-1765.* (New York).
POST, LYDIA M. 1970. *Personal Recollections of the American Revolution: A Private Journal.* Edited by Sidney Barclay (Port Washington, N.Y.).
Proceedings of the Convention of Delegates Held at the Town of Richmond, Friday, 1 December, 1775 and Afterwards by Adjournment in the City of Williamsburg. 1816. (Richmond).
Proceedings of the Convention of Delegates Held at the Capitol . . . 6 May, 1776. 1816. (Richmond).
RANDOLPH, EDMUND. 1970. *History of Virginia.* Edited by Arthur H. Shaffer, *VHS Documents.* **9** (Charlottesville).
REED, WILLIAM B. 1847. *Life and Correspondence of Joseph Reed.* **1** (Philadelphia).
Report on the Manuscripts of Mrs. Stopford-Sackville of Drayton House, Northamptonshire. 1910. **2** (Hereford, England).
"Revolutionary Army Orders 1778-1779 [Order books VHS]. 1906. *VMHB* **13**: pp. 337-350; 1914. **22**: pp. 6-13.
"Revolutionary Letters." 1928. *Tyler's Quarterly.* **9**: pp. 245-248.
RILEY, EDWARD M., ed. 1963. *The Journal of John Harrower: An Indentured Servant in the Colony of Virginia, 1773-1776* (Williamsburg, Va.).
ROCHAMBEAU, VICOMTE DE. 1936. "The War in America: An Unpublished Journal, 1780-1783," in Weelen, Jean-Edmond, *Rochambeau: Father and Son,* translated by Lawrence Lee (New York).

Ross, Charles, ed. 1859. *Correspondence of Charles, First Marquis Cornwallis.* 1 (London).

Rutland, Robert A., ed. 1970. *The Papers of George Mason, 1725-1792* (3 v., Chapel Hill).

Ryden, George H., ed. 1933. *Letters to and from Caesar Rodney, 1756-1784* (Philadelphia).

Scheer, George F., ed. 1962. *Private Yankee Doodle, Being a Narrative of . . . a Revolutionary Soldier* [Joseph Plumb] (Boston).

Scull, G. D., ed. 1881. *The Montresor Journals. Collections of NYHS.* 14 (New York).

Shelley, Fred, ed. 1954. "The Journal of Ebenezer Hazard in Virginia, 1777." *VMHB.* **62**: pp. 400-423.

Showman, Richard K., ed. 1976. *The Papers of General Nathanael Greene.* 1 (Chapel Hill).

Simcoe, Lt. Col. John G. 1787, 1844. *A Journal of the Operations of the Queen's Rangers from the End of the Year 1777 to the Conclusion of the Late American War* (New York).

Smyth, J. F. D. 1784. *A Tour in the United States of America* (2 v., London).

"Some Washington Memoranda." 1896. *VMHB.* **3**: pp. 200-203.

Sparks, Jared, ed. 1853. *Correspondence of the American Revolution being Letters of Eminent Men to Washington* (4 v., Boston).

Stevens, Sylvester K. et al., eds. 1940-1943. *The Papers of Col. Henry Bouquet* (ser. 21643-21645, 21647, and 21655, Harrisburg).

Stoudt, John J. 1963. *Ordeal at Valley Forge: a Day-by-Day Chronicle from 17 December, 1777 to 18 June, 1778* (Philadelphia).

Sturgill, Claude C., ed. 1970. "Rochambeau's Memoire de la Guerre En Amerique." *VMHB.* **78**: pp. 34-64.

Syrett, Harold C., ed. 1961. *The Papers of Alexander Hamilton.* 1 and 2 (New York).

Tarleton, Lt. Col. Banastre. 1787, 1967. *A History of the Campaigns of 1780 and 1781 in the Southern Provinces of North America* (Spartanburg, S.C.).

Trumbull, Benjamin. 1899. "Journal of the Campaign at New York 1776-1777." *Collections of the Conn. Hist. Soc.* **7**: pp. 175-218.

Tyler, Lyon G., ed. 1931. "The Old Virginia Line in the Middle States During the American Revolution." *Tyler's Quarterly.* **12**: pp. 1-42 and 90-141.

[Waldo] "Valley Forge 1777-1778: Diary of Surgeon Albigence Waldo of the Continental Line." 1897 *Pa. Mag. Hist. and Biog.* **21**: pp. 305-323.

Watson, Winslow C., ed. 1857. *Men and Times of the Revolution, or Memoirs of Elkanah Watson, including his Journals . . ., 1777-1842* (New York).

[Weedon, George]. 1971. *Valley Forge Orderly Book of General George Weedon of the Continental Army under Command of General George Weedon in the Campaign of 1777-1778* (New York).

Weight, John W., ed. 1926. "Pickering's Letter on Washington." *Tyler's Quarterly.* **7**: pp. 16-45.

Whiting, Henry, ed. 1844. *Revolutionary Orders of General Washington . . . 1778, 1780, 1781, & 1782, Selected from MSS of John Whiting* (New York).

[Wild] "Journal of Ebenezer Wild." 1890. *Proceedings of the Mass. Hist. Soc.*, ser. 2, **6**: pp. 78-160.

Williams, Samuel, ed. 1948. *Lieut. Henry Timberlake's Memoirs, 1756-1765* (Marietta, Ga.).

Wright, W. E., ed. 1971. *Memoirs of the Marshal Count de Rochambeau Relative to the War of Independence of the United States* (New York).

Wyllie, John C., ed. 1966. "New Documentary Light on Tarleton's Raid: Letters of Newman Brockenbrough and Peter Lyons." *VMHB.* **74**: pp. 452-461.

SECONDARY WORKS AND REGISTERS

ALBERTS, ROBERT C. 1965. *The Most Extraordinary Adventures of Major Robert Stobo* (Boston).

ALDEN, JOHN R. 1951. *General Charles Lee: Traitor or Patriot?* (Baton Rouge, La.).

AMBLER, CHARLES S. 1936. *George Washington and the West* (Chapel Hill).

AMMON, HARRY. 1971. *James Monroe: The Quest for National Identity* (New York).

BAKER-CROTHERS, HAYES. 1928. *Virginia and the French and Indian War* (Chicago).

BASS, ROBERT D. 1957. *The Green Dragoon: The Lives of Banastre Tarleton and Mary Robinson* (New York).

BELLAMY, FRANCIS R. 1951. *The Private Life of George Washington* (New York).

BERG, FRED A. 1972. *Encyclopedia of Continental Army Units* (Harrisburg).

BILL, ALFRED H. 1952. *Valley Forge: The Making of an Army* (New York).

BOATNER, MARK M. 1966. *Encyclopedia of the American Revolution* (New York).

BOOGHER, WILLIAM F., compiler. 1903. *Gleanings of Virginia History: An Historical and Genealogical Collection* (Washington, D.C.).

BOOKER, J. MOTLEY. 1969. "Annals of the Northern Neck of Virginia." *Northern Neck of Virginia Historical Magazine.* **19**: pp. 1912-1925.

"Books in Colonial Virginia." 1903. *VMHB.* **9**: pp. 389-405.

BOWMAN, ALLEN. 1964. *The Morale of the American Revolutionary Army* (Port Washington, N.Y.).

BRIDENBAUGH, CARL. 1965. *Myths and Realities: Societies of the Colonial South* (New York).

BROWN, JOHN H. 1966. *Early American Beverages* (Rutland, Vt.).

BROWN, STUART E. 1965. *Virginia Baron: The Story of Thomas 6th Lord Fairfax* (Berryville, Va.).

BRUCE, PHILIP A. 1907. *Economic History of Virginia in the Seventeenth Century* (New York).

BUCK, WILLIAM J. 1877. "Washington's Encampment on the Neshaminy." *Pa. Mag.. Hist. and Biog.* **1**: pp. 275-284.

BURGESS, LOUIS A. 1973. *Virginia Soldiers of 1776* (3 v., Spartanburg, S.C.).

BURK, JOHN and continued by Skelton Jones and Louis H. Girardin. 1805 and 1816. *The History of Virginia* (v. **3** and **4**, Petersburg, Va.).

CAJETT, DORA. 1928. *Minor Sketches of Major Folk and Where They Sleep: The Old Masonic Burying Ground, Fredericksburg, Virginia* (Richmond).

CAMPBELL, T. E. 1954. *Colonial Caroline: A History of Caroline County, Virginia* (Richmond).

CANBY, HENRY S. 1941. *The Brandywine* (New York).

CARRINGTON, HENRY B. 1881. *Battles of the American Revolution, 1775-1781* (New York).

————. 1881. "Lafayette's Virginia Campaign." *Mag. Amer. Hist.* **7**: pp. 340-352.

CARSON, JANE. 1965. *Colonial Virginians at Play* (Williamsburg, Va.).

————. 1964. "The Fat Major of the F. H. C.," in Rutman, Darrett, ed., *The Old Dominion: Essays for Thomas Perkins Abernethy*, pp. 79-95 (Charlottesville).

————. 1965. *James Innes and his Brothers of the F. H. C.* (Williamsburg, Va.).

CHAMPAGNE, ROGER J. 1975. *Alexander McDougall and the American Revolution in New York* (Schenectady, N.Y.).

CHITWOOD, O. P. 1967. *Richard Henry Lee: Statesman of the Revolution* (Morgantown, W. Va.).

COMETTI, ELIZABETH. 1964. "Depredations in Virginia During the Revolution," in Darrett Rutman, ed. *The Old Dominion: Essays for Thomas Perkins Abernethy*, pp. 135-151 (Charlottesville).

CONWAY, MONCURE D. 1892. *Barons of the Potomack and the Rappahannock* (New York).

CORKRAN, DAVID H. 1962. *The Cherokee Frontier: Conflict and Survival, 1740-1762* (Norman, Okla.).

CRESSON, W. P. 1946. *James Monroe* (Chapel Hill).

CULVER, FRANCIS B. 1921. *Blooded Horses of Colonial Days* (Baltimore).

CUNEO, JOHN R. 1959. *Robert Rogers of the Rangers* (New York).

DARLINGTON, MARY C. 1920. *History of Colonel Henry Bouquet and the Western Frontiers of Pennsylvania, 1747-1764* (priv. printed).

DARTER, OSCAR H. 1957. *Colonial Fredericksburg and Neighborhood in Perspective* (New York).

DAVISON, BERTHA. 1963. "A History of Washington Parish." *Northern Neck of Virginia Historical Magazine.* **13**: pp. 1195-1211.

DAWSON, HENRY B. 1886. *Westchester County, New York During the American Revolution* (New York).

DE KOVEN, MRS. REGINALD. 1913. *The Life and Letters of John Paul Jones* (2 v., New York).

"Descendants of Francis Gray." 1904. *WMQ*, ser. **1**: 12: pp. 267-270.

DUKE, JANE T. 1949. *Kenmore and the Lewises* (New York).

EATON, DAVID W. 1942. *Historical Atlas of Westmoreland County, Virginia: Patents* (Richmond).

ECKENRODE, H. J. 1916. *The Revolution in Virginia* (Boston).

ENGLISH, WILLIAM H. 1896. *Conquest of the Country Northwest of the River, Ohio, 1778-1783* . . . (v. **2**, Indianapolis).

EVANS, EMORY G. 1975. *Thomas Nelson of Yorktown, Revolutionary Virginian* (Williamsburg, Va.).

FLAGG, C. A. 1912. "Virginia's Soldiers in the Revolution." *VMHB.* **20**: pp. 52-68, 181-194, and 267-281.

"Fredericksburg in Revolutionary Days." 1919. *WMQ.* ser. 1, **27**: pp. 73-95, 164-175, and 248-257.

FREEMAN, DOUGLAS S. 1949-1954. *George Washington* (v. **1-6**, New York).

GARNETT, JAMES M. 1909. "James Mercer," *WMQ*, ser. 1, **17**: pp. 85-99 and 204-223.

——————. 1907. *John Francis Mercer, Governor of Maryland* (Baltimore).

Gloucester County, Virginia: A Bicentennial Perspective. 1976 (Gloucester, Va.).

GOOLRICK, JOHN T. 1906. *The Life of General Hugh Mercer* (New York).

GOOLRICK, JOHN T. (Jr.). 1936. "Letter to the Editor." *Free Lance Star* (Fredericksburg), 9 April, 1936.

——————. 1976. *The Story of Stafford: A Narrative History of Stafford County, Va.* (Stafford, Va.).

GOTTSCHALK, LOUIS. 1942. *Lafayette and the Close of the American Revolution* (Chicago).

——————. 1937. *Lafayette Joins the American Army* (Chicago).

GREENE, FRANCIS V. 1911, 1967. *The Revolutionary War and the Military Policy of the United States* (Port Washington, N.Y.).

GREENE, GEORGE W. 1871. *The Life of Nathanael Greene* (3 v., New York).

GREENE, KATHERINE G. 1926. *Winchester, Virginia, and its Beginnings, 1743-1814* (Strasburg, Va.).

GROCE, GEORGE C., and DAVID H. WALLACE. 1957. *The New-York Historical Society Dictionary of Artists in America, 1564-1860* (New Haven).

GWATHMEY, JOHN H. 1938, 1973. *Historical Register of Virginians in the Revolution: Soldiers, Sailors, Marines* (Baltimore).

HARRELL, ISAAC S. 1926, 1965. *Loyalism in Virginia: Chapters in the Economic History of the Revolution* (New York).

HARRISON, FAIRFAX. 1927. "The Equine F. F. Vs." *VMHB.* **35**: pp. 329-370.

HARTLEY, CECIL B. 1859. *Life of Major General Henry Lee* (Philadelphia).

HATCH, CHARLES E., Jr. 1940. "Gloucester Point in the Siege of Yorktown, 1781." *WMQ*, ser. 2, **20**: pp. 265-284.

——————. 1966. "The Washington Pope's Creek Plantation was a 'Living Farm.'" *Northern Neck of Virginia Historical Magazine.* **16**: pp. 1668-1670.

HAYNIE, MIRIAM. 1959. *The Stronghold: A Story of Historic Northern Neck of Virginia and Its People* (Richmond).

HEITMAN, FRANCIS B. 1914, 1973. *Historical Register of Officers of the Continental Army during the War of the Revolution, April 1775 to December, 1783* (Baltimore).

HERNDON, JOHN W. 1943. "Applications of Virginians for Office During the Presidency of George Washington, 1789-1797." *WMQ*, ser. 2, **23**: pp. 162-205.

HIGGINBOTHAM, DON. 1971. *The War of American Independence: Military Attitudes, Policies, and Practice, 1763-1789* (New York).

HOCKER, EDWARD W. 1936. *The Fighting Parson of the American Revolution: General Peter Muhlenberg* (Philadelphia).

HOPPIN, CHARLES A. 1926. "The House in which George Washington was Born." *Tyler's Quarterly.* **8**: pp. 73-103.

————. 1923. "The Washington-Wright Connection and Some Descendants of Major Francis and Anne (Washington) Wright." *Tyler's Quarterly.* **4**: pp. 153-314.

HUGHES, RUPERT. 1930. *George Washington: The Saviour of the States, 1777-1781* (v. **3**, New York).

HUME, EDGAR E. 1940. "Memorial to George Hume, Esquire, Crown Surveyor of Virginia and Washington's Teacher of Surveying." *Tyler's Quarterly.* **21**: pp. 70-120.

————. 1934-1935. "The Virginia Society of the Cincinnati's Gift to Washington College." *VMHB.* **42**: pp. 103-115, 198-210, and 304-316 and **43**: pp. 47-58.

HUME, IVOR. 1966. *1775: Another Part of the Field* (New York).

HUNTER, WILLIAM. 1960. *Forts on the Pennsylvania Frontier, 1753-1758* (Harrisburg, Pa.).

JAMES, ALFRED P. 1963. *George Mercer of the Ohio Company* (Pittsburgh).

JOHNSON, MONROE. 1929. "James Monroe, Soldier." *WMQ,* ser. 2, **9**: pp. 110-117.

JOHNSTON, HENRY P. 1878. *The Campaign of 1776 around New York and Brooklyn. Memoirs of the Long Island Historical Society* (v. **3**, Brooklyn, N.Y.).

————. 1881. *The Yorktown Campaign and the Surrender of Cornwallis, 1781* (New York).

KEBLER, ELEANOR. 1960. *Weedon Genealogy* (mimeographed, LC).

KEENE, JAMES S. 1908. "Hugh Mercer." *The John P. Branch Papers of Randolph-Macon College.* **2**: pp. 198-213.

KEGLEY, F. B. 1938. *Kegley's Virginia Frontier: The Beginning of the Southwest: The Roanoke of Colonial Days, 1740-1783* (Roanoke, Va.).

KING, GEORGE H. S. 1956. "Further Notes on Captain George Buckner and the Caroline County Buckners." *VMHB.* **64**: pp. 358-372.

————. 1940. "General George Weedon." *WMQ,* ser. 2, **20**: pp. 237-252.

————. 1940. "Memorial to Henry Fox, Gentleman, of 'Huntington,' King William County, Virginia." *Tyler's Quarterly.* **21**: pp. 217-290.

————. 1960. *The Register of Saint Paul's Parish, 1715-1798* [Stafford and King George Counties] (Fredericksburg).

KNOLLENBERG, BERNHARD. 1940. *Washington and the Revolution* (New York).

KOONTZ, LOUIS K. 1925. *The Virginia Frontier, 1754-1763. Johns Hopkins University Studies in Historical and Political Science,* ser. 43, no. 2 (Baltimore).

La Fayette's Second Expedition to Virginia, 1781. 1891. Maryland Fund-Publication No. 32 (Baltimore).

LAMDIN, ALFRED C. 1877. "Battle of Germantown." *Pa. Mag. Hist. and Biog.* **1**: pp. 368-403.

LANCASTER, BRUCE. 1955. *From Lexington to Liberty: The Story of the American Revolution* (New York).

LEE, HENRY. 1869, 1969. *Memoirs of the War in the Southern Department of the United States* (New York).

LEWIS, CHARLES L. 1945. *Admiral De Grasse and American Independence* (Annapolis).

LOSSING, BENSON J. 1860. *The Pictorial Field-Book of the Revolution* (New York).

LOWELL, EDWARD J. 1884. *The Hessians and the other German Auxiliaries of Great Britain in the Revolutionary War* (New York).

LYNES, RUSSELL. 1970. *The Art-Makers of Nineteenth Century America* (New York).

MATTESON, DAVID M. 1941. "The Fredericksburg Peace Ball." *VMHB.* **49**: pp. 152-156.

McALLISTER, J. A. 1913. *Virginia Militia in the Revolutionary War* (Hot Springs, Va.).

MAYS, DAVID J. 1952. *Edmund Pendleton, 1721-1783* (2 v., Cambridge, Mass.).

MEAD, BISHOP WILLIAM. 1857. *Old Churches, Ministers and Families of Virginia* (2 v., Philadelphia).

MONTROSS, LYNN. 1967. *The Story of the Continental Army, 1775-1783* (New York).
MOORE, CHARLES. 1932. *Wakefield: Birthplace of George Washington* (Washington, D.C.).
MORGAN, GWENDA. 1973. "Virginia and the French and Indian War." *VMHB*. **81**: pp. 23-48.
MORTON, RICHARD L. 1960. *Colonial Virginia* (2 v., Chapel Hill).
MUHLENBERG, HENRY A. 1849. *The Life of Major-General Peter Muhlenberg of the Revolutionary Army* (Philadelphia).
MYERS, WILLIAM S. 1927. *The Battle of Monmouth* (Princeton, N.J.).
NICKLIN, JOHN B. C. 1930. "The Strother Family." *Tyler's Quarterly* **11**: pp. 113-141, 182-199; **12** (1931): pp. 42-66.
O'MEARA, WALTER. 1965. *Guns at the Forks* (Englewood Cliffs, N.J.).
PALMER, JOHN M. 1937. *General von Steuben* (New Haven).
"Past is Prologue:" Gloucester County, Virginia. 1973. (Gloucester County, Va.).
PAYNE, BROOKE and GEORGE H. S. KING. 1933. "The Monroe Family." *WMQ*, ser. 2, **13**: pp. 231-241.
PECKHAM, HOWARD H. 1964. *The Colonial Wars, 1689-1762* (Chicago).
PICKERING, OCTAVIUS. 1867 and 1873. *The Life of Timothy Pickering*. (v. **1-2**, Boston).
PIERCE, MICHAEL D. 1972. "The Independence Movement in Virginia, 1775-1776." *VMHB*. **80**: pp. 442-452.
PINKOWSKI, EDWARD. 1953. *Washington's Officers Slept Here: Historic Homes of Valley Forge and Its Neighborhood* (Philadelphia).
PRYOR, MRS. ROBERT. 1903. The Mother of Washington and her Times (New York).
QUATTROCHI, ANN. 1962. "Thomas Hutchins, Provincial Soldier and Indian Agent in the Ohio Valley, 1758-1761." *West. Pa. Hist. Mag.* **45**: pp. 193-207.
QUENZAL, CAROL H. 1951. *The History and Background of St. George's Episcopal Church* (Fredericksburg, Va.).
————. 1947. *Preliminary Checklist for Fredericksburg, 1778-1876*. Virginia Imprint Ser., no. 1 (Richmond).
QUINN, S. J. 1908. *The History of the City of Fredericksburg, Virginia* (Richmond).
————. 1890. *Historical Sketch of Fredericksburg Lodge #4* (Richmond).
"Reverend Roderick McCulloch." 1929. *VMHB*. **37**: pp. 344-347.
RICHARDSON, ROBERT N. 1975. *Valentine Peers* (Hamilton, Ohio).
RILEY, EDWARD M. 1949. "Yorktown During the Revolution." *VMHB*. **57**: pp. 22-43, 176-189, and 274-285.
ROWLAND, KATE M. 1892, 1964. *The Life and Correspondence of George Mason, 1725-1792* (New York).
RUSSELL, T. TRIPLETT, and JOHN K. GOTT. 1976. *Fauquier County in the Revolution* (Warrentown, Va.).
SCHEER, GEORGE F., and HUGH F. RANKIN. 1957. *Rebels and Redcoats* (pbk. ed., New York).
SELLERS, CHARLES C. 1947. *Charles Willson Peale* (v. 1, Philadelphia).
SIPE, C. HALE. 1927. *The Indian Wars of Pennsylvania* (Harrisburg).
————. 1925. *Mount Vernon and the Washington Family* (Butler, Pa.).
"Sir Thomas Lunsford." 1900. *WMQ*, ser. 1, **8**: pp. 183-186.
SLAUGHTER, REV. PHILIP. 1847. *A History of St. George's Parish in the County of Spotsylvania* (New York).
SMITH, SAMUEL S. 1976. *The Battle of Brandywine* (Monmouth Beach, N.J.).
SMITH, WILSON C. 1881. "The Roger Morris House: Washington's Headquarters on Harlem Heights." *Mag. Amer. Hist.* **6**: pp. 90-106.
"The Society of the Cincinnati in Fredericksburg Marks its Birthplace . . . . 30 March, 1940." 1941. *Tyler's Quarterly*. **22**: pp. 22-34.
STANARD, MARY N. 1917. *Colonial Virginia: Its People and Customs* (Philadelphia).
STANARD, W. G. 1895. "Racing in Colonial Virginia." *VMHB*. **2**: pp. 293-305.
STEDMAN, CHARLES. 1794. *The History of the Origin, Progress, and Termination of the American War* (2 v., London).
STEVENS, JOHN A. 1881. "The Allies at Yorktown, with Appendix of Contemporary Letters . . . ." *Mag. of Amer. Hist.* **6**: pp. 1-53.

_____. 1880. "The Battle of Harlem Plains, with Appendix of Original Documents." *Mag. of Amer. Hist.* 4: pp. 351-374.

STEWART, MRS. CATESBY WILLIS. 1973. *The Life of Brigadier General William Woodford of the American Revolution* (2 v., Richmond).

STRYKER, WILLIAM S. 1898. *The Battles of Trenton and Princeton* (Boston).

_____. 1927. *The Battle of Monmouth* (Princeton).

SYDNOR, CHARLES S. 1952. *Gentlemen Freeholders: Political Practices in Washington's Virginia* (Chapel Hill).

TEBBEL, JOHN. 1954. *George Washington's America* (New York).

THANE, ELSWYTH. 1972. *The Fighting Quaker: Nathanael Greene* (New York).

THAYER, THEODORE. 1960. *Nathanael Greene: Strategist of the American Revolution* (New York).

THOMPSON, RAY. 1974. *Washington at Whitemarsh: Prelude to Valley Forge* (2nd ed., Fort Washington, Pa.).

TOWER, CHARLEMAGNE. 1894, 1971. *The Marquis de La Fayette in the American Revolution* (v. 2, Freeport, N.Y.).

TYLER, LYON G. 1884. *Encyclopedia of Virginia Biography* (v. 1, Richmond).

_____.1895. "Washington and His Neighbors." *WMQ*, ser. 1, 4: pp. 28-43.

_____.1931. "The Old Virginia Line in the Middle States During the American Revolution." *Tyler's Quarterly.* 12: pp. 1-43, 90-141, 198-203, and 283-289.

VALENTINE, ALAN. 1969. *Lord Stirling* (New York).

WAINWRIGHT, NICHOLAS B. 1959. *George Croghan: Wilderness Diplomat* (Chapel Hill).

WALLACE, WILLARD M. 1954. *Traitorous Hero: The Life and Fortunes of Benedict Arnold* (New York).

WARD, CHRISTOPHER. 1952. *The War of the Revolution* (2 v., New York).

WARD, HARRY M. 1961. *Department of War, 1781-1795* (Pittsburgh).

_____, and HAROLD E. GREER, JR. 1977. *Richmond During the Revolution, 1775-1783* (Charlottesville, Va.).

"Washington's Opinions of His General Officers." 1879. *Mag. of Amer. Hist.* 3: pp. 81-88.

WATERMAN, JOSEPH M. 1941. *With Sword and Lancet: The Life of General Hugh Mercer* (Richmond).

WATKINS, C. MALCOM. 1968. *The Cultural History of Marlborough, Virginia* (Washington, D.C.).

WEIG, MELVIN J. 1957. *Morristown National Historical Park, New Jersey: A Military Capital of the American Revolution* (Washington, D.C.).

WEIGLEY, RUSSELL F. 1973. *The American Way of War: A History of United States Military Strategy and Policy* (New York).

_____. 1967. *History of the United States Army* (New York).

WHITTEMORE, CHARLES F. 1961. *A General of the Revolution: John Sullivan of New Hampshire* (New York).

WICKWIRE, FRANKLIN and MARY. 1970. *Cornwallis: The American Adventure* (Boston).

WILDES, HARRY E. 1938. *Valley Forge* (New York).

_____. 1941. *Anthony Wayne: Trouble Shooter of the American Revolution* (New York).

WILLCOX, WILLIAM B. 1946. "The British Road to Yorktown: A Study in Divided Command." *Amer. Hist. Review* 70: pp. 1-35.

_____.1964. *Portrait of a General: Sir Henry Clinton in the War of Independence* (New York).

WILSTACH, PAUL. 1932. *Potomac Landings* (Indianapolis).

_____. 1929. *Tidewater Virginia* (Indianapolis).

WOODMAN, HENRY. 1922. *The History of Valley Forge* (3d ed., Oaks, Pa.).

WRIGHT, JOHN W. 1931. "Some Notes on the Continental Army. *WMQ*, ser. 2, 11: pp. 81-105 and 185-209.

WRIGHT, LOUIS B. 1964. *The First Gentlemen of Virginia . . .* (Charlottesville, Va.).

WRIGHT, MARCUS J. 1905. "General Lafayette's Campaign in Virginia, April 1781-October, 19, 1781." *Publications of the Southern Hist. Assoc.* 9: pp. 234-240 and 261-271.

INDEX